CW01022410

V&R unipress

National Taiwan University Press

Reflections on (In)Humanity

Volume 6

Edited by
Sorin Antohi, Chun-Chieh Huang and Jörn Rüsen

Jörn Rüsen (ed.)

# Approaching Humankind

## Towards an Intercultural Humanism

V&R unipress

National Taiwan University Press

This book series is sponsored by the Berendel Foundation.

Published in cooperation with the Institute for Advanced Studies in Humanities and Social Sciences, National Taiwan University.

Bibliographic information published by the Deutsche Nationalbibliothek

The Deutsche Nationalbibliothek lists this publication in the Deutsche Nationalbibliografie; detailed bibliographic data are available in the Internet at http://dnb.d-nb.de.

ISBN 978-3-8471-0058-4 [Print, without Asia Pacific]
ISBN 978-986-03-6608-2 [Print, Asia Pacific only]
ISBN 978-3-8470-0058-7 [E Book]


Cover image: Inga Rüsen: Approaching Humankind 2012/13
Page 2: Engraving by Johann Heinrich Meyer for the title page of Johann Gottfried Herder, *Briefe zur Beförderung der Humanität*

## Contents

# Preface

This book has come into existence as part of a project on "Humanism in the Era of Globalization, an Intercultural Dialogue on Humanity, Culture and Values". The project was carried out with the financial support of the Mercator Foundation, at the *Kulturwissenschaftliches Institut* (Institute for Advanced Study in the Humanities) in Essen (KWI) during the years 2006 to 2009 and has resulted in a considerable number of publications.[1] Some texts from the German collections of essays[2] dealing with the central aspects of the project are in this volume made accessible in English translations. The editor hopes that this will advance the cause of the international as well as intercultural work in the topic of humanism.

When the project was initiated, the topic of humanism was of no particular relevance in the humanities and appeared to be only of interest to experts on Western cultural history. The intercultural widening of the scope of a not irrelevant theme in Western cultural history was not being considered at the time. This has changed over the last few years, not least of all since this research project has spawned other projects with different affiliations as regards the institutions or the individuals involved, which are specifically concerned with the intercultural dimension.[3] Occasionally there is even mention made of a 'humanistic

1 Cf. the series *Being Caught in the Web of Culture – Humanism in the Era of Globalization*, published by Transcript-Verlag, Bielefeld. Cf. also: Rüsen, Jörn/Laass, Henner (Eds.): *Interkultureller Humanismus. Menschlichkeit in der Vielfalt der Kulturen*, Schwalbach/Taunus 2009.

2 Esp. – in a shortened version – from Rüsen, Jörn (Ed.): *Perspektiven der Humanität. Menschsein im Diskurs der Disziplinen*, Bielefeld 2010 [Rüsen, Antweiler, Dux, Straub, Lenz, Schmidt-Glintzer] and from: Rüsen, Jörn/Laass, Henner (Eds.): *Interkultureller Humanismus. Menschlichkeit in der Vielfalt der Kulturen*, Schwalbach/Taunus 2009 [Cancik, Macamo, Roetz, Kozlarek]. – The contributions of Hüther, Oesterdiekhoff, Chattopadhyaya have not been published before.

3 I am referring here to the relevant projects initiated by the Berendel Foundation in London in the initiative of Sorin Antohi, especially the annual conference at Oxford University which are devoted to the topic of intercultural humanism.

turn' in the humanities.[4] In this respect the book might meet with a growing interest in the theme of humanism and contribute to providing a stimulus for new approaches to the topic through the results of the older project.

I would like to thank the Mercator Foundation for funding the project, the Institute for Advanced Study in the Humanities in Essen for its institutional support and the Berendel Foundation for financially supporting further research and publication ventures dedicated to humanism, in an intercultural perspective.

A special thanks go to Erhard Reckwitz and Shari Gilbertsen for their empathetic and competent translation. Thanks are also due to the authors who have gone to the trouble of reducing their texts to the limitations that were unavoidable in view of the wealth of material. I am also grateful that instead of translations of existing texts new texts could be admitted that the authors have made available instead of the ones originally envisaged. My special thanks are due to Sorin Antohi for his untiring effort on behalf of numerous projects on humanism and for his friendship while we jointly initiated and completed some of them.

I would like to give my express thanks to Angelika Wulff for her competent and tireless effort in completing the manuscripts and the editing of the book. Finally thanks are due to the colleagues from the publishing house which, thanks to its series "Reflections in (In)Humanity", has provided a site for research for humanism within the international landscape of the humanities.

Bochum, January 2013 Jörn Rüsen

4 Kozlarek, Oliver: "Towards a Humanist Turn", in: *The Unesco Courier* (October-December 2001): 18–20.

Jörn Rüsen

# Introduction: Enquiring about Mankind

It is an essential part of being human not only just to exist and live one's life, but in one's existence and with regard to all aspects of life to constantly enquire about who one is and to organize one's life in accordance with the answer to this question and to regulate one's dealings with the world, with oneself and with one's fellow human being. Man is unthinkable without this enquiry about himself and without seeking and finding an answer to this. He is forced – and that defines him as a cultural being – to make some kind of sense of his world and himself, of nature and others, because human life is only thinkable within the context of such meaningful orientation. Some kind of self-awareness of being a person only as a person forms part of this orientation indispensable for leading one's life. This is commonly understood as a concept of humanity. In shaping the cultural conditions of his life man creates his own image. His life is thereby a reflective process. This type of reflection is to be found in all cultures, at all times and in all kinds of places, and of course it manifests itself in various shapes and forms. Depending on the context in which the question of what man is gets posed, the answer can vary. This variety has an *historical*, but also a *cognitive* dimension. From an historical perspective it manifests itself as the multifariousness of cultural life styles, and in the cognitive dimension the knowledge about mankind takes on the form of various cognitive practices. These days those practices are embodied by the sciences. Both dimensions are closely interwoven and cannot be clearly separated. Although certain scientific disciplines have evolved world-wide and within different cultural traditions, they nonetheless have to come to terms with the vitality of these traditions, not least of all because their insights have to be absorbed by the various life practices at work in different cultural contexts. In addition to this, the provenance of the humanities from the tradition of Western thought is becoming increasingly problematic. In a critical perspective their normative demands are contextualized, historicized and thereby potentially relativized. The knowledge about mankind accumulated by the humanities is about to be destroyed by the relativism of its cultural conditioning factors without there being a viable alternative in sight. What is therefore required is to critically reconnect the insights gained by the humanities with their various cultural contexts. Such a reconnection need not necessarily lead to surrendering all the normative clams made by the various human sciences, but on the contrary: it can enrich these claims with the enormous wealth of cultural experience, which itself is the primary object of research in the humanities. The explicitly intercultural reflection upon the hermeneutical tools the humanities have to develop for this purpose has begun by now and there is no reason to doubt that they are going to be successful. The final aim should be a deepening and an extension for those methods for understanding which the humanities have evolved over the last 200 years of their existence and development.

It would be problematic, however, to regard the insights provided by the humanities as absolutely decisive or as the sole source for our existential orientation, thereby confirming the idea of being human to those forms of the cultural production of meaning the humanities are capable of providing. They are, indeed, necessary but not indispensible, even less so in view of the cognitive status of the epistemology underlying the human sciences currently undergoing a process of critical revision. Furthermore, it should not be overlooked that the normative claims of scientific knowledge derived from employing certain methodological procedures is based upon premises that have a limiting effect upon the meaning-making potential of the sciences. Human self-interpretation is not confined to rational acts of cognition but goes far beyond these, for instance in the sphere of the arts, in the field of everyday knowledge and also, of course, in that of religious belief, which even in the secular culture of modern civil society has not entirely lost its appeal. But without systematic thought, without the cognitive potential of reason, a useful self-awareness of human beings is not possible.

Another limitation of the cognitive achievements of the humanities as regards providing some practical orientation for human life consists in their multifariousness and high degree of differentiation, i.e. they appear as forms of knowledge that cannot be immediately equated with certain practical applications. For such a purpose those sciences that are focused on man as their object are too varied and too heterogeneous in terms of their approach and methodology. A comprehensive anthropology capable of viewing and explaining mankind in its totality does not exist: this applies even more because man as a cultural being is also part of nature, and hence nature and culture are thematized and researched in two completely incompatible epistemologies.

And yet, what is required is a comprehensive synthesis, or else the cultural orientation indispensible for human life-practices would have to have recourse to a kind of knowledge whose fragmentariness and heterogeneity runs counter to the demands made upon its ability to provide some orientation. Orientation in this context means supplying a horizon of meaning for human life both in theoretical and practical terms, i. e. making part of the general objective guiding human action and of the way in which human beings cope with the experience of suffering. Horizons encompass the entire world and provide some point of reference for the human beings living in this world so that they know where they are, where and whence they move, and how their paths intersect with those of other humans.

If it is our concern to thematize humanity within a cognitive horizon and thus produce some knowledge about mankind that, though its form of scientific procedure, fulfils certain basic cultural criteria of plausibility (*Wissenschaftlichkeit*) – which is indispensible for the culture of modern societies – then we are confronted with the fundamental problem of cultural orientation: the integration of the entire accumulated stock of knowledge into a coherent form which would correspond to an "idea of mankind" capable of informing all our activities.

These days the question of what it means to be human poses itself as part of the unbroken continuity of self-probelmatization mankind has been undergoing with regard to its cultural status, and also within the context of new challenges. Among these can be counted the provocations issued by new insights on the part of the natural sciences. Those have extended and deepened the disposal of man over his own nature tight down to interfering with his genetic equipment as well as making the processes of his mental activities visible, and thereby rendering them capable of manipulation. Another challenge is issued by the conflictual potential resulting from intercultural interaction through the process of globalization: here ideas of mankind are competing – and quite often – clashing with one another. Such conflicts can go so far as to annihilate the other side in order to force upon it one's own idea of humanity. The sciences – if they want to or not – are involved in this clash. They can either supply it with intellectual weaponry, or they can also enter the fight in their own specific way, i. e. with the intention of reflecting upon its causes and showing up ways of its peaceful resolution. What is to be done within the continuity of our cultural enquiry into what fundamentally constitutes the humanity of human beings in the face of these challenges from the natural sciences? First of all it is important to investigate the humanity of mankind from the multiple perspectives opened up by a variety of disciplines, but also from that of the diversity of cultural traditions, in order to come to cognitive grips with humanity. The demand for the totality of cultural orientation is thereby confronted with the multi-perspectivism of scientific research and – in a completely different dimension – diverse cultural traditions (which can also influence the scientific disciplines). The first move away from this irritating plurality of perspectives to the concept of total meaning consists in acknowledging perspectivism as such. This realization and acceptance of the ineluctable persepctivism of all scientific knowledge is the first step towards a higher coherence of meaning. Because in accepting this, the limits of particular insights are made visible and – in doing so – already transgressed in the direction of other disciplines and their respective forms of cognition.

Knowledge alone is incapable of fulfilling the need for orientation required by the mental effort of producing meaning. What is also needed for such an orientation are norms and values and meaningful symbols (such as those provided by art) that go beyond the rational reach of the sciences. If one want to raise modern culture (and it has to be raised because it is of vital importance), then one also questions the ability of scientific knowledge to be connected and mediated with other achievements human anatomy, and whether it can be integrated into the horizon of cultural self-definition.

The following texts are attempting to supply an answer to the question after the humanity of human beings that take both aspects into consideration: the multiplicity of perspectives from which man has to be studies, and in an equal measure the aspects under which one can attempt to integrate this plurality into a whole. One should not expect more than just a sketchy outline of the entire field of human self-thematization because the gaps in the argumentative context of various disciplines and traditions are only too obvious. For instance there are no contributions on religion or economics, and philosophy is only referred to somewhat obliquely. Also the cultural diversity of such powerful traditions in the need for orientation that the process of globalization and the effect of technological-scientific civilization upon people's lives have given rise to could only be addressed by way of example.

In spite of the sketchiness and temporariness of the arguments presented here there are some more comprehensive themes emerging that are capable of lending the intercultural debate on the future perspectives of cultural science-making about man and his world a specific profile. It appears that the new challenges so forcefully issued to human self-understanding by globalization demand a response whereby the different traditions ascribing an intrinsic value to human beings can be summarized under the heading of *new humanism.*

The essential features of this kind of humanism are evident: it is grounded upon anthropological universals; it integrates new insights into human nature as the basis for mankind's cultural achievements; it develops cross-cultural perspectives on historical development; finally it opens up human self-understanding to the multifariousness and changeability of the cultural life forms mankind has evolved.

In the *first part* of the volume the anthropological, neuro-biological and evolutionary aspects are presented that form our idea of being human at the interface of three research-paradigms – biology, ethnology and sociology.

Biology comes first. The concept of 'humanity' and most all of 'humanness' designate a human quality that mark man as a cultural being, which serves all his ties with natural conditioning factors. Nonetheless man as a cultural being also remains part of nature. The interdependence of both, nature and culture, their synthesis through the humanity of humans, is a fact, but fully grasping this fact meets with great difficulties. These are principally caused that nature is the object of a branch of science which, for methodological reasons, is not concerned with the question of meaning that is so relevant for the humanities. How can such a way of thinking possibly comprehend the nature of man that is constantly being converted into culture if exactly that aspect of nature is not mentioned at all which defines culture? Conversely, those branches of science that occupy themselves with culture are, for epistemological reasons, incapable of systematically transcending the horizon of mankind's cultural dimension towards its natural qualities. This would, indeed, be beyond the scope of the cultural sciences.

This tension also manifests itself in the current discourse about human nature and its influence on determining man's cultural life practices. Recent insights into the genetic equipment of man and the genetic structure as well as function of his brain have led scientists to assume that mankind's cultural aspirations are determined by nature. This went so far that some of the key-terms of man's cultural self-reflection, such as freedom, have had their cognitive relevance abrogated. There is of course no doubt about the conditioning of human life by the natural equipment he has come endowed with as a member of the species of *homo sapiens*, but the extent of this conditioning is still a matter of controversy.

The essay by *Gerald Hüther* shows in an impressive manner that it would be rather more appropriate to speak of the cultural conditioning of natural processes in the brain than conversely to regard the cultural activities initiated by the brain as being conditioned by nature. It is culture, the social context into which human beings have been born, in which they grow up and spend their lives that largely determine the formation and structure of the brain. In Hüther's argument the entity 'brain' is not conceived as an object among other objects, but in terms of its quality and in specific contribution to organizing human life it stands revealed as an essentially social phenomenon. Only within a social context does the brain evolve into the natural locus of what constitutes human life.

From the perspective of brain research being human is a life-long process of becoming human. Through this insight the category of education acquires a new degree of plausibility. With such research findings anthropological study comes close to a synthesis of body and mind, nature and nurture, which has to be taken into account and explained more than ever. Due to the insights provided by brain research, nature as a category external to man and something he has to come to term with, especially in views of today's urgent environmental problems, in order to safeguard his humanity is thereby shifted into man himself. This is exactly where a new understanding of man's relationship with nature becomes visible which one could apply to the ecological problems of securing the survival of the species.

Any attempt at determining the humanity of human beings in such a way that transcultural features we all have in common are to serve as the basis for intercultural understanding meets with massive objections. These are grounded on the undeniable fact that there exist fundamental cultural differences which are not just empirically obvious, but which are also deeply embedded within the mental processes of every human being and which serve as a specific quality by means of which it distinguished itself from other people, whether as an individual, whether as the member of a larger community. Nevertheless, anthropological universals might be drawn upon in order to render more plausible the attempt to use a universalizing idea of mankind for resolving the current problems arising from globalization. *Christoph Antweiler* is supplying strong arguments in support of this view. His argument runs counter to the tendency to make cultural difference into the paramount aspect of intercultural communication, as a result of which anthropological universals (if they are perceived and recognized at all) on the one hand, and the particularity and difference of concrete human life styles ('cultures') on the other are played off against each other as supposedly unbridgeable opposites. Only if universals and differences can thought of in terms of their complementarity, when they are thought 'into one another', as it were, is it possible to gain a proper perspective on mankind that is both empirically enriched and normatively promising by way of serving as a point of reference for cultural orientation. Antweiler emphasizes the complexity of difference and similarity, thereby not denying the power of difference while at the same time integrating it into a referential system of transcultural communality among humans.

*Georg Oesterdiekhoff*'s contribution fulfils a similar function in the way of supplying a foundational system for understanding human beings in the multifariousness of their life forms. In doing so he focuses on one capacity for dealing with the world. Taking as his starting point the insights of developmental psychology such as they have been evolved by Jean Piaget and others he develops a theory of cultural evolution whereby our understanding of what it means to be human is placed within the context of the universal unfolding of our cognitive capacity. In doing so he generalizes the insights of modern developmental psychology through widening its scope to such an extent that it can serve as the universal history of the way in which our human life forms have evolved. Thus the variety of human life forms can be categorized by subsuming them under the different stages of our cognitive development, and as such they can be understood as stages within a structured genetical process. The notion of such a developmental process refers back to the old enlightenment trope of progress as the on-going change mankind is made to undergo in the course of history, while additionally supporting it by supplying a lot of empirical data. Universal history is thereby conceived as a continuous process of 'humanizing humankind' with our current understanding of humanity, i.e. the abstract norms of universal ethics, serving as the standard.

Oesterdiekhoff's main argument, i.e. of distinguishing between premodern and modern life forms and using this distinction by way of proving the evidence of social evolution, would have to be historicized much more extensively in order to be able to analyze more closely the differences between various historical epochs and, of course also between cultures and civilizations.

In the *second part* of the book, as opposed to the transcultural, generalizing and fundamental concerns of the first part, the focus will be on cultural difference by drawing on the example of some selected large civilizations. This is all about confronting Western civilization with non-Western cultural developments which can justifiably be regarded as contributions to the understanding of humanity or humanness.

*Hubert Cancik* gives a survey of Western humanism. He makes it clear that humanism in all its varieties cannot be understood without taking into consideration its roots in classical antiquity, especially by the Greek and Roman one. He elaborates on the special and temporal dimensions of Western humanism while emphasizing the special role played by education in the process of forming the humanity of humans (or more precisely, for the becoming human of mankind both onto- and phytogenetically). However, Western humanism is not just reduced to some basic assumptions as a result of which these assume the quality of an invariable historical phenomenon. Such sweeping characterizations are nothing but generalizations compared to the multiple and differentiated manifestations. In this regard it is not only regional but also epochal differences that play an important role. Admittedly, the central concepts of humanist thinking have been evolved in Roman antiquity and has remained an important point of reference for this kind of thought right up to the threshold of Modernity; however, as an identifiable intellectual movement, as a discourse delimiting itself from other intellectual discourses it did not come into existence until the early Modern Age. In Modernity it finally acquires not only its name but also its own people, and at the same the dynamism inherent in its divergencies and tension.

In his contribution on Confucianism *Heiner Roetz* indicates the possibility of historically locating and making plausible a genuinely non-Western humanism. This has systematic implications for the current treatment on the topic of humanism far exceeding the isolated case of China. Although the term bears a Western imprint, but when one considers the essential elements of this concept with regard to the relationship of man with himself (as man) the whole issue attains a universal dimension: Culturally different concepts of humanity can be examined and critically compared with each other. Roetz develops Chinese humanism within the context of the specific historical situation that gave rise to Confucianism and its varieties. However, he is not so much concerned with historically distinguishing it from the Western tradition (as is frequently the case with Chinese authors who maintain a critical stance vis-à-vis the West). On the contrary, for him Chinese humanism with its historical particulars is nothing but a variety of human thought that came into existence with the epochal rupture of axial time in diverse cultures. Little though the specifically Chinese character of Confucianism can be denied, it is on the other hand relevant to point up those of its features that it has in common with other versions of human thought, especially as regards its universalizing tendencies. It is this very universalism which lends Chinese humanism its intercultural relevance, however, only without its nationalist overtone whereby it gets instrumentalized as the cultural means of securing political power. Roetz is positioning himself in the current confrontation of the Confucian with the Western tradition often to be found among East Asian intellectuals. He does not do this just with regard to human rights, but he also introduces bioethical aspects into a debate in which normative claims connected with the Western concepts of human dignity are often refuted. Without playing off Western arguments against East Asian ones he shows that the Confucian tradition can be interpreted in a different way that is compatible with Western arguments. In doing so he implicitly introduces a humanist dimension into the intercultural controversy over different varieties of humanist thought.

*Umesh Chattopadhyaya* presents Indian humanism in view of its long historical development from the classical texts of the Vedanta via the critical debate with Western culture up to the concept of a new humanism. Against the background of a long tradition with a strong religious bias Indian humanism is marked by its attempt to conclusively connect the essential elements of this tradition with those aspects that systematically take into account the historical specifity of Modernity. In this respect Indian humanism indeed distinguishes itself from the Western and other varieties of humanist thought, but at the same time this distinctiveness acknowledges the fact that what had been distinguished was not outright rejected or limited off but integrated and adapted. Especially with regard to India the traditional distinction made in the discourse on Hinduism are thus becoming obfuscated: secular and religious elements no longer appear as strict opposites but appear in different constellations. In an intercultural perspective this raises the question if our traditional understanding of religion is at all adequate for interpreting (Western) humanism when it comes to growing awareness of the immanent and transcendent dimensions in several versions of humanism (not only the Western variety) and being able to appreciate the relevance of their mediation in an idea of humanity. Something similar applies to the clear-cut distinction between Western and non-Western aspects of humanist thought. Can the political humanism of Mahatma Ghandi or the poetical one of Rabindranath Tagore at all be understood in terms of such a difference? Especially with regard to Indian culture interculturality can be defined as one of those intellectual operations whereby opposites are not just removed, but where non-oppositional thinking becomes viable. In the context of the question whether an inclusive humanism is at all possible India therefore acquires not only an historical degree of relevance but also in systematic-theoretical terms. My own contribution is the attempt to delineate the development of the concept of being human and humanity, and to show how it culminates in the rise of modern humanism. In doing so I am guided by a theoretical intention. The historical particularity of humanism, such as it manifested itself as the humanist concept of the European Modern Age, is to be placed within the general context of the philosophy of history, which will make it interculturally relevant.

The argument is based on an outline of the various periods as defined by the philosophy of history, which relies on the concept of axial time. This concept makes it possible to combine cultural variety with a universal history common to all, which would – beating in mind the notion of Modernity as a 'second axial time' – secure for the present historical scheme of things as regards the idea of humanity and humanism. This historical reconstruction results in a problematic whereby the current thinking about mankind in an intercultural perspective is faces with the task of being renewed in conceptual terms: the various and usually exclusive idea, regarding mankind so far evolved in different cultural traditions have to be reinterpreted and developed further on the basis of their inclusive features because these can be regarded as the highest form of any internal universalism. Through this manoeuvre the temporal distancing that the historicizing of the category of humanity and humanism inevitably entails is capable of paving the way for a future perspective, which makes historiography into an indispensible partner in the current discourse about the humanity of humans.

*Oliver Kozlarek* expounds the Latin American variety of humanist thought by referring to its most distinguished exponents. It is composed of a peculiar combination of Western and indigenous tradition or ways of thinking. In Latin America, and Kozlarek does not leave this in any kind of doubt, Western thought can be perceived itself in the mirror of critique in which its dark sides stand out much more clearly than in its usual historical self-perception that totally excluded non-Western humanism on trial before the court of ideological critique, but by pointing up its limitations its potential for further development is also indicated. Its alienation from itself by being absorbed into colonial forms of life can therefore be seen as a chance for its enrichment, which can also be made productive for the intercultural debate on a new humanism.

The *third part* is concerned with making the philosophizing about mankind, together with its humanist aspirations, applicable to present-day problems, i.e. relating concepts of humanity, within the context of Modernity, to those problems of orientation caused by the process of globalization. Of course not all the issues within this context can be addressed, but in an exemplary way questions will be raised concerning economic distributional justice, gender-relations and the attendant overcoming of inequality, as well as the psychological dimensions in which humanity can articulate itself in the context of Modernity. In conclusion we shall ponder the chances of an intercultural humanism for the future.

In his article *Günter Dux* combines insights from the fields of cognitive theory, the idea of history as well as sociology and the theory of history. His argument takes its point of departure the current problems of orientation resulting from the threat to long-established humane life forms posed by the development of market-economy (capitalism). Modern thought, which revolves around man as the source, the end and the be-all of his orientation in the world, is positioned within the comprehensive framework of the evolution of mankind's cultural self-definition, and this in turn is made understandable by resorting to the decisive cognitive move of relating it to the cognitive achievements of the natural sciences. On the basis of these no orientational norms whatsoever can be proclaimed that would be grounded upon, as it were, meta-anthropological presuppositions. Humanity is the fundamental category of a 'recursive' definition of mankind. Cognitively enabled by nature, man constructs his own world and makes himself, so to speak, at home in it. This process of accommodation occurs over a long historical process of development also definable as evolution, which sits athwart the development of cultural difference. Dux sets out the logic of this evolution as the unfolding of cognitive competence inherent in all human action.

This humanity, from a theoretical perspective enriched with empirical data is described as an historical process. This finally leads to certain human life practices that we today perceive as being specifically humanist. According to Dux, humanism can be defined as the self-determined relationship man establishes with himself. This relationship gets, through the dominance of market economy, into an inner contradiction between the economic production of material riches and the political demand for human self-determination. The potential inclusion of all individuals, due to their being human, in life forms that are considered to be humane by all concerned is fundamentally put in question by distribution of wealth produced in a capitalist system. From this insight Dux derives political strategies for a humanization that remains loyal to the standards of humanity achieved in the course of universal history.

In *Ilse Lenz'* contribution the fundamental fact that being human is principally and always and everywhere conceived in terms of gender occupies center stage of her argument. For a long time (and occasionally still today) mention has been made of 'man as such', thereby completely leaving the gender-specific aspects of being human out of the picture. This resulted in viewing human beings first and foremost as a generalized male being, as a result of which the human potential of being female has been totally marginalized. In a detailed overview of modern feminist movements and the political and academic discourses associated with these, a vast and highly complex vista of being human is opened up in which inequality and difference become visible both as a danger to, as well as a chance for, humanity.

The dangers – in the form of a structural imbalance in the relation between the genders along with serious discrimination – are evident and still virulent. At the same time, however, the sociological perspective in the global dimension of gender inequality among humans alters us to the experience of a fundamental change that is occurring world-wide. It is definitely moving in the direction of doing away with this imbalance.

Within the context of an unconditional recognition of cultural difference transcultural phenomena like gender inequality as the source of conflict and violence are easily lost sight of or are at least played down in their importance from a culturally relativist point of view. That is the reason why Ilse Lenz expressly comes out in favor of not subsuming social difference, along with its central feature of gender difference, under cultural difference, thereby permitting the culturalist legitimization of evident inhumanity. At the same time she pleads in favor of a hermeneutical sensitivity in dealing with gender-determined life forms and their changes. In this regard Lenz develops the concept of a 'reflective universalism' that systematically takes cognizance of 'cultural difference', while at the same time adhering to transcultural experiences and perspectives in terms of their interpretation (along with the practice al strategies allied with these).

With the concept of personal identity *Jürgen Straub* analyzes one of the principal notions for understanding human beings within the context of modern societies. The psychological phenomena coming within the purview of this concept for him amount to a specific configuration of those mental forces that constitute human subjectivity and make it into a project for those involved that they have to cope with on an individual basis. Thereby he introduces a differentiation that is relevant for the historical analysis of humanism: No longer can there be any talk of an essentializing anthropological definition of mankind without referring to or even subverting the specific discourse in which it was first formulated. Straub reconstructs the historically specific situation of human beings in the context of the living conditions in the age of Modernity and systematically characterizes the complex psychological make-up of human subjectivity corresponding to this situation. In this manner he analyzes a type of human behavior that is specific of our epoch and that has to become the object of all our remedial efforts in creating a sustainable humanism by way of providing a cultural orientation in the current of process of globalization. As opposed to traditional historicism and its different variations Straub explicitly emphasizes the high level of complexity of subjectivity in the modern world (without being oblivious of this cultural type's confinement to certain areas in an inter- as well as intracultural comparison). Especially the fragility, fragmentariness, openness, inner dynamic and the high degree of self-reflectiveness that the permanent awareness of a precarious relation with alterity involves render this type into a highly attractive option. Any attempt at rethinking humanism as a cultural compass for a new and viable orientation of human practices in the face of the modern challenges of globalization would be well advised to consider this approach.

The conclusion of this volume is formed by the essay of *Helwig Schmidt-Glintzer.* The intercultural perspective of this contribution is influenced by the topical problems of the situation in our world and therefore focuses on the difficulties of orientation attendant upon the process of globalization. At the same time reference to this presence is complemented and completed with numerous digressions into the past with its historical dimension. The first one of these revolves around the question of the historical preconditions. Schmidt-Glintzer explicitly inquires the opportunities and limitations of a new humanism (a question informing the concept of this entire volume). This humanism does not do away with the vital distinction between the self and the other. On the contrary, it rests upon the fundamental recognition of cultural difference and multifariousness. But this multitude of differences is circumscribed by the notion of a universal humanity that can assume different shapes. All endeavors to realize humanity must aim at unlocking this potential through a successful process of education. The forces running counter to such an education are addressed and differentiated by Schmidt-Glintzer so that his plea for a new humanism is counterbalanced by a realistic appraisal of mankind's potential for humanity, thus arming us against possible disappointments. This works all the more in favor of those arguments that positively assess the chances of working towards a new and viable intercultural humanism.

# I. Foundations

Gerald Hüther

# Neurobiological Approaches to a Better Understanding of Human Nature and Human Values

## 1. The Unique Plasticity of the Human Brain

By far the most significant finding in the field of neurobiological research in recent years is what we refer to today as experience-dependent or use-dependent plasticity: It is the discovery that the neuronal and synaptic connections in the human brain can be altered. The complexity of these connections and their stabilization depend to a far greater extent than previously believed on how – or rather, for which purpose – an individual uses his brain, the goals pursued, the experiences made in the course of his life, the models used for orientation, the factors which provide emotional stability and a sense of commitment. All this is shaped by an individual's family relationships, the abilities passed on to him and the guiding ideals and the goals conveyed by the thoughts and aims, by the myths, legends and belief systems of the particular culture in which a person grows up. The neuronal connectivity patterns in the human brain are continuously adjusted to these social and cultural factors, at least in all those areas which are shaped and structured postnatally. In other words, the individual human brain in its mature state is a social construct.

Therefore, it is not astonishing that neuroscientists by their modern imaging techniques are able to identify numerous differences between the brains of differently encultured and socialized subjects at both, the structural and the functional level. These differences are most pronounced in the very slowly developing higher cortical association areas. Examples of such use dependent adaptive modifications and reorganizations of neuronal connectivity have been observed throughout lifetime, even in the brains of elderly subjects. The degree of brain plasticity is of course highest at younger ages, but the networks and connections between nerve cells can apparently be restructured and adjusted to new demands throughout lifetime. A prerequisite for such experience-dependent changes is the activation of the emotional centers (limbic system). This leads to the release of trophic, hormone-like substances, which stimulate the growth and the reorganization of nerve cell contacts and connections. Such emotional activation, i. e. situations which "go deeply under the skin", are most often experimented during childhood and adolescence, but much less frequently during adulthood, when a person has learned to master almost all challenges of daily life routinely.

The most important triggers for the adaptive modification and reorganization of neuronal networks and synaptic circuitry at any age are the problems encountered and the experiences made by an individual in the course of the so called stress-response. Therefore, the first part of this contribution will focus on the adaptive self-organization of neuronal connectivity through the mastery of challenges and of stressful experiences. In the second part, the influences of early affective relationships and of a culture of peace and non-violence on the developing brain will be somewhat more closely examined.

## 2. Stress and the Experience-dependent Organization of Neuronal Connectivity

Current stress research is characterized by fascinating insights into the mechanisms involved in the activation and the regulation of the neuroendocrine stress response and the consequences of this activation on the body and the brain. This progress is contrasted by a considerable degree of conceptual confusion. Until now, a generally accepted concept of stress is still elusive. Initially the term "stress" was used synonymous to "stressor" and no clear distinction was made between this stimulus and the reaction to it, the "stress-response". This concept has now been replaced by the recognition that stimulus and response cannot be regarded as two independent, stable entities but rather represent two closely linked components mutually affecting each other in the course of the stress-reaction-process. This conceptualization explicitly implies important aspects, such as the character of the strain, the appraisal and the psychological as well as the emotional changes which occur in the course of this process. It implies that, if an individual is able to terminate a certain stressor by his own efforts, a *controllable* stress response is elicited, whereas an *uncontrollable* stress response is initiated when no adequate coping strategies are available or can be applied to terminate the stressor.

A controllable stress response is typically elicited when an individual has the subjective feeling that a certain demand or challenge can be met in principle by its own action but when this action is not (yet) ready, efficient or adequate enough to avoid the activation of his central stress responsive systems. The initial stages of the controllable and the uncontrollable stress response are identical. Both start with the recognition of a novel, unexpected, challenging or threatening stimulus which causes the generation of a nonspecific pattern of arousal in the associative cortex and in the limbic structures. Through descending excitatory efferences, this activation is propagated to lower brain structures, especially to the central noradrenergic system. If the stressor is felt to be uncontrollable, the arousal of the higher cortical and limbic brain structures will not only persist but is even potentiated by the increased firing of noradrenergic afferences. Above a certain threshold, the sum of excitatory cortical and limbic, as well as of noradrenergic inputs to the neurosecretory hypothalamic nuclei will ultimately stimulate the release of corticotropin releasing hormone and vasopressin, and thus, activate the HPA-system and stimulate adrenal glucocorticoid secretion. However, if the stressor is felt to be controllable, the nonspecific pattern of arousal in the associative cortex will be funnelled into a specific activation of those neuronal pathways and circuits which are involved in the behavioral response to that stressor. Under these conditions, the enhanced noradrenergic output acts to facilitate the neuronal pathways activated in the course of this response. The reverbatory stimulation of the central stress responsive systems is no longer propagated, and the HPA-system is not at all or only slightly stimulated. Therefore, the controllable stress response may be regarded as an incompletely built up activation of the central stress responsive systems. It is characterized by a preferential activation of the central and the peripheral noradrenergic system.

Due to its extensive projections and the fact that adrenergic receptors are expressed not only by neurons but also by glial and endothelial cells, the central noradrenergic system is capable of modulating a great number of different brain functions:

Stimulation of neuronal adrenoreceptors increases the signal-to-noise ratio of cortical information processing, and contributes to the gating and to the facilitation of neuronal output patterns. Stimulation of adrenergic receptors of cerebral blood vessels leads to enhanced perfusion, increased brain glucose uptake and elevated energy metabolism. Activation of astrocytic adrenoreceptors stimulates glycogenolysis and the release of glucose and lactate as well as the formation and the release of various neurotrophic factors. Through these different effects, the increased noradrenergic output in the course of a controllable stress response contributes to the stabilization and facilitation of those neuronal pathways and connections which are activated in response to a certain controllable stressor. Repeated exposure to one and the same controllable stressor will thus lead to the successive facilitation of the neuronal circuitry involved in the behavioral responding. The noradrenaline-mediated stimulation of the synthesis and the release of neurotrophic factors by astrocytes will additionally favor structural adaptations through experience-dependent plasticity. Such stepwise adaptive modifications of the neuronal circuitry will automatically be triggered in the course of the controllable stress response until the original stressor can be adequately met by an efficient response. To some extent, this adaptive modification of associative cortical networks is comparable to catecholamine-mediated, peripheral structural adaptation processes, such as the increase of fur density in mammals upon repeated exposure to cold.

The particular importance of the repeated activation of noradrenergic neurons in the course of the response to controllable stress for central adaptation processes is further supported by the fact that specific mechanisms evolved in mammals which increase the output efficacy of the noradrenergic system in the course of future stress responses in individuals exposed to different kinds of controllable stressors. This up-regulation of noradrenergic activity upon exposure to different controllable stressors is seen at several levels: The firing rate of noradrenergic neurons increases, the synthesis, storage, and release of noradrenaline by noradrenergic nerve endings rises, and even axonal sprouting and intensification of noradrenergic innervation in certain brain areas, e.g. in the cortex, have been observed.

Evidently, controllable stress of very complex and diverse character is a prerequisite for the optimal expression of the individual's genetic potential and for the elaboration of a very complex neuronal circuitry in the brain. An impressive illustration of the complex and persistent effects of multiple experiences of many different controllable stress responses on brain structure and brain function are the influences of "enriched environments" on the development of the cortex of young experimental animals. Enriched environments provide many different stimuli which are novel and which can be explored. Rats which had grown up under such complex stimulatory environments show a thicker cortex, enhanced vascularization, elevated number of glial cells, enlarged dendritic trees of pyramidal neurons, and an increased density of synapses in the cortex. Additionally, in adulthood, they show diminished anxiety in novel environments and an increased response of their HPA-system under conditions of severe stress.

An uncontrollable stress response is elicited when the activation of the central stress sensitive systems cannot be terminated by an individual's own efforts, because his previously acquired strategies of appraisal and coping are not appropriate or cannot be employed. Under such conditions, the initial arousal of cortical and limbic structures will persist and contribute to escalate the reverbatory activation of the central stress responsive systems culminating in the activation of the HPA-system and adrenal glucocorticoid secretion. Because of their lipophilicity, circulating glucocorticoids can easily enter the brain and bind to the glucocorticoid receptors expressed by neurons and glial cells. As in the periphery, it is their main function to attenuate the activation of immediate stress responsive systems and to prevent these initial reactions from overshooting. However, glucocorticoids do not directly suppress the immediate central responses in the course of the stress response, e.g., the release of excitatory amino acids or of monoamines. Instead, most actions of glucocorticoids in the brain are delayed and involve changes at the level of gene expression. These alterations have longer-lasting consequences on neuronal and glial cell function and metabolism. Certain functions will be affected in a way such that the targets of the immediate stress response are better protected against the potential damage caused by an overshooting future activation. This is achieved at several different levels: through the suppression of c-AMP formation in response to adrenergic stimulation, through compromising cerebral energy mobilization or through the reduced formation of neurotrophic factors, growth of processes and synaptogenesis. Glucocorticoids have been shown to potentiate the glutamate-induced damage to neurons and their dendrites and are therefore able to interrupt the neuronal circuits involved in the initiation and propagation of the central stress response. The hippocampal pyramidal neurons are endowed with the highest density of glucocorticoid receptors and are therefore especially vulnerable to long-lasting elevations of circulating glucocorticoids caused by the uncontrollable stress. Also the noradrenergic axons and nerve terminals in the cortex appear to be particularly susceptible under such conditions and tend to retract and to degenerate. At the behavioral level, high concentrations of circulating glucocorticoids have been shown to facilitate the extinction of previously acquired reactions. The common feature of all these different effects caused by the activation of the HPA-system in the course of the uncontrollable stress response is their destabilizing influence on the previously established neuronal connectivity. The facilitation and stabilization of neuronal circuitry triggered in the course of previous controllable stress response is thus opposed, attenuated or even reversed in the course of an long-lasting uncontrollable stress. The destabilization of the previously established neuronal connectivity in cortical and limbic brain structures may lead to fundamental changes in cognition, emotion and behavior and, at least in the adult brain, may be a prerequisite for the acquisition of novel patterns of appraisal and coping and for the reorganization of the neuronal connectivity in cortical and limbic associative networks.

Throughout life, the repeated experience of the controllability of stressors is normally alternated by feelings of loss of control. The central adaptations resulting from the repeated exposure to controllable stressors are thus at least partly destabilized during periods when the loss of control is experienced. The activation of the central stress responsive systems by repeated experiences of controllable stress facilitates neuronal circuits and synaptic connections mainly through the activation of the central noradrenergic system. The neuroendocrine changes associated with the experience of uncontrollable stress, on the other hand, favor synaptic regression and the destabilization of previously established synaptic pathways and neuronal circuits. As long as the activation of the central stress system can be terminated by a cognitive, emotional or behavioral reaction, the neuronal circuits involved in this response become facilitated. If no cognitive, emotional or behavioral responses are available to terminate the activation of the central stress response system, the underlying neuronal networks become destabilized. This may provide novel opportunities for the reorganization of neuronal circuits and the acquisition of novel coping strategies for a more efficient control of the novel environmental demands. But more often such destabilization processes pave the way into the manifestation of various kinds of psychopathologies.

The nature of what an individual considers life threatening, stressful challenges changes together with, and as a result of his improving sensory cognitive and intellectual realization of, and interaction with, the outside world. In infants, a stress response is initially only elicited in situations that demand the satisfaction of a basic need. Later, the central stress-responsive systems are most frequently activated by the recognition of certain social and cultural rules which prohibit the satisfaction of such a need. In the course of their socialization, individuals develop additional needs which are no longer basic but culturally acquired. The strategies which are chosen by an individual to meet each one of these challenges are strictly dependent on his previous experiences. "Successful" behavioral strategies, i.e. the neuronal networks involved in the activation and execution of certain cognitive, emotional or behavioral reactions which make a certain type of stressor subjectively controllable, become increasingly reinforced and facilitated. Inadequate strategies which repeatedly fail to suppress and to silence the central stress responsive systems will either be eliminated or will become a constant source of dysregulation. By this self-optimization process, the cognitive, behavioral and emotional reactivity of an individual is fitted in a stepwise, trial-and-error manner to its changing environmental demands.

All newborns possess a certain repertoire of behavioral reactions which are activated in the course of, or together with, the activation of the central stress responsive systems when their homeostasis is threatened by cold, hunger, thirst etc. Thus, they all make the repeated early experience that their reactions are suited to terminate the central responses elicited by stressful experiences. This early recognition of the controllability of a stressor by an own action is one of the earliest associative learning experiences of a child and it has a strong imprinting impact on the developing brain. It is the prerequisite for the acquisition of an ever increasing repertoire of more and more specific and refined behavioral strategies for the control of stressors. This repeated experience of the controllability of stress is a prerequisite for the acquisition of behavioral strategies which allow an individual to act and not simply to react. The more successful these actions are, the more will the neuronal pathways and synaptic connections involved in a certain type of adaptive behavior become strengthened and efficient coping skills for certain types of stressors be developed. The ability to deal successfully with stressors strengthens the self-esteem and feelings of self-efficacy as much as the range of problem-solving skills of an individual. Consequently, the experience of the controllability of stress is the predominating experience and the driving force for the later development of those individuals of a social group which, within the socio-cultural and age-specific context of this group, will become the most successful, the most clever, but not necessarily the most flexible and the most stable ones.

Such personal qualities emerge already at rather young ages. They can only be developed on the basis of secure stable affectional relationships during early childhood and favorable temperamental attributes. It is important, that stressful experiences are encountered at a time and in a way that allows the feeling of the controllability of stress to increase through appropriate responses. Reinforcing interactions with and responses from other people are important prerequisites for the promotion of self-confidence and self-esteem. A child's ability to cope successfully with stress is therefore never due to the buffering effect of some supportive factor. Rather it is determined by the chain of sequential experiences made under the prevailing conditions of a given familial and socio-cultural context.

## 3. The Influence of Early Affectional Relationships on Brain Development and Behavior

Secure emotional relationships between the child and its caregivers are of uttermost importance for the integration of novel experiences into the already existing patterns of neuronal connectivity in the developing brain. When a new stimulus reaches the brain, it will elicit a certain kind of arousal in the associative networks. If this arousal pattern is identical with the pattern of arousal formed by the activation of already established neuronal connections (founded by earlier experiences), the new stimulus will be reorganized as already known and responded as usual, i. e., routineously. If the novel arousal pattern is at least a bit similar to the already existing patterns formed by earlier experiences, it may be integrated into these old patterns and will thus become stabilized as an extended, more complex pattern of neuronal activity. This is the way, how children (and adults) learn. If this integration is impossible, because the novel arousal pattern is too strange and cannot be associated with any already existing pattern, the child may either neglect the challenge or – if the stimulus or the problem is large enough and does not disappear – activate an emergency reaction. All mammals process such very old, genetically programmed emergency reactions: fight, flight – and if neither the activation of one or the other does solve the problem – freezing. The latter is associated with a so-called uncontrollable stress response, which causes a massive and long-lasting release of stress hormones which may cause destabilization of already existing neuronal connections and hamper the formation of new ones. Under such condition of helplessness, nothing can be learned and already stored knowledge cannot be activated and the respective neuronal connectivity patterns may even get lost permanently.

Secure emotional relationships provide the most potent protection against such overload and its consequences on the brain. They act to resilience the stress-system under conditions of massive arousal by too strange experiences or too strong stimulation. In the other extreme, when the novel stimulus is not very strong, secure emotional relationships act as "emotional enhancers of arousal". The child is thus encouraged and motivated in its attempts to realize and integrate a novel (otherwise too weak) stimulus. If such support by secure attachment relationships are not available to a child, it is easily either flooded by an overload of stimuli (no stable activation patterns can then be formed and integrated in the brain structures) or it is insufficiently aroused (and therefore no sufficiently strong activation patterns are build up and can be integrated in the brain). Therefore, the quality of the relationship to its caregivers my either favor or hamper the acquisition of own knowledge and competence by the child and affect the complexity of the structural maturation of its brain in a beneficial or detrimental manner.

It is during the first three years of life when the vast majority of synapses is produced. The number of synapses increases with astonishing rapidity until about the age three years and then holds steady throughout the first decade of life. A child's brain becomes super-dense, with twice as many synapses as it will eventually need. Brain development is, then, a process of pruning, i.e. use-dependent structuring. This is why early experience is so crucial: those neuronal networks and synaptic pathways that have been stabilized by virtue of repeated early experience tend to become permanent; the synapses that are not used often enough tend to be eliminated. In this way early experiences – positive or negative – have a decisive impact on how the brain is wired.

Compared to other primates, the maturation of the human brain, especially of the higher frontocortical brain regions is enormously prolonged in our species. It reaches a much higher degree of complexity and is much more affected by early experiences, by use- and disuse- dependent plasticity. The most delicate neuronal networks of the frontal cortex are the sites where the most complex, most sophisticated and the most human-specific brain functions will be generated: goal-oriented behavior and motivation, self-concept and self-efficacy, impulse-control, consciousness and the ability to transcend own thoughts and intentions into larger contexts. Also the ability to feel what others feel, and to experience feelings of connectedness, peace and love are generated by the most intricate neuronal networks located in the frontal (frontoorbital) cortex. These networks and the abilities mediated by them are not preformed by an inherited genetic program. They all must be acquired, stabilized and facilitated by experience dependent plasticity, i. e., by education, socialization and enculturation.

Genetically driven are only the enormous offerings made in individual brain areas (including the frontal cortex) at certain periods in the form of an overproduction of neuronal dendritic and axonal processes and an overabundance of synaptic contacts (critical periods). How many and which of these offerings can be maintained and become integrated into larger functional networks is dependent on their stabilizing inputs, i. e. the complexity of experiences made by a child during these early critical periods of brain development. But the most complex and most slowly developing neuronal networks in the frontal cortex are not only vulnerable to the lack of stabilizing inputs. They are at least as vulnerable to overstimulation and to the destabilizing influences mediated by ascending projections from subcortical (limbic, hypothalamic and brain stem) stress-sensitive systems. The enduring activation of an uncontrollable stress response will seriously hamper and suppress the elaboration and stabilization of the complex neuronal and synaptic connections in higher cortical association areas.

If a child experiences constant stress and anxiety, e. g. from not being able to structure and understand the world around it, or from the absence of grown-ups relieving the anxiety, the structuring of the brain risk be destabilized and regressing. Instead of structures enabling problem solving, the experience of own inability and incompetence is then structurally anchored in the developing brain. The part of the brain that is particularly open to the outside influences is the frontal cortex in which the experiences of learning and socialization are structured.

## 4. A Neurobiological View on the Prerequisites for a Culture of Peace and Non-violence

The development of the human brain is much less (pre-)determined by genes than previously thought. Our brain is a self-organizing, open system, characterized by an enormous degree of experience-dependent plasticity. Especially in the higher brain regions, the connections between nerve cells are structured by use and disuse, i.e. by activity patterns which are generated in the brain by sensory inputs. The more complex the situations we learn to deal with, the more sophisticated are the experiences we make, and the larger will be the degree of connectivity formed between the nerve cells in our higher brain centers.

When novel demands cannot properly responded by the activation of an already established pattern of connectivity in the higher brain regions, emotional centers in the midbrain become activated. Without this activation new experiences cannot be made and anchored in the brain structures. The stronger the activation, the more firm the structure. E.g. when parents play "hide and seek" with their baby, the baby feels anxiety because the parent disappear and it doesn't know how to rectify the situation. When the parent reappears the anxiety is relieved. When the baby experiences this again and again a firm structure is formed from the experience that "my parent is able to relieve my anxiety and I will be fine". This structure is stored in the brain enabling the child to face future situations with anxiety with the experience that "if I involve my parent the anxiety disappears", i.e. a problem solving skill is learned, enabled by brain structures.

It is paramount for the development of the brain (and thus for the ability to internalize emotional, social and intellectual knowledge) that the child is surrounded by grown-ups that help it relieve anxiety and stress by teaching it how to master problem solving in challenging situations thus creating new experiences. Since the brain cannot stimulate itself to develop the needed functionality, and the child won't know how to, the child depends on the grown-ups around it to provide the stimuli. Secure emotional relations with the primary care takers are therefore so important.

Animal experiments have shown that even newborn rats which are raised by a "bad" or less "competent" mother will themself become "poorly gifted" mothers, even if they were born by a "good" mother. Parental competence is obviously not inherited but acquired already in rats, and definitely even more so in humans. Here, parents must provide almost every competence, skill and cultural achievement to their children. Without their example, children would not even learn to stand upright or to speak. The better the competences of the parents, the greater the chance that they will be transmitted from one generation to the next. However, this process is only efficient if the parents are also able to engage emotionally in their relation to the child. This ability is also largely determined by their own experiences with emotional relationships during early childhood.

During early childhood, aversive or insecure attachment relationships are the most important trigger for the activation of uncontrollable stress-responses. Therefore, insecurely attached children are unable to develop a highly complex neuronal and synaptic connectivity in their brain, especially in the frontal cortex. They have difficulties to acquire a broad spectrum of different coping strategies, to maintain a high level of creativity and curiosity, to constructively interact with others, and to develop feelings of connectedness, love and peace. Instead such emotionally labile children will tend to use and facilitate various less sophisticated, pseudo-autonomous, egocentric and even autistic behavioral strategies. They have difficulties to feel what others feel and to accept social rules. They are unable to control their impulses and they tend to various forms of violent destructive behavior. Because of their poorly developed self-concept and their lack of self-efficacy, such children can easily be manipulated by "strong others", e.g. a "Führer". Therefore all totalitarian regimes have always made special affords to systematically disrupt the formation of secure early attachment relationships between mothers and their children.

In order to prevent such negative effects of aversive early childhood experiences on later individual life and on the society, and to pave the way to a culture of peace and nonviolence, particular efforts must be made to strengthen the relationship between parents and their children as early as possible, i.e. already during pregnancy, and to protect children against insecurity, anxiety and stress during early childhood. Since most parents are not aware of the sculpturing influences of their own relationships on the developing brains of their children, education programs may help and should be installed to overcome this deficit. These programs should aim to strengthen the affectional relationship between parents and their children, to inform the public about the negative influence of psychosocial and other stressors on brain development, and to help to prevent distortions of the relationship between parents and their children by aversive, traumatic or neglecting experiences. Particular effords must be made to support secure attachment relationships and the feeling of emotional stability in our children, if we want to create a more peaceful world. Only then human subjects will have a chance to unfold their full potential.

Thus, modern brain research confirms an old Indian proverb: putting on pressure and inducing fear are not only unsuitable strategies for improving performance; they also strangle curiosity and creativity in schools, businesses and civil administration. It's high time to think about a new relationship culture. And slowly but surely, this is starting to be implemented as a successful leadership concept everywhere. This concept is called "Supportive Leadership", and it aims at the promotion of the readiness to achieve through support, recognition and encouragement. What should grow better has to be adequately watered and fertilized.

Unfortunately, the strange notion has set in the minds of many people that it is or indeed must be tiring to achieve, whether to learn a lot in school or to work successfully later. Therefore in school or at work, it is all too often attempted to improve achievement through reward and if this doesn't work, by threat of punishment.

These learning by rote methods appear at first glance to work quite well. But on closer examination and particularly in the long term, they turn out to be extremely problematical. Through these forced methods, the achiever senses a feeling: he or she feels that they are being put under pressure.

Neuronal patterns thus activated in the brain are then coupled and connected with all that required to attain the achievement concerned. Who goes through this once or even repeatedly, always feels, even at a later date, this same unpleasant feeling in his stomach, whenever he faces a similar challenge.

In order to get rid of this, one can only try to keep well clear of the work or even to seek an even bigger reward. The enthusiasm for achievement, the enthusiasm for learning and to do it your way is usually gone forever. The seedling shrivels, because it has been pulled instead of being watered.

## Summary

The most important finding made in the field of neurobiological research during the last decade is the discovery of the enormous experience-dependent plasticity of the human brain. The elaboration and stabilization of synaptic connectivity, and therefore, the complexity of neuronal networks in the higher brain centers depend to a far greater extent than previously believed on how – or rather, for which purpose – an individual uses his brain, the goals pursued, the experiences made in the course of his life, the models used for orientation, the values providing stability and eliciting a sense of commitment.

The transmission and internalization of culture-specific abilities and of culture-specific values is achieved primarily during childhood by nonverbal communication (mirror neuron system, imitation learning) as well as by implicit and explicit experiences (reward system, avoidance and reinforcement learning). Therefore the structural and functional organization of the human brain is crucially determined by social and cultural factors. Especially the frontal cortex with its highly complex neuronal networks involved in executive functions, evaluation an decision making must be conceptualized as a social, culturally shaped construct.

The most important prerequisites for the transgenerational transmission of human values and their deep implementation into the higher frontocortical networks of the brains of subsequent generations are secure affectional relationships and a broad spectrum of different challenges. Only under such conditions, children are able to stabilize sufficiently complex networks and internal representations for metacognitive competences in their brains. This delicate process of experience-dependent organization of neuronal connectivity is seriously and often also persistently hampered or prematurely terminated by uncontrollable stress experiences. This danger ought to be minimized by education programs aiming at the implementation of values of connectedness to others and to nature during the period of brain maturation, when the frontocortical circuitry for such metacognitive competences is established.

## References

This contribution is a comprehension and a framework constructed on the basis of numerous original articles that have been publishes in the field of brain research, developmental neurobiology and psychology in recent years. For the sake of clarity, citations of original work and references to related articles are not included here. The reviews may serve as guidance to these original references are found in the bibliography of this book.

Christoph Antweiler

# Pan-cultural Universals – a Foundation for an Inclusive Humanism

More and more people are becoming dissatisfied with defining culture predominantly in terms of its differences and using a word like identity exclusively in its plural form. In view of world-wide conflicts between cultures being additionally fuelled by the debate surrounding globalism there is, however, an increasing demand – both on the part of politicians and the general public – for research contributions that empirically enquire into what constitutes the unity of humankind. Fundamental statements concerning human nature are currently the specific domain of bio-science. On the other hand, there exists a mounting critique of approaches that exclusively focus on biological factors. Therefore, contributions are called for that take a more holistic – in actual fact – a bio-cultural view of human culture.

The conceptualization of a cross-cultural humanism is an urgent project for the human species. Within the framework of current policies that lay the emphasis on cultural difference or culturalism and ethnicity, respectively, and in the process frequently inventing their own separate histories, an intercultural dialogue meets with fundamental opposition. This is due to there seeming to exist an unbridgeable gap between cultural difference and particularity on the one and a universalist discourse on the other hand. In this context the careful search for commonalities is capable of making an important contribution to the cause of cooperation and humanism in the era of globalization.[1]

What is at stake here is to develop a form of humanism which emphasizes cross-cultural unity and whatever cultures have in common while not neglecting the differences that are indispensable for the formation of identity. To this end, and this is the leading assumption underlying this essay, concepts of cultural diversity that are constantly invoking some kind of universal quality will prove to be the

1 Bielefeldt, Heiner: "Menschenrechtliche Universalität und Entwicklungszusammenarbeit", in: Habisch, André/Pöner, Ulrich (Eds.): *Signale der Solidarität. Wege christlicher Nord-Süd-Ethik*, Paderborn etc. 1994, pp. 31–47; Kulturwissenschaftliches Institut Essen (KWI) 2005: "Graduiertenkolleg 'Der Humanismus in der Epoche der Globalisierung. Ein interkultureller Dialog über Kultur, Menschheit und Werte'", in: *Die Zeit* 52 (21.12.2005): 38.

most suitable ones. They are more fruitful than the usual focus on cultural difference and interculturality, with its tendency to posit cultural difference as an absolute given, and at the same time they are more realistic than the total denial of any limits currently en vogue in cultural studies.[2] Figuratively speaking, this amounts to the question of how to visualize the world in its entirety, thereby regarding it less as a globe, which would be to emphasize difference, but more as a planet, which would open up the perspective of commonality.[3]

## Universals and the Project of a New Humanism

The search for common elements among the great philosophical traditions and the great religions that might prove to be useful towards developing a new humanism thus forms an important aspect of the humanism project at the KWI. Of central relevance in this process is the question of whether the great traditions, religions or civilizations, in spite of all their differences, have certain elements in common, especially when it comes to defining what it is to be human. Particularly if one could locate in all of these certain concepts of humanity that purport to be of a universalist nature themselves, these might contribute to the formation of an inclusive concept of humanity.[4] We have little systematic knowledge of such ubiquitous universalist concepts of humanity within the great traditions of thinking. Much less do we know about shared attributes between the thousands of cultures, societies or ethnicities, especially when it comes to common norms, values or ideals. To verify these is exactly the aim of this essay. I am attempting, by drawing on the resources of cultural anthropology, to empirically search for a commonality among numerous, if not all cultures: Cultural universals that in the following I am referring to in short as 'universals'.

The argument of this article proceeds in seven stages. In section 1 I define universals as common human properties on a collective level while proposing that universals, though they differ from the concept of 'human nature', can prove useful for conceptualizing a realistic bio-cultural idea of humanity. In part 2 a wider concept of diachronic universals will be presented, and I will attempt to

2 Antweiler, Christoph: *Grundpositionen interkultureller Ethnologie.* (= Interkulturelle Bibliothek, 79), Nordhausen 2007.

3 Sicks, Kai Marcel: *Bericht zur Konferenz 'Das Planetarische. Kultur – Technik – Medien im postglobalen Zeitalter' an der Universität zu Köln, 8.10.–10.10.2008.* H-Soz-u-Kult, http://hsozkult.geschichte.hu-berlin.de/tagungsberichte/id=2351< (consulted: 11.2.2013)

4 Gieselmann, Martin/Seebold, Irmtraud: *Der Humanismus in der Epoche der Globalisierung. Ein interkultureller Dialog über Kultur, Menschheit und Werte. Arbeitspapier,* Essen: Kulturwissenschaftliches Institut (KWI), unpubl. mscr., n.y. (ca. 2006), p. 1 (http://humanismus@kwinrw.de/cms/index.php?t=126&sid=a622b977f26d7e992c78ffd0bfd7b648; consulted: 13.10.2011)

provide a stimulus for clarifying universals of development. In part 3 I want to emphasize the potential for inclusive definitions of humanity, while at the same time warning against falling a prey to wishful thinking in the search for common values. I am exemplifying this by drawing on concepts of humanity such as 'the family of mankind'. At the same time I would like to point out the possibility of not defining humanity via a rigid catalogue of certain qualities but would rather proceed genealogically via cross-generational links between human beings. In the methodological section 4 I am elucidating the comparison between species and cultures as being the central procedure when researching universals. However, while ethnology is capable of providing synchronic comparisons between ethnicities and while historical studies are contributing diachronic comparisons between societies and civilizations it is nevertheless highly relevant to make a comparison between various species, such as they have been made by behavioral research, primatology, socio-biology and evolutionary ecology, in order to arrive at an empirically based concept of humanity. This leads to the causes of universals set out in part 5. What is emphasized here is that our biotic equipment constitutes only one among numerous indicators of universals. In section 6 it is argued that cultural theories should not be concentrated on the differences between (ethnic) cultures, national culture or civilizations but should instead take into account intra-cultural diversity on the one hand and pan-cultural universals on the other. In part 7 I am setting out some of the universals that might be useful for an inclusive humanism. This specific area, which is one of the still incomplete projects of this contribution and where a lot of research still remains to be done, will be explained by drawing on the example of world-views. The final result will be that universals provide an empirical access to humanity that is an alternative both to extreme cultural relativism and to the absolute givens stipulated by some schools of thought.

## 1. Pan-cultural Patterns vs. 'Human Nature'

Universals, cultural universals, human universals (French: *universaux*) are elements or phenomena to be found regularly in all or almost all societies known to us.[5] More specifically these are patterns that we come across not only in the present day but in all cultures independent of their time and place. By this definition universals are intentionally understood as mere phenomena without naming any causes.

From an empirical perspective the decisive questions are the following: Do

5 Brown, Donald Edward: *Human Universals*, New York etc. 1991; Antweiler, Christoph: *Was ist den Menschen gemeinsam? Über Kultur und Kulturen*, Darmstadt ([1]2007), [2]2009.

human beings act everywhere in such a way as to enhance their own advantage? Or is this different in i.e. Asia? Does there exist in all cultures a concept like justice? Do all humans generally think in terms of dichotomies? Do people everywhere prefer their close relations? Are all societies classified according to roles and status? Does the incest-taboo hold for all groups of people everywhere in the world? Do adolescents feel insecure in all societies? Have people everywhere mastered the art of sensing minute differences when they want to look down upon somebody? Do humans from all cultures possess the faculty of mutually recognizing the expression of their emotions? And finally: Which are the forms and the contents of learning and teaching that are similar in all cultures – in spite of their obvious differences?

The well-known examples of universals that are more commonly postulated are the Oedipus-complex, the dominance of men in politics and in public life and especially the incest-taboo. This universal, which would be more aptly termed 'incest-avoidance', mainly implies the prevention of sexual congress or marriage and procreation among persons who are related plus norms, prohibitions and sanctions regulating this. The popular term 'incest-taboo' only refers to one facet of the whole complex issue. Incest-avoidance is one of the few universals that are uncontested, as is evidenced by the following quotation: "If ten anthropologists were asked to name one universal institution, nine would be likely to name the incest prohibition; some have expressly named it as the only universal one."[6]

- Anthropomorphic concepts
- Nepotism
- Specific gender-roles, -states, -ideals
- Wedding rites
- Categories or terminology to designate age-groups
- Contraceptive practices
- Magical concepts
- The linear concept of time as an arrow (besides other time-concepts)
- Ethnicity and ethnocentrism
- Practices of weather-forecasting
- The concept of romantic love
- Music, dances, performances
- Art as 'making special'
- Politeness by means of long introductions
- Pauses of appr. 2.8 seconds in text-recitals (independent of stanzas)

Figure 1: Selected examples of universals

Universals can take on a variety of manifestations: in the general conditions of life, in behavior, thinking and feeling as well as in facial expression, social institutions and certain objects. In figure 1, I am giving a few examples in order

6 Kroeber, Alfred Louis: "Totem and Taboo in Retrospect", in: *American Journal of Sociology* 55 (1939): 446.

to demonstrate the multifariousness of universals with regard to their content and specificity. The examples chosen are only a small selection of universals either postulated or proven.[7]

One usually differentiates various forms and types of universals, for which the most precise terminology and taxonomy has been compiled in linguistics.[8] Without dwelling on this point more extensively,[9] I am briefly naming the most important ones. One distinguishes absolute or true universals (German: '*echte Universalien*'), i. e. features to be found in all known societies, from near universals, i. e. phenomena encountered in a great number of known societies but not in all of them. The so-called implicational universals form a specific group. They consist of a relationship between two characteristics in such a way that whenever one specific feature (which itself is not a universal) exist in a society, another related feature is also to be found (but not vice versa). A simple example: all languages that have a plural form also have a dual form.

The universality or ubiquity that lends a phenomenon its status as a universal always applies to cultural units, e. g. societies, nations or ethnicities, not, however, to individuals. Because they manifest themselves throughout all cultures, though not necessarily in all individuals, such universals are also designated as 'cultural universals'. These are distinct from other forms that refer to general human characteristics, i. e. features that are to be found in all individuals, the entire species and all of mankind. Contrary to common opinion universals are therefore not to be simply equated with human nature or the general attributes of *homo sapiens*, although they are partially related with these.

Human universals have a status that is different from the characters defining various species of animals. With animals the universalizing designation of a species comes very close to the findings one would expect from an ethogram (inventory of all behavior) of any population of that species. This means that one could investigate different populations of a given species, with due consideration of environmental parameters, from which one would derive generalizing pro-

7 Cf. various catalogues of universals that have been published subsequent to the first list of universals drawn up by George Peter Murdock in 1945: Murdock, George Peter: "The Common Denominator of Cultures", in: Ralph Linton (Ed.): *The Science of Man in the World Crisis*, New York 1945, pp. 123 – 140; Sherry, John F. Jr.: *Contemporary Marketing and Consumer Behavior. An Anthropological Sourcebook*, Thousand Oaks etc. 1995, 288 f., Eibl, Karl: *Animal Poeta. Bausteine der biologischen Kultur- und Literaturtheorie*, Paderborn 2004, pp. 353 – 358 and the comparative documentation of various such lists in *Was ist den Menschen gemeinsam?*, 393 – 409. For a more popular presentation of various examples of pancultural patterns in the context of cultural diversity cf. Antweiler, Christoph: *Heimat Mensch. Was uns alle verbindet*, Hamburg 2009.

8 Holenstein, Elmar: *Zur Begrifflichkeit der Universalienforschung in Linguistik und Anthropologie*, Cologne 1979.

9 Cf. Antweiler: *Was ist den Menschen gemeinsam?*, ch. 8.

nouncements about the entire kind. However, even with some primates this is only possible within limits, as the differences in behavior among various populations of free-living Chimpanzees and Orang-Utans have shown. With human populations such generalizations are even less viable. The research of universals can therefore count as a specific empirical contribution to resolving the problem of what it is that constitutes our human nature, a human nature that would include our biotically inherited disposition towards, and need of, culture.

## 2. Diachronic Universals and Developmental Universals

In a slightly different sense, universals are phenomena that are not only found in all recent cultures but are a common feature of all known human societies. Such diachronic universals thereby exist in cultures across time and space (fig. 2): In such an understanding universals can be regarded as common properties that are timeless. Even our ethnographic knowledge of more recent cultures is rather incomplete. Even our knowledge of prehistoric cultures is extremely fragmentary. Hence it will be particularly difficult to define exactly such universals. This, however, should not prevent us from investigating diachronic universals since our fragmentary empirical knowledge can be supplemented by other methods such as deduction or retrodiction. This determination of universals is reminiscent of Kroeber's above-mentioned very broad definition of anthropology as a discipline that is synchronic as well as diachronic. Accordingly Donald Brown defines human universals as transcultural and transhistorical:

> "Human universals comprise those features of culture, society, language, behavior, and psyche for which there is no known exception to their existence in all *ethnographically or historically* recorded human societies."[10] (my emphasis)

> "Human universals – of which hundreds have been identified – consist of those features of culture, society, language, behaviour, and mind that, *so far as the record has been examined*, are found among all peoples known to ethnography and history."[11] (my emphasis)

Cultural universals always exist as isolated features of certain communities or societies, and not as the sum total of their features. To claim that societies are similar with regard to one feature "a" does not preclude that in terms of other feature "b","c", … – or even all other characteristics – there exist significant differences. The determination of a universal therefore does not diminish the

10 Brown, Donald Edward: "Human Universals", in: Wilson, Robert Anton/Keil, Frank C. (Eds.): *The MIT Encyclopedia of the Cognitive Sciences*, London 1999, p. 382.

11 Brown, Donald Edward: "Human Universals, Human Nature/Human Culture", in: *Daedalus* (Fall 2004): 47.

uniqueness of certain objects, persons or societies. It simply means that the examined object is not unique in every respect. Following Kluckhohn and Murray one could say: Every human being is like all other humans, like some other humans, like no other humans.[12] This is borne out by recent studies on the psychological diversity of human beings: all are the same, and everybody is different.[13]

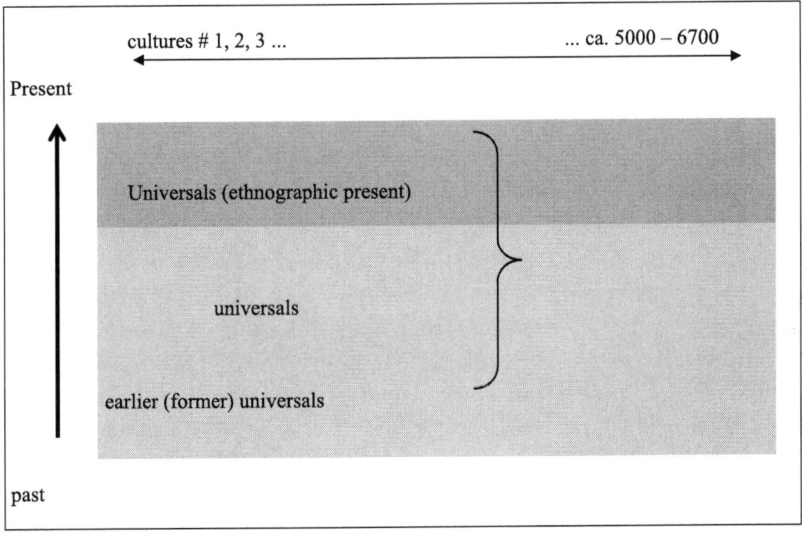


Figure 2: Synchronic and diachronic universals

The definition of universals as existing across all human societies does expressly not imply the assertion that such characteristics do not also exist among populations of other primates. This needs emphasizing since some authors' understanding of universals implies that these are characteristics exhibited by all human beings as individuals, but are not to be found among animals. Such characteristics should be distinguished as 'species-specific features' from universals. One of the few features fulfilling this additional condition is that of 'secret copulation'. It is not only ovulation that is covert among humans, but also sexual intercourse in all cultures does not usually take place *coram publico* but in

12 Kluckhohn, Clyde Kay Maben/Murray, Henry A.: *Personality in Nature, Society and Culture*, New York 1953.

13 Lewontin, Richard Charles: *Menschen. Genetische, kulturelle und soziale Gemeinsamkeiten*, Heidelberg 1986; Grossmann, Klaus E./Grossmann, Karin: "Universale Bedingungen für die Entwicklung kultureller Vielfalt: Eine verhaltensbiologische Perspektive", in: Trommsdorff, Gisela/Kornath, Hans-Joachim (Eds.): *Theorien und Methoden der kulturvergleichenden Psychologie*, Göttingen etc. 2007, pp. 249–254.

private (being associated with secrecy and inhibition[14]), whereas among all other primates this is totally different.[15]

A specific type of universal is constituted by developmental universals or so-called evolutionary universals. They are of particular relevance within the framework of globalized processes of development. In the early 1960s Talcott Parsons – after his conversion from a convinced anti-evolutionist ("who nowadays reads Spencer?") to a theoretician of evolution – formulated universals of macro-social development. With his concept of 'evolutionary universals' he defines certain civilizatory inventions as the specific achievement of complex societies, as e.g. writing, market economy, bureaucratic organization, common law and democracy as well as increasing social mobility. There are six evolutionary universals in particular that are held to be of great relevance by Parsons: social stratification, cultural legitimization (e.g. social ideals and social identity), administrative bureaucracy, monetary systems, generalized and universally applicable norms and democratic forms of association.[16]

Parsons' main emphasis was on their significance for the long-term adaptability of macro-societies, and this is where they acquire a particular importance for an inclusive humanism. He considers these evolutionary universals as highly relevant social structures as well as individual forms of behavior that have arisen in a variety of societies over a long period of time as well as independently of each other and that historically evolved over a long period of time. This implies the assumption that their formation as a conglomerate of institutions was the precondition for reaching a more complex stage of social evolution. As a social structure and as individual forms of behavior they have severally evolved independently of each other and have prevailed over long periods of time. Thereby, via the genre-specific abilities of individuals, all societies potentially share in certain pan-human cultural elements. Within this context, however, various cultures have only availed themselves of these possibilities more or less completely.[17] With reference to the entire world one would therefore have to speak of near-universals.

Developmental universals are currently also under discussion in disciplines

14 Duerr, Hans-Peter: *Nacktheit und Scham*, Frankfurt/Main 1988.

15 Schröder, Inge: *Wege zum Menschen. Theoretische Beiträge zur evolutionären Anthropologie*, Göttingen 2000, p. 59; Ehrlich, Paul R.: *Human Natures. Genes, Cultures, and the Human Prospect*, Harmondsworth 2002, pp. 187 f.

16 Parsons, Talcott: "Evolutionary Universals in Society", in: *American Sociological Review* 29 (1964): 339 – 357; Sanderson, Stephen King: *Evolutionism and Its Critics. Deconstructing and Reconstructing an Evolutionary Interpretation of Human Society*, Boulder, Col./London 2007, pp. 133 f.

17 Schöfthaler, Traugott: "Kultur in der Zwickmühle. Zur Aktualität des Streits zwischen kulturrelativistischer und universalistischer Sozialwissenschaft", in: *Das Argument* 139 (1983): pp. 337 f.

other than macro-sociology and universal history. Evolutionary psychologists and ecologists are dealing with the implications of what in a macro-historical perspective can be regarded as the unusual size of modern societies, i. e. the phenomenon of ultrasociality. Modern human societies, be they ethnographic groups or states, are both in demographic and spatial terms considerably larger than anything known to us from other primates or from anthropogenesis. They represent highly complex forms of society or are parts of these. In addition, most groups of humans dispose of a considerable amount of material objects. Frequently these are artifacts of a trans-generational durability. On top of this there are intensive and also trans-generational changes in our physical environment. Almost everywhere on earth people live in anthropogenically shaped landscapes and thereby in environments that are predominantly formed by cultural factors. Societies which are larger and more complex than those that were typical of the Holocene with its small groups comprising up to about 150 individuals are designated as 'ultrasocial'.[18]

In the perspective of universal history and the history of evolution humans have only lived in large and complex communities since fairly recently. For the larger part of history *homines sapientes* lived in small groups. This fact is only thematized in evolutionary psychology where, as distinct from sociobiology, it is not so much the common ground existing between mankind and animals is of interest but where instead the special characteristics of human beings are emphasized.[19] Evolutionary psychologists are focused on how the human psyche has been shaped by such environments. This circumstance has far-reaching consequences for the understanding of universals. Not only were these groups of people small but they also used comparatively few artifacts, nor did they effect lasting changes on their physical environment. A special feature of early society which makes up the larger part of human history is that there were very few material and non-corporeal media of information. Particularly writing or monuments as trans-generational transmitters of social memory were not yet in existence.

The phenomenon of ultrasociality can lead to the formation of universals because the sheer size and complexity of such societies lead to specific needs and

18 Dunbar, Robin I.M.: "Coevolution of Neocortical Size, Group Size, and Language in Humans", in: *Behavioral and Brain Sciences* 16 (1993): 681–694; Dunbar, Robin I.M.: *The Human Story. A New History of Mankind's Evolution*, London 2004; Campbell, Donald T.: "The Two Distinct Routes Beyond Kin Selection to Ultrasociality: Implications for the Humanities and Social Sciences", in: Bridgeman, Diane L. (Ed.): *The Nature of Prosocial Developoment. Interdisciplinary Theories and Strategies*, New York 1983, p. 12.

19 Eibl, Karl: "Warum der Mensch etwas Besonderes ist. Einige evolutionsbiologische Aspekte", in: *Literaturkritik.de* 2 (2007): (http://www.literaturkritik.de/public/rezension.php?rez_id=10428&ausgabe=200702%3E; consulted 11.2.2013).

requirements. In order to be able to function, complex societies need complex institutions that go beyond the organizational level of kinship relations.[20] Socioeconomically complex societies of large extension and demographic density require the division of labor as well as subsystems, such as a bureaucracy. Such societies have to adapt to the problems both of their own complexity and that of their environment, which latter also comprises complex neighboring societies. It can therefore be expected that groups of people, no matter what their specific culture may be, from a certain degree of extension, size and density of population as well as complexity are bound to exhibit certain similarities. Another requirement is media, to the extent that mass-media can be regarded as a fairly recent near-universal, in whose products in turn one can investigate other specific universals.[21]

In this context one can postulate universals, which can be qualified as implicational universals that are closely linked with the conditions of ultrasociality. Since today's societies have all exceeded Dunbar's threshold of ultrasociality, a number of near-universals can be expected to arise from this. The focus on ultrasociality is capable of widening the important perspective on the small 'tribal' group by means of which the disciplines of socio-biology and evolutionary psychology have attempted to evolve psychological universals, by focusing on the more comprehensive dimension of larger societies. This would specifically lead to a deeper understanding of universals that are the result of long-term social development. I would like to elucidate this by means of a speculation on a typical theme of classical sociology and ethnography, i.e. the nexus of kinship, altruism and sexuality. In ultrasocial communities the following scenario would be thinkable:

> "Altruism vis-à-vis relatives (friends) as a bio-evolutionary universal is stabilized by the cultural norm of kin solidarity and thus functions as a – universal – bonding agent of culturally *variable* social structures. The practical freedom from, and the elimination of kinship relations in the functional subsystems that are being formed is an *evolutionary universal* on the way towards a modern type of society. In the same process the gratification of undoubtedly universal sexual desires is freed from social constraints and expresses itself with less inhibition."[22]

---

20 Richerson, Peter J./Boyd, Robert: "Complex Societies: The Evolutionary Origins of a Crude Superorganism", in: *Human Nature* 10 (1999): 253–290; idem: "Institutional Evolution in the Holocene: The Rise of Complex Societies", in: Runciman, Walter Garrison (Ed.): *The Origin of Human Social Institutions*, Oxford etc. 2001, pp. 201 ff; idem: *Not by Genes Alone. How Human Culture Transformed Human Evolution*, Chicago/London 2005.

21 Uhl, Matthias/Kumar, Keval J.: *Indischer Film. Eine Einführung*, Bielefeld 2004; Hejl, Peter M.: *Introduction – Culture: Universals and Particulars.* Paper, Conference "Media and Universals 2005, Focus on Film and Print", SFB/FK 615 Medienumbrüche, Teilprojekt A 3: Soziale und Anthropologische Faktoren der Mediennutzung, Siegen: 3.2.–5.2.2005.

22 Hejl, Peter M./Antweiler, Christoph: "Kooperation und Konkurrenz", in: Roth, Gerhard

Through this speculation it can be demonstrated that (1) universals are generally evolved in a systemic context and are thereby useful for the understanding of cultures as social systems, that (2) biotic universals are capable of interacting with non-biotic ones, and that (3) universals are not only of a static nature but also exist in the form of a dynamic process. Such evolutionary universals might be an extremely interesting object for the future research of universals.

## 3. *The Family of Man:* the Problematic Nature of Normative Humanism Exemplified by Popular Concepts of Humanity

Scientists or scholars research certain themes and phenomena not exclusively because they are motivated to know something, but their pursuit of knowledge goes beyond this. This is why there are extrinsic motivations that sometimes cause an author to fall into a trap, and especially the theme of universals is replete with such traps. One of the dangers inherent in our humanist concern is that one might wish certain universals into existence. The idea of considering humanity as a cosmopolitan community of interest is very important[23] but can be extremely seductive for political institutions as well. An example of this is the motif of 'One World' currently prevalent in German development aid, which as the humanist version of an ethics of planetary responsibility has gained the status of a guideline for action. In view of the anxiety of a cultural break-up and the problem of fast increasing globalization the search for universals that are capable of supplying arguments against xenophobia or racism becomes only too understandable. If all over the world the ideology of individualism and competition is propagated, critics are only too prone to succumb to the tendency to prove the universal existence of a counter-trend. What is then sought after are the more positively valued qualities of mankind or of all cultures, like sociability and altruism.

Whenever human beings compare each other in an everyday context, most people are initially struck by the extraordinary variability of humanity, especially as regards their facial features, less so, however, by their similarities. Even when entire cultures are under comparison the differences are foregrounded, and this is what dominates the world-wide discourse: culture as difference. Whatever cultures have in common only gets mentioned after their difference has first of all been emphasized or any common features have even been rejected

(coord.): *Antrag auf eine internationale Konferenz Transkulturelle Universalien am Hanse-Wissenschaftskolleg in Delmenhorst*, unpubl. ms. (Delmenhorst) 2004, p. 11.

23 This topic is developed in Antweiler, Christoph: *Inclusive Humanism. Anthropological Basics for a Realistic Cosmopolitanism*, Göttingen and Taipei 2012.

from the outset. The perception of relative differences is strongly dependent on the level of comparison. When humans compare themselves and their societies with animals and animal populations rather than with other people and their cultures, the differences observable between groups of people tend to disappear from view almost completely. In such circumstances what is perceived in the first place is the communality of the *conditio humana*, and thus the contrast gets emphasized that exists even with regard to our closest biological relations, the higher primates.[24] The *conditio humana*, however, also lends itself to being transfigured into a naturalistic mystique. The longing for positive universals appears to be harmless at first sight. However, it does pose a few problems, as is evidenced by an example taken from the area of visual popular culture.

Over the last few years projects for visually documenting the world-wide diversity of human life-forms have proliferated.[25] At a first glance these books seem to show how multifarious humans are and how diverse their ways of life are capable of being. More subliminally, however, the universal themes of mankind and transcultural problems are referred to. Similar projects are aimed at documenting universals for didactic purposes and have for some time been accessible via internet.[26] Even more than ten years ago a 'GeoSphere Project' funded by UNESCO came up with a CD-ROM giving an insight into data and answers on questionnaires of thirty families 'randomly chosen' from all over the world.

The classical precursor of these projects was the highly successful photographic exhibition that Edward Steichen (1879–1973) in his capacity as curator of the Museum of Modern Art (MoMa) compiled in New York. Following the formulation of the 'General Declaration of Human Rights' in 1948, there are 503 black-and-white photographs by 278 amateur and professional photographers from 68 countries put on exhibition. Employing the medium of photography as a world language the show demonstrates in 24 categories that everywhere the same universal human themes and similar problems dominate, such as play, work, birth, illness, old age and death. What Steichen aimed at was to create a "mirror of the fundamental similarity of the human species".[27] The photos are supplemented with seemingly timeless quotations, e.g. proverbs or lines from the Old Testament for each of the categories.[28] 'The Family of Man' went on tour through

24 Lewontin, Richard Charles: *Menschen. Genetische, kulturelle und soziale Gemeinsamkeiten*, Heidelberg 1986, p. 1 f.

25 Ommer, Uwe: *1000 Families. Das Familienalbum des Planeten Erde. The Family Album of Planet Earth. L'album de famille de la planète Terre*, Cologne 2000.

26 Payne, Harris/Gray, Susan: "Exploring Cultural Universals", in: *Journal of Geography* 96 (1997): 220–223.

27 Steichen, Edward: *The Family of Man. The Greatest Photographic Exhibition of All Time – 503 Pictures From 68 Countries*, New York 1955.

28 For the details cf. Philipp, Claudia Gabriele: "Die Ausstellung 'The Family of Man' (1955).

67 countries as a travelling edition and it turned out to be a sensational success. In the age of the Cold War the exhibition was fostering the idea of the unity of mankind. The numerous divisions of mankind thus are made to appear as the mere surface, as something contingent, under which the substantial identity becomes manifest. The intermingling of human diversity and the essential unity of their actions and emotions fascinated millions of spectators. This even applied, when starting in 1993, a revised version of the exhibition was put on show again in numerous countries of the world, among others, in Japan. In a day and age of cultural upheaval this fascination in conjunction with universalist utopias has certainly inspired some more recent and similar exhibitions and books.

Behind such projects there often is lurking wishful thinking, sentimentality, a hidden political agenda or crypto-religious ideologies. In Berlin the exhibition bore the title 'Wir alle' ('We all') and in Paris 'La Grande Famille des Hommes', i.e. 'The Great Family of Man'. On the occasion of the Parisian tour Roland Barthes in his 'Mythologies' criticized the show right from the start as moralizing, sentimental and pseudo-religious. In his view the pictures are in actual fact highlighting or 'babelizing' the differences between peoples through their very presentation of skin-color and customs, in order to then arrive in an almost magical fashion at the unity of mankind:

> "...man is born, works, laughs and dies everywhere in the same way, and if there does become visible some ethnic specificity in these activities, one immediately suggests that behind them lies an identical 'nature' and that diversity is only of a formal character which does not contradict a common substance. That of course leads to postulating a human essence, and already God has been reintroduced in our exhibition...".[29]

In 1994 the exhibition, which had been presented to the Duchy of Luxemburg as early as 1964 by the American government, has found a permanent home in a revised form in Clervaux Castle in Luxemburg. While the contributions to the jubilee edition published on this occasion mostly amount, with very few exceptions, to an homage to Steichen, there subsequently ensued an intensive discussion in which Barthes' arguments were supported.[30] What the exhibition was criticized for was both the involuntary emphasis on physical difference on the one hand as well as the universalizing message on the other. The monumental fraternization amounted to a denial of any kind of social difference. The latter was regarded as an instrument of American imperialism during the Cold War.

Fotographie als Weltsprache", in: *Fotogeschichte* 23 (1987): 45–61; Schmidt, Julia: "Edward Steichens 'The Family of Man'", in: *Kunstchronik* 8 (1996): 365–370.

29 Barthes, Roland: "Die große Familie des Menschen", in: idem: *Mythen des Alltags*, Frankfurt/Main 1974, p. 16.

30 Schmidt: "Edward Steichens 'The Family of Man'", in: Back, Jean/Schmidt-Linsenhoff, Victoria (Eds.): *The Family of Man –2000. Humanism and Postmodernism. A Reappraisal of the Photo Exhibiton by Edward Steichen*, Marburg 2004.

Not only was the exhibition obfuscating any problems of social inequality, but especially of the Jewish Shoa. Some voices were critical of the implicit patriarchal overtones of the 'Family of Man'; the American 'normal' family was the unadmitted ideal of the show. Others blamed it for its obtrusive didacticism. The exhibition in its present form was, they opined, an early version of consumer-oriented theme-parks and the 'United Colours' campaign by Benetton.

Upon a closer look at the exhibition there is much about these critiques that seems justified, whereas in other respects they are somewhat exaggerated. What is easily forgotten is that the concept of the 'Family of Man', in spite of being problematic, possesses a serious potential, as elucidated by Gernot Böhme. The metaphor of the family does not, of necessity, have to be understood in a Christian, Jewish or patriarchal sense, and furthermore it does not need to be understood as consolatory or sentimental. The metaphor can also be read in a historical or phylogenetic sense. The membership of each individual to the genres of mankind is particularly emphasized by the concept of 'family' with its connotation of kinship, connectedness and unity. "One is a human being because one is descended of human beings".[31] In that way one could define humanity in terms of its interrelatedness, and one could conceive of it as an *extensional* concept which would admit diversity. A definition of humanity that makes the membership of the human race conditional upon certain qualities (*intensional*) would hardly permit of such latitude.

An extensional understanding of humanity, inspired by the familial metaphor, could also be inserted into the recent debate about the universalist dimension of world-wide cultural diversity. A new 'cultural universalism' under the heading of 'world culture' or 'global culture'[32] would no longer be concerned about Euro-American dominated homogenization. The world-culture approach is more about how cultural diversity is organized globally by means of establishing relationships throughout the world at large, as is the case e.g. with the Olympic Games or the world-wide movement of Non-Governmental Organization (NGOs) in civil society. What is decisive in this process are 'universalist elements' which are presented in such a way as though they were of universal relevance, e.g. the DSM IV-classification of mental diseases. In Lechner and Boli's definition of cultural universalism an important aspect of numerous universalist approaches becomes apparent: Wishes, values and norms.

31 Böhme, Gernot: "Kant und die Family of Man. Wie begründet sich die Universalität der Menschenrechte?", in: *Lettre Internationale* 25 (1999): p. 26.

32 Robertson, Roland: *Globalization. Social Theory and Global Culture.* (= Theory, Culture & Society), London etc. 1992, pp. 108–114; Lechner, Frank J./Boli, John: *World Culture. Origins and Consequences*, Oxford etc. 2005, pp. 22–25, 44 ff.)

> "The element is presumed to have universal (world-wide) scope; it is presumed to be interpretable in a large uniform way and to make sense both cognitively and, often normatively, in any particular local culture or social framework."[33]

## 4. Methods of an Empirical Search for Universals: Comparison between Species and Intercultural Comparison

The most relevant method of empirically documenting universals consists in diverse forms of comparison between species and intercultural comparison. I would, however, like to mention a few other methods that have been of relevance for the research on universals: Theories, case histories and archaeological methods. First of all theories are important because universals are often deductively postulated. Secondly case studies can be most instructive. They permit the refutation of implicitly assumed universals or supposedly impossible phenomena ('In no culture are there any…') by supplying evidence of extreme varieties of human culture that contradict these generalizations. In this respect curious or odd phenomena prove their worth. The verification of one single well-documented case of a marriage between women (gynaegamy) would be sufficient to upset Eurocentric notions of supposedly fully universal marital or family relations. A further example would be the search for societies in which women dominate the public political sphere. Archaeological methods become relevant when they are capable of demonstrating the historical emergence of similar cultural features or patterns independently of each other. Thus there are to be found correspondences in the complex societies of the Old and the New World, especially with regard to their institutions. In a kind of historical experiment similar but independent structures can be shown to emerge from the same Palaeolithic heritage.

Charles Darwin and Konrad Lorenz can be regarded as the founding fathers of comparisons between humans and (other) animals. Especially comparisons between humans and primates are relevant in this respect. Such comparisons only make sense when the phenomena compared possess a degree of analogy, e.g. when the causes of the phenomena are identical and there exists some common ground. Converging developments, i.e. similarities that are due to a different genealogy, have to be excluded. In the case of phenomena that are strongly determined features such as language, this method has proved to be effective, e.g. with regard to genealogy in comparative biology or relations of parentage in comparative linguistics. This procedure becomes problematic with

33 Lechner/Boli: *World Culture. Origins and Consequences*, pp. 21 f.

phenomena whose genealogy is complex.[34] It is the common properties that enable a comparison in the first place, and it is the differences that make these interesting.[35]

The central method in the research into universals, the comparison between species, consists of the comparison between humans and the higher primates. This poses the problem of what the qualities are that primates actually have in common (*ape universals*[36]). Some primatologists therefore consider the comparison across the entire range of apes to be of prime importance in order to be able to understand the differences between e.g. Chimpanzees and Bonobos as well as the similarities of both as against other apes.[37] Other authors go even further in seeing the Rubicon between monkeys and apes rather than between primates and humans. Accordingly they criticize any 'primatocentrism' and demand explicit comparisons with other animals because even non-primates such as whales, birds and rats possess protocultural abilities.[38] Such inter-species comparisons not only permit the establishment of homologies or phyletic connections. Additionally analogies or convergences that are due to similar environments or similar functional contexts can be explained via the comparison of species. Therefore, contrary to common opinion, not only comparisons between closely related species can be of use.

In the social science the fundamental method for supplying the empirical proof of the existence of universals is the systematic as well as world-wide cultural comparison or cross-cultural comparison. This is the central approach of ethnology with regard to the research on universals. For this purpose the synchronic comparison of ethnology can be supplemented with diachronic comparisons such as they are supplied by historical research (fig. 3) – something that has happened far too rarely until now. In comparative cultural research particular a phenomenon is observed across the range of numerous, or at least,

34 Markl, Hubert: *Evolution, Genetik und menschliches Verhalten. Zur Frage wissenschaftlicher Verantwortung*, Munich and Zürich 1986, p. 83.

35 Cf. Antweiler, Christoph: "Analogisierung als spezielle Form von Vergleich: eine nützliche Methode der interdisziplinären Evolutionsforschung", in: *Erwägen, Wissen, Ethik. Deliberation, Knowledge, Ethics* 16.3 (2005): 370–371.

36 Silverman, Sydel: *The Beast on the Desk. Conferencing with Anthropologists*, Walnut Creek, Cal., etc. 2002, p. 186.

37 Strier, Karen B.: "Beyond the Apes: Reasons to Consider the Entire Primate Order", in: de Waal, Frans B.M. (Ed.): *Tree of Origin. What Primate Behavior Can Tell Us about Human Social Evolution*, Cambridge, Mass., and London 2001, p. 72; cf. Byrne, Richard W.: "Social and Technical Forms of Primate Intelligence", in: de Waal, Frans B.M. (Ed.): *Tree of Origin. What Primate Behavior Can Tell Us about Human Social Evolution*, Cambridge, Mass./London 2001, p. 170.

38 McGrew, William C.: "The Nature of Culture. Prospects and Pitfalls of Cultural Primatology", in: de Waal: *Tree of Origin. What Primate Behavior Can Tell Us about Human Social Evolution*, p. 232.

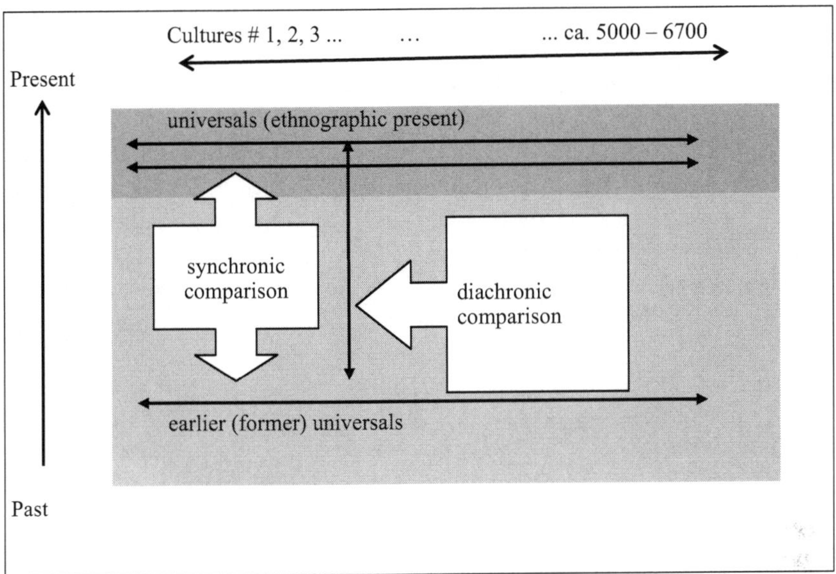


Figure 3: Synchronic and diachronic cultural comparison related to variously broad concepts of universals

several cultural units. Comparative inquiries in the fields of ethnology, sociology and political science can conduct their comparison on various levels:

- Within one culture (intracultural comparison)
- Between various specific cultural units, such as ethnicities, societies and nations (intercultural comparison)
- Between a larger number of societies right up to world-wide samples (systematic intercultural to holocultural comparison)

Instead of dwelling more extensively on the methodological problems one is confronted with in such empirical comparisons of cultures[39] I would like to highlight two contrasting views of typological cultural comparison:[40]

1) Cultures are distinguished by means of features only they possess, i. e. by distinctive features, or under certain conditions even by exclusive features. Cultures are discontinuous with regard to each other
2) Cultures are distinguished by means of the relative importance of features that are also to be found elsewhere; thus the differences are gradual and the

39 Cf. Antweiler: *Was ist den Menschen gemeinsam?*, pp. 206 – 233.

40 Holenstein, Elmar: "Interkulturelle Beziehungen – multikulturelle Verhältnisse. Im Ausgang von Japan-Berichten in der westdeutschen Presse", in: Holenstein, Elmar: *Menschliches Selbstverständnis. Ichbewußtsein – Intersubjektive Verantwortung – Interkulturelle Verständigung*, Frankfurt/Main 1985, p. 139.

relation between cultures is continuous. Features are not exclusive but graded according to their relative status. The predominant feature is decisive of the relative importance of all the others.

These two views have a strong influence on how cultural similarities or differences are conceptualized, with the first view being the one that currently represents the mainstream in cultural and social studies. The second view is of a more optimistic bent, but might be caused by wishful thinking. In spite of this I hold the second mode of comparison to be more adequate in theoretical and more realistic in empirical terms.

## 5. The Causes of Universals: Evolution... and Much More!

When a phenomenon occurs in all or nearly all cultures it is initially quite obvious to attribute the causes to natural factors. This is designated by terms such as 'human nature' or 'the human psyche'. In this context one might ascribe related causes to the structure and function of the human organism and assume the ultimate cause to be rooted in the evolution of mankind. 'The mental uniformity of mankind', for instance, can be held responsible for some or even a large number of universals, as Stephen Pinker argues: "Through the discovery of those profound parallels in the languages of French and the Germans, of the Arabs and the Israelis, of the East and the West, of people from the age of the internet and people from the Stone Age one catches a glimpse of the mental uniformity of mankind."[41]

The ubiquity of this phenomenon, however, cannot automatically – *contra* Pinker – be ascribed to a biotic basis because besides biotic or evolutionary factors there do exist other possible causes of universals. Global cultural phenomena can be caused by their world-wide diffusion. Such diffusion has occurred long before the advent of Globalization in our modern sense. Universals can also be due to historically early forms of diffusion that were the result of the spread of *homo sapiens* across the globe (so-called 'archoses'). Finally universal types of behavior or of mental tendencies can originate from the fact that human beings as culturally dependent organisms are confronted, wherever they go, with similar circumstances and problems of ordering their lives. This results in universal patterns without there being any specifically genetic disposition. The same applies to social universals that are the response to universal functional requirements.

Considering the essentially bio-cultural nature of humans, any study of

41 Pinker, Steven: *Wörter und Regeln. Die Natur der Sprache*, Heidelberg/Berlin 2000, p. 287.

universals is generally faced with the theoretical as well as methodological problem of conflating culture and bios. The capacity for culture in the form of non-genetic factors when it comes to organizing human existence represents a biotic given that is necessary for survival. Hence there can be no empirical version of mankind that would be 'natural' in the sense of being entirely devoid of culture. The still prevailing dichotomy of nature and nurture – whether it may take the form of an opposition, a complement or an interaction – has proved to be one of the most serious obstacles in the research on universals. Culture and nature as decisive factors have to be seen separately from the context of similarities and differences. On principle genes can be held responsible for similarities as well as differences, just as much as culture can lead to similarities and differences.

The resolution of a strict dichotomy between a biotic substratum and a cultural 'veneer' by attributing the universals to a non-variable biotic stratum and the more specific features to a variable cultural layer is erroneous. Universals do not necessarily have to be conditioned by genetics. The causes may be multiple and interwoven. If mankind is to be thematized in all its aspects, cultural and biological research will have to complement each other. This can only be effective within the framework of a world picture that is informed by an inclusive naturalism rather than by biologism. There are different suggestions as to how this is to be achieved; a naturalist world picture cannot simply be equated with a socio-biological or psychology-of-evolution one. This can be demonstrated by comparing Bernhard Rensch's 'universal world picture' (1991) with Edward Wilson's 'consilience' (1988).

## 6. Towards a Realistic Theory of Culture: Universals within the Context of Intra- and Intercultural Diversity

Reflecting upon and investigating universals is capable of making a contribution to a realistic concept of culture. In my view the current theoretical debate is dominated by somewhat extreme positions. On the one hand cultural differences are over-emphasized in a radically relativist manner. This obsession with alterity is opposed by an equally unrealistic tendency to obfuscate the borderlines between cultures. Both approaches are to be found in several concepts of hybrid cultures. This is not the place to discuss the concept of culture at any greater length. Instead I shall give a brief sketch of my ideas on this as far as they are relevant within the topic of universals. For the sake of tying up the modern non-essentialist notion of culture[42] with the theme of universals I am having recourse

42 Hauck, Gerhard: *Kultur. Zur Karriere eines sozialwissenschaftlichen Begriffs*, Münster 2006,

to insights provided by the linguistic research on universals as it has been evolved by Elmar Holenstein in the context of cultural theory.[43]

The currently dominant position among ethnologists and other researchers in cultural studies is – in spite of all difference between various approaches – founded on the idea that cultures are not sharply delineated, not static, not homogenous and internally coherent. I am sharing this implicit critique of a static and monadic concept of culture, but I also believe that in current cultural theory the baby is often poured out with the bath-water. Cultures are definitely not 'containers', but on the other hand they do not just amount to a mere cluster of elements which is an entity totally open, unlimited and without contours. As the research on ethnicity has shown, individual cultures are usually kept strictly separate from the internal perspective (-emic) of their members. From an external research perspective (-etic), however, and going beyond the confines of such a cognitive/emotional as well identity-giving delimitation (which in its turn is also part of social reality) cultures are only rather imperfectly kept separate from one another. In today's view cultures are not like Herder's incommensurable 'spheres'.[44]

Cultures are not distinct entities that are utterly separate, closed and independent from one another.[45] Cultures are not logically consistent or coherent structures, as postulated by an exaggeratedly holistic understanding of culture. In culture each element is by no means exclusively understandable as part of its entire context (like a system "où tout se tient"). Such a notion is implicit in the hermeneutical principle of the interrelatedness of part and whole, and holism and the metaphor of 'culture as text' are also based on this. Cultures rather conform to the metaphorical model of tinkering (*bricolage*) suggested by Lévi-Strauss for understanding 'primitive' cultures that – within their given environment – have to 'muddle through'[46] with their limited means – a concept that the biologist François Jacob later on adapted for biology.[47] What goes against an understanding of cultures as closed systems is the fact that most individuals have

pp. 178–188.

43 Holenstein, Elmar: "Interkulturelle Beziehungen – multikulturelle Verhältnisse. Im Ausgang von Japan-Berichten in der westdeutschen Presse", in: idem: *Menschliches Selbstverständnis. Ichbewußtsein – Intersubjektive Verantwortung – Interkulturelle Verständigung*, pp. 104–180; idem: *Kulturphilosophische Perspektiven. Schulbeispiel Schweiz, Europäische Identität auf dem Prüfstand, Globale Verständigungsmöglichkeiten*, Frankfurt/Main 1998, pp. 257–287.

44 Wiredu, Kwasi: *Cultural Universals and Particulars. An African Perspective.* (= African Systems of Thought), Bloomington/Indianapolis 1996; Wiredu, Kwasi: "Gibt es kulturelle Universalien?", in: Hejl, Peter M. (Ed.): *Universalien und Konstruktivismus*, Frankfurt/Main 2001, p. 76, 81.

45 Holenstein: *Kulturphilosophische Perspektiven*, p. 239.

46 Lévi-Strauss, Claude: *Das wilde Denken*, Frankfurt/Main 1968, p. 26.

47 'Tinkering', Jacob, François: "Evolution and Tinkering", in: *Science* 196 (June 1977): p. 1161.

inherent non-conformist inclinations, and – negatively speaking – that without these any kind of individual action would be possible. I shall revert later to some more positive reasons for this that are based on empirical observation, e.g. intuitive world models.[48]

Cultures are heterogeneous or internally diverse ('intracultural diversity'[49]). Except for positive law there is hardly anything that one would (a) find only in one culture, (b) with all its members and (c) with no other member of another culture. Cultures are not differentiated in such a way that culture A has a number of features that are totally absent in culture B, and that conversely B is marked by an exclusive bundle of features. Properties belonging to culture A are also to be found (at least marginally) in (almost all) other cultures. Cultures therefore are not differentiated on the basis of specific qualities or bundles of features that are their exclusive property. Cultures differ instead via the status or degree of relevance given to certain of their features. Thus it is rather the relative importance or hierarchical position of largely shared qualities that causes cultures to differ. This is confirmed by the more recent research findings on individualistic (and analytically separating) vs. collectivist (and holistically unifying) styles of thinking and mentalities.[50] An insight like this is specifically relevant for the understanding of universals in general and important in methodological terms for the various ways of cultural comparison in particular:

> "...the assumption of discontinuous, mutually exclusive types of culture has to be corrected by the insight into continuously merging types."[51]
>
> "Two cultures are less differentiated by the presence or absence of certain features rather than by the differing dominance of almost universally given features".[52]

The variations within one and the same culture (e.g. in terms of age, occupation, social class, region or epoch) are nearly as pronounced as the ones between cultures ('intercultural diversity'), often even more so.[53] Subcultures and non-conformity are something normal; in addition there are usually considerable inter-individual differences, even if only on account of persons belonging to

48 Holenstein: *Kulturphilosophische Perspektiven*, p. 243.

49 Boster, James Shilts/D'Andrade, Roy: "Natural and Human Sources of Cross-Cultural Agreement in Ornithological Classification", in: *American Anthropologist* 91 (1989): 132–142.

50 Nisbett, Richard E.: *The Geography of Thought. How Asians and Westerners Think Different ... and Why*, New York etc. 2003; London 2003.

51 Holenstein, Elmar: "Interkulturelle Beziehungen – multikulturelle Verhältnisse. Im Ausgang von Japan-Berichten in der westdeutschen Presse", in: idem: *Menschliches Selbstverständnis. Ichbewußtsein – Intersubjektive Verantwortung – Interkulturelle Verständigung*, p. 104.

52 Holenstein, "Interkulturelle Beziehungen – multikulturelle Verhältnisse. Im Ausgang von Japan-Berichten in der westdeutschen Presse", p. 137 ff.

53 Antweiler, Christoph: *Was ist den Menschen gemeinsam? Über Kultur und Kulturen*, Darmstadt [2]2009.

different age-groups. Holenstein goes so far as to maintain that the differences within societies and between societies are identical with regard to kind, degree, function and consequence. The intracultural diversity within a culture is analogous to the intercultural variability of mankind.[54] What this amounts to is the abolition of the difference between intra- and intercultural difference, which in my opinion is going a bit too far. However, his insight is worth considering, especially in contrast with a pronouncement by the early Habermas, because this represents the currently dominant opinion in cultural studies:

> "It is easier to make generalizing statements about mankind as a specific species, i. e. statements that hold true for all human beings and no other creatures than it is to make generalizing statements about individual cultures as a specific population, i. e. statements that apply to all the members of a culture, and only to them and no member of another culture."[55]
>
> "Mankind as such, and in an equal measure language as such, do not exist. Because human beings only make themselves into what they are and this is done in the specific ways demanded by the given circumstances, there do exist societies and cultures about which generalizing pronouncements can be made in the same way as about species of plants or animals, but not about mankind in general."[56]

However, cultures are not – as mentioned above – just 'clusters' of elements that are totally pervious to external influences. That is my objection to earlier versions of the concept of transculturality as represented by Wolfgang Welsch.[57] Even though there are cultural manifestations that go right across the existing old container-types of culture,[58] such as patterns of consumerism and occupational forms of behavior, this does not cause cultures just to be dissolved as definable units. Cultures maintain relations with their surroundings and are dynamic, and yet in a limited fashion they are integrated systems. Cultures are

54 Holenstein: "Interkulturelle Beziehungen – multikulturelle Verhältnisse. Im Ausgang von Japan-Berichten in der westdeutschen Presse", p. 159; idem: *Kulturphilosophische Perspektiven*, p. 240, 279, 285, 326.

55 Holenstein: *Kulturphilosophische Perspektiven*, p. 326.

56 Habermas, Jürgen: "Philosophische Anthropologie. Ein Lexikonartikel", in: idem: *Kultur und Kritik. Verstreute Aufsätze*, Frankfurt/Main 1973, p. 106.

57 For a revised version cf. Welsch, Wolfgang: "Über den Besitz und Erwerb von Gemeinsamkeiten", in: Brinkmann, Claudia/Scheidgen, Hermann Josef/Voßhenrich, Tobias/Wirtz, Markus (Eds.): *Tradition und Traditionsbruch zwischen Skepsis und Dogmatik. Interkulturelle philosophische Perspektiven*, Amsterdam/New York 2006, pp. 113 – 145.

58 Welsch, Wolfgang: "Transkulturalität. Lebensformen nach der Auflösung der Kulturen", in: Luger, Kurt/Renger, R. (Eds.): *Dialog der Kulturen. Die multikulturelle Gesellschaft und die Medien*, Wien 1994, p. 147; cf. Welsch, Wolfgang: "Wandlungen im humanen Selbstverständnis", in: Schmidinger, Heinrich/Sedmak, Clemens (Eds.): *Der Mensch – ein 'animal rationale'? Vernunft – Kognition – Intelligenz.* (= Topologien des Menschlichen, 1), Darmstadt 2004, pp. 48 – 70; Hepp, Andreas: *Transkulturelle Kommunikation*, Konstanz 2006, p. 63 f.

systematic organizations, but they are not uniform. Individual subsystems are capably of acquiring a certain degree of autonomy, like in the way of modules.

Insights of this more recent synthetic thinking (figure 4) have consequences for the definition of universality. The relative autonomy of substructures in all cultures is a precondition for the comparability of cultures across time and space. Not only are universalism and pluralism compatible, but they are mutually illuminating: "Intracultural diversity (incoherence, plurality) facilitates intercultural unity (invariants, universality)."[59]

Some basic theses concerning the relationship between universality and diversity:

| | Platonic | Romantic | Synthetic |
|---|---|---|---|
| 1. Types of universality | Essential universals at a profound level | No trivial or abstract universals | Contingent universals at profound and superficial levels, e.g. universals of expression (form) |
| 2. Extent of variability | Essential unity of mankind and contingent heterogeneity of cultures | External heterogeneity of mankind and internal homogeneity of cultures | Contingent homogeneity of mankind and internal heterogeneity of culture (modular and limited) |
| 3. Relationship between form and content | Mutually dependent | Mutually dependent because part of total structure | Meaning and expression mutually dependent, but not completely as regards text and context |
| 4. World picture | Ontically invariant, phenomena are accidental | Without structure, chaotic or randomly variable ('anything goes') | Naturally limited variability ('constraints') |
| 5. Value system | Hierarchical, harmonious, stable | Instable and boundlessly relative ('relativism of values') | Heterarchical network of values including hierarchies and conflict ('polytheism of values') |
| 6. Structure of languages | Variable, particular accidental and superficially different | Radically different due to historical influences | Due to phylogenetic influences similar at all structural levels |
| 7. Factors determining world view | World structure → language structure; universals | Language structure →experience, world picture; particular | Brain → experiential capacity and language; universal |

59 Holenstein: *Kulturphilosophische Perspektiven*, p. 244.

*(Continued)*

| | Platonic | Romantic | Synthetic |
|---|---|---|---|
| 8. Possibility of intercultural under-standing | Return to ideas as such | Hardly, if at all through assimilation | Possible through change of perspective |

Figure 4: The relationship between universality and diversity by comparing between antique, early modern and modern concepts (strongly modified after Holenstein: *Kulturphilosophische Perspektiven:* 265 – 274)

Universals are not capable of being understood without taking cultural diversity seriously, just as much as cultural difference can be properly understood without an appreciation of similarities (even going so far as to postulate universals.) This may be illustrated by drawing on an example.[60] In a study by López et al.[61] the knowledge of mammals and their categorization was made the object of a study comparing the Itza-Maya from Pètus (Guatemala) and students from Michigan. On the one hand there were some striking similarities concerning their classification, which in both groups came very close to Carl von Linné's division. The inductive method used in order to justify their choice was similar; thus both groups used taxonomic assumptions. However, there were significant differences with regard to the reasons given for their respective categorization. The Maya were often relying on their ecological knowledge while the American students were mostly advancing taxonomic arguments. Are therefore the divergences simply to be attributed to cultural difference, whereas the similarities point to the existence of universals? This is clearly not the case because other studies have shown that causal logic is dependent upon experience. Thus the differences may well be less culturally specific than purpose- and problem-specific. Experts from different cultures resemble one and other much more closely than lay-persons, even though they may also follow cultural models.[62] This in turn raises the question whether the similarities between them might themselves be regarded as universals.

## 7. Pancultural Structures in World Views Relevant for Humanism

I would like to briefly elucidate some universals that may be made relevant for a humanism project. I am proposing to do this by drawing on the example of world

60 Following Ross, Norbert: *Culture and Cognition Implications for Theory and Method*, Thousand Oaks etc. 2004, p. 13.

61 López, Austin A. et al.: "The Tree of Life. Universals in Folk-Biological Taxonomies and Inductions", in: *Cognitive Psychology* 32 (1997): 251 – 295.

62 Medin, Douglas L. et. al.: "Categorization and Reasoning in Relation to Culture and Expertise", in: *The Psychology of Learning and Motivation* 41 (2002): 1 – 41.

views and the idea of humanity underlying them.[63] World views, i. e. concepts of how the world is structured and works show several transcultural similarities. Thus the cosmology of a uniform world and the cosmology based on this are fairly widespread. What unites all these world concepts is their shared claim of explaining how the world is ordered. Myths from all over the world that supply theories of how the world came into existence and how it developed have a lot in common, even when it comes to details.

In almost all societies the following fundamental differences between human beings and animals are made either explicitly or implicitly. Firstly, only humans make fire not only to warm themselves but also for cooking; secondly they only have sexual congress with other humans, and thirdly they alter their bodies by means of painting, mutilation or clothing.[64] The tendency to anthropomorphize and reify nature seems to be another universal.[65] The same might apply to the dichotomization of nature and culture.[66] This has, however, not yet been verified empirically; it might just be a projection of the ancient Western Cartesian dualism. So ethnologists have strong doubts as to whether the distinction of nature as a reality that exists independently from culture is actually universal. Their argument is that 'nature' itself is a culture-specific category that denies its own cultural conditioning. Josephus Platenkamp writes the following on this:

> "... (the) idea nature was a universal reality totally uninfluenced by our social and moral activities is a fairly recent idea in Western thought..." (and it is) "... at best an idea ...that is specific for only a small number of societies and only ... for a relatively limited period of time."[67]

World-pictures consist of concepts concerning the macro-, meso-, and micro-levels of the world. Among these, the concepts pertaining to individuals as agents are of most immediate interest to the individual in the process of experiencing itself. The cognitive capacity for this seems to be already congenital to some higher primates. This seems at least implicit in some studies on second-order intentionally, even though the extent of this capacity is a matter of contention.[68] Concepts of agency are to be found in all human cultures:

63 Cf. Müller, Klaus E.: "Das Unbehagen mit der Kultur", in: idem (Ed.): *Phänomen Kultur. Perspektiven und Aufgaben der Kulturwissenschaften*, Bielefeld 2003: pp. 13 – 47.

64 Leach, Edmund Ronald: *Social Anthropology*, London 1982, p. 118.

65 Wilson, Edward Osborne: *Die Einheit des Wissens*, Berlin 1998, p. 205; Kennedy, John Stodart: *The New Anthropomorphism*, Cambridge 1992.

66 Dissanayake, Ellen: *Homo Aestheticus. Where Art comes from and why?*, New York etc. 1992, 72 f., cf. Freud, Sigismund Schlomo: *Vorlesungen zur Einführung in die Psychoanalyse*, Frankfurt/Main [5]1969.

67 Platenkamp, Josephus D.M.: "Natur als Gegenbild der Gesellschaft. Einige Betrachtungen zu einer paradoxen Idee", in: Mohrmann, Ruth-Elisabeth (Ed.): *Argument Natur – Was ist natürlich?*, Münster 1999, p. 6.

68 Tomasello, Michael: "The Human Adaptation for Culture", in: Wuketits, Franz M./Antweiler,

> "initially what seems fundamental is the urgent need of every human being to develop an idea of its own personal identity and to maintain its integrity and autonomy, i. e. to dispose of an adequate measure of self-control and to resist any excessive interference of control form without".[69]

Geertz emphasized that the distinction 'self' vs. 'other' is universal, as well as the idea of persons as object and subject, i. e. persons are not only understood to be reactive.[70] Another universal is the concept of intention, i. e. the assumption that agents desire something, that they make plans and that they can make decisions. Connected with this is the universal concept of the actor who is at least partially responsible for his actions. Equally wide-spread is the distinction of actions over which we have influence from those where we have not. The problems surrounding decisions and responsibility make it clear to people from all cultures how ambivalent actions are capable of being, and accordingly we find everywhere the idea that actions, and especially decisions, are always ambivalent.[71] The actor-concept even influences our metaphors: everywhere one comes across the manner of talking of social institutions in terms of actors, such as in "the legislative punishes the university".

Most ethnologists share the opinion that – as distinct from actor-concepts – the more specific concept of personhood as an individual endowed with autonomy and a long-term identity is universal. This is why studies arguing that in all likelihood the concept of autonomous personhood is not known among all cultures have to be taken particularly seriously. There are numerous indicators of this in ethnographies of regions of the Pacific.[72] Some Western theorists, even

Christoph (Eds.): *Handbook of Evolution*, vol. 1: *The Evolution of Human Societies and Cultures*, Weinheim 2004, pp. 1–23; Schiefenhövel, Wulf: "Kognitions- und Entscheidungsmuster in Melanesien", in: Schmidinger, Heinrich/Sedmak, Clemens (Eds.): *Der Mensch – ein "animal rationale"? Vernunft – Kognition – Intelligenz*, Darmstadt 2004, 275–292; De Waal, Frans B.M.: *Der Affe und der Sushimeister. Das kulturelle Leben der Tiere.* Munich 2005; De Waal, Frans B.M.: *Der Affe in uns. Warum wir sind wie wir sind*, Munich 2006 (orig. *Our Inner Ape. A Leading Primatologist Explains Why We are Who We are*, New York 2006).

69 Markl, Hubert: *Evolution, Genetik und menschliches Verhalten. Zur Frage wissenschaftlicher Verantwortung*, Munich/Zürich 1986: 84–85.

70 Geertz, Clifford James: *The Interpretation of Cultures*, New York 1972.

71 Cf. Boehm, Christopher: "Ambivalence and Compromise in Human Nature", in: *American Anthropologist* 91 (1989): 921–939.

72 Loizos, Peter/Heady, Patrick (Eds.): *Conceiving Persons. Ethnographies of Procreation, Fertility and Growth.* (= London School of Economics Monographs on Social Anthropology), London 1999; Strathern, Andrew J./Stewart, Pamela J. (Eds.): *Identity Work. Constructing Pacific Lives.* (Association of Social Anthropologists of Oceania Monograph), Pittsburg 2000; Gregor, Thomas A./Tuzin, Donald F.: "Comparing Gender in Amazonia and Melanesia: A Theoretical Orientation", in: Gregor/Tuzin (Eds.): *Gender in Amazonia and Melanesia. An Exploration of Comparative Method*, Berkeley 2001, pp. 1–16, cf. also Köpping, Klaus-Peter et al. (Eds.): *Die autonome Person. Eine europäische Erfindung?*, Munich 2002.

when their argument is otherwise universalizing, are not unanimous concerning the universality of personhood. In Marxism, for instance, the subject is constituted by the historically specific mode of production, which is why there can be no universal person.

What universally held ideas are there concerning the meso- and macro-world? On the basis of comparative cultural research and deductive arguments of the cultural materialist type Michael Kearney has developed a general model of world-views.[73] In doing so he has resumed the ancient question of the mental unity of mankind by referring to a specific aspect. Kearney's concept of generalizing "world view universals"[74], in many respects corresponds to an early model of universals proposed by Redfield.[75] According to both models the most fundamental and universal differentiation is the one between Self and Other. Kearney emphasizes the logical connection existing between this dichotomy (figure 5). Accordingly all other dualistic differentiations are largely derived from this basic one. The concepts of time and space are more closely dependent on the concept of causality than they are on each other.

Whereas Redfield's interest in world view universals was largely inspired by the idealist tradition, Kearney is more focused on their genesis and function. His interpretation is based on historical-materialist research and thus views them as practical and social phenomena.[76] According to Kearney world view universals are a reflection of the most general human experience in dealing with the practical circumstances of life. As a result e.g. the space-time concept is pre-Einsteinean in viewing space and time as distinct categories. The categories defined by Kearney are largely correspondent with the results of Piaget's genetic psychology concerning the development of logical thinking in children.[77] So far there have been few inquiries that explicitly research the universals to be found in the biographical development of children plus the necessary mental performance involved in this. The studies conducted so far point towards an increasing complexity of world views and the substitution in early adulthood of an autonomous identity by one dependent on mutuality.[78]

73 Kearney, Michael: *World View*, Novato, Cal. 1984; idem: "World View", in: Levinson, David/ Ember, Melvin (Eds.): *Encyclopedia of Cultural Anthropology*, vol. 4., New York 1996, pp. 1380–1384.

74 Kearney, *World View*, pp. 65–107; "World View"; p. 138; cf. also Wrightsman, Lawrence S.: *Assumptions about Human Nature. A Social-Psychological Approach*, Monterrey, Cal., 1975.

75 Redfield, Robert: *The Primitive World and Its Transformations*, Ithaca, N.J., 1953; cf. Kearney, *World View:* 39; cf. figure 1 with 1984: 106, figure 6.

76 Kearney: *World View*, p. 66, 119–121, figure 7.

77 Kearney: *World View*, pp. 84–91, 208.

78 Oerter, Rolf: "Das Menschenbild im Kulturvergleich", in: idem (Ed.): *Menschenbilder in der modernen Gesellschaft. Konzeptionen des Menschen in Wissenschaft, Bildung, Kunst, Wirtschaft und Politik.* (= Der Mensch als soziales und personales Wesen, 15) Stuttgart 1999, pp.

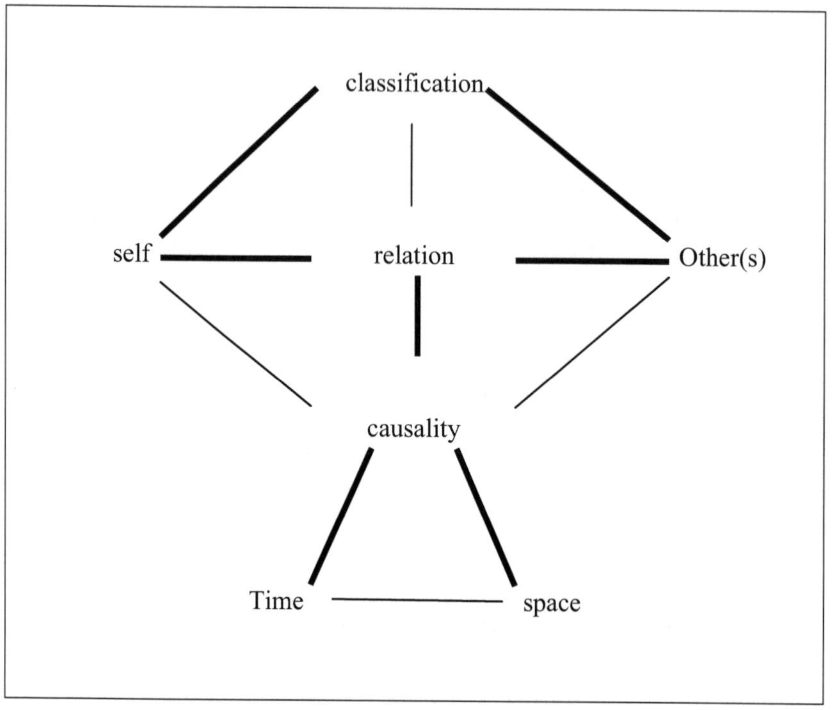


Figure 5: Integrating world view universals [According to Kearney, *World View*, p. 106; redrawn.]

A universal that is intimately connected with the world-view is the one about the existence of natural law. These are concepts concerning types of behavior or norms/ideals of action which are held to be the universal achievement of all peoples. There are many different concepts of natural law. It is supposed to be grounded upon such different entities as God, reason, human nature or social constraints. In oral societies it is often present in an implicit form; it is usually exemplified by contrasting it with manmade positive law.[79] As a general concept natural law is a near-universal, as Adams[80] maintains: "…in one sense or other it is surely universal." The various and rather divergent concepts of natural law exhibit as their common feature the thought pattern that there exists an "essential unity" between the law and the highest manifestation of nature. The

pp. 192–197; idem: "Menschenbilder im Kulturvergleich", in: Trommsdorff, Gisela/Kornath, Hans-Joachim (Eds.): *Theorien und Methoden der kulturvergleichenden Psychologie*, Göttingen etc. 2007, 508–522.

79 Adams, William Yewdale: *The Philosophical Roots of Anthropology*, Stanford, Cal. 1998, p. 117 ff.

80 Adams: *The Philosophical Roots of Anthropology*, p. 121.

universality is, according to Adams,[81] indicated by its being natural, and vice versa its naturalness is an indicator of its rightness or verity.

A variety of authors have postulated the existence of universals in world views and speculated as to their existence. I am giving just a few examples: Everywhere, they say, there are theories about the weather, about good luck or bad luck and health or illness. Everywhere there exists the notion of a causal nexus between illness and death, and also the interpretation of certain circumstances and events through minor indicators (animals, illnesses). In all cultures there is magic for securing the vital necessities of life or the attention of the opposite sex. It was further speculated on the ubiquitous existence of sympathetic magic, i. e. the idea that by manipulating symbols or images the symbolized or represented objects could be influenced. Even some highly specific ideas were claimed to be near-universals. According to Edward Leach e. g. the symbolism of hair in general and especially the equation of hair with the genitals is universal).[82]

However, numerous questions concerning similarities and differences in world views or patterns of thought still remain unanswered. Keesing and Strathern are therefore justified in saying:

> "The gulfs between cultural models of reality of different peoples cannot be aptly characterized as either superficial or deep. The process of thought, perception, and memory by a *Homo Sapiens* brain that is the same in Amazonia or Nigeria or New York or the Trobriand Islands. The range of cultures that are thinkable and learnable by members of species is probably – in terms of formal organization and logic – quite narrow. But on the other hand, the variation in content and substance (as opposed to structure and organization) of culturally constructed world, is striking."[83]

Besides the similarities of world views there are, among the hundreds of universals that have been so far documented, quite a few which might be relevant for a project on humanism. In figure 6 I have listed some of them.

81 Adams: *The Philosophical Roots of Anthropology*, p. 115 ff.

82 Leach, Edmund Ronald: "Magical Hair", in: *Proceedings of the Royal Anthropological Institute of Great Britain and Ireland* 88.2 (1958): p. 147 ff.

83 Keesing, Roger M./Strathern, Andrew J.: *Cultural Anthropology. A Contemporary Perspective*, Fort Worth etc. 1998, p. 341 ff.

- Concept of human beings (e.g. as an organism and human qualities, e.g. the capacity for suffering)
- Concepts of mankind (currently only widely shared, a probably emerging universal)
- Concepts of actors with limited autonomy (agency)
- Concepts of history, the historicity of human culture, natural history
- Cooperation
- Reciprocity (behavior and social norms)
- A minimum of fairness in competition (at least as a tendency)
- Capacity for empathy
- Concepts, norms and ideals of education
- The family as a combined sphere of biotic propagation and social reproduction
- Concepts of adolescence and other age groups and rites of passage
- Gender differences in behavior during adolescence
- Tendentially dichotomous gender-concepts, -norms and –ideals
- Locally and empirically founded knowledge and performative learning
- Thinking in metaphors
- Nepotism-tendency
- Egoism-tendency
- Social control of deviant behaviour

Figure 6: Universals relevant for an inclusive humanism: a selective list

## Summary: a Universalizing Approach vs. Relativism and Absolutism

Universals are not simply the counterparts to the diversity of human cultures. Universals only acquire their real relevance when they are viewed as a common pattern against the common background of the diversity of ways humans regulate their existence. Research into universals opens a fruitful perspective on so-called human nature. It is an approach that offers a middle-course between speculation and wishful thinking on the one hand and the unsystematic gathering of assumed similarities on the other. I am interested in a non-metaphysical access to human nature. The leading idea is that one can reduce human beings neither to their nature nor their culture and that, secondly, culture cannot be confined to the intellectual sphere but that it is something inherently social. This essay is understood as a contribution to an anthropology that could act as the smallest common denominator of those sciences that are concerned with human beings. Anthropology in my mind is "… the understanding of the humanly possible – and the limits of what is humanly possible."[84] Thus conceived the research into universals is capable of making a contribution to a human science understood in a more comprehensive sense, to an anthropology that is an em-

84 Hauschild, Thomas: "Ethnologie als Kulturwissenschaft", in: Stierstorfer, Klaus/Volkmann, Laurenz (Eds.): *Kulturwissenschaft interdisziplinär*, Tübingen 2005, p. 61.

pirically oriented but at the same time theoretically informed science of "the whole man."

Research into universals can grant important insights into the similarities between the approximately 7000 cultures existing in this world. Universals are not to be seen as the contrary of cultural particularity and difference or the diversity of the entire human race. Universals are not to be mistaken for absolutes. The frequent, more than accidental emergence of a phenomenon is sufficient in order to raise the question of universality. However, universals only derive their real interest from being perceived against the background of cultural diversity. They cannot be verified by some kind of 'opinion poll' among peoples. What is called for in methodological terms is the formation of a theory on the basis of evolutionary and social science for the purpose of making judicious intercultural comparisons.

Universals are simply not to be equated with the *conditio humana* or "anthropological constraints", such as they are discussed in philosophy. In the same measure they are not to be equated with "the physical unity of mankind". Universalism understood as an absolute is just as untenable as a one-sided particularism that has mutated into relativism. In a dogmatic universalism cultural anthropology would be superfluous, because the familiar and strange would just be the facets of something identical. On the other hand an extreme insistence on cultural difference is a dead end. The obsession with alterity makes culture into an unquestionable given, and this can be politically dangerous.[85]

A careful and empirically grounded universalist approach is opposed to both relativism and absolutism. In order to once more underline the special status of this approach, figure 7 will give a rough and ready overview of the position of universalism vis-à-vis absolutist and extremely relativist positions. The two important issues here are the emphasis given to commonalities within human experience and the weight given to cultural context. Similarities and specifics are of equal importance. The main challenge posed by universalism lies in empirically verifiable congruences between cultures that have been resulted from intercultural comparison.

I have spoken of 'universals' instead of 'cultural universals' in this essay. This is not only suitably shorter, but it also permits to keep the definition of the phenomenon clear of any foregone conclusion – in this instance a culturalist one. However, universals are also called 'cultural universals' because they are only universal at the level of cultures or societies, and not on the individual level. This is why they are not to be confused with bio-psychological universals. That does

85 Van der Walt, Sibylle: "Die Last der Vergangenheit und die kulturrelativistische Kritik an den Menschenrechten. Ursprung und Folgen der westlichen Alteritätsobsession", in: *Saeculum* 57.2 (2006): p. 237.

not, of course, preclude a causal nexus between them, especially because some cultural universals are the direct result of bio-psychological universals, but this applies to only some of them.

| | | Are specific ways of life relevant for establishing an inclusive humanism? | |
|---|---|---|---|
| | | no | yes |
| Are pan-cultural commonalities relevant for an inclusive humanism? | no | „Nihilism": very limited possibilities of human science and humanist politics | Radical Relativism |
| | yes | Absolutism: e.g. human nature, anthropic constants, psychic unity | Universalizing Approach; empirically based Cosmopolitanism |

Figure 7: Basic orientations of human sciences relevant for an inclusive humanism [Strongly modified after Adamopoulos, J./Lonner, W.J.: "Absolutism, Relativism and Universalism in the Study of Human Behavior", in: Lonner, Walter J./Malpass, Roy S. (Eds.): *Psychology and Culture*, Boston etc. 1994, p. 130, and Lonner, Walter J.: "The Psychological Study of Culture: Issues and Questions of Enduring Importance", in: Friedlmeier, Wolfgang/Chakkarath, Pradeep/Schwarz, Beate (Eds.): *Culture and Human Development. The Importance of Cross-Cultural Research to the Social Sciences*, Hove and New York 2005, p. 16; idem: "Das Aufkommen und die fortdauernde Bedeutung der kulturvergleichenden Psychologie", in: Trommsdorff/Kornath (Eds.): *Theorien und Methoden der kulturvergleichenden Psychologie*, pp. 97 – 117.]

Georg W. Oesterdiekhoff

# Man on the Way Towards Intellectual Growth and Humanity – Anthropological Foundations of History and Social Change

## Introduction

In this article I am going to present and outline the theoretical program I have evolved over the past 30 years, which I have come to call "structural-genetic sociology". This theoretical program lays claim to have found a new key on which to base the humanities and social sciences, not only sociology and sociological theory. It entails a comprehensive theory of the humanities, relevant to almost all or even all the disciplines that belong to the branches of the humanities and social sciences. Additionally, this theoretical program can be used to reconstructs the cultural history of humankind. It supplies a new reference system, based on anthropological foundations, to describe and to explain the history of economy, society, culture, politics, sciences, religion, law, manners, and morals. I regard this program as a radical breakthrough with reference to the endeavor to explain scientifically the social evolution from the early Paleolithic to modern times.

Since their beginnings, the social sciences have tried to determine the relationship between man and society, person and environment, subject and object, in order to explain social changes. Previously, certain classical sociologists supplied their contributions in order to clarify this relationship. It is within this context that sociologists nowadays speak of the necessity to develop a micro-sociological theory on which to elaborate and base macro-sociology. Due to these same reasons and intentions, historians have established approaches such as "historical anthropology", "historical psychology", or "mentality research", to better understand cultures and history.

All these efforts revolve around the question of which part the historical changes of psyche and personality have with regard to the social and cultural changes of humankind. We cannot understand the changes in society, economy, and culture without the consideration of those changes which have taken place in the minds and hearts of people. Karl Marx, pointing to this fact, spoke about the historical dialectics of subject and object; Norbert Elias about the causal interrelationship between psycho- and socio-genesis.

Some scholars had already come up with the idea a few generations ago that developmental psychology could offer the best solution for analyzing this relationship between subject and object and to supply the definitive answer to the question of the psyche's role in history and social change. The founder of sociology, Auguste Comte, and the last classical author of sociology, Norbert Elias, based their theories on assumptions derived from developmental psychology. Both authors maintained that childlike anthropologic structures may characterize adults living in pre-modern societies, whereas only those adults living in modern industrialized countries might establish more elaborate, mature psycho-cognitive structures. A multitude of sociologists, ethnologists, and historians shared this core assumption to the extent that they often contributed interrelated research papers.

## Developmental Psychology and Piagetian Cross-Cultural Psychology

Developmental psychology originated as a serious discipline around 1880, and has developed an all-encompassing, detailed theory of human development from infancy to adulthood. The human nervous system requires roughly two decades in order to reach a fully developed, mature status. The physical growth of the brain is regarded as the basis for the development of the psyche and personality, that is, the entire development from neonates to children and from teenagers to adults. Adults differ from infants mainly with regard to their divergent brain capacities. The increase of brain functions carries the ontogenetic transformation of the psycho-neurological system and the related augmentation of achievement of mental and social skills. Humans developed from animal-like organisms into thinking and reflective beings. This transformation is by no means limited to an increase of knowledge and experience but implies a change of anthropologic structures that process knowledge and constitute experiences. This increase of consciousness and reflectivity implies an ongoing reorganization of psyche and personality. Higher stages of consciousness replace the lower, more primitive ones. This removal of the earlier stages entails the loss of these forms of psychological constructs in a person's memory. The mature psyche no longer has access to its primitive predecessors. Therefore, the child cannot retrieve the mind she had when she was a nursing infant; the adult cannot reproduce the consciousness he or she had as a small child. The higher stages cannot reproduce the lower stages but have lost the entrance to their specific structures.

Jean Piaget (1896 – 1980) delivered the most famous and most detailed description of ontogenesis and human development, mainly following in the steps of James Mark Baldwin. Piaget distinguishes four stages of human development. The sensory-motor stage describes the first 18 months of life. The conquest of language and thinking characterizes the second stage of life, or the pre-operational stage. Children between their sixth and twelfth year of life develop the concrete operations, that is, the logical coordination of material objects. Only adolescents, who grow up in industrial societies establish step by step the formal-operational thinking; the fourth stage is characterized by reflectivity, formal logic, systematic coherence, combinatorial and abstractive capabilities.

Every new stage reorganizes the entire experience of reality, social environment, morals and customs, physics and nature. The stages diverge in their constitution of language, thinking, consciousness, reality, causality, chance, probability, space, time, self-image, intentions, religion, morals, and justice. Developmental psychology has shown that children experience the world in completely divergent patterns from adults. There is no other theory (or branch of science) that has delivered such deep-rooted and comprehensive insights into human nature as developmental psychology has done.[1]

Piagetian Cross-Cultural Psychology (PCCP) designates cross-cultural examinations and applications of Piagetian developmental psychology encompassing thousands of empirical studies carried out in more than 100 cultures and milieus all over the world, executed from about 1930 up to now. The overall result is that humans from all cultures reveal the answers and reactions Western developmental psychology has described. This implies that developmental psychology (and Piagetian stage theory) is appropriate to all peoples, even those from very exotic and archaic cultures. Infants around the world show the features that correspond to the known characteristics of sensory-motor and pre-operational stages. Humans, even adult humans, raised in developing regions, establish concrete operations only on an incomplete level. The values diverge with regard to fields of experience in these examined populations as well. Frequently only 30, 50 or 80 % of people within a certain population develop at the level of concrete operations which refer to a specific task or field of experience.

In contrast, however, modern, industrial populations completely develop concrete operations with regard to all fields of experience and contents. Addi-

1 Stern, William: *Psychology of early childhood up to the sixth year of age*, New York 1924; Werner, Heinz: *Comparative psychology of mental development*, New York 1948; Piaget, Jean: *The psychology of intelligence*, London 1950; Piaget, Jean/Inhelder, Bärbel: *The psychology of the child*, New York 1969.

tionally, industrial populations develop at least the basic phases within the stage of formal operations. Only 30 to 50 % of industrial populations will also develop the higher phases of formal operations though.

Populations from developing regions, meaning from backward, illiterate, and socio-economically weaker milieus within developing countries, establish even lower phases of formal operations which are either scarcely present or not present at all. Whenever the higher stages are missing and inactive, then the lower stages and their specific patterns are at work and in force. We can therefore always ascribe the test behavior to the known stages.

The empirical studies could demonstrate that school education and admission to patterns of cultural modernity are the most important incentives to evoking operations respectively at higher stages. I summarize the main conclusions we have drawn from the empirical studies.

(1) People from Europe, America, Asia, Africa, or Australia, living or having lived in pre-modern societies, do not mentally systematize at the stage of formal thinking. People from all continents who are (or were) socialized within modern milieus usually develop at least the lower phases of formal operations. The link between pre-modern social structures and lower stages on the one side, and between modern social structures and higher stages on the other, refutes racial theories and relativistic approaches as well. The relationship between culture and anthropological level is relevant to all human groups at basically the same rate.[2]

(2) Roughly half of all Europeans, Japanese and North Americans never achieve the higher stages of formal operations, as I have just mentioned. That means that their developmental age (or anthropologic summit) is scattered somewhere between their twelfth and fifteenth year, whereas the developmental age of the other half that achieves the formal stage shows a more diffuse pattern of between the fifteenth and twentieth years of age.

(3) Adults having lived in Europe or the USA 100 years ago or earlier usually mastered the level of formal operations either only partly or not at all. Correspondingly, we can estimate the developmental age of adults from other pre-

2 Dasen, Pierre/Berry, John W. (Eds.): *Culture and cognition. Readings in cross-cultural psychology*, London 1974; Dasen, Pierre (Ed.): *Piagetian psychology. Cross-cultural contributions*, New York 1977; Hallpike, Christopher: *Foundations of primitive thought*, Oxford 1978; Oesterdiekhoff, Georg W.: *Kulturelle Bedingungen kognitiver Entwicklung. Der strukturgenetische Ansatz in der Soziologie*, Frankfurt/Main 1997; idem: *Zivilisation und Strukturgenese. Norbert Elias und Jean Piaget im Vergleich*, Frankfurt/Main 2000; idem: *Kulturelle Evolution des Geistes. Die historische Wechselwirkung von Psyche und Gesellschaft*, Hamburg/Münster 2006; idem: *Mental growth of humankind in history*, Norderstedt 2009; idem: *The steps of man towards civilization. The key to disclose the riddle of history*, Norderstedt 2011; idem: *Die Entwicklung der Menschheit von der Kindheitsphase zur Erwachsenenreife*, (forthcoming); idem: *Traumzeit der Menschheit. Ursprung und Wesen der Religion*, (forthcoming).

modern cultures whose developmental age or anthropologic summit often levels off at around the tenth year.

(4) Christopher Hallpike, in this context, introduced the distinction between qualitative and quantitative development. Adults whose developmental age has only reached that of children aged eight or ten years nonetheless diverge from children strongly in that they possess more knowledge and life experience than children. Children (from all cultures) and adults from pre-modern cultures share the same qualitative developmental summit but diverge quantitatively. The subsequent examples, however, demonstrate that the qualitative development has a much stronger effect than the quantitative one.

(5) Children raised in industrial cultures are, by developmental parameters, only ten years old once in their lives. Adults who have grown up in a pre-modern society remain at more or less the developmental age of ten years throughout their entire lives. For example, children brought up in a modern culture think in magical and animistic terms until approximately their tenth year of life. Adults of pre-modern cultures share these childlike belief systems lifelong, however. Only children (not adults) in modern cultures believe in ghosts and sorcerers; adults of pre-modern cultures are concerned with and frightened of ghosts and magicians throughout their entire lives. Children in modern cultures and adults in pre-modern cultures understand dream contents as reports of real occurrences, not as illusionary images as we do. I could refer to some hundreds additional phenomena which illuminate the psychological identity that are typical of anthropologic stage of children and primitives the same way. Adults of pre-modern societies, the so-called primitives, astonishingly do not establish the stage of formal operations, not even in their third, fourth, or fifth decade. They do not enter the anthropologic stage modern adolescents develop between their tenth and twentieth year of life. Thus, their anthropologic summit remains bound to previous, childlike stages. We need to refer to the theory of the developmental window in order to be able to explain this kind of impasse. Whenever certain psychological expansions are not activated by socializing factors within the crucial childhood years, they will never arise in later years. It is nearly impossible to establish these skills in the later phases of life. Whoever believes by the age of twenty that the waves of the sea move by their own power will still assert the truth of this assumption even at the age of forty or sixty.

(6) All the knowledge developmental psychology has accumulated with respect to the psycho-cognitive development of children and adolescents can be used and applied to describe the thinking of adult humans living in various cultures around the world. The comparison of the corpus of insights won by ethnography about the thinking and worldview of pre-modern societies with the insights which have been accumulated by developmental psychology about children reveals abundant concurrences and incredible similarities. Whatever

ethnographers have written about the experience of space, time, causality, chance, nature, physics, dream, magic, superstition, and fear of ghosts, must be recognized and attributed to the concepts expanded upon by developmental psychology. Developmental psychology delivers the theoretical basis and the scientific framework for the knowledge collected by ethnography and related disciplines.

(7) The influence of culture on human development is therefore much greater than is widely estimated. Various social and environmental influences upon brain, psyche, and personality have considerable effects. The notion of the historical development of anthropological stages within the psycho-neurological system not only provides the foundation of historical anthropology and micro-sociology, but also the decisive key to a true understanding of the history of humankind; not only confirming the early assumptions of so many classical authors, but also fulfills the Marxian formula of the historical dialectics of subject and object.

(8) We can understand the cultural achievements of ancient societies only by referring to the childlike characteristics of the pre-formal psyche, whereas the rise of modern societies is accountable for the respective emergence of higher anthropologic stages of the formal operations and related phenomena. Some authors, such as Jürgen Habermas, Jean Piaget and Christopher Hallpike have already pointed out these consistencies.

## Logical and Abstract Thinking

Alexander Lurija, ostensibly the father of neuro-psychology, is considered to have originated the clearest and most concise evidence of the fact that illiterate and pre-modern populations remain bound to childlike anthropologic stages. This judgment is correct even if one considers that Lurija himself was not really aware of this appraisal of his work. In 1932 and 1933, he and his team exposed various age groups of the Kashgar people from Uzbekistan to a set of classical test procedures in order to examine their ability to think in hypothetical terms, to use formal-operational problem solving, their self-awareness, etc. The result was that adult illiterates reveal the same patterns and process mental tasks in the same way as children do. However, had the adults some years of school experience, according to modern curricula, then they found the proper solutions to the tasks. Especially in the sixties and seventies of the last century Lurija's tests had been replicated among groups in Asia, Africa, and America. The results, won on different continents, confirmed those made among the Kashgar in Uzbekistan.[3]

The test procedures convincingly demonstrate the basic reasoning structures common to all pre-modern populations around the world, that is, their ways of deducing, interpreting, and thinking. Lurija's study demonstrates the implications of what it means when people are not able to think on formal-operational levels. I present here only one example to show the huge difference between pre-formal and formal thinking styles. The example refers to syllogisms, something that appears as an inevitable peculiarity of the human brain, but is indeed chargeable only to forms of operational thinking. Therefore, most adult humans in world history never mastered syllogisms. A man of the of the Kashgar people, aged 37, answered as all illiterates from developing regions and as most people in world history have done:

> "The following syllogism is presented: In the Far North, where there is snow, all bears are white. Novaya Zemlya is in the Far North and there is always snow there. What color are the bears there?
> Answer: There are different sorts of bears.
> Commentary: Failure to infer from syllogism.
> The syllogism is repeated.
> Answer: I don't know; I've seen a black bear. I've never seen any others ... Each locality has its own animals: if it's white, they will be white; if it's yellow, they will be yellow.
> Commentary: Appeals only to personal, graphic experience.
> Question: But what kind of bears are there in Novaya Zemlya?
> Answer: We always speak only of what we see; we don't talk about what we haven't seen...".[4]

Lurija explained the failure of illiterates the same way as child psychologists are doing with regard to children in industrial societies. Children under their tenth year of life raised in industrial societies have not yet mastered syllogisms. Children in all societies and primitives (adult illiterates) share this cognitive failure. Only school-educated people, adolescents and adults within modern milieus are able to perform these tasks. Children and unsophisticated adults do not understand the meaning of "some" and "all" and they do not regard any logical relationship between the phrases. They do not understand the sentences as parts of a logical system but only as single and isolated pieces of information.[5] The questionnaire reveals a good working intelligence which isn't yet capable of

3 Cole, Michael/Scribner, Sylvia: *Culture and thought*, New York 1974; Oesterdiekhoff, Georg W.: *Kulturelle Evolution des Geistes. Die historische Wechselwirkung von Psyche und Gesellschaft*, Hamburg/Münster 2006.

4 Lurija, Alexander R.: *Cognitive development. Its cultural and social foundations*, Cambridge, Mass., 1982, p. 108 f.

5 Piaget, Jean: *Judgment and reasoning in the child*, New York 1959.

formal-operational thinking. Unsophisticated populations are encapsulated in divergent forms of imagination and representation which are not answerable to logical deductions and hypothetical conclusions. These forms of deficiency may arouse tremendous negative effects on communication and social life.

## Rationality and Superstition

The thinking which goes on beneath the stage of formal operations, the pre-formal stage, is characterized by a duality of rational adaptations and autistic thinking as well. The extent and the level of rationality and adaptation, however, remain restricted to the peculiarities of pre-formal thinking. Formal operational thinking enlarges the possibilities of rationality and adaptation on the one hand and removes autistic thinking patterns on the other. Therefore, the forms of autistic thinking among children and primitives additionally indicate the developmental range and limitations of their rational adaptations.[6]

The pre-modern cultures' accomplishments and achievements arose within the framework of pre-formal structures. The rise of formal operations within modern societies is the overall precondition for the increase of rationality generally, and the attainment of new levels of sciences and technology, that is, of adaptation especially.

Autistic thinking is shaped and constituted by wishful thinking, a psyche bound to fairy tales, overabundant religiosity, superstition, magic, belief in teleportation and telepathy, and other forms of illusionary thinking. These patterns of thinking are autistic because they are based on egocentrism and the missing boundaries between fantasy and reality. These peculiarities characterize the psycho-neurological structure of the child.

Magic, animism, and artificialism are the essentials of the pre-formal and childlike worldview. *Animism* means the belief that objects may become animated and are equipped with a soul; rivers, mountains, stars, and plants may be fit by reason and willpower. *Magic* implies the belief in the direct and mystical power of persons and divinities, nature, and reality. *Artificialism* expresses the idea that personalities may have created nature and the cosmos through magic, and all occurrences in reality and history may result from magical influences. Children and primitives share this archaic worldview.

Only adolescents and adults raised in industrial societies can supersede this mystical construction of reality by using empirical-causal and rational mecha-

6 Piaget, Jean/Inhelder, Bärbel: *The psychology of the child*, New York 1969; Werner, Heinz: *Comparative psychology of mental development*, New York 1948; Stern, William: *Psychology of early childhood up to the sixth year of age*, New York 1924.

nisms and by the concomitant mechanical worldview. This dis-enchantment, literally, of the worldview took place analogously in the seventeenth and eighteenth centuries in Europe. The rise of formal operations in the brains of contemporary adolescents and the educated classes of the early modern era is the cause of these parallels. The evolution of mechanical philosophy and the physical sciences displaced the magical worldview of the middle ages, which consisted of magic, animism, and artificialism.[7]

## Ordeals and Oracles

I am going to present now, by reference to two examples, the tremendous practical consequences these forms of mystical and pre-formal thinking had on social life within pre-modern societies. The so-called "immanent justice" is an inevitable ingredient of the pre-formal psyche of children up to their tenth year of life. Children initially believe that occurrences are made by mystical and magical influences. When, for example, a bridge collapses at a moment while children, who had stolen apples in an orchard, are running over its planks, then children will usually say the bridge collapsed intentionally in order to punish them. They argue that the wind may have told the bridge about the theft or the bridge had known about it due to its own telepathy, or God may have ordered the bridge to disintegrate. 86 % of children aged six, 73 % of children aged seven and eight, 54 % of children aged nine and ten, and 34 % of teens aged eleven and twelve answered in this way, according to Piaget's survey conducted in Switzerland in 1932.[8] "Immanent justice" is the direct result of animism, magic, and artificialism, of the total lack of empirical causality and chance, and immaturity of reflectivity and consciousness.

Children and adults from contemporary developing regions around the globe answer according to "immanent justice" and do not transcend this phase as teenagers of modern societies do, as all the empirical results of PCCP repeatedly evidenced.[9] Moreover, one of the most influential judicial procedures in the history of humankind is based on "immanent justice". Ordeals and oracles are namely a direct manifestation of "immanent justice". They have been a part of

7 Piaget, Jean/Inhelder, Bärbel: *The growth of logical thinking from childhood to adolescence*, New York 1958; Piaget, Jean: *Introduction à l'épistémologie génétique*. Vol. 1: *La pensée mathematique*, vol. 2: *La pensée physique*, vol. 3: *La pensée sociologique*, Paris 1950; Oesterdiekhoff: *Kulturelle Evolution des Geistes*; idem: *Mental growth of humankind in history*, Norderstedt 2009; idem: *The steps of man towards civilization. The key to disclose the riddle of history*, Norderstedt 2011.

8 Piaget, Jean: *The moral judgment of the child*, New York 1997.

9 Oesterdiekhoff: *Mental growth of humankind in history*: pp. 344–368.

human culture across all pre-modern societies around the globe up to recent times.

A person accused of having committed a crime is forced over a red-hot iron or to hold it in his hands, or has to swallow a poison potion, must fight a duel, or suchlike. The assumption was that those who were injured or worse, lost the contest, were guilty of the charges, whereas unharmed or triumphant defendants were regarded as innocent.[10]

Edward Evans-Pritchard[11] and Lucien Lévy-Bruhl[12] found evidence that the confidence invested in ordeals is unlimited among the primitives. Millions of innocent people may have lost their lives due to the irrational practices of such ordeals. Moreover, the consequences of these ordeals to human advancement were low rates of population growth throughout world history for millennia.

## Magic

The belief in the power of magic has played an enormous role across all pre-modern societies according to the related surveys of ethnographers and historians. The books of R.F. Fortune on the Dobu of Melanesia[13] and of E.E. Evans-Pritchard on the Zande in Sudan[14] illuminate convincingly the strength of belief and its huge practical consequences. These people believe that supernatural causes are behind every seemingly irregular incident such as the cracking of a pot during its fabrication, an unusually powerful rain storm, a failed shot, meal preparation that did not come off well and/or a nasty quarrel with the husband. Particularly sickness, accident, war and murder are always interpreted according to paranormal causation. The thinking of children and primitives does not follow the operational categories of causality, chance, and probability but obeys mystical influences which are believed to exist everywhere and to have control over everything.

God, divinities, ghosts, humans, animals and even objects play their part as active magicians, all having more or less the same occult influence on cosmos and life. The primitives surmise that neighbors, relatives, fellow village dwellers, or other persons may cause the smaller and bigger mishaps of their everyday life.

10 Oesterdiekhoff, Georg W.: "Das archaische Prozeß- und Beweisrecht und die immanente Gerechtigkeit", in: *Zeitschrift der Savigny-Stiftung für Rechtsgeschichte, Germanistische Abteilung* 119 (2002): 175–192.

11 Evans-Pritchard, Edward Evan: *Witchcraft, oracles, and magic among the Azande*, Oxford 1976.

12 Lévy-Bruhl, Lucien: *How natives think*, Princeton 1985.

13 Fortune, R.F.: *Sorcerers of Dobu*, London 1932.

14 Evans-Pritchard: *Witchcraft, oracles, and magic among the Azande.*

When somebody is unable to sleep at night or loses a dog, he will then ask his oracle to divine the name of the malevolent magician who caused these things. After having established the identity of the magician responsible, he addresses him, demanding an end to the attacks or some reimbursement; sometimes bringing him in front of a court or in extreme cases, killing him.

Primitives usually employ daily magical practices in order to secure success in life and to protect themselves against damage from magic malevolence. Only magicians or shamans can guarantee good weather, abundant harvests, safe childbirth, sanity, peace, success in love and wealth. Practical work and empirical measures have no effect without magical assistance. Magic is the foundation of life, therefore, all primitives are experts in magic, not just priests, sorcerers, and witches.

Even the best theoreticians such as Evans-Pritchard or Lévy-Bruhl[15] could only describe these phenomena but were unable to explain their sources and essence. Not one ethnologist in the history of the discipline has ever answered the question in a convincing and encompassing manner: which psychological preconditions must be given in order to enable humans to believe in the crucial role played by magic in life and the cosmos? Imagine that there is no brainwashing, no method of conditioning or acculturation that could ever induce an adult person, living in an industrial culture, no matter from what social class or job background, to believe that he or she is able to rouse a storm on the Atlantic Ocean or to defeat a hostile army only by aid of some magic spell. People must regress to a state of consciousness and reason which characterizes a child of about eight years in psychological development from an industrial culture in order to be able to share in these magical belief systems. The whole field of child psychology over the past century has collected verifiable data that children in industrial cultures believe in magic only up to their seventh or eighth year.[16] By this time pre-adolescents of modern cultures aged twelve and up, due to their higher intellectual maturity, would ridicule the magical practices of ancient cultures. They would at least smile or, more probably, pour their derision on ordeal practices and magical rites.

Thus, it is impossible to explain the belief in magic without the application of developmental psychology. So far, only structural-genetic sociology has com-

15 Evans-Pritchard: *Witchcraft, oracles, and magic among the Azande* or Lévy-Bruhl, Lucien: *Le surnaturel et la nature dans la mentalité primitive*, Paris 1931; idem: *L'éxperience mystique et les symboles chez les primitives*, Paris 1938.

16 Piaget, Jean: *The child's conception of the world*, New York 1975; Zeininger, Wolfgang: *Magische Geisteshaltung im Kindesalter und ihre Bedeutung für die religiöse Entwicklung*, Leipzig 1929; Werner, Heinz: *Comparative psychology of mental development*, New York 1948.

pleted the task of integrating the belief in magic into the theoretical framework of developmental psychology.[17]

## Religion

The explanatory power of my structural-genetic sociology is remarkable especially with regard to religion and religiosity. Archaic cultures believed that gods and ancestors created *in illo tempore* the whole cosmos by magic. As children do, they believed that divinities made the cosmos with their own hands, with spells or metamorphosis. The Australian aborigines for example, imitate in their rites all objects and beings in the certainty that in this way their existence will be sustained and replenished. In doing so, they manifest the conviction that only the magic of humans and divinities may secure the foundation of the cosmos' existence. Jean Piaget in his unique "The child's conception of the world" demonstrated that exactly this belief is central to a child's philosophy up to their seventh or eighth year. I have worked out these parallels between children's ideas and archaic religion to the minutiae.[18]

Magic brought forth the entire cosmos and all subsequent occurrences which are running through it. Therefore, in the eyes of primitives, even now the quotidian experience of reality and life is deeply mystical and religious. Whoever experiences thunder and lightning literally as the vital expression of god's life, as it is common among the primitives, is addicted to religion to an extent that no Christian or Islamic fundamentalist could ever achieve. The believer raised in an industrial culture still has an empirical-causal and mechanical understanding of nature without much space left for divine interventions. Though he believes in occasional divine interventions, he has lost the idea that god creates every neonate by his own hand or makes the Sun shine and the rain fall. The literal disenchantment of the world, the decline of magic and the weakening of religiosity are interrelated phenomena which influence the beliefs of any person living in a modern society, even the beliefs of all fundamentalist factions.

The ancient cultures, however, understood unhappy incidents as magical attacks or divine punishments and correspondingly fortunate occurrences as rewards. Happiness and mishap both on earth and in heaven were interpreted as

17 Oesterdiekhoff: *Mental growth of humankind in history*, pp. 203–260; idem: *The steps of man towards civilization:* pp. 110–132; idem: *Die geistige Entwicklung der Menschheit*, Weilerswist 2012.

18 Oesterdiekhoff: *The steps of man towards civilization*, pp. 147–161; idem: *Die Entwicklung der Menschheit von der Kindheitsphase zur Erwachsenenreife*, (forthcoming); idem: *Traumzeit der Menschheit. Ursprung und Wesen der Religion*, (forthcoming); idem: *Mental growth of humankind in history*, pp. 261–277, 224–260.

punishment or reward. Belief in hell and heaven were universal fantasies around the globe, both in tribal and civilized societies. These ideas reflect wishful thinking which thoroughly indicates the prevalence of the childlike psyche. Only the pre-formal anthropological stage is capable of a graphic belief in the immortality of the soul and the existence of a hell and paradise.

Developmental psychology explains the structure and development of divinities as well. The idea of a father god who rules cosmos and heaven has been a universal across the globe for millennia. Ancestor worship, to be found in every tribal society and pre-modern civilization, exists as a parallel phenomenon. Even in Christianity by the age of Enlightenment the cult of the dead has played a role in the lives of backward groups throughout Asia, Africa, and South America up to recent times. The ancestors commonly have a bigger role in cults and rites than god-the-father or the gods of Olympus. The primitives attribute the same power and knowledge to the ancestors as to god-the-father or to the Olympic deities. Ancestor worship actually means veneration of one's deceased parents, grandparents or great-grandparents as gods, who are believed to have originated the cosmos and world, ruling all occurrences in a literal sense. Primitives can naturally only then venerate their dead family members when they loved and feared them even before their death.[19]

According to the studies of Pierre Bovet and Jean Piaget,[20] all children up to their sixth or seventh year of life regard their parents as almighty and omniscient gods, ruling household and cosmos, even if they have already formed an idea of god-the-father in their minds. During their sixth and seventh year of life, children in industrial societies run into their first crisis of skepticism, beginning to doubt the magical power of their parents, and from this point onward will save any religious feelings only for the official god of their culture.

I have already demonstrated that this childlike attitude alone can explain the entire phenomenon of ancestor worship. Children of all cultures and adults of pre-modern cultures venerate family gods and father-gods as well, whereby the family gods play a stronger role in the minds of both groups. A modern adult could never be manipulated or conditioned to believe that his grandparents created the cosmos and were its true masters. A regression to the anthropological stage of children aged five or six is necessary in order to reawaken ideas of this kind.[21]

Primitives experience neither the first nor the second skeptical crisis. Teenagers of modern cultures run through the second skeptical crisis during their

19 Oesterdiekhoff: *Traumzeit der Menschheit.*

20 Bovet, Pierre: *Le sentiment religieux et la psychologie de l'enfant*, Neuchâtel/Paris 1951 and Piaget, Jean: *The child's conception of the world*, New York 1975.

21 Oesterdiekhoff: *Traumzeit der Menschheit.*

thirteenth year or later on.[22] The idea of god becomes more abstract and bloodless and the transition to agnosticism and atheism takes place roughly among half of adolescents nowadays. Only 15 % of German adolescents find "religion is important to my life". About half of Europeans at present have lost the belief in god and paradise. All empirical indicators used to measure religiosity testify to this continuous decline over more than 100 years. Only 7 % of the members of the American Academy of Sciences and only 3 % of the members of the Royal Society of London still confess to being religious. Moreover, 79 % of the latter "deny religion completely".[23] Thus, religion has died out almost completely within the most intellectual milieus. The reverse conclusion is that religiosity strengthens in proportion to lower intellectual levels. Developmental psychology, therefore, explains both religion and atheism. My structural-genetic sociology is the first all-encompassing approach to have explained religion on the basis of developmental psychology,[24] acknowledging only Ludwig Feuerbach[25] as a predecessor.

## History of Philosophy and Sciences

Jean Piaget, in addition to other authors, demonstrated in numerous books and articles that only developmental psychology can explain the history of philosophy and sciences.[26] Ancient and medieval philosophy consisted predominantly of artificialism, animism, and magic. A theological understanding of the world formed the center of pre-modern philosophies. Piaget, along with some other authors repeatedly determined that only the philosophy of the early modern times manifested an understanding of nature corresponding to the adolescent stage of formal operations. It was not before the 17th and 18th centuries that the educated classes and the scientists of Europe first elaborated on the stage of formal operations. The evolution of the physical sciences is therefore the direct result of formal operations arising in the brains of scientists. Thus, the emergence of science "*im eigentlichen Sinne*" originates from the interrelationship of education and cognition, an interrelationship that PCCP has found as the de-

22 Bovet: *Le sentiment religieux et la psychologie de l'enfant*, Neuchâtel/Paris 1951 and Piaget, Jean: *The child's conception of the world.*

23 Dawkins, Richard: *The god delusion*, London 2006.

24 Oesterdiekhoff: *Traumzeit der Menschheit*; idem *The steps of man towards civilization:* pp. 147–161; idem: *Mental growth of humankind in history:* pp. 224–260; idem: *Die geistige Entwicklung der Menschheit.*

25 Feuerbach, Ludwig: *The essence of Christianity*, New York 1985.

26 Piaget, Jean: *Introduction à l'épistémologie génétique.* Vol. 1: *La pensée mathematique*, vol. 2: *La pensée physique*, vol. 3: *La pensée sociologique*, Paris 1950; Piaget, Jean/Garcia, Rolando: *Psychogenesis and the history of sciences*, New York 1989.

cisive engine propelling cognitive growth. The conditions of education, curricula, libraries, book printing, schools, and universities underwent dramatic improvement in the early modern era, and thus stimulated the evolution of the formal operational stage. The rise of the anthropological phase (including increased cognitive ability) is the single cause, during the 18th century, of the rise of the sciences, both the physical sciences and the humanities.[27]

The transformation of alchemy to chemistry, of magic treatments into medicine, of astrology to astronomy, of theology to physics, biology, geology, and the liberal arts or humanities are developments that indicate the transition from pre-formal to formal-operational thinking. The pre-formal disciplines consist totally of artificialism, animism, and magic. The alchemist believes in a living soul within any form of matter and chemical elements and then tries to transform and create them. During the Renaissance period the astronomer still believes the stars may be gods maintaining their orbits of their own volition, and thereby sending their occult influences earthward. Shamanism understands disease to be caused by the occult assaults of ghosts and sorcerers. Both causes and treatments of sickness must be, therefore, magical in nature. The etiology corresponds to the therapy: treatment consists of the exorcism of ghosts.

By the 18th century, sick persons in Europe still frequently preferred to patronize wise men and witches instead of consulting a medical man of the academic school of thought.

It was about 1750 when the formal scientific structures had comparatively outweighed some of the surviving autistic forms. By the 19th century, all forms of autistic and pre-formal thinking in the sciences had been ruthlessly eliminated.

## The Rise of Industrial Society

By this time Jean Piaget[28] and Jürgen Habermas[29] were pointing to the causal interrelation between the emergence of industrial society and formal operations. The rise of formal operations started among the educated classes during the 18th century and had subjugated the lower classes continuously during the 20th century.[30] The steady ascent of anthropological levels from generation to generation resulted in the elevating of cultural milieus and preceded the increase in

27 Oesterdiekhoff: *Die Entwicklung der Menschheit von der Kindheitsphase zur Erwachsenenreife*; idem: *Die geistige Entwicklung der Menschheit.*

28 Piaget: *La pensée sociologique.*

29 Habermas, Jürgen: *Zur Rekonstruktion des Historischen Materialismus*, Frankfurt/Main 1976.

30 Oesterdiekhoff, Georg W./Rindermann, Heiner: *Kultur und Kognition*, Hamburg/Münster 2008; Flynn, James: *What is intelligence?*, London 2007.

methodological efficiency of technological civilization as well. The installment of compulsory school attendance laws in Europe were not completed until around 1900, and the improvement of curricula prepared the rise of management culture over the last 200 years. The improvements in education and cognition support the evolution of professionalism; these three factors explain economic growth and the rise of modern society. Anthropologic ascent, the evolution of the educational system, advancements in the sciences and the implementation of their techniques for production with increases in productivity, the diversification and stringent requirements for professional organizations along with continuous economic growth built up a coherent and complex network we call modern industrial society.

By now the key technology of the first phase of industrial revolution, the steam engine of Watt and Boulton, was an immediate result of the new physical sciences. James Watt was a leading chemist and mathematician of his time, not a craftsman as is sometimes surmised. He could have never built his engine without vast scientific knowledge. From its very beginnings, the industrial revolution essentially consisted of the incorporation of scientific knowledge into the production system. According to the studies of Margaret Jacob,[31] the sciences made the difference between Europe and Asia regarding the evolution of industrial modernity. Nobody in antiquity 2,000 years ago or Asia 200 years ago could have had the skills to build Watt's engine.

Commerce and trade were much more highly developed in Asia than in Europe of the 18th century. Japan and China had all socio-economic and political preconditions for an industrial revolution of their own. Property rights, political security, banks, commerce, trade, mining, metallurgy, infrastructure and transportation were by no means inferior in Asia in comparison with Europe. Asia diverged from Europe only by its lack of the physical sciences, Enlightenment thought and by the unbroken intransience of ancestor worship and a magical-animistic worldview. The perseverance of the childlike anthropologic stage is the singular cause for Asia's failing to develop an industrial revolution and co-development of a modern society by own ideas and means.[32]

The effects brought about through increase of the anthropologic level are not restricted to the development of one social stratum or subsystem but influence all spheres of life and society. The development of humanism and democratic rights, modern music and literature, white pedagogic and distinguished morals on the one hand and the surpassing of witchcraft, superstition, laws which call

31 Jacob, Margaret: *Scientific culture and the making of the industrial west*, Oxford 1997.

32 Oesterdiekhoff: *Kulturelle Bedingungen kognitiver Entwicklung*; idem: *Mental growth of humankind in history*; idem: *The steps of man towards civilization*; idem: *Die Entwicklung der Menschheit von der Kindheitsphase zur Erwachsenenreife.*

for brutal punishments and barbarian customs on the other hand, result from this level of anthropological development. The anthropologic factor is the decisive factor with regard to the evolution of modern society.

To understand this better, we should consider if people who bring animals before a court of law as defendants and then punish them as felons, who spend large sums of money to buy magical spells or who venerate their grandparents as divinities could ever create and run an industry-based society; and in fact, this would be impossible. First of all people must be routed through an educational process which reorganizes their psycho-neurological systems in order to be able to face the tasks modern humans have set themselves to accomplish.

## The Historical Development of Morals

Needless to say, anthropologic differentiation affect morals and violent behavior, too, and it not need be said that highly civilized people are also capable to violence and brutality, whereas conversely, more simply structured peoples can be peaceful and helpful. However, it is statistically significant that thresholds of violence and harsh customs are lower among humans whose anthropologic stage is five or ten years lower compared to civilized humans operating on formal operational levels. Empirical surveys among people living in developing regions are evidence of this fact. The surveys cite testimonies that household quarrels, adultery, theft, and insults are legitimate justifications for killing someone.[33] Surveys among modern populations reveal quite different ideas. Ethnographic descriptions show abundantly that primitives actually kill other persons for exactly these superficial excuses which are taken as legitimate reasons when only considered and discussed.[34]

According to ethnographic statistics, a full third of all humankind over the past millennia have been victims of homicide. Even during the 20th century death rates across tribal societies due to homicide in Australia, South America, Papua-New Guinea and elsewhere amounted to around 33 %[35] while the corresponding death rate in North America and Europe (minus Russia) in the 20th century was around 1 % which after 1945 actually decreased to 0,1 %. Thus, the probability of getting killed has been 330 times higher in tribal societies than in the most advanced contemporary societies. What causes this difference is not only psychology, as I evidenced with reference to the surveys, but is also due to in-

33 Oesterdiekhoff, Georg W.: *Zivilisation und Strukturgenese. Norbert Elias und Jean Piaget im Vergleich*, Frankfurt/Main 2000, p. 301.

34 Hallpike, Christopher: *The evolution of moral understanding*, London 2004.

35 Kelley, Lawrence: *War before civilization*, Oxford 1996, pp. 185–202.

stitutional conditioning. Trained police forces and justice systems built upon the armature of professionalism effect a highly efficient culture of control and deterrence. Thus, Norbert Elias[36] was right in saying the higher violence rates of primitive societies were caused by institutional and psychological factors as well.

Wild and crude manners are more pronounced and widespread among primitive societies than in modern ones as people frequently had to face mortal duels or combat as a normal aspect of their social milieu. The punitive customs of tribal societies and civilizations is predicated as well upon an almost casual attitude of utmost brutality and boundless sadism. Wolfgang Schild[37] described it simply as a form of butchery. The Roman arena games are defined by a combination of warrior culture, animal fights and the executions of criminals, that is, by the elements found in every pre-modern society. The uniqueness of the Roman games resulted from a constellation of these elements and by showcasing them within a splendid spectacle. Millions of humans and animals met their deaths through these games, watched by anywhere from 20,000 to 70,000 spectators. These staged spectacles were the most famous element within Roman entertainment culture, and the pleasure people enjoyed watching humans and animals fighting and being torn to pieces was the single biggest reason for their existence. I maintain that populations of modern, industrial cultures could neither enjoy nor stomach seeing how armed-to-the-teeth dwarves fare against women identically armed, or the particulars of how lions go about slaughtering young girls, and, as a finale, how hundreds of criminals being compelled to hack away at each other all end up lying sprawled, bloody and dead, in the sand of the arena floor. The civilized psychic construct has completely rejected such forms, and any civilized person would become hysterical if exposed to such demonstrations through force or other unwanted circumstances. The complete resistance of the modern psyche to such atrocities is the single reason these forms of entertainment are no longer tolerated to exist in a modern society. The civilization of the psyche (the anthropologic rise) is the single reason that brutal punishments, along with a dueling culture – both components of the Roman games – were abolished during the era of Enlightenment 200 years ago. It would be unimaginable that a modern population (or culture) could re-establish Roman-style games, with members of government and parliament in the first rows – applauding the already-mentioned horrors – as was common in ancient times. Whoever tried to re-establish such things nowadays would be stopped immediately, it should go without saying, whereas there was no ancient abolitionist movement, no popular moral impetus then in existence either to

36 Elias, Norbert: *Power and civility*, New York 1982.
37 Schild, Wolfgang: *Alte Gerichtsbarkeit*, München 1980.

level accusations or to force their closure. There does exist clear proof of the fact that moral refinement, empathy, sensibility, humanity, and a growing culture of nonviolence is due to the ascent of anthropologic stages in effecting these transformations of morals and social behavior.[38]

The development of modern humanism is understandable only within the framework of these abstract considerations and by inserting these historical facts: Jörn Rüsen[39] sees the rise of modern humanism as the heritage of Enlightenment thought and philosophy. I would like to add that the philosophy of Enlightenment and the birth of humanism are, respectively, clear manifestations of the anthropologic stages accelerating the formal operations, which in turn, are rewiring the brains of millions of individual humans.

Future social sciences will be better in understanding the history of wars as a part of the human psyche's evolution. By way of example, the two World Wars were by no means inevitable due to situational logic, military policy, economic motives or political circumstances in any strict sense, but emerged from political motives understandable only against the backdrop of politicians' (and populations') mind-sets. Politicians had the power, and could have prevented the beginning of both wars – if they really had had the slightest motivation to do so. Furthermore, they always retained the power to call off hostilities at any point during the course of either of these wars.[40] The *readiness* to prevent or to stop hostilities results in a direct way from the anthropologic level, respectively, from the layers of responsibility, empathy, morals, emotional intelligence, as well as intellect. In our own time, an overwhelming segment of the population can no longer understand the political decisions leading to wars and conflicts, and would make quite different decisions from the political leader class if asked to be involved in the processes of disentangling the of conflict together with their contexts.[41]

The psycho-neurological system entangled in, as well as provoking, two world wars, was, by current standards, amazingly primitive (contemporary European politicians hurled back in time to Europe as it was 80 years ago, would make radically different decisions from those of their ancestors) but not as primitive as

38 Oesterdiekhoff, Georg W.: "The arena games in the Roman empire: a contribution to the explanation of the history of morals and humanity", in: *Narodna Umjetnost. Croatian Journal of Ethnology and Folklore Research* 46.1 (2009): 177 – 202; idem: *Mental growth of humankind in history*, pp. 310 – 332; idem: *Die geistige Entwicklung der Menschheit.*

39 Rüsen, Jörn: "Traditionsprobleme eines zukunftsfähigen Humanismus", in: Vöhler, Martin/ Cancik, Hubert (Eds.): *Humanismus und Antikerezeption im 18. Jahrhundert.* Vol. 1: *Genese und Profil des europäischen Humanismus*, Heidelberg 2009, pp. 201 – 216.

40 Baker, Nicholson: *Human smoke. The beginnings of World War II, the end of civilization*, New York 2008, evidences this convincingly.

41 Oesterdiekhoff: *Zivilisation und Strukturgenese*, pp. 301 – 314; idem: *Die geistige Entwicklung der Menschheit.*

that still simpler psychic-system that inaugurated cannibalism, the Roman arena games, the Spanish atrocities in the Americas, and in 1994, the genocidal incidents in Ruanda. It is necessary to measure the anthropologic summit not just with reference to the extent of damage, but also with reference to just how primitive are the level of motives and actions.

Richard Dawkins[42] presented convincing evidence of an increased moral sentiment in industrial populations since 1945. Imagine in this context the current deep-rooted pacifism of the Japanese, the total unreadiness of the US to accept its own casualties (compare D-day with the war on Iraq, which was said to have claimed initially not one American victim), the impossibility of wars for territorial conquest nowadays (there is not one country worldwide over the past few decades that was able to gain and maintain new territories by war), and the measurable decline in the number of wars in recent decades. In the considered opinion of August Comte and Herbert Spencer, that wars may be a phenomenon conjoined to pre-industrial societies and would inevitably die out in modern times, describes not a utopia but is more and more apposite to the real developments of the international political system.[43]

## Freedom and Democracy, Slavery and Dictatorship

Slavery and feudalism were typical components of the social structure of premodern societies across Asia, Europe, Africa, and America. Slavery is not a phenomenon bound only to civilizations, but is also common among tribal societies such as those of the North American Indians, African tribes or ancient Germans. Ancient philosophy usually had no problems justifying slavery and other forms of lost or absent freedom, such as the dependent status of women and children. The ways and means in which a person's freedom can be denied have dominated on most continents up to the rise of modernity and partly later on. Social sciences and the humanities are correct to ascertain that the invention of freedom is limited to European developments, of the past 200 years in particular. The abolishment of slavery and feudalism within the social system and of autocracy within the political systems of Europe over the past 200 years are developments whose theoretical explanation has been incomplete until now. The attainment of freedom both in the political and social system seems to manifest in coherencies which hint at a common causality. Social scientists emphasize both intellectual and economic factors which are believed to have caused this

42 Dawkins, Richard: *Der Gotteswahn*, Berlin 2008, pp. 367 – 377.

43 Oesterdiekhoff: *Zivilisation und Strukturgenese*; idem: *Die geistige Entwicklung der Menschheit.*

breakthrough. I have shown that this breakthrough in the cause of freedom is primarily accountable to the psycho-cognitive evolution of humankind and not to economic factors.[44]

For example, the abolition of the slave trade by European nations in the first half of the 19th century directly resulted from Enlightenment ideas and by no means from economic changes.[45] Nations such as England and Denmark fought against the slavery trade, thus investing means to hinder it, for example by controls and blockades across the Atlantic Ocean. Thus, the fight against slavery and feudalism belongs to the same political movement, which directed against monarchy and dictatorship and supported the establishment of the constitutional state and democracy. The ideas of the Enlightenment and humanism are the motives behind the abolition of autocratic systems and the establishment of systemic emancipation.

Jean Piaget[46] established that the idea of freedom evolved from the cognitive development and maturation of the adolescent psyche. In his unique book on moral development he showed that small children initially believe that rules are unchangeable and made by god or father. The children believe that they can only obey but by no means influence legislation or create the rules which govern their lives on their own. Only by the beginning of the second decade of life do adolescents begin to understand that rules are changeable and man-made. From this point on they regard the democratic process as the only legitimate source of rules. This implies that the counterweight of democracy in relation to autocracy is caused by the rise of anthropologic stage corresponding to the development of formal operations.

I showed that the evolution of freedom and democracy over the past 200 years has gone the same way due to the same reasons. I worked out the parallels between the ontogenetic and historical developments. The philosophy of law and legislation, the ideologies of monarchy, the ideas and practices of rulership in pre-modern societies all fit in every respect the childlike ideation which gave rise to autocracy and inflexible rulemaking. The revolutions in France and the USA, the humanistic philosophy of the Enlightenment, the innovations which gave rise to the constitutional state and democracy in the West fully represents anthropologic rises and cognitive evolutions.

Autocracies, monarchies and dictatorships can only exist and survive when a majority of the population supports them. Their existence depends on maintaining legitimacy through loyalty. Primitive populations deny the concept of

44 Oesterdiekhoff: *Mental growth of humankind in history*, pp. 277–285; idem: *Kulturelle Evolution des Geistes*, pp. 243–277; idem: *Die Entwicklung der Menschheit von der Kindheitsphase zur Erwachsenenreife*.

45 Porter, Roy: *The creation of the modern world*, New York 2000.

46 Piaget: *The moral judgment of the child.*

democratic self-determination and will demand a strong and unidirectional leadership, believing as they do that democracy leads to anarchy and chaos, immorality and inefficiency. Even the Catholic Church in the first half of the 20th century objected to democracy on these same grounds. The support of fascism among Europeans resulted from the childlike attitudes Piaget[47] called "moral heteronomy" that are bound to lower anthropological stages.

Thus, the advent of democracy in Europe in the past 100 years originates in anthropologic rises. Advanced populations view the legitimacy claims of dictatorship, monarchy and autocracy with the greatest suspicion and skepticism and are consequently unwilling to accept any other form of political life than democracy, as also did the adolescents Piaget described. Thus, democracy, the constitutional state and humanism originate in higher forms of communication and social life, morals and responsibility. The humanitarian breakthroughs represented by individual freedoms and civil rights is a manifestation of the attainment of higher anthropological summits.

Around 1975, dictatorships ruled over two thirds of the nations worldwide. Nowadays, democracy has achieved a counterweight among 200 nations. The roots of the current Arab Spring do not stem from suppression, poverty, and overpopulation, as is often maintained, but from anthropologic rises within the minds of the more educated younger generation.

Therefore, I make the assertion that my structural-genetic sociology has provided the theoretical basis which would explain the universality of slavery and autocracy in pre-modern societies and the evolution of freedom and democracy in modern societies which we experience and enjoy today.[48]

## Conclusions

(1) Developmental psychology in respect to structural-genetic sociology provides the key to understanding anthropological structures in all cultures. The tremendous and unique insights into thinking and behavior on different developmental plateaus that research into developmental psychology has collected is now available to explain the thought processes and behavior of populations across different cultures. My theoretical program secures an understanding of the specific psycho-cognitive structure of modern man, whose historical origins and particularities become apparent only when contrasted with those of pre-modern man. Only with this theoretical program can we illuminate what pre-

47 Piaget: *The moral judgment of the child.*

48 Oesterdiekhoff: *Kulturelle Evolution des Geistes*, pp. 243–277; idem: *Die Entwicklung der Menschheit von der Kindheitsphase zur Erwachsenenreife.*

vious theories of pre-modern humankind did not provide about complete layers of consciousness, reflectivity, and operational structures that only emerged piecemeal in more recent history. The application of developmental psychology mediates an entrance into a new universe of scientific possibilities and resolutions.

(2) Pre-modern humans lived inside a completely different set of social dynamics, corresponding to fairy tales worlds and childlike myths, possessing as they did different forms of consciousness in their quest to experience humans, society and nature. Only developmental psychology delivers the key to reveal these foreign forms.

(3) This theoretical program explains the historical development of the basic thought structures, worldview, religion, philosophy, science, law, customs, morals and social behavior. Without reference to this program we can scarcely explain any relevant social phenomenon, neither long-term social change nor the history of violence, nor developmental and educational policy.

(4) This theoretical program is heir to the classical sociology represented especially by Auguste Comte and Norbert Elias, classical British Anthropology, and the approaches of Ernst Cassirer and Lucien Lévy-Bruhl. It delivers a new basis to "historical anthropology" and the micro-sociology of social change. Moreover, the program provides a new framework and foundation to all the humanities and social sciences.

(5) Hermann Schneider wrote in his book on the ancient Egyptians[49] that his time would understand more completely that developmental psychology delivered the key to a true comprehension of the history of mankind. Karl Lamprecht, the most widely read historian in Germany at this time, shared this opinion. Schneider predicted a future scientific breakthrough in the humanities due to the application of developmental psychology. Only then, Schneider said, would the humanities attain that level which the science of biology had achieved in consequence of the contributions of Charles Darwin.

(6) The idea of a pre-formal cognitive level in humans living in pre-modern societies and the discovery of anthropologic levels about five or ten years ago is the most fundamental scientific breakthrough within the fields of humanities and social sciences; a discovery which reveals the potential for even more breathtaking and fascinating scientific insights on the horizon.

49 Schneider, Hermann: *Kultur und Denken der alten Ägypter*, Leipzig 1909.

# II. Cultural Manifestations

Hubert Cancik

# Europe – Antiquity – Humanism

## 1. Orientation

'Humanism' is a fairly recent, an open and somewhat indeterminable concept. That may be an advantage, but it can also carry the temptation of vagueness, of empty phrase, cant on festive occasions.

The word derives from the university and school system. The term originally designates a program for the reform of secondary education ('Gymnasium') in Germany (Friedrich Immanuel Niethammer, 1808). Later on it was used to characterize a period of Italian history (14.–16. century, the so-called Renaissance). Finally humanism has come to denote the basis of humanitarian practice across the world.

The German loan-word 'Humanität' itself is a bit older. It is taken from French (*humanité*). Johann Gottfried Herder (1744 – 1803) has legitimized it for the German language and has established it in the semantic field of 'mankind, human rights, human dignity, philanthropy'.

Both terms 'humanism' and 'humanity' are derivations of the Latin word *humanitas.* This word means 'humankind', 'being human', 'education' and 'charity'. M. Tullius Cicero (106 – 43 B.C.) has supplied the classical quotations.

The name 'Europe' is very ancient, in fact so ancient that it is not clear whether it is of Greek or Semitic origin. It originally designates a figure from Greek mythology, and subsequently, a diversity of geographical entities with numerous languages and religions (Celtic, Germanic, Slavonic; Jewish, Christian, Islamic; deistic, pantheistic; atheistic, pagan). Finally, Europe is the name of the political principle that after the Second World War (1945) and after the demise of the political blocks (1989) has led to the creation of an ever-growing European Union.

The word 'antiquity' implies both an epoch and a norm: on the one hand the ancient era of Greeks and Romans (appr. 800 B.C. to 800 A.D.), on the other everything that is 'classical', the antique 'canon', the model or example of those who went 'before us' (lat. *ante nos*), the *antiqui.* Parts of this culture and history are regarded as the common 'heritage' of Europe: Roman roads (lat. *stratum*) and urban settlements (Aachen, Cologne, Mainz, Regensburg, Trier), writing and money, ethics and politics, law and philosophy, myths, art, science. This heritage is received, made use of or rejected; it is processed, adapted, vernacularized, nationalized and synthesized with something 'new' or 'alien'. This processing of the antique tradition forms an important aspect of the religious and intellectual history in all European cultures after the period of antiquity. But not every reception of antiquity is, as such, humanism.

## 2. Europe

### 2.1. Myth-History

'Europa', 'the far sighted one', is the name of a Phoenician princess from Tyros (Lebanon). Greeks are supposed to have abducted her, as the 'father of historiography' relates it, at the beginning of his history. The ancient chronographs date the abduction around the year 1435 B.C., thus indicating the mythic-historic beginning of Europe. The great war between the Persians and the Greeks (500–479 B.C.) is perceived by him as a conflict between the continents of Asia and Europe, between Orient and Occident. This is why Herodotus' (484-ca.420 B.C.) account of the abduction of females from mythical times is so detailed: Phoenicians steal Io, the Greeks Europa; then the Greeks abduct Medea from Kolchis, and Paris of Troy in Asia (Minor) carries off Helen. This abduction of women thereafter escalates, against all political reason, into a great war, i. e. the Trojan War – according to Herodotus's reckoning around 1250 B.C. The historian digs so deep into the mythical early history in order to illustrate the relevance of the contemporary conflict between Hellenics and Persians in the fifth century. In this process Herodotus creates the idea of Europe. The historian constructs it from the material of geography and myth, politics and war. He opposes Greek freedom with oriental despotism, and against the superiority in numbers from Asia he sets the cunning, the pathos of freedom and the absolute fearlessness of the few in the battles of Marathon (490), Salamis (480) and at Thermopylae (480).

The myth of the virgin on the bull and Herodotus' construct of the idea of Europe are reminiscent of the provenance of Greek culture from the great, rich and alien orient and thus are formative of the European sense of identity. This idea is mediated through fascinating images and forceful texts. They form the very core of European humanism.

## 2.2. The Space

The old Europe is a continent like Asia and Libya (Africa). According to ancient views its border is formed by the Dardanelles and the Tanais (the river Don in Russia). Asia Minor (Turkey), although densely populated by Greeks from early onwards ($2^{nd}$ millennium), belongs to Asia. After Kiev and Moscow had laid claim to the political as well as religious heritage of the Byzantine empire ('the Second Rome') and reclaimed the title of 'The Third Rome' for themselves, the Modern Age advanced the border of Europe to the Urals.

The name Europe is also connected with a small area at the Dardanelles. It is delineated as the territory of Constantinople (Istanbul in Turkey), the 'New', the 'Second Rome'. In late antiquity the small province of Europe belonged to the diocese 'Orient' and to the Eastern part (*praefectura Orientis*) of the Roman Empire. The Europe of antiquity is up to now located in Turkey, of all places.

Europe lies in the West, where the sun sinks into the Ocean (Occident); this is where the land of darkness is situated (Hesperia/ 'Abendland'). In accordance with the geographical logic of astronomy it always forms the counterpart to the Orient, to the Eastern world where the sun goes up on the horizon. Europe is a small continent, the western tip of huge Asia. It is a continent divided into small sections. For a long time this prevented the formation of large centralized empires such as in Mesopotamia and on the Nile. Numerous small islands, an ocean in the middle that did not separate so much as it invited voyages of discovery, commerce, and the founding of colonies. Everywhere along the coastline settlements were founded by Phoenicians, Greeks, Romans. Ulysses, the 'much-enduring', the 'man of many devices', is a person typical of this landscape. Homer (Odyssey 1,3) sings his praises: "He has seen the cities of many people and has understood their mind (Greek *égno*)." Ulysses stands at the very beginning of the genealogy of European mankind;[1] he was, so it is said, "the first self-determined [...] man of world literature". This is why Homer was made into a set text at schools both in Antiquity and the Modern Age, and Ulysses became a paradigm of the humanist image of man.

## 2.3. The Empire

The political-military and cultural energy of Europe was not limited by its geographical boundaries. The empire of Alexander (336–323 B.C) and his successors extends via Syria, Iraq and Afghanistan all the way to the Indus and

1 Cf. Andreae, Bernard: *Odysseus. Archäologie des europäischen Menschenbildes*, Frankfurt/ Main $^{2}$1984, p. 18.

Ganges. The Roman Empire comprises northern Africa and the western parts of Alexander's empire. Thus the Mediterranean became the inland lake of the Empire. Pompey finally triumphs over the three continents (61 B.C.). But the Roman *imperium* wants unbounded power. Vergil composes (Aneid 1,278 f.) the following lines:

*His ego nec metas rerum nec tempora pono,*
*Imperium sine fine dedi.*
On these (Romans) I impose neither spatial nor temporal limits of power,
I gave them an empire without end.

Already in antiquity Vergil became a schoolbook author, and he has remained so in the latinized West until the present day. It is he who has put into the most beautiful verse, which has been frequently commented on by all the humanists, Europe's claim to dominance. Vergil is, also because of this, "the father of the Occident".

The economic, political and cultural unity of the Roman Empire is destroyed by two ruptures. The Greek eastern part is split off from the Latin West of Europe (395 A.D.). The political split is deepened by the religious one. The great schism (1054) separates the Roman Catholic from the orthodox Greek and Slavonic churches. Christianity was not capable of fulfilling its supra-national claim. It cemented national politics and ancient, deep-seated cultural differences.

The second rupture of the circum-mediterranean and multi-religious Roman Empire was occasioned by the expansion of the Arabs into Syria and Egypt (640 A.D.), northern Africa and Spain (711 A.D.).The originally unifying inland sea becomes a hostile one. This horizontal division of the Roman Empire around 800 marks the end of antiquity. The new centres of Europe have shifted to the north, the east, and to the Atlantic coast. The new Cesar Augustus resides in Aachen and Vienna (up to 1806), the Second Rome (until 1453) is supplanted by Moscow, the New, the Third Rome (since 1523/24). In huge colonial empires on all four continents European culture aggressively and irresistibly spreads all over the globe: Christianity, technologies, educational systems, and political ideologies spread, and along with them the antique tradition, both idealist (I. Niethammer) and realist (K. Marx) humanism, the concepts of human dignity, liberty and equality as well as human right.

## 3. Antiquity

### 3.1. The Epoch and the Model

1. 'Antiquity' is an epoch (ca. 800 B.C.–800 A.D.) and an idea (ideal, norm, canon, model). It is a common European heritage partially through the historical process because numerous regions of Europe were part of the *imperium Romanum*, partially through reception because all regions of Europe, also the Slavonic and temporarily Arabian ones (Sicily, Malta, Andalusia), have assimilated ancient culture. Classical antiquity, both in terms of factual history and as an idea has been the basis and omnipresent impetus for a European humanism in all its multiple and contradictory manifestations. 'Antiquity' is a promise of happiness, the scope for human fulfilment, a longing, arcadia and utopia all in one: "There, there will I go…" (J.W. Goethe) So much enthusiastic love of antiquity is capable of fostering illusions and escapism, it obstructs the view of actual history and of the task of having to mediate between dream and reality, antiquity and our respective present without disavowing the dream. In antiquity the traumatic experience of inhumanity and destructiveness, both individual and collective, have been cast in the most striking moulds and been transmitted in a variety of mythical configurations (Antigone, Medea, Niobe), in epic (the Theban and Trojan wars) and in tragedy (Aeschylus, The Persians; Sophocles, Oedipus; Euripides, Hekabe), in historiography and historicizing poetry: Thucydides about the plague in Athens, Tacitus about the fall of the Roman republic, Lucan about Caesar's civil war.

2. Greek antiquity originates as a marginal culture of the late ancient Orient and becomes the centre of the *Méditerranée.* In myths and historiography the Greeks have commemorated this dependency: Europe comes from Tyros, Priamos from Troy is a vassal of Ninos, the king of Assyria. Thales, the first philosopher of nature (1st half of 6th cent. B.C.) is said to have been of noble Phoenician descent. With him it is that the science of the principles of nature and the cosmos takes its beginnings. Three foreign words – principle (Greek *arché*), nature (Greek *physis*), cosmos (Greek *kosmos* – 'the ordered world') – encompasses the fundaments of a theoretical exploration of the sky and the earth that is untainted by magic.

The Greeks have a culture of learning. They take over everything from the barbarians – and improve on it. Even their gods and rites they have "learnt" from the Egyptians and Phoenicians. What is conspicuous is their reluctance to learn foreign languages; it is understandable, though, that for them "education comes before everything" (*próton paídeusis*)[2] and that the techniques of oratory

2 Cf. Antiphon, frg. 60 (Diels, Hermann/Kranz, Walther (Eds.): *Die Fragmente der Vor-*

(rhetoric) became a part of general education. The Romans learn from the Greeks – language, art, myth, philosophy, rhetoric, history – and they try to "surpass" them. This makes them into the very model of European culture in general. But also the principle of competition (Greek *agón*), "always to be the best and excel among others" is Greek (Homer Iliad 6, 208). The intercultural dialogue is a practice inscribed in the structure of both cultures.

3. Ancient culture is political and public. Man is defined as a "state-orientated" social being (Greek *zoon politikón*, lat. *animal sociale*).[3] The political space is extensive as well as differentiated. There is the market-place (Agora) where the apostle Paulus meets philosophers with whom he can discuss the divine and the resurrection of the flesh; the court of law (Areopag); the 'theatre' in which the body politic can represent and celebrate itself; they are spaces for plays, receptions, speeches for display, public assemblies. Most sacral spaces are freely accessible, even to foreigners (non-citizens). Here artwork and votive gifts are exhibited, complete with the inscription and names of the donors, and a great many people are able to read these.

Athens is the paradigm (Greek *parádeigma*) of all this.[4] The *pólis* ("city state") is completely autonomous and therefore free. During its classical period (5$^{th}$-4$^{th}$ cent. B.C.) several types of "people's rule" (Greek *demo-kratiá*) are invented here. That is why Athens offers "the most varied forms of life". This city becomes an "educational institution" (Greek *Paídeusis*) for all of Greece, of antiquity, and beyond.

This is where new ideas of freedom and equality are conceived and practiced – not without conflict and failure. In a new branch of science, politology, these concepts are researched and criticized: What is the best constitution, what are the best modes of living for as many states and people as possible?[5] What types of democracy are there? Freedom, as Aristotle defines it, is most effectively realized in a democracy, because everybody, according to the law applying to all, equally participates in the state (Greek *politeía*).

4. Antiquity is a complex culture. In some regions and epochs there exist a fully developed monetary market, the division of labour, manufacture, foreign trade, i. e. the whole structure typical of early modernity. The cultural sectors – the legal system, art, religion, philosophy, education, science, wisdom – are highly differentiated, theoretically founded and reflected upon in terms of their historicity. Through an unusual creativity and energy a "second nature" (Cicero) is created. Prometheus, who shaped the first human beings, and Icarus, who flies

*sokratiker*, Berlin 1952/60).

3 Cf. Aristotle, *Politics* 3,6,1278b: "By his very nature man is a 'political animal'".

4 Thucydides, 2,37,1.

5 Aristotle, *Politics* 4,11.

into the sun, until today have remained mythical emblems of a "titanic" force:[6] "Many things are tremendous. But nothing/ Is more tremendous than man."

Religion is loosely connected with culture and science. The temples possess little economic power. Priests and priestesses are well respected but do not form an organized clergy. Speculative theology becomes the province of philosophers. There is no sacred book, no general, state- or church-organized religious instruction. During the conflict with Judaism and Christianity certain religious "privileges" are construed (Lat.: *privilegia Iudaeorum*) and religious freedom as a human right (*ius humanum*) is demanded from the state. Towards the end of ancient history the tolerance-laws from the time of Constantine (306 – 337 A.D.) through Julian (360 – 363) once more create the conditions for a multi-religious society that also includes the Christians.

## 3.2. Contradictions

Antiquity is the culture of a layered society with great differences between the city and the country, between Greece and Rome, between the polis and the empire. It cannot be compressed into a brief physiognomic sketch of its culture. Deconstructivist disenchanters would have easy play: Antiquity, the Greek, the Roman do not exist. The attempts at achieving equality and liberty, democracy and tolerance can be easily exposed as being ideological and having failed or may be qualified by ancient alternatives. Democratic Athens was defeated by Sparta; the Roman republic of the aristocracy that was based on inequality proved to be superior in military and political respect; a lot of philosophers praised the monarchy; towards the end of the ancient world, the religious totalitarianism of Christianity prevented the religious freedom of a multireligious society. Slavery was not abolished, not even with Jews and Christians, nowhere were women granted the active or passive right to vote. 'Antiquity' was open to the world, biophile, full of curiosity and the liking for empiricism. But it also invented the Great Beyond (Greek *ep-ékeina*), the chasm (*chorismós*) between the world and the realm of ideas. 'Antiquity' is sensuous and erotic; the plastic arts are its special art form: the figure of the "pure person", without insignia and uniform. But the Romans, as common wisdom has it, are sober, dry, prudish, rather unartistic, anti-mythical. The gods of antiquity are numerous and of human shape. But the philosophers are thinking of the one God, the "one and all" (*hen kai pan*), the spirit that moves and guides the world. Roman law amounts to a

6 Sophocles, *Antigone* (performed ca. 442), first song of the chorus (vv. 332 – 375); the German translation by Friedrich Hölderlin runs: "Ungeheuer ist vieles. Doch nichts/ Ungeheuerer als der Mensch."

cultural revolution: no divine judgement, the restraints on humiliating and cruel punishment; the foundation of law in the principles of justice, fairness, legal security, nature and reason (Cicero, *About Laws*). But there still remains justice based on class, torture, the penalty of crucifixion and *ad bestias.*

In view of such and numerous other contradictions it is small wonder that those who want to attack the ideal or real, the ethical or emancipatory humanism can also cite ancient authorities and paradigms. Antiquity is, they claim, the very proof against humanism as such. After all, antiquity holds that slavery was part of "the essence of culture": "The misery of people living laboriously must be increased", not abolished; the talk of human dignity and basic rights is an illusion, a lie; the enlightenment was "un-Germanic", war is necessary, modern man has grown soft. Thus spoke Friedrich Nietzsche,[7] teacher and professor of Greek in the great old humanist city of Basel on the Rhine.

## 4. Tradition – Reception – Renaissance

### 4.1. Italy

1. Around 1500 there exist "humanity studies" (*studia humanitatis*) in numerous Italian cities, in Padua, Venice, Pisa, Bologna, Milan, Florence and Rome. This is where the *(h)umanista* teaches ancient literature and rhetoric. He becomes a member of the faculty in which the "seven liberal arts" are taught. The arts faculty is a "lower faculty" devoted to preparatory studies. These are a preparation for the professional studies at the three "high faculties" (medicine, jurisprudence, theology). The lowly position of the *umanista* stands in striking contrast to the demanding subjects he has to teach and the objective to be achieved: nothing less than forming the mind (*conformatio*) towards humanity by studying the texts of the famous rhetoricians, historians, poets and philosophers. The name and syllabus of the *studia humanitatis* have become well established in Italy and legitimized by their ancient provenance. Coluccio Salutati (1331 – 1406), chancellor of Florence (1375 – 1406), explains to Carlo Malatesta, Lord of Rimini, the meaning of 'humanity' (*humanitas*).[8] The word signifies 'forming the mind' (*eruditio, litterae, scientia*) and 'mildness' (*mansuetudo, comitas, benignitas*). Cicero defines it likewise. The 'studies of humanity' of the Italian Renaissance are a conscious and legitimate reception of

7 Nietzsche, F.: "Der griechische Staat. Weihnachtsgabe an Cosima Wagner, 1872", in: Colli, Giorgio/Montinari, Mazzino (Eds.): *Friedrich Nietzsche. Sämtliche Werke. Kritische Studienausgabe*, Munich 1980, vol. 1, pp. 764 – 777.

8 Coluccio Salutati to Carlo Malatesta, September 10th, 1401 (Epistle 12, 18, in: *Epistolario III*, pp. 534 – 536).

ancient pedagogy and 'moral science' (*scientia moralis*). The *studia humanitatis* were only much later nobilitated by having an 'ism' attached to them, thereby becoming elevated to the status of a pedagogical system: "humanism" (1808). However, the dual determination of humanity by "(mental) refinement" (*eruditio*) and "(active) mercifulness" (*philanthropia*), the very core of humanism, has been effective in the Italian Renaissance from the very beginning.

2. The extension of "humanity studies" and the slow ascent of the arts faculty to the status of a high philosophical faculty is the apex, a terminologically fixed point, but by no means the beginning of the humanist movement in Italy (ca. 1300 – 1600). The rise of the Italian cities and states, the decline of feudalism and the success of bourgeois economy, of republican and democratic constitutions in various cities begin before and independent of this movement. Francesco Petrarch (1304 – 1374) is considered to be its first representative. He has studied jurisprudence, is temporarily in the employ of Cardinal Giovanni Colonna, travels to see Emperor Charles IV in Prague (1336) by order of the Visconti (Milan). Petrarch learns the Greek language from Barlaam, a monk from Calabria, who had lived in Constantinople for a long time. The Capitol in Rome is the stage for crowning the poet with a laurel wreath (*poeta laureatus*, 1341). This is where the ancient "Capitolinian Games" are renewed, where a cultural-political signal to all of Europe is emitted. Following the ancient custom Petrarch receives the laurel wreath and Roman citizenship. The antique ruins of the Eternal City for him are a sign of hope that goes far beyond the improvement of the Latin style, the enrichment of Italian literature or the further study of Cicero's speeches and letters. Thus he writes to Cola di Rienzo, who in 1347 had been elected tribune by the Roman people:[9]

> "Brutus has freed the city of one single tyrant, you of many. Camillus resurrected the city from still existing, yes, still smouldering ruins, you from ruins decayed since long ago."

The new freedom was due to the long absence of Emperor and Pope, but also to ancient traditions and relics, such as the inscription that Cola di Rienzo found in the Lateran (Rome) and publicized as an exemplar of the good old law of the Roman Empire in the Lateran basilica. The "law on the rule of Vespasian" from the middle of the first century after Christ demonstrates to the surprised inhabitants of Rome the majesty of the Roman people and the power of the Senate to nominate emperors and to restrain them by legislative means.[10]

---

9 Petrarch to Cola di Rienzo, *Epistolae variae* 48; cf. Petrarca, *Epistolae familiares* 11, 16, 1 (Defense of Cola).

10 The inscription is published: *Corpus Inscriptionum Latinarum* VI 930; *Inscriptiones Latinae Selectae* 244; McCrum, M./Woodhead, A.G.: *Documents of the Principates of the Flavian Emperors* (A.D. 68 – 96), Cambridge 1966, no. 1.

The history of ancient Rome – Brutus, Camillus, Vespasian – is capable of inspiring new political visions: the unification of torn-apart Italy. Petrarch writes to Cola di Rienzo: "Be welcome, founder of the freedom, the peace, the calm of Rome". Cola is "the prophet of the Italian renaissance" (F. Gregorovius).[11]

3. The poetical and political commencement of the Renaissance, Petrarch's coronation as a poet (1341) and the tribuneship of Cola di Rienzo (1347), is not accidentally linked with the City of Rome. Her monumental remains were still greatly in evidence even in the 14th century: ancient columns everywhere, the ruined aqueducts, the road-system, the huge thermal baths of Diocletian and Caracalla, the Aurelian wall, the long rows of sepulchres outside the city gates. A later visitor writes:[12] "[...] with this place (i.e. Rome) the entire history of the world is linked, and I account the day that I entered Rome a second birthday, a veritable rebirth."

But not only in Rome and not only as late as the 14th century does the reception of ancient science, philosophy, art, history and poetry acquire the dimension of a rebirth. Even as early as the 12th century the concept of a natural knowledge of God and morality had been evolved and had Plato, Cicero and Seneca been rediscovered as the heralds of reason, nature and virtue proceeding from a natural sense of ethics (Abaelard, John of Salisbury, William of Conches). The philosopher makes a reappearance and represents a position of his own in the religious debate with Jews and Christians.[13] John of Salisbury (ca. 1120–1180) has preserved a saying by Bernard of Chartres (around 1126):[14]

*Pigmei gigantum umeris impositi*
*Plus quam ipsi gigantes vident.*
Dwarves placed on the shoulders of Giants
See more than the giants themselves.

The saying in its brevity and conciseness combines the self-confidence of the century with the respect for the achievement of those who went before, the belief in progress (*plus*) with the necessity of tradition ("on the shoulders").

---

11 Gregorovius, Ferdinand: *Geschichte der Stadt Rom im Mittelalter* (1859/1860), Darmstadt 1953/1957 (=Munich 1978), II 2, p. 744.

12 Goethe, Johann Wolfgang: "Italienische Reise", 3rd Dec. 1786, in: Goethe, Johann Wolfgang: *Sämtliche Werke*, Zürich 1977 (=1950), vol. 11, p. 160; cf. p. 157; p. 179.

13 Abaelard, Peter (1079–1142): *Gespräch eines Philosophen, eines Juden und eines Christen.* Latin-German edition: *Peter Abailard.* Ed. and transl. by Hans-Wolfgang Krautz, Darmstadt 1995.

14 John of Salisbury, *Metalogicon* 3,4 (900 C), (ed. C.C.J. Webb, Oxford 1929, p. 136). Cf. Merton, R.K.: *Auf den Schultern von Riesen* (1965), Frankfurt/Main 1983.

## 4.2. Byzantium and Slavonic Culture

1. Byzantium, an ancient Greek city on the Dardanelles, in the $4^{th}$ century becomes Constantinople, the "New Rome", the "Second Rome".[15] The city of Constantine, founded in 330 A.D., acquires the same relevance for the Eastern part of the imperium as Old Rome had for the West. It is from here that the traditions of antiquity are transmitted, via Christian Syria to the Persians, Arabs, and finally to the Osmanic-Islamic cultural region. Through the politics and culture of Byzantium, Bulgarians and Slavs become acculturated and christianized. Their Glagolitic and Cyrillic script is developed from the Greek one. After the seizure of Constantiople by Mohammed II (1453) the title along with the imperial and cultural idea of 'Rome' was available again. After the 'Old' and the 'Second' now followed Moscow, the "Third Rome". The theology and ideology of the "Third Rome" is set out in three circular letters sent by Philotheus of Pleskow (Filofei of Pskow, Russia) to the Russian Grand Princes Micheal G. Misjur' Munechim (died 1528), Vasilij III (1503 – 1533), Ivan IV (1533 – 1574): "For two Romes have fallen, but the Third stands firm, and there will not be a Fourth".[16] Roman and Christian traditions become conflated: "The Roman Empire is indestructible because the Lord (Christ) was registered under the reign of Rome". The Third Rome – "that is the New Great Russia".

2. The Hellenic educational system continues to exist in the Byzantine Empire, in the same way as in the West, even after the christianization of the ruling house as well as of the population. Civil servants require a solid general education (Greek *enkyklios paideía*, Latin *studia liberalia*), because the "knowledge of literature", according to the emperors Constantius and Julian, "is the greatest of all virtues"; only the person excelling at this gets promoted.[17]

In Byzantium the ancient literature is preserved in large quantities and in excellent quality. The diplomat, ecclesiastic prince and scholar Photios documents the Greek literature available to him in his 'Bibliotheca' (written about 845).[18] He describes and makes excerpts from 239 Christian and Jewish works plus 147 Hellenic ones, among which there are multi-volume historians like Diodorus Siculus and Cassius Dio. 110 texts still read by Photios have gone missing completely in the meantime. School text-books and standard literature are not listed in the 'Bibliotheca' because they are assumed to be generally known: Homer, Hesiod, the three tragedians, Aristophanes, Pindar, Theognis;

15 Themistios, Oratio III; Oratio XII. Cf. Schaeder, Hildegard: *Moskau, das Dritte Rom. Studien zur Geschichte der politischen Theorien in der slawischen Welt*, Darmstadt $^{2}$1957, (thesis Hamburg 1927; first printing Prague 1929).

16 The German translation of the texts in H. Schaeder, loc. cit.

17 Cf. Codex Theodosianus 14,1,1 (February 24th, 357 [360]).

18 Treadgold, Warren T.: *The Nature of the 'Biblioteca' of Photius*, Dumbarton Oaks 1980.

Thucydides and Xenophon, Plato and Aristotle, Euclid, and the Bible. This negative list shows the extraordinary level of education of the Byzantine upper class. That way, it becomes understandable why Photios has become designated as a 'humanist' and his entire epoch as 'Macedonian Renaissance' (9th-11th century). The temporal delimitation is, however, somewhat unclear; criteria like 'autonomy of the individual, extensions of the Christian-medieval world-picture, creative advancement of art and science, new forms of life' are hard to define. Almost the same applies to the "Proto-Renaissance" (11th–13th century), the so-called renaissance or restoration under the Komnenes (11th–12th century) and the Palaiologoi (13th–15th century). Without a precise typology and phenomenology of 'renaissance' it is difficult to decide whether the term ist applicable. In any way, the differences from the social, political and cultural development in the West are obvious, especially because the West owes the Byzantinian scholars, teachers and copyists a lot of thanks.

### 4.3. Arabian-Islamic Culture

1. Syria (alongside Lebanon, Palestine/Judaea), the empires of the Arsacids und Sassanids in Mesopotamia (Iraq) and Iran had been a part or come under the influence of Hellenist culture ever since Alexander and his successors (Seleucids and Ptolomaians).[19] As a consequence of the conquest made since the death of Mohammed (632) these and some other strongly Hellenized regions came under Arabian rule. This Arabian-Islamic cultural space gave rise to a comprehensive Greek-Syrian-Persian literature in translation, whose influence and importance, however, is doubtful.

The most important authors of the "science of the ancients" (Greeks) are well known in the Arabian world: Aflatun, Aristutalis, Arsimidis, Batalamyus, Buqrat, Galinus, Suqrat, Uqlidis.[20] Whereas the sciences, above all medicine and philosophy, predominantly Aristotle, were translated and revised, literature – the great Greek epics, poetry, drama – is a conspicuous absentee. The Arabian reception is quite different from the Roman one, which begins with the absorption of art and myth, script and law, Homer and drama. Roman culture became bilingual. The Arabian intellectuals do not have the desire to go back "to the sources" (*ad fontes*) themselves. They are content with what translators, philologists and organizers like Hunain ibn Ishaq (803 – 873) have transmitted.[21]

19 Arsacids (427 B.C.–226 A.D.); with Ardashir I (226 – 241) the empire of the Sassanids took its inception (until 651).

20 Plato, Aristotle, Archimedes, Ptolomaios, Hippocrates, Socrates, Euclid.

21 Bergsträsser, Gotthelf: *Hunain ibn Ishaq und seine Schule*, Leiden 1913.

Through their translations Hunain and his school have a great influence on forming the Arabian scientific terminology – a lasting as well as unobtrusive nationalization (arabisation) of the Greek tradition. Even though literature in the sense of imaginative writing and the myths of the Greeks were not taken over, Aristotle's poetics, as part of the 'organon' and of 'logical' writing, have been translated. Ibn Sina (Avicenna, died 1027) and Ibn Rusd (Averroes, died 1198) have revised it and have speculated about the meaning of "imagination" and "mimesis". Hazim al Qartaganni (died 1256) has founded his Arabian poetics on this Greek-Arabian tradition.

Only a few of the authors of the *jumatrija, asturnumija, falsafa/al-falasifah* that are known in Arabian culture should be mentioned here: Euclid, Heron, Nicomachus, Archimedes, Aratus, Dorotheos, Ptolomy; Aristotle (analytica, ethics, metaphysics), Alexander of Aphrodisias, Polemon (physiognomics), Porphyry (history of philosophy), Plotinus, Proklos, Pseudo-Menander (wisdom), Pseudo-Plutarch ("teachings of the philosophers"), Pythagoras ("golden words"), Theophrastus. The entire body of Greek medical writings is made known to the Arabs: Galen (translated by Hunain ibn Ishaq) and Hippocrates, Dioskurides ("On medicinal herbs"), John Philoponus ("On the history of medicine"). Even the "Hippocratic oath", the basis of the ethics and humanism of the medical profession, was translated:[22]

> "I swear by God, the master of life and death, [...] and I swear by Asclepios [...]".

The ethics of professional responsibility, the scientific approach to healing, the discretion and the primacy of the patient's well-being are inscribed here, whereas abortion and euthanasia are forbidden.

2. The after-effects and significance of this reception of Greek learning and philosophy for Arabian culture are contested. In any case the search for the "ancient heritage" in the modern culture of Europe will and cannot disregard the specific traditions and the innovations contributed by these cultures (nations, ethnicities). The ideal construct composed of a specific form of life and concept of humanity, of human compassion and the professional ethics of teachers, writers, officials, judges, doctors and scholars, which in the West goes by the name of "humanism", can, of course, also be conceptualized in terms of its culture- specific provenance. Thus one could speak of a "Salomonic" or "Confucian" humanism. According to Hans-Heinrich Schaeder (1896–1957) the reception of Greek culture in the Orient has not "borne fruit" so that a real "renaissance" or a "sustainable humanism" never came into existence,[23] whereas

22 Ibn Abi Usaibiah, *Ujun al-anba* (History of medicine), I, pp. 25–26. – Rosenthal, Franz: *Das Fortleben der Antike im Islam*, Zurich/Stuttgart 1965, pp. 250 f.

23 Schaeder, Hans-Heinrich: "Der Orient und das griechische Erbe" (1928), in: idem, *Der*

Franz Rosenthal (1914 – 2003), a disciple of Schaeder's, holds that the reception of Greek antiquity during the Caliphates of the 8th to 10th century "comes by far closest to the spirit and essence of the European Renaissance among all those movements to which in recent decades the name 'Renaissance' had been so fashionably applied"; the "Renaissance of Islam" via the influence of the Greek heritage cannot, according to him, be overlooked.[24]

Anyone who is not a specialist will be well advised not to decide between these two opposite opinions. This is why a statement by an Arabian historian of philosophy and the Fatwa of a legal expert should conclude this problem sketch.[25] Said al-Andalusi (1029 – 1070) writes: "The Greek philosophers belong to the highest class of humankind and to the greatest philosophers". And as-Subki (1284 – 1355) maintains: "Anyone who claims that logic is unislamic and therefore forbidden is a dunce".

## 5. Humanity

### 5.1. The Human Condition

1. In the 18th century there occurs a second "Copernican turn", the turn to "anthropology" (J.G. Herder, 1765). The ancient oracle from Delphi "know thyself" (Latin *nosce te ipsum*) is brought up-to-date:[26]

> "Know then thyself, presume not God to scan;
> The proper study of mankind is Man."

With the advent of Deism, Freemasonry and Enlightenment, the word *humanity, humanité, Humanität, gummanostj* used emphatically with a positive connotation, is spread throughout all European languages, also in its vernacular form: *Menschlichkeit, lidskost, tschellawjatschnostj.* Their joint origin in the Latin *humanitas* and the continuous reception of classical texts, especially Cicero, has the consequence that the meaning in the different European languages is very much alike: a) human nature (being human), b) mankind (the human race), c) humanity (empathy, understanding, compassion, humanitarian

*Mensch in Orient und Okzident. Grundzüge einer eurasiatischen Geschichte*, Munich 1960, pp. 107 – 160.

24 Rosenthal, *Das Fortleben der Antike im Islam*, p. 28. – Cf. Mez, Adam: *Renaissance des Islam*, Heidelberg 1922; Kraemer, Joel L.: *Humanism in the Renaissance of Islam*, Leiden 1986.

25 a) Said al-Andalusi (1029 – 1070), Tabaqat al-umam 22 – 26 (in: Rosenthal, *Das Fortleben der Antike im Islam*, 61). b) as-Subki (1284 – 1355), Taqi-ad-din: Fatawi as Sbuki, Cairo 1355 – 1356, II, 644 f. (in: Rosenthal, *Das Fortleben der Antike im Islam*, 116).

26 Alexander Pope, *Essay on Man* (1733), II, 1 – 2.

aid). In France *humanité* becomes one of the central terms of an enlightened ethics. The definition supplied in the *Encyclopédie* is as follows:[27]

> *"Humanité [...] c'est un sentiment de bienveillance pour tous les hommes, qui ne s'enflamme guère que dans une âme grande & sensible. Ce noble & sublime enthousiasme se tourmente des peines des autres & du besoin de les soulager, il voudroit parcourir l'univers pour abolir l'esclavage, la superstition, le vice & le malheur."*

2. In Germany Johann Gottfried Herder (1744 – 1803) has made the French loanword familiar and determined it semantically, although against considerable resistance. In the 27[th] of his "Briefe zur Beförderung der Humanität" (1792) he writes:

> "Sie fürchten, daß man dem Wort Humanität einen Fleck anhängen werde; könnten wir nicht das Wort ändern? *Menschheit, Menschlichkeit, Menschenrechte, Menschenpflichten, Menschenwürde, Menschenliebe?*"

These fears are dispersed in the letter, and Herder concludes:

> "Also wollen wir bei dem Wort *Humanität* bleiben, an welches unter Alten und Neuern die besten Schriftsteller so würdige Begriffe geknüpft haben. Humanität ist der *Charakter unsres Geschlechts*; er ist aber nur in Anlagen angeboren, und muß uns eigentlich angebildet werden."

When Herder speaks of humanity he means the idea of the equality and dignity of all human beings, their being endowed with reason and natural rights, but he also points to the fact that neither equality nor human rights have become fully realized yet: "The human race", says Herder, "as it is now and probably will be for a long time, for the larger part possesses no dignity. [...]" It should, however, "be educated towards the true nature of its character, and hence towards its worth and dignity".

The "ancients" Herder is referring to are, above all, Epictetus, Marcus Aurelius, Lucretius and Homer. According to him they have contributed to his definition of "humanity" the following elements: a) the concepts of 'mankind, humanity, humanitarianism, human rights, human dignity, philanthropy'; b) the idea that human beings are incomplete, hence capable of progress and of "acquiring the true character of our species"; c) for this end an extensive anthology of ancient authors is required as well as d) a separate section on Greek art, which Herder defines as the "school of humanity".

27 S.v. "Humanité" (Mallet), in: Diderot/d'Alembert (Eds.): *Encyclopédie ou Dictionnaire raisonné des sciences, des arts et des métiers* (1751 – 1780), vol. 8, 1765, p. 438.

## 5.2. *Humanitas* – "Cultivation and Compassion"

1. The unity of the lexical field 'humanity' in the European languages is founded in the tradition of Latin language. The Latin word *humanitas* is first documented as existing in public speech at the beginning of the 1st century B.C.[28] In classical texts (Cicero, Seneca, Pliny) it carries the following meanings; a) the human condition (*condicio humana*), man's mortality as opposed to the immortality of the Gods, and his weakness compared to (wild, cruel) animals; man is distinguished by his reason, but is yet unformed when entering the world; b) the human race (*genus humanum*); c) humanity in feeling and acting: compassionate, helpful, tolerant, tactful, skillful in dealing with people, urbane, full of decency and wit. These definitions are universal and apply to everybody, men and women alike. Its incompleteness and frailty enforce upon humankind lifelong learning, social behavior (sociability in family, state and cosmopolis) and mutual assistance (*mutuum auxilium*).

"Cultivation" and "compassion", or in modern terminology "education" and "humanitarian practice" are the two necessarily inseparable definitions of Roman *humanitas* and, accordingly European humanity.[29]

2. Roman *humanitas* merges the universally applicable arguments of philosophical anthropology and ethics with the social standards of the urban upperclasses of Rome. The classical quotations pertaining to this fusion are supplied by Marcus Tullius Cicero (106 – 43 B.C.). This wealthy, highly educated lawyer, politician, orator and philosopher, is a figure of great eminence.

His comprehensive as well as varied œuvre consisting of letters, speeches, rhetoric, philosophical dialogues and treatises made him into the style model and much-used source of many European humanists. In Cicero's texts they came across the earliest references to the term "human dignity" (*dignitas hominis*).[30] The German translation of Cicero therefore contains the first reference to the word "Menschenwürde" in the German language (J. Neuber, 1488). In Cicero they found a graphic model for the way the human 'person' is made up of universal as well as individual "masks" (Latin *personae*): the masks of reason, individuality (singularity), historicity, the will. Cicero supplied them with a survey of the philosophical systems of the Greeks in a clear and precise language, focusing on ethics, religion, law and politics. From natural law the human rights could be derived – "by nature free" –, and the universality of reason was the foundation for the cosmopolitan right of the citizen of the world.[31] Cicero's

28 Auctor ad Herennium (ca. 84 B.C.), 2,16,23 f; 2,17,26; 2,31,50; 4,8,12; 4 (5), 16, 23. – M. Tullius Cicero, *Pro Sexto Roscio Amerino* (80 B.C.), 154 (final paragraph).

29 Cf. Gellius, *Noctes Atticae*, 13,17.

30 Cicero, *de officiis* (44 B.C.), 1,30,106.

31 Cicero, *de legibus* (ca. 54 – 51 B.C.), 1,14,40; 1,15,43; 2,1,2.

dialogues and letters also provided the exemplary model for an urbane culture of conversation – a villa with a park, the formation of a circle (the so-called circle of the Scipios) and a theory of friendship. To the established Roman patricians Cicero was a social climber (*homo novus*), whose erudition was a means of overcompensating this deficiency; a translator and mediator of Greek culture with a great educational commitment, who managed to reconcile the requirements of the *vita civilis (activa)* with the *vita contemplativa.*

Cicero postulates rhetoric as a universal education. He demands the comprehensive command of diverse areas, like perfect linguistic abilities, a knowledge of psychology, literature, philosophy, history, a specialist expertise in legal matters and a self-assured public appearance (*actio*):[32] this amounts to a European program of education. His writings on the philosophy of religion treat of an atomistic and pantheistic theology, mild skepticism (Cicero himself) as well as a state-affirmation and conservative fideism (Aurelius Cotta, Supreme Pontifex).[33] Cicero defines the humanist underpinnings of all humanitarian practice as follows:[34]

> *Natura praescribit, ut homo homini quicumque sit, ob eam ipsam causam, quod is homo sit, consultum velit.*
> "Nature prescribes that man should care for another man, whoever he may be, just because he is a human being."

## 5.3. Philanthropy

The humanitarian aid ("charity", *clementia*) that is based on a natural "love of mankind" and "compassion" forms a necessary part of humanity. In accordance with this, in the 18th century the word and concept of 'humanity' lead to the spread of the Greek word *phil-anthrop-ía* – 'love of mankind' in the European languages. Mythology, some passages in the Bible and deep-going changes in the understanding of poverty, begging and alms in the bourgeois societies of the Modern Age gave rise to a new language of euergetism (Greek '*doing-good-work*').[35] After all Prometheus, who had created mankind and stolen the heavenly fire for them, was the first 'philanthropist' (Aeschylus, *Prometheus*).

In Greco-Roman antiquity poverty – as different from 'simplicity'– does not constitute a personal religious value or God-given state. To the humanists and philanthropists it is an often self-inflicted disgrace which, so they hope, can be

32 Cicero, *de oratore* (55 B.C.), esp. 1,5,17 – 18 (definition of rhetoric).
33 Cicero, *de natura deorum* (44 B.C.).
34 Cicero, *de officiis* (44 B.C.), 3,6,27.
35 Sachße, Christoph/Tennstedt, Florian: *Geschichte der Armenfürsorge in Deutschland*, Stuttgart/Berlin 1980.

remedied through education and discipline. The declericalization and modernization of the school-system is a way of achieving this objective. Through the foundation of the "Philantropin" in Dessau (1774) by Johann Bernhard Basedow a "modern pedagogy" becomes established – vocationally orientated, practical, middle-class. He demands that education should be state-controlled and founds seminaries for teachers who are no longer private tutors or clerics.[36] The success of Basedow, Joachim H. Campe, Christian G. Salzmann provokes the formation of a contrasting approach: Friedrich Immanuel Niethammer names it by a new word – 'Humanismus'.

## 6. Humanismus

### 6.1. The Pedagogical and Political Definition of the Term

1. The term 'humanism' was coined by the philosopher and educationalist Friedrich Immanuel Niethammer (1766–1848). It designates the traditional "studies of the *humaniora*" at secondary schools (4.1.1) as reformed by himself. The title of his programmatic tract is:[37] "Der Streit des Philantropinismus und Humanismus in der Theorie des Erziehungs-Unterrichts unserer Zeit" (1808). The pedagogical term 'humanism' is used as the very antithesis of the "modern pedagogy" as enunciated by the philanthropists. The humanist approach to education is not aimed at providing a quickly completed practical preparation of the pupil for his occupation or a specialized course of studies, i. e. the adaption of the child to the "mechanical nature" of the machine age. What Niethammer's humanism wants to achieve is a general education, i. e. the formation of the entire human being (p. 276), of its reason and its humanity, "Menschenbildung" (p. 183):

> "die Bildung des Menschen als Menschen, abgesehen von aller Verschiedenheit individueller Beschaffenheit […], oder die Bildung der Menschheit im Individuum."

The subjects taught have to possess a "classical form"; "true classic form, however, in all kinds of representations of what is true, good and beautiful (will) be found in its greatest perfection only in the classical nations of antiquity" (p. 18). Niethammer aims to create a new 'class of the educated' taken from all social classes and status groups, with the exception, however, of women. The modern age requires "well-educated" civil servants, scientists and artists. The "hu-

36 Basedow, Johann Bernhard: *Vorstellung an Menschenfreunde und vermögende Männer über Schule, Studien und ihren Einfluß in die öffentliche Wohlfahrt* (1768), Leipzig 1893 (Neudrucke pädagogischer Schriften 14).

37 Newly edited by Werner Hillebrecht, Weinheim 1968 (= Kleine pädagogische Texte 29).

manistische Gymnasium" (humanist high-school), although "anti-modern" by intent, initially turned out to be successful against all expectation and against the growing resistance of the representatives of the mathematical, scientific and technical subjects, and the opponents of these elitist bourgeois schools and their exclusive privilege of granting the 'Abitur' (university entrance requirement), thereby providing the formation of the civil servants and the intellectual aristocracy of the educated bourgeoisie.

2. Karl Marx (1818–1883) was a typical product of this type of "humanistisches Gymnasium" (Trier, 1830–1835). This is where he learnt his maxim: *nihil humani a me alienum puto*; later on he read Homer to his children, and, for himself, every year, Aeschylus' tragedies. In some passages of his early writings (ca. 1843–1848) he does use the term 'humanism'. He has freed it of its bond to pedagogy and antiquity, radicalized its humanitarian energy, reconceived it in anthropological and social terms, and concretized and modernized it in the form of a political program. He designates this as "real humanism", in order to emphasize the antithesis to "spiritualism and speculative idealism", "which in place of the real, individual person substitutes *self-consciousness* or the *spirit*".[38] The real individual, however, exists in concrete, often destructive circumstances as "a being that has been humiliated, oppressed, that is lost and contemptible": This is why "living conditions have to be humanized".[39]

These conditions are based on the division of labor in an industrialized society, full-fledged capitalism and the exploitation of the fourth estate. The final aim, however, is "the real appropriation of the human essence by and for man", i.e. "humanized man".[40] Marx no longer uses this term in his later writings and has castigated its use by Arnold Ruge (1803–1880) as a "phrase".[41] He has shifted the focus of his research from a critique of idealist philosophy to economy, history and technology. This shift in emphasis should not lead to the conclusion that Marx actually performed an 'anti-humanist turn'. The research into the human condition with its "alienation", its genesis and the possibility of overcoming it remained the focal point of his scholarly and political endeavors.

38 Engels, Friedrich/ Marx, Karl: "Die heilige Familie" (Paris, Brüssel 1844/1845), in: *Marx-Engels-Werke* (MEW), vol. 2, Berlin 1958; Landshut, Siegfried (Ed.): *Karl Marx - Die Frühschriften*, Stuttgart 1964; full text MEW 2 online: http://www.dearchiv.de/php/brett.php?archiv=mew&brett=MEW002&menu=mewinh.

39 MEW vol. 2, pp.138 f.; Landshut, p. 235; http://www.dearchiv.de/php/dok.php?archiv=mew&brett=MEW002&fn=82-151.2&menu=mewinh.

40 Marx, Karl: "Ökonomisch-philosophische Manuskripte" (1844), in: MEW, Suppl. vol.: Schriften, Manuskripte, Briefe bis 1844, 1., Berlin 1968, p. 536; http://www.dearchiv.de/php/dok.php?archiv=mew&brett=MEW040&fn=530-588.40&menu=mewinh.

41 Marx/Engels: "Die großen Männer des Exils" (Manchester 1852), in: MEW vol. 8, Berlin 1969, p. 278; http://www.dearchiv.de/php/dok.php?archiv=mew&brett=MEW008&fn=233-335.8&menu=mewinh).

## 6.2. Humanism with an Adjective

1. The term 'humanism' proved to be highly successful in Germany. Around the middle of the 19th century the period-term 'humanism' makes an appearance alongside the idealist, pedagogical or realist definitions. The literary scholars Karl Hagen (1841/44) and Georg Voigt (1827–91) use it to designate the beginning of the Italian Renaissance. Voigt's title is quite striking: "The Revival of Classical Antiquity or the First Century of Humanism" (1859).[42] The title consciously avoids the epoch-term "*la renaissance*" introduced by Jules Michelet (1855).[43] The term 'humanism' is obviously quite natural: Voigt does not seem to feel that it needs any justification. The new era after the "age of darkness" (Petrarch) begins with Petrarch (1304–1374) and is concluded with the spread of "humanism" in the republics and courts of Italy around 1500. What Voigt means by 'humanism' is the ancient "heritage" as revived in Italy, the liberation of the individual, the strengthening of the laity vis-à-vis the power of the Church. Voigt is focusing almost exclusively on literary history – there is very little said concerning art or economy (cf. 4.1). But the book was a success, also outside Germany, and managed to internationalize the new 'ism'. The ensuing multiplication of humanisms, though, now required a distinction by means of adjectives and numerals.

Friedrich Paulsen (1846–1908), professor of philosophy and pedagogy in Berlin, was critical of the humanist *Gymnasium* from a realistic point of view: it was not sufficiently "nationalist" and "modern".[44] In his history of scholarly education he distinguishes between the two humanisms as "the old humanism" (15th-17th century) and "the new humanism" (from 1740 onwards). This terminology forced all his successors into using a number whenever they themselves wanted to propagate a new humanism. Eduard Spranger (1887–1963) followed the first and second one up with a "third humanism" (1921), i.e. one that was modern as well as classical and that was more suited for understanding the irrational, dionysical and political aspects of the Greek mind than Goethe, Friedrich August Wolf or Wilhelm von Humboldt had done.[45]

---

42 The second enlarged edition appeared in Leipzig in 1880, the third, revised by Max Lehnhardt, in 1890; Italian transl.: Firenze 1888; French transl.: Paris 1894.

43 Michelet, Jules: *Histoire de France*, vol. 7, Paris 1855; cf. Burkhardt, Jacob: *Die Kultur der Renaissance in Italien* (1860), Frankfurt/Main 1989.

44 Paulsen, Friedrich: *Geschichte des gelehrten Unterrichts auf den deutschen Schulen und Universitäten vom Ausgang des Mittelalters bis zur Gegenwart. Mit besonderer Rücksicht auf den klassischen Unterricht*, Berlin (1844; ²1895) 3rd enlarged edition, ed. by Rudolf Lehmann, Leipzig 1919–1921.

45 Spranger, Eduard: "Aufruf an die Philologie" (1921), in: idem: *Der gegenwärtige Stand der Geisteswissenschaften und die Schule*, Leipzig 1922, pp. 5–13. This talk was dedicated to

The contemporaneous rise of the "Third Reich" was responsible for getting Spranger's and Werner Jaeger's (1888 – 1961) humanism into murky waters because of its "feeling of racial affinity" between Greeks and Germans and its "essentially" political understanding of humanism.[46]

2. The gradual separation of the term "humanism" from its pedagogical origin, from antiquity and classicism sets it free for a multitude of combinations. A small selection: Western humanism, atheist, Christian, classical, critical, dialectical, ethical, evolutionary, existential, Hebrew, socialist, secular. The connection of philosophical anthropology or theology or ideology with 'humanism' can yield the most diverse results: harmonious syntheses; the mere take-over and neutralization of a successful brand-name; the sophisticated further development of a respected tradition. Accordingly, the critique of humanism and a strict anti-humanism can focus on numerous points of attack: the humanist concept of mankind; the irresolvable tension between historical reality and the normative claim of an ancient tradition; the educational program and the success (or failure) of the humanistic *Gymnasium*; the futility of all humanist endeavor vis-à-vis open structural violence, religious intolerance, the "forces of evil", the supposed constraints of markets and monopolies. The belief in the essential goodness of humans, the utopian and Arcadian potential of the world and of history, the promise of beauty and happiness, of a free, rich and perfect life, the cultivation of one's personality – all these collide with the harsh realities of the wide-spread need for the bare necessities of life, the fight for water and affordable medication, for rice and a minimum of security.

## 6.3. Theory and Practice

1. Humanism, as the list of hyphenated humanisms shows, is not a philosophy, not a closed system of anthropology and ethics exclusively compatible with itself, but a lesson in "tolerating an incomplete world-view".[47] Humanism is not a religion, not even a substitute religion. Humanism is first and foremost a pedagogical program and part of the European reception of antiquity. On the one hand humanism is a cultural and educational movement that is closely connected with the "free arts", with the study of ideas, culture, the humanities and history (*studia humaniora*), on the other it is the foundation of all humanitarian

Werner Jaeger (1888 – 1961), who in March 1921 had become the successor of Ulrich von Wilamowitz-Moellendorff.

46 Jaeger, Werner (with preface from 1935): *Paideia. Die Formung des griechischen Menschen* (1933/34; 2nd edition 1936), Berlin 4th ed. 1959, vol. I, p. 4; 9; 16; cf. Jaeger, Werner (Ed.): *Das Problem des Klassischen und die Antike* (1933), Darmstadt 1951.

47 Mach, Ernst: *Die Mechanik in ihrer Entwicklung*, Leipzig 1883, p. 479.

practice. Its most relevant exponents were and are male and female teachers (pedagogists, educationalists), doctors, lawyers (judges, notaries, administrators), scholars, artists, the intelligentsia.

Humanism has always been a controversial tradition, a continuous dialogue of texts and images conducted with historical paradigms (Athens, Sparta, Rome, Byzantium), with philosophemes (nature, reason, liberty) and the declaration of human rights, with symbolic places (Troy, Olympia, Kythera, Florence, Wörlitz), with martyrs and confessors (Socrates and Seneca, Erasmus and Thomas More), with mythical figures (Helena and Medea, Antigone and Medusa), with a specific architecture (the Parthenon in Athens, the Pantheon in Rome, the Brandenburg Gate in Berlin) and with figurative art (the Apollo of Belvedere in the Vatican, Michelangelo's David in Florence).

Not every reception of antiquity is inspired by humanism. Ancient achievements (grammar, logic, rhetoric, medicine) can be used for inhumane purposes. On the other hand a humanism without Athens and the Stoa would be like Christianity without Jerusalem and Tenach.

2. No humanism without humanity, no 'education' without 'compassion', without humanitarian practice. The corporeality, incompleteness, frailty, fragility of man invariably and on principle necessitate the immediate, special and timely help, instruction, healing, consolation and protection. Beyond this any humanitarian practice is necessarily and in an ambivalent way connected with the inherent deficiencies, the destructiveness and dysfunctionality of the state, the economy, the military, the legal system and society. The Red Cross or the Red Crescent may be able to care for injured people or refugees, but they cannot prevent wars and ethnic cleansing. World Hunger Aid may be capable of mitigating humanitarian catastrophes, but not of abolishing a fundamentally wrong agricultural policy. The need for, and ambivalence of, humanitarian practice have increased due to the deficiencies of the welfare state and the demand for a streamlined 'deregulated' state that permits public goods and services (education, public transport, water, energy, healthcare) to come under the control of private investors.

The welcome increase in the obligatory nature of human rights in international law has made possible, under certain conditions, the "humanitarian intervention" in order to prevent "humanitarian catastrophes", but at the same time it has led to an improper and world-wide military interventionism in the guise of humanitarian aid (Somalia, Kosovo, Burma).[48]

A large number of institutions are concerned with these internal and external, European and global, theoretical and practical tasks and problems: the "Euro-

48 Documentation and analysis in Noam Chomsky, *The New Military Humanism. Lessons from Kosovo*, London 1999.

pean Humanist Federation" (EHF, founded in 1991), humanist universities, institutes and academies (Brussels, Utrecht, Essen, Berlin) and numerous Non-Governmental Organizations (NGOs).

## 7. 10th December – Human Rights Day

1. Sixty years ago, on 10th December 1948, the "General Declaration of Human Rights" was proclaimed in Paris, Palais de Chaillot, by the General Assembly of the United Nations.[49] The declaration belongs to the fundamental texts of modern humanism. The first article runs as follows:

> "All human beings are born free and equal in dignity and rights. They are endowed with reason and conscience and should act towards one another in the spirit of brotherhood."

The article and the various concepts it contains have a long and multicultural past history. The membership of the commission and its secretariat was cosmopolitan. China, the Middle East, South America and the Soviet Union were also represented.[50] As can be seen from the minutes of the secretariat, the diaries and the reports by John Humphrey (1905 – 1995, Canada), René Cassin (1887 – 1976, France), Charles Malik (1906 – 1987, Lebanon/Saudi Arabia), the tradition of human rights in legal history and philosophy were taken into account and reflected upon, "speculative" debates of a philosophical or theological nature, however, were consciously avoided. The "philosophy behind" (Humphrey) was not made explicit. In 1948 the "auspices of the Supreme Being" or "Nature that has endowed man with certain rights", such as they are inscribed in the preamble of the French "*Déclaration des droits de l'homme et du citoyen*", are therefore not invoked. And yet the French declaration of 1789 was a "starting point" (Cassin) and a template for the General Declaration of 1948, and the references to the "natural rights" of mankind were the result of a long-standing discourse in the philosophy of law. In classical antiquity religious freedom (*libertas religionis*), for example, has been legally claimed against the Roman state as a "human right

49 Resolution 217 A (III), 10 – 12 – 1948. The UNO at that time had 56 member states; 48 approved of the resolution; 8 nations abstained; no votes against.

50 Cf. Yearbook of the United Nations, *Special Edition – UN Fiftieth Anniversary*, 1945 – 1995; Humphrey, John P.: *Human Rights and the United Nations: A Great Adventure*, New York 1984; Hobbins, A.J. (Ed.): *On the Edge of Greatness: The Diaries of John Humphrey, First Director of the United Nations Division of Human Rights*, Montreal 1995 – 2001; Cassin, René: *La pensée et l'action*, Boulogne-sur-Seine 1972. (A selection of Cassin's texts by François-Joachim Beer, among others on: "Eleanor Roosevelt", pp. 80 – 83; "Montesquieu et les droits de l'homme", pp. 89 – 95; "La tradition libérale occidentale des Droits de l'homme", pp. 139 – 150).

(*humanum ius*) and the natural faculty of each individual".[51] Philosophical and legal texts from antiquity supplied central concepts of the modern discourse: "natural law" (*ius naturale*) "human right" (*ius humanum*), "human dignity" (*dignitas hominis*), liberty and equality.

"By law of nature", says the Roman statute book, "all men are born free" and "all equal".[52]

The French declaration says (article I): "Les hommes naissent et demeurent libres et égaux en droits".

The "General Declaration of Human Rights" formulates it as follows (article I): "All human beings are born free and of equal dignity and rights".

The "General Declaration" is evidence of both the strength of the tradition as well as the huge "revolutionary" (Humphrey) progress of modern international and social law, of citizen's and human rights. The implementation and realization of this progress, however, meets with great difficulties. The ban on torture (art. 5) is questioned even by some of the first signatories of the "General Declaration"; neither the death penalty nor degrading, humiliating forms of corporeal punishment have been abolished.[53] Not even the freedom to change one's religion has become a matter of course.[54]

Sixty years after this declaration was proclaimed, admiration and satisfaction are commingled with the insight that many of the promises from the euphoric phase after the Second World War have not been realized, and that new, serious threats to human rights, to humanitarian practice, and to European and any other humanisms have arisen.

51 Tertullian, *Ad Scapulam* (about 214 A.D.) 2; idem, *Apologeticum* (197 A.D.), 24, 5–6.

52 Cf. Ulpian, in: *Digest* 1,1,4 = Justinian, *Institutiones* 1,5 pr.; 1,2,2: *iure enim naturali ab initio omnes homines liberi nascebantur.*

53 Art. 5: "No one shall be subjected to torture or to cruel, inhuman or degrading treatment or punishment."

54 Art. 18: "freedom to change his religion or belief."

Heiner Roetz

# Confucian Humanism

The categorical imperative pronounced by the young Karl Marx according to which "all those conditions have to be abolished under which man is a humiliated, a subjected, a forlorn, a contemptible creature"[1] can be counted among the classical formulations of a humanist utopia. One must be either blind or cynical to deny that today's world is still in need of such a utopia. However, can the aim propounded by Marx be universalized at all, or is it just the expression of a specific tradition? Is it possibly the secularized version of the Christian religion, and does it not reveal itself as such because the Marxist "imperative" takes its declared "departure" from "the positive suspension of all religion"? Does it loose its safe ground without this background, and did humanism perish in the 'real' Marxism of the Eastern European or Chinese brand because in both of these a different "oriental" or "Asiatic" heritage prevailed?

Critics steeped in the tradition of Western Marxism had asked these questions fairly early on.[2] What they designate as "Asiatic" or "oriental" is, as Marx likewise saw it, a "barbaric" order of society in which 'central despotism' is responsible for uniting scattered village communities under an authoritarian government. 'Asiatic' here is primarily understood in an historical sense, but the borderline with a trans-historical term in the sense of a deep-seated cultural residue is not sufficiently clear.

As distinct from the ambivalent perception of "Asia" in Western Marxism, in today's social sciences the category of 'culture' has played a leading role in describing the great 'civilizations'. The cultural turn is based on the justified critique of a conceptual universalism that takes the opportunity of universalizing 'Western' concepts simply for granted. This critique, however, leads to aporias because its proponents claim to be conducting a meta-discourse which itself is not subject to any cultural affiliation. There is also the additional danger of replacing the old

1 Marx, Karl: "Zur Kritik der Hegelschen Rechtsphilosophie", in: *Marx Engels Werke*, vol. I, Berlin 1976, p. 385.
2 An example is Dutschke, Rudi: *Versuch, Lenin auf die Füße zu stellen*, Berlin 1974.

conceptual hegemony with the local despotism of particular 'cultures'. Both approaches are hard to reconcile with a consensual resolution of those problems which the world-community is currently facing, i. e. the challenge to create a global ethical framework for the exercise of political and social power, and to curb the economic and technological imperatives, the out-of-control nature of which is threatening to destroy the planet. This project can be termed 'humanist' in the truest sense of the word since it stems from mankind's desire to live in a just society and an intact environment, and not under demeaning circumstances. But do we not, in making these demands, already take up a culturally specific position that gets us embroiled in the 'clash of civilizations'?

And indeed, the definition of what 'man' is and what is his due, along with its practical consequences, is at the very center of all conflicts fought out in the name of culture. The competition among political ideologies has not been replaced with a global normative consensus after the end of the Cold War. Instead particularizing notions of culture are now prevailing. The campaign for 'Asian values' of the 1990s, but also the attempts on the part of the People's Republic of China to culturally legitimize its political course are typical of this. The fact that it appears as though China could substitute the old socialist ideology with a new culturalist one without any change in the political system seems to confirm the 'Asian' theory of Western Marxism.

The Chinese arguments that pose a challenge to the project of global humanism are above all concerned with the question of human rights, but also with the ethics of medical research.

Modern biotechnology, with all its possibilities and promises, has once again caused to be put on the agenda the question of how mankind seeks to deal with itself. It has by now become a factor of global economic and socio-political relevance; especially in the Asian States of the Pacific Rim and the Indian Ocean the new 'life sciences' are subsidized with massive investment schemes. World-wide transnational cooperation exists alongside national competition among countries. Following the attraction of diminishing regulation, research is increasingly shifted from countries with restrictive legislation to those with a more permissive one. Ethical objections are all too often countered with a relativistic argument. The German legislation protecting embryos, e. g., has been accused of claiming a non-universal Christian concept of man as an absolute given. Chinese scientists and institutions in their turn are advocating a 'cultural context' which is hampered less by ethical qualms than many Western states.[3] What allegedly makes research

3 Cf. e.g. Yang Xiangzhong: "An embryonic nation. Liberal views on human-embryo technology make China ideal to become a world leader in this field", in: *Nature* 428 (11 March 2004): 210–212, quoted in Roetz, Heiner: "The end of ethical universalism? Bioethics in the age of globalization and the case of China", in: Sitter-Liver, Beat (Ed.): *Universality: From*

conducted with 'human material' less problematic is a view of man as a social being distinct from "Western individualism". According to this, man only acquires his full human status as a member of a community, and not before birth. Research using embryonic stem-cells would thereby be ethically unproblematic, as maintained by Qiu Renzong, the Nestor of Chinese bioethics, who is referring to a cultural consensus supposed to be rooted in Confucianism.[4] This definition of man as a social being does not only weaken the status of life before birth but by analogy also at the end of life: according to the Taiwanese bioethicist Lee Shui-chuen (Li Ruiquan) patients who are incapable of interacting with their environment only enjoy a moral status if accorded to them by their relations, but not in and by themselves.[5] Furthermore, Lee is of the opinion that in terms of Confucian understanding, man does not have the responsibility to preserve nature, a notion resulting from the biblical idea of the world being created by God. Invoking the classical Confucian text *Zhongyong*, Lee instead declares man to be a "co-creator" of the universe who gets away with "playing God". In the same vein, cloning in all its forms and other types of genetic intervention are to be welcomed in order "to improve upon the deficiencies of nature".[6] Max Weber's theory that China, as distinct from the West, has been incapable of unhinging the world because of its lack of religions transcendence is thereby turned upside down.

The concept of man ascribed to Confucianism is also a constant point of reference in the debate about how Chinese culture positions itself with regard to human rights. Since 2004 human rights in China have been inscribed in the constitution. What China, however, insists on is a special interpretation whereby the fundamental human right is one of 'subsistence', i. e. of securing the material basics of life. But because this right can only be secured by communal effort, the collective 'right of development' follows from this, which in turn presupposes a state endowed with the 'right of sovereignty'. In the terms of this logic, human rights are subordinated to those institutions from whose very power they should give protection.

China's argument in favor of this position is predominantly pragmatic, but it is at the same time invoking the 'factor of culture' in the name of a collectivist interpretation of Confucianism, thus following the 'Asian values' campaign. In accordance with this an exaggerated individualism, a one-sided insistence on

*Theory to Practice, An intercultural and interdisciplinary debate about facts, possibilities, lies and myths*, Fribourg 2009, pp. 177–190.

4 Qiu Renzong (Ed.): *Bioethics in Asia – a Quest for Moral Diversity*, Dordrecht 2006, Introduction. Cf. Roetz: "The end of ethical universalism? ", 180–181 and 182–183.

5 Lee Shui-chuen: "A Confucian Assessment of 'Personhood'", in: Döring, Ole/Chen Renbiao (Eds.): *Advances in Chinese Medical Ethics: Chinese and International Perspective*, Hamburg 2001, p. 176.

6 Li Ruiquan (Lee Shui-chuen): *Rujia shengming lunlixue* (Confucian Bioethics), Taipei 1999, pp. 130–132. Cf. Roetz: "The end of ethical universalism?", p. 183.

rights over duties and an atomistic view of society are rejected as being Eurocentric.

Does there then exist a traditional Chinese view of man that is capable of justifying an illiberal policy and a liberal bioethics at the same time? And, furthermore, does the hope for a globalized humanism have to be replaced with a pragmatic process of negotiation? Any idea of humanism would actually be bound to fail if the definition of what constitutes man were to be at the free disposal of particular cultures. It would, however, be confirmed if it were possible to show that the great ethical systems that humans have produced independently from one another are grounded in joint intuitions ensuring the respect due to man. China can therefore be regarded as a challenge as well as a test-case for the program of 'Humanism in the Era of Globalization'.

In my view a culturalist position like the one I have outlined is not really convincing: Firstly, the idea of man being a socially constituted animal is not specific to China but also an essential part of Western theories of development. Secondly, the social nature of the human being by no means necessarily entails a collectivist ethic. It can be reconciled with the acknowledgement of human individuality.

On the other hand the Chinese voices concerning bioethics and human rights I have quoted, although they do represent a mainstream, also meet with contradiction, particularly by authors who are aligning themselves with the same cultural tradition. Thus for the bioethicist Nie Jingbao, Confucianism, as far as the need to protect life before birth is concerned, is located more within the conservative than the liberal camp.[7] The "New-Confucian" philosopher Lee Ming-huei in turn emphasizes that it is not the individualist but the collectivist human rights which are irreconcilable with Confucian ethics.[8] This exposes one of the fundamental problems of invoking cultural traditions: They need to be interpreted. The individual interpreter cannot hide behind a tradition, but in referring to it he is, as it were, responsible for it or the way in which it is understood. He can refute it, but he can also attempt to bring it up to date in order to transform it, e.g. for the program of a global humanism. Chinese traditions are in no way less suitable for this purpose than Western ones. In this context it has to be borne in mind right from the start that the ethics which have been handed down to us could not possibly address all the problems we are beset with nowadays, nor could they dispose of the accumulated knowledge available to later generations. If they still do have any meaning for today this is because

7 Nie Jing-Bao: "The Plurality of Chinese and American Medical Moralities", in: *Kennedy Inst Ethics J* 10 (2000): 250 and 251. Cf. Roetz: "The end of ethical universalism?", p. 185.

8 Lee Ming-huei [Li Minghui]: "Rujia chuantong yu renquan" [Confucian tradition and human rights], in: *Yuandao* 7 (2002): 36 – 55.

they have – under the pressure of existential challenges – reflected on the problems of the *conditio humana* in an exemplary fashion. Both aspects involve having to think with and against them at the same time.

Already ancient China has had a profound grasp of these issues through the experience of a fundamental break in its tradition. In the following we will have a look at classical Chinese philosophy, especially the concept of humanity propounded by Confucianism, which in the cultural debates of today is continually being referred to.

Philosophical thinking in China emerges as a reaction to the far-reaching social crisis taking place against the background of the total collapse of the feudal reign of the Zhou dynasty ($11^{th}$-$3^{rd}$ cent. B.C.). The loss of traditional certainties leads to the search for a new orientation. The main tendencies in Chinese philosophy originate in attempting to answer the question of how the world could possibly have been inundated by the deluge in which it is about to go under and what should be done in order to save it. Above all, three of these answers have been of historical consequence: that of Confucianism, of Legalism and of Daoism. The Confucians identify the problem of their time as a moral one that is most suitably countered by cultivating the personality. They are primarily focused on the individual and place their entire trust in its malleability. This places them in the context of traditional mores while at the same time founding it on the new basis of a morality in the inner 'self' of each individual or in his moral nature: This amounts to an inward turn of the focus of attention. The Legalists refute this as a fatal illusion – for them man is a coolly calculating egoist who has to be restrained by institutional means. They view the problem as an organizational one and therefore direct their focus on the political system, from which all traces of personal relationship have to be expunged in favor of the mechanical application of rules and regulations. The focus is now directed forward to the present and the future: The path to a peaceful world is not to be sought for in precedents of the past or in moral reflection, but solely in a novel and rigid technology of domination adapted to the problems of the present. As far as the Daoists are concerned the reason for the collapse lies in the formation of an artificial human world that is no longer in unity with nature and is therefore a problem caused by human civilization itself. Their gaze faces backwards beyond the beginnings of history to an indivisible and forever lost naturalness that required neither an ethics nor institutions. They tend to idealize man in his unspoilt, childlike state of nature, but consider him as a dangerous stray as soon as the destructive energies of his calculating reason have been awakened. The three main tendencies of classical Chinese thought thus follow, according to a distinction drawn by the new-Confucian philosopher Tang Junyi (1909 – 1978), a humanist, an anti-humanist and a supra-humanist course.[9]

All these philosophies are marked by their critical and reflective relationship with the failed traditional ethos. All the previously recognized guiding ideas and authorities – parents, teachers, princes, religions, powers, the convictions held by "the majority", the modes of the past, the traditional forms of moral behavior – are subjected to a systematic scepticism. New criteria like Usefulness (*li, yong*), the Good (*shan*), the Natural (*tian*) or the Practicable (*ke*) that seek to come to terms with the Here and Now are being conceived. Reliable knowledge is no longer to be found in what is distant but rather in what is close, in what one has experienced and seen oneself instead of hearsay, in the present instead of antiquity. All these shifts culminate in a new vision of what is close at hand and most immediate: 'Man' himself. The positions of Legalist and Daoist philosophers with their critique of humanism can be read as the dialectical counterpart of this anthropocentric turn. Therefore, the discovery of the theme of 'Man' is the result of a crisis, which was the reason for a fundamental critique of tradition. Man loses the support of the culture he is part of and finds a new point of reference in reflecting upon himself. It is of great relevance to realize that all of classical Chinese philosophizing, irrespective of its content, is grounded in this dialectical structure, because this renders the attempt at taking in a view of mankind indiscriminately based on 'Chinese thinking' for a calculating culturalism extremely doubtful. With this attempt the most important potential offered by a way of thinking that is capable of distancing itself from its own origins is gambled away, i. e. in passing beyond what is familiar to enter into an open and non-isolationist relationship with what is alien.

The centrality of the theme 'Man' in classical Chinese philosophy and its embeddedness in a critique of tradition is documented in the ensuing passage from the chapter *Cha jin* (Examine the Present) of the *Lüshi chunqiu* ("The Almanac of Mister Lü") from the middle of the 3rd century B.C.:

> "Why should the ruler not take the standards (fa) of the early kings as a model? It is not that the former kings were not wise. It is because they cannot be taken as a model. The standards of the former kings have come upon us by passing through the remote ages. Some men have added to them, and some have omitted parts from them. How could they be taken as a model then? Even if nobody would have added to or omitted something from them, they could still not be taken as a model. […] The standards of antiquity and of today are different in their language and their statutes. The words of antiquity, therefore, frequently do not correspond with the expressions of today, and

9 Tang Junyi: *Zhongguo renwen jingshen zhi fazhan* [The development of the Chinese humanistic spirit], Hongkong 1958, partly translated in T'ang Chun-I, *Essays on Chinese Philosophy and Culture*, Taipei 1988, pp. 257 – 289.

the standards of today frequently do not accord with the standards of antiquity. It is like people having different customs. […]

How could the standards of the early kings be taken as a model? Even if this were possible, it would still not be proper. The standards of the former kings were somehow required by the times. But the times have not come down to us together with the standards. Thus, even if the standards should have come down to the present, it would still not be proper to take them as a model.
Therefore, we should abandon the fixed standards of the early kings and take as a model how they set up their standards. But how did the early kings make their standards? When making standards, they followed man. But we ourselves are men, too. Therefore, by examining oneself one can know others. By examining the present one can know the past. The past and the present are one, and the others and I are the same. A scholar who is in possession of the Dao appreciates knowing the distant by the near, knowing the past by the present, knowing what he has not seen by what he has seen. Therefore, look at the shadow below the hall, and you know the course of sun and moon and the change of yin and yang. Look at the ice in a vase, and you know that it is cold under heaven and fish and turtles will hide. Taste one mouthful of meat and you know the flavor of the whole cauldron and the seasoning of the whole vessel".[10]

The *Lüshi chunqiu* unites classical topoi of the critique of tradition formulated during the late Zhou-period. The orientation by way of past example has become unreliable, the process of handing down involves a process of change, and temporal distance is responsible for the difficulty of understanding as well as for new problems that are no longer amenable to the old solutions. This causes any normative point of reference beyond the Now to disappear. The transition from the observation of pre-established norms towards the establishment of norms involves a reorientation from the past to the present, from imitation to innovation. Such a fundamental shift of emphasis is the typical formal characteristic of "axial age" thought in the sense of Karl Jaspers.

Where, however, does one derive the new norms from? The text is consistent in following its anti-historical line: It strongly argues in favor of the sameness of the Human regardless of time and place, which everyone has access to just by means of reflecting upon it. A timeless anthropological paradigm thereby replaces the paradigm of history that forms the basis of all traditionalist thinking. This corresponds to an old tenet of European humanism: The movement of the human spirit transcends space and time.

The manner in which the chapter *Cha jin* of the *Lüshi chunqiu* is referring to the present is certainly not equally characteristic of all schools of thinking during the Zhou period. But they are all deeply affected by the new temporal paradigm, even Confucianism with its idea of being a guardian of tradition. Even there man is no longer understood to be merely the member of a specific historical community

10 *Lüshi chunqiu* 15.8, *Zhuzi jicheng*, Hongkong 1978, vol. 6, p. 177.

interwoven with the fabric of his cultural context – he still remains in this role, but not exclusively. This is made evident by two of the key elements of Confucian ethics: Confucius' Golden Rule and Mengzi's moral anthropology.

Confucius' (551 – 481 B.C.) response to the crisis in China consists in an internalization of morality. It takes the form of a conspicuous self-reference of the agent, who by constantly monitoring his thoughts for their probity, thereby developing a sense of self-respect, shapes himself into an autonomous moral person, and all this without sanctions from outside and without any hope of happiness in the hereafter. Furthermore, the traditional values and norms become the object of reflection. This inward turn does not suspend the traditional rules of moral behavior (*li*), which – strictly stratified in terms of social position, gender, age and role – regulate everyday life right down to the minutest of details. The *li*, the very epitome of the Zhou tradition, may have lost their power of providing communal coherence during the social upheaval of the time, but without them, as Confucius emphasizes in his "Collected Sayings" (*Lunyu*), one would be "left without any ground to stand on" (*Lunyu* 8.8, 16.13, 20.3).[11] Nevertheless, now the direct, abstract relationship with a generalized 'other', alongside the action determined by one's role, becomes one of two complementary basic components of moral practice: Besides *li*, i. e. custom and tradition, *ren*, i. e. "humanity", appears on the scene. Even though it would be untypical of Confucianism to overemphasize the tension between these two, in case of a conflict humanity would take precedence over the obligatory role imposed by *li*. Dong Zhongshu (179 – 104 B.C.) gives a striking example of this: He comes out in defense of a general who contrary to an order concludes peace with a besieged city on his own initiative because he feels pity towards the population. This constitutes an offence against the code of *li* that does not permit such unauthorized action. But it would have been a more serious offence to sacrifice humanity and remain unmoved by the sight of human suffering. That the suspension of the moral code is justified for Dong Zhongshu proceeds from the following saying of Confucius': "When humanity is at stake, one should not give precedence to one's teacher."[12]

As opposed to the assumption that Confucius did not possess an abstract concept of man, none of his uses of the term 'humanity' clearly admits of a reading implying a social or ethnic restriction. Humanity, says Confucius, "cannot be renounced even while living among the Yi and Di (barbarian people in the eyes of the Chinese)." (*Lunyu* 13.19) What is referred to here is evidently a

11 The *Lunyu* is quoted after *Harvard-Yenching Sinological Index Series, A Concordance to the Analects of Confucius*, reprint Taipei 1972.

12 *Lunyu* 15.36; Dong Zhongshu: *Chunqiu fanlu* 2.3, Taipei 1975, pp. 3a–4a. Cf. Roetz, Heiner: *Konfuzius*, Munich 2006, p. 92.

general concept of mankind that may well have been brought about by the crisis in traditional China.

Confucius' Golden Rule, which is one of the striking explications of 'humanity', shows most clearly the link between the general reference to man and the distancing from tradition implicit in it. Asked if there was anything "consisting of only one word that could be followed for a whole life", Confucius responds with the sentence: "Whatever one does not wish oneself, one should not do unto others." (*Lunyu* 15.24) *Lunyu* 5.12 is even more precise: "If I do not wish that others do something to me, then I do not want to do it to them." This is obviously not a concrete rule applicable only to specific practices, but a rule of general validity. The "method of humanity" simply consists in "taking what is close at hand as an example" (*Lunyu* 6.28), which means that one projects one's own likes and dislikes onto an Other with whom one exchanges the roles of agent and patient. A single thought experiment is capable of showing the right way to behave, as Han Ying (2nd century B.C.) explains: One "measures the world by one's own feelings" and thereby knows that no one wants "to starve and freeze" or live a life of "toil and bitterness".[13] In these terms the Golden Rule implies the fundamental equality of all humans as vulnerable creatures of need, something to be realized unbounded by time and space and without requiring the values of a particular tradition. These may be as little dispensed with as the unequal roles of a hierarchical society. But in establishing the analogy between self and other a formal criterion has been brought into play by which these values have to prove their worth.

It becomes obvious now why the *Lüshi chunqiu* in the passage quoted above was able to evolve the basic pattern of the Golden Rule – to see the other by seeing oneself – as the procedure for setting up the non-traditional norms. Confucius' Golden Rule likewise paves the way for the principle of "mutual exchange of benefit" expounded by Mo Di, the founder of 'Mohism', who presents a utilitarian adaptation in his quest for a new criterion for what constitutes 'the good',[14] as well as for Mengzi's (ca. 380 – 290 B.C.) introduction of another non-traditional paradigm into Confucianism: the paradigm of natural spontaneity.

Mengzi searches for an answer to the rebellion against morality in the name of nature, instigated by the philosophers belonging to the Daoist circle. For the Daoist, morality is a constraint of natural man, which in the best case amounts in the helpless attempt to compensate for the loss of naturalness, in the worst case the means to an end that even keeps together a gang of robbers. The moralists are the helpmates of tyrants. Thus it says in book 2 of the Daoist classic *Zhuangzi:*

13 Han Ying: *Hanshi waizhuan* 3.38; Lai Yanyuan: *Hanshi waizhuan jinzhu jinyi*, Taipei 1972, p. 14, cf. Roetz: *Konfuzius*, p. 92.

14 Cf. Roetz, Heiner: *Confucian Ethics of the Axial Age,* Albany 1993, pp. 234 – 247.

> "The great original virtue has fallen apart, and innate nature and life have fallen into a state of confusion. The world loves knowledge, and the people are driven to exhaustion. Ever since axes and saws (corporal punishment) rule, regulations kill and hammer and chisel (torture) decide. The world is in great chaos, and the stirring up of the human heart is guilty of this. [...] In our age the people executed are amassed in big piles, dense crowds of people are driven onwards in neck collars and foot-chains, and the mutilated see their fellow victims. And only now, amidst all the chains and fetters, Confucians and Mohist are rolling up their sleeves. Indeed, this is too much! I know of no ingenuity and intelligence that have not procured neck collars and foot-chains, not the justice and humanity that have not contributed to the making of foot- and hand fetters. How does one know that it is not the moralists who are the harbingers of tyrants and robbers? Put an end therefore to sagacity and intelligence! Then perfect order will reign in the world".[15]

The *Zhuangzi* is just as much outraged by the suffering inflicted by man upon man as by the suffering done to nature. Its response, however, is not that of a moralizing critique in the name of whatever kind of humanism. The application of a specifically human standard is itself rather something wrong and an outgrowth of calculating reason that is dissolving the unity of the world. Humanity and justice themselves are the products of calculating. Over against this Daoism sets a purely naturalist form of goodness: One gives oneself over to "primordial virtue" and the "essence of one's nature and one's physical existence."[16] Against the human standardization of the world the Daoists idealize the unspoilt infant and enthuse about the harmonious unity of the 'highest antiquity' when man is finally losing his contours. The *Lüshi chunqiu* has confronted the universal humanism of the Confucians with the universal naturalism of the Daoists in an ingenious parable:

> "A man of Jing lost his bow. Instead of seeking it, he said, 'A man of Jing has lost it, a man of Jing will find it. Why should I seek it, then?' When Confucius heard about it he said, 'If he leaves out 'Jing', it will be all right.' When Lao Dan heard of it, he said, 'If he leaves out 'man', too, it will be all right.' Thus Lao Dan was the most impartial".

Confucianism has advanced two arguments against the Daoist idealization of nature. According to Xunzi (ca. 310 – 230 B.C.) Daoism removes man backwards to the animal kingdom, in which he cannot survive because as a deficient creature he cannot do without culture. Mengzi, however, tries to outdo Daoism on its very own terrain: If natural man is 'good', then in terms of Confucian ethics. This moral anthropology at the same time affords Mengzi with a basis for attacking the inhumanity of his time.

Like Xunzi Mengzi is a philosopher in the 'warring states period', in which the

15 Guo Qingfan: *Zhuangzi jishi*, *Zhuzi jicheng*, vol. 2, pp. 172 f.

16 *Zhuangzi* 8, p. 148.

states that resulted from the collapse of political feudalism were decimating each other in merciless wars. These wars and their consequences most emphatically raised the question of what constitutes just rulership. It was posed the first time when the Zhou proved to be victorious over the preceding dynasty of the Shang. The answer was that all rule required a 'mandate' from 'heaven' that is revocable and that is to be exercised in the interest of the people by a person of virtue. Due to this, politics starts to become subordinated to the primacy of morality. Later on the political discourse becomes more radicalized with the emergence of the centralized state with its military and authoritarian structure, whose ruler is only answerable to his own coldly calculated advantage and to no higher authority: no longer is he answerable to the king of the Zhou as the supreme feudal lord, nor to tradition, to 'heaven' or the expectations of the people. The central issue of the system, whose theoretical underpinnings are provided by the legist school, is pure self-interest, manipulated for the benefit of the state by the two 'mechanisms' of reward and punishment; any trace of morality would be an alien element in this context. Ruler and subject have to get agreed on not being 'humane' or 'loyal' to each other; laws and regulations alone are in force.[17] Man as a human being is of no account in such a system; the ruler "keeps him like a domestic animal and uses him like a plant."[18] Confucianism, by contrast, is suspected of being in collusion with the personal rule of the past.

Through the rise of the militarist state the question of proper rule, which the Confucians as the heirs of the religion of 'Heaven' had always had their focus on, becomes intensified. Confucius pleads in favor of government by virtue instead of administration and violence (*Lunyu* 2.3). Since the Confucians are insistent when it comes to this difference they are considered as trouble-makers. Mengzi designates those princes as murderers "who lust after killing people" and who "sacrifice human flesh for territorial gain" (*Mengzi* 1 A4, 4 A14).[19] Both Mengzi and Xunzi legitimate the removal of tyrants by violent means. Their justification for this rests on the argument that the ruler has lost the 'world', i. e. the people, upon whose at least passive support he is dependent.[20] Mengzi indicates to the princes that they can achieve this support on condition that they themselves are humane and just, but that – by contradistinction – "if they regard their subjects as so much dirt, these will consider them as robbers and mortal enemies" (*Mengzi* 4B3). He accords to the people the right to "retaliate" against what has been done to them (*Mengzi* 1B12). What precedes the legitimate rebellion is the violation of the expectation of reciprocity whose moral sublimation is the

17 Cf. Roetz: 1993, p. 262.

18 *Guanzi* 6; Dai Wang: *Guanzi jiaozheng, Zhuzi jicheng*, vol. 5, p. 30.

19 The *Mengzi* is quoted after *Harvard Yenching Institute Sinological Index Series, A Concordance to Meng Tzu*, reprint Taipei 1973.

20 Cf. Roetz: *Confucian Ethics of the Axial Age*, p. 75.

Golden Rule. Xunzi has later on evolved a dialectical theory based on this, which is supposed to bring 'balance' into a hierarchical society by integrating both equality and inequality in such a way that even the lowliest person can accept it, provided he can derive some advantage from it – i. e. the relief from strife and want through participating in the 'shared benefit'.

Mengzi, however, does not base his demand for a world that is less violent exclusively on the contract of reciprocity linking those who are powerful with those who are weak, but even more so on his concept of human nature. He maintains that human beings do not have the fundamentals of moral orientation "infused from outside", but that they have these "firmly in themselves" already in the form of dynamic "roots" (*Mengzi* 6 A6). This is the very apex of an internalization of morality far removed from traditional thinking that starts with the continuous self-reference of the 'gentleman' and the Golden Rule in the *Lunyu*. Yet Mengzi is not here envisaging the immediacy of a thought-experiment but that of spontaneous inclination. He discerns two sources of morality grounded in natural emotions. The one is that of familial affection, especially the love of children for their parents:

> "What man is capable of without having learned, is his good capacity. What man knows without having to think, is his good knowledge. Among the children still babbling like babies and carried on the arm, there is not a single one which would not know how to love its parents. And when they have grown up, there is not a single one which would not know how to respect the eldest brother. To love the parents is humaneness, and to respect the elders is justice. There is nothing else, and this should be extended to the whole world". (*Mengzi* 7 A15)

Embedding morality in the family is not to be misunderstood as a plea for an ethics of kinship – Mengzi's concern is the foundation of morality, not its limitation. By 'extending' familial sentiment to other areas he prevents morality from becoming a merely internal affair; the family should be the seat of special and primary, yet not of exclusive responsibility. At this juncture Mengzi not only transcends the limits of kinship, but also of an affective ethic confined to sensual experience and therefore limited in its range. In his critique of a king who managed to sacrifice not only his people but also his son in the 'war for territory' Mengzi says:

> "A humane person extends his attitude towards those he loves to those he does not love. An inhumane person extends his attitude towards those he does not love to those he loves". (*Mengzi* 7B1)

Mengzi formulates the same idea with regard to the second natural source of morality – the feeling of 'unbearability':

> "For all human beings there is something which they cannot bear. To extend this [attitude] to what they can bear is humaneness.... If one can bring to the full this inner attitude of not wishing to harm others, there will be humaneness in abundance". (*Mengzi* 7B31)

The most important trigger for feeling something to be unbearable is provided by witnessing the suffering of others. This is something everybody possesses whose natural emotions are still intact:

> "All men have a heart which cannot endure the suffering of others. The early kings had this heart, and they therefore also had a government which could not be cruel to men. If one practices such a government with such a heart, then one can rule the world as if making it turn round on the palm.
> My reason for saying that every man has a heart which cannot endure the suffering of others is this. Suppose a man suddenly sees a child about to fall into a well. In such a situation, everybody will have the feeling of alarm and compassion. This is not because he wants to enter into good relations with the parents of the child, or because he wants to gain praise in his neighborhood and among his fellow students and friends, or because he dislikes the cry of the child (or: a bad reputation).
> In view of this, he who has no feeling of compassion would not be a human being. He who has no feeling of shame and disgust would not be a human being. He who has no feeling of courtesy and modesty would not be a human being. He who has no feeling of right and wrong would not be a human being.
> The feeling of compassion is the beginning of humaneness. The feeling of shame and disgust is the beginning of justice. The feeling of courtesy and modesty is the beginning of propriety. The feeling of right and wrong is the beginning of knowledge. Man has these four beginnings, just as he has his four limbs. [...] In general, he who has these four beginnings in himself also knows how to expand and bring to completion all of them, like a spring just welling out, or like a fire just lit. If one knows how to bring them to completion, it will suffice to protect all within the four seas. If one does not bring them to completion, it will not even suffice to serve one's parents". (*Mengzi* 2 A6)

In his doctrine of the "fort beginnings" Mengzi describes man as *ens morale* that is capable of acting and judging morally all by himself, provided his natural capacities have had the chance of developing freely. In this case the quasi-biological impulse set off in him causes him to empathize with the entire human race, and not only his next of kin: It is not his own but a strange child's predicament that acts as a trigger. The analogy drawn between the "four beginnings" and the four extremities shows that Mengzi's thinking remains focused on humans as a species – morality by its very nature is not the product of a particular period in cultural history.

This does not require Mengzi to totally delete the model function of the early heroes of Chinese civilization; the only thing, however, that does cause them to stand out is the fact that they managed to fully preserve the talents all human beings are initially endowed with in an equal measure. Their behavior shows in an exemplary fashion how the spontaneous impulses of unspoilt human nature work – they are responsible for feelings of empathy with the fate of *every individual.* All human beings are connected with one another by nature, not by being part of society. "Whenever somebody in the Empire was drowned," says Mengzi about Yu, the founder of the Xia dynasty, "it was as if he himself had drowned him." The same goes for Ji, the forefather of the Zhou: "When someone in the Empire was starving it was as if he himself had starved him." (*Mengzi* 4B29) The chancellor Yi Yin is idealized in a similar fashion: "When a single simple man fell by the wayside he used to say: This is my fault." (*Shujing, Yueming*) Every man bears all others within himself. The climactic points in history so far have been nothing but the highlights of the working of human nature.

For Mengzi the 'four beginnings' of morality are evidence of 'Heaven' (*tian*) being represented in every human being. Thereby man possesses a quality within himself that has a specific 'dignity'. The dignity of his moral nature is to be distinguished from the dignity that an institution can either confer or take away:

> "To desire dignity is an aspiration all men have in common. But every single human being has a dignity within himself which he only does not think of. What men [normally] esteem as dignity is not the good dignity. To whom [a potentate like] Zhao Meng can confer dignity, Zhao Meng can also degrade". (*Mengzi* 6 A17)

In analogy with this argument Mengzi has put the "heavenly ranks" of morality, and primarily of humanity, above the ranks of political hierarchy (*Mengzi* 6 A16) and proclaimed the authority conferred by virtue to take precedence over the authority granted by a person's political position (*Mengzi* 2B2). It is his demand that politics should be made totally subservient to the moral potential of mankind. Through "humane governance" it should create the optimal conditions for fostering man's moral capacity: Securing his material sustenance, furthering the common good, renouncing wars and unjust taxation and the institution of a public school system. But it is not the main task of the state to restrain man by institutionalized force. A ruler even loses the right to punish if he has driven his people into want and then into crime – as someone "who has set up a trap" he himself is to be held responsible (*Mengzi* 1 A7).

It is, however, questionable if the dignity man according to Mengzi has "within himself" can be identified with the dignity of the human being as such or whether an important distinction is to be made here: Is the dignity of his moral nature only conferred upon him if man lives up to his moral capacity? Can he, if he fails to do so, otherwise be treated like an animal? At least one passage can be read as contradicting such an interpretation: Thus a person who has not sufficiently cultivated his innate "good knowledge" (knowledge of goodness), is referred to in the following manner:

"When others see him being animalish, they think that there was never any endowment in him. But how would this be man's true condition (*qing*)! " (*Mengzi* 6 A8)

According to this, man is obviously determined by his moral possibilities and not by his actual performance. Even though he may behave in an inhumane way, either due to his own fault or the force of circumstance, this would not detract from his essential nature – i.e. his ability for moral behavior, which may have become stunted but can be reactivated on condition that one should "look for it" (*Mengzi* 6 A6). This very idea could have influenced a humane provision in premodern Chinese law: the assurance of impunity or extenuating circumstances in case of a self-accusation before the official prosecution of a crime had begun. This is based on the assumption that man is a being capable of remorse and self-correction and thereby of improvement, which until today informs the most cogent objection against capital punishment. The same argument is the motivation for abolishing the penalty of mutilation in 167 B.C. by the Han emperor Wen. Ti Ying, the daughter of a condemned person, successfully pleaded in favor of her father:

"A dead person cannot be brought back to life, and a mutilated person cannot be sown together again. In case he wanted to correct his mistakes and reform himself he would have no opportunity of doing so. I am prepared to expiate my father's guilt as an official slave to enable him to reform himself".[21]

Correcting one's mistake is a motif from the *Lunyu*, whereas the notion of "self-reformation" goes back to Mengzi's theory of the inalienable "true condition" (*qing*) of the human being. Mengzi's moral anthropology is addressed to everybody, but above all it is a means of exerting pressure on those in power. As members of the human race they are capable of humanity – no one can use the lack of natural abilities as a pretext (*Mengzi* 6 A6). Mengzi thus lays the foundation for obliging those in power to behave like human beings. If they did otherwise they would not only act against their own nature but also against that of those who are the objects of their actions. The obligation to act morally obviously corresponds to the right of being treated like a human being. This goes to explain Mengzi's indignation at rulers treating their people like animals or worse. Thus he attributes to the king of Qi a 'humane' disposition because he showed his pity for a cow about to be sacrificed. "What, however, are we led to think", he asks, "when kindness is only shown towards animals but is never extended to the people?" (*Mengzi* 1 A7) A compassionate action can be applied to an animal, but it only finds its true object in a human being, and what distinguishes man from animals is that "little something" (*Mengzi* 4B19) of his moral capacity. This, however, is a major distinction. Animals in Confucianism

21 *Shiji* 10, Hong Kong 1969, p. 427.

are not the object of respect, and, conversely, respect is the specific quality distinguishing the treatment of humans from that of animals (*Lunyu* 2.7). This distancing of non-human nature is the reverse of Confucian humanism.

Thus Mengzi obviously expresses the idea of man as an autonomous *ens morale* that is essentially different from a thing or an animal. Such an interpretation fits in with the attempts, frequently documented in early Confucian literature, to guarantee a moral life via the self-respect of the individual and less so via the judgment of 'others' or the expectation of reward or punishment by some divine authority. This contradicts the theory mentioned initially whereby for Confucianism a human being does not exist at all before becoming an active member of a community. This view reduces man to a merely relational quantity by equating the constitution of human individuality with that of the human being. Yet to make a sharp distinction between biological and social man is tantamount to overlooking that especially for the Confucianist Mengzi biological man is already an incipiently moral being. Additionally culturalist ethics tend to view sociability as conditioned by a particular community and to link the norms of social life to its traditional values. This means that the 'Dao', the 'right way', which Mengzi still located in the natural impulse of man granted from Heaven, now becomes immanent to a specific culture. Not only does this contradict Mengzi's essentially non-traditional approach to ethics resembling the idea of natural law, but it also tends to overlook the conflictual situation the ancient, continually misunderstood Confucian 'gentleman' finds himself as an autonomous moral agent confronting his community.[22]

Not only does Mengzi's moral anthropology open up possibilities of self-responsible action for the individual without any constraints imposed from the outside, but also of a humane, ultimately democratic system which derives its guiding principles from such an ethics. It is no coincidence that his ethical principles should nowadays form the most important link with the idea of individual human rights, against the official line held in China, with the Chinese cultural tradition. Mengzi's concept of man as a being that through his membership in the human species is by nature distinct from animals is also apt to put in question the 'Chinese' position in bioethics whereby a human being that does not yet form part of a community has a lower moral status than one already born into it. As one can show by Mengzi's example, Confucianism neither gives license to the restriction of human rights nor to an "anything that goes" ethos in biotechnology.

That Mengzi himself would presumably not have been willing to draw the progressive consequences inherent in his theory is another matter. In many respects he is a child of his times. Like all pre-modern Confucians he is a

22 Cf. Roetz: *Confucian Ethics of the Axial Age*, pp. 162 and 172 – 173.

monarchist and elitist, and his political ethics tend towards a benign paternalism. He is intolerant of "wrong teachings" (*Mengzi* 3B9), his thinking is distinctly paternalistic, and the proudest proclamation of his uncompromising stance vis-à-vis the powers-that-be is made explicit in his gender-role as a man (*Mengzi* 3B2). All this, however, is due to historio-sociological circumstances and does not proceed from constraints systematically inherent in his theorizing. In order to make it suitable for a globalized humanism one would have to rid Confucianism, like all other traditional ethics, of such residues. This not least of all applies to the dark side of his humanism, i. e. his denigration of non-human nature. And yet there is more in it than its representatives were historically willing to implement, especially after they had installed themselves as officials at the imperial court.

The fact that Mengzi's teachings at the time were much more at odds with the prevailing hierarchical understanding of politics than he himself realized is evidenced by the polemics of his ancient opponents who were charging him with having betrayed the tradition and its institutions to natural spontaneity. The extent to which Mengzi is far ahead of his times has been proven by the 'New-Confucianism' of the 20$^{th}$ century, which in spite of its cultural conservatism that is not always in line with Mengzi's principles, is tantamount to the attempt at bringing the ancient teachings up to the level of modernity. For the New-Confucian Tang Junyi, this is the task of a self-correction of Confucian humanism.

Ever since it has been in existence in China, the notion of 'humanism' belongs to the vocabulary of Confucian self-description. Tang Junyi regards 'humanism' as the central idea of Confucianism per se and the spirit of Chinese culture that has to be regained. He differentiates 'humanist' from 'a-humanist', 'super-humanist', 'sub-humanist' and 'anti-humanist' thinking. For 'humanist' thinking the existence and the 'value' of man and human nature is of supreme importance. A-humanist thinking, which Tang regards as being the operative principle of Western science, objectifies the world of non-human nature. Supra-humanist thinking is focused on transcendent powers, such as in Christian religion. Anti-humanist thinking reifies man himself, as in Legism, the socio-technological law-and-order school of ancient China, as well as in modern materialism. Sub-humanism is located between humanism and anti-humanism and derives from a limited view of human nature; following Tang Junyi all utilitarian ethics, such as ancient Mohism, belong within this category.[23]

According to Tang Junyi Confucian humanism does have certain deficits that eventually caused its demise. Its central feature is the one-sided perception of

23 Tang Junyi: *Zhongguo renwen jingshen zhi fazhan* [The Development of the Chinese Humanist Spirit], Hongkong 1958, partly translated in T'ang Chun-I: *Essays on Chinese Philosophy and Culture*, Taipei 1988, pp. 257–289.

man as a 'moral subject'. But the 'moral subject' also has to be realized as a 'political subject', an 'epistemological subject' and 'technological-practical subject'. Confucianism therefore has to be remodeled in such a way that the ideas of science and technology and of democracy, which for historical reasons had remained undeveloped, can be absorbed by it. This necessitates the acceptance of 'a-humanist' and in certain respects also of 'sub-humanist' thinking inasmuch as a democracy is also an arena of conflicting interests. On the other hand the humanist core of Confucianism should not be forfeited, especially under modern conditions, since science and democracy in their turn require a moral framework to operate in. For this purpose Mou Zongsan (1909–1995) has developed the idea of a 'self-negation' of the 'good knowledge' postulated by Mengzi (*Mengzi* 7 A15, see above): Of its own volition and until revoked, the 'moral subject' withdraws and delegates responsibility to science and technology, politics and law.[24]

With regard to the constitution of the 'moral subject' Tang Junyi delimits Confucian humanism in two directions: He neither accepts the materialist reduction of human beings as creatures of necessity nor does he tolerate the 'supra-humanist' subordination to the judgement and grace of a transcendent divinity. Tang even views the Christian doctrine of sin along with its threat of eternal damnation as a form of anti-humanism that is demeaning to mankind. Confucian religiousness, on which Tang insists in order to keep materialism at bay, should by contrast be part and parcel of humanism: 'Heaven' is manifesting itself *completely* in man's moral nature, and 'spirituality' is nothing but realizing this nature. If man makes full use of this nature of his, then – so Tang says following Mengzi, "he also knows Heaven" (*Mengzi* 7 A1), and there is no numinous rest. Confucian humanism would thus amount to embodying the highest form of humanism. Man does not have to orientate himself by some pre-given doctrine of salvation but solely by the creative strength lying within himself.

In the New-Confucianism of the present, the 'unity of heaven and man' as the culminating point of a 'holistic humanism' is seen, notably by Tu Weiming, as the expression of an ecological vision which is contrasted with the 'Western' aggressiveness towards nature. Raised to the level of 'anthropocosmism', Confucian humanism makes man into a 'partner of heaven' in order to halt the destructiveness immanent to the 'Faustian drive' of modern 'secular humanism'.[25]

24 Mou Zongsan: *Zhengdao yu zhidao*, p. 58.

25 Tu Weiming: "A Confucian Perspective on the Core Values of Global Community", in: *The Review of Korean Studies* 2 (1999): 55–70, and "The Ecological Turn in New Confucian Humanism: Implications for China and the World", in: *Daedalus* 130.4 (2001): 243–264. Cf. my article "Confucianism between Tradition and Modernity, Religion, and Secularization: Questions to Tu Weiming", in: *Dao* 7.4 (2008): 367–380.

For this end Tu Weiming invokes the argument of a classical Confucian text, *Zhongyong*, according to which man forms a "trinity together with heaven and earth".[26] This very thought, however, motivated Lee Shui-chuen to justify biotechnology (see above). It is also to be found with Xunzi in the context of his doctrine of the 'victory' of man over nature. For Xunzi nature in its original state represents no value in itself but only the material basis for man's sustenance, who has to work on it and transform it before it can be put to any use at all. A new, anthropogeneous order is superimposed upon the order of a nature that is 'tailored' to suit the needs of man who originally has no real home in it. Another object of 'artifice' disposable to mankind is its own congenital and natural constitution. Because this constitution, so Xunzi states in his critique of Mengzi, is 'bad' in a moral as well as, compared to animals, a functional sense.[27]

The end Xunzi pursues with this theory is primarily an ethical and socio-political one and not a technical or scientific one. His concern, along with all other Confucians, is the moral cultivation of mankind and society, which however is conditional upon departing from the continuity with what is natural. However, the total liberation of blind instrumental rationality for Xunzi would equal a relapse into mere nature. All the same, his teachings show how ambivalent Confucian humanism actually is when it comes to preventing the violation of nature for human purposes.[28]

To come to a conclusion and to answer the question posed at the beginning, humanism, also in view of its ambivalence and inconsistencies, is not the sole property of the biblical-Greek West. And an exclusively Chinese, notably Confucian, view of mankind that involves a culturally limited concept of ethics and politics, which would render a global humanism impossible, does not exist. But even if the variety of cultural traditions should sit athwart this project the last word on it would not have been pronounced yet. Because humanism is by no means the exclusive and secure *property* of one particular culture but is the unending *task* of creating and forming culture. The resources for this are offered by the various traditions, which only have to be submitted to a humanist reading so that they can offer a humanist response. And yet, as the ancient Chinese already knew, the logical site for locating humanism is not the past of the traditions, but the here and now and the future.[29]

26 *Zhongyong* 22; Zhu Xi: *Sishu jizhu*, Hong Kong 1986, p. 20.

27 *Xunzi* 17 and 23, cf. Roetz: "The end of ethical universalism?", p. 186 f.

28 Cf. my articles "On Nature and Culture in Zhou China", in: Dux, Günter/Vogel, Hans Ulrich (Eds.): *Concepts of Nature. A Chinese-European Cross-Cultural Perspective*, Leiden 2010, pp. 198–219, and "Chinese Unity of Man and Nature – Reality or Myth?", in: Meinert, Carmen (Ed.): *Nature, the Environment and Climate Change in East Asia*, Leiden 2013.

29 An extended version of this article has appeared in: Hennigsen, Lena/Roetz, Heiner (Eds.): *Chinesische Menschenbilder*, Wiesbaden 2009.

Umesh C. Chattopadhyaya

# Indian Humanism

## 1. Introduction

Humanism as a philosophical and cultural movement has a long history in Europe. The movement intensified and assumed a global dimension in the past several decades as a result of various historical and political developments following the World Wars and their presumed negative impact on human existence. The conventional form of humanism with a number of variants attempts to universalize a particular understanding of mankind and its concerns. To be specific, it is the homogenized 'modern' Western understanding of mankind and this kind of humanism has generally remained conservative in accommodating ideas from the marginalized majority of the world. Many modern humanist associations complain of falling membership in the age of globalization that necessitates serious self-reflection and contemplation on the possible flaws underlying such movements.

So there is a necessity to form a new world body of Humanism based on fresh insights acquired from history and intercultural debates, that should also be free from the influence of both religious dogmatism and politico-economic ideologies – socialism, capitalism, etc. – with powers to review and decide humanitarian cases round the world. Humanism is one that sublime theme where all ideologies have to converge.

The 'New Humanism' envisaged by Jörn Rüsen in Germany is a fresh and timely response to the problem of humanism in the age of globalization. It is a welcome departure from the earlier forms of Western Humanism as it shows far greater broadness and openness in outlook. The central point here is "unity in difference" and, therefore, it is open to intercultural perspectives. While opposing such divisive and dangerous themes as the "clash of civilizations",[1] this

1 Huntington, S.: *The Clash of Civilizations*, New York 1996. In a subsequent publication, *Who Are We?*, London 2004, Huntington legitimizes the Biblical concept of evil/Satan, manifested in the form of external enemies, as of paramount importance for the internal integration of the

new liberal humanism evolves a method of creative engagement between different cultures and to delineate common points in all the major civilizations for a constructive dialogue. The idea is to recognize differences and work out on the shared features towards a better understanding of humankind and developing a systematic program for a legitimate place of humanism and its active role in the service of mankind through new education. This also adequately justifies the need for the incorporation of ideas from India and other traditional countries with rich cultural/intellectual heritage. India is amongst the countries that will benefit most from New Humanism because, despite a long tradition of humanitarian concerns as elaborated below, there is a tremendous gap between theory and practice. Here the inhumanitarian trends are on the rise, and there is a fear of its further aggravation in the age of globalization.

## 2. Humanistic Ideas in India

### 2.1 Understanding India

Any understanding of Indian humanism raises the question of 'what India is'. By common consent, India constitutes a world in miniature. It offers all the major climatic regimes of the world and faces the same situation of enormous diversity at ethnic, cultural, economic, religious and linguistic levels that the modern world faces. Some of the intriguing problems, connected with the central question of Indian humanism are 1) how to explain unity in diversity, if there is any, and 2) how Indian civilization maintained its continuity through special adaptive mechanisms at least over the last five thousand years. Attempts at reducing her into straight-jacketed categories by both traditional scholars and those equipped with modern analytical temperament are routinely made with diametrically opposite results and provide at best partial, contesting pictures. Only those exposed to both traditional and modern approaches know how difficult it is to define India as she resists any pigeonholing attempts at all levels. There is a 'mystique' element in India, as also in her culture, that prevents clear-cut definitions, and since its center and boundaries cannot be firmly located, India is also spared as a target of total subjugation and annihilation.

Nevertheless, attempts at understanding India should be made not in isolation but in a global context. India's distinctive personality, if any, is shaped largely by her long cultural tradition that had an element of openness to con-

United States. This is an example of negative creativity where certain emotive feelings like hatred and animosity are generated for the suffering of mankind – to transfer one's own problems onto others.

temporaneous ideas from Iran, Greece, Rome, China and so on. According to many, toleration constitutes a vital feature of India, but according to Amartya Sen, a better term is "*svikrti*" (acceptance).[2] Because of her dynamic and most adaptive nature, she appreciated and accepted many elements of the Islamic civilization of the medieval period, such as arts, literature and philosophy (of Sufism, for example), as well as of the modern Western civilization. Like the ancient Chinese, Indians have been able to synthesize apparently contradictory ideas – materiality and spirituality, for example. It is interesting, though, that whenever modern Indians, trained in the Western line of education, are confronted with deeper issues of life, they turn to their traditional mode of philosophical thinking and often effectively combine the best in the Western and the Indian thoughts towards a unique solution. An example can be cited in the form of M.N. Roy, whose radical humanism has been elaborated below.

William Dalrymple, the famous historian and novelist, writes:

> "Indians live in so many worlds at the same time. You will find McDonald's and KFC in New Delhi. But a few miles down the line in Madhya Pradesh you will find 3,000 kinds of *saris!* All over the world there is anxiety about our times being of one-world, one-culture. But Indians will remain more diverse. India has always had its uniqueness. Indians have successfully moved forward while embracing each new age, [...] Some traditions get lost, others survive. India is never going to lose its soul in its quest for globalisation. [...]
> There is a danger of globalisation, yes, but there is awareness to what is our own here. It is better to be modern than purely traditional".[3]

Since such complex patterns of life style pose problems at clear-cut understanding of India and her peoples, systematic attempts are made at intellectual levels to wipe out the traces of ancient Indian cultural tradition (wherein lay India's originality) and substitute the same by certain modernist ideologies. But the uniqueness of India lay neither in her excellence in borrowing and transplanting Western ideologies that a section of Indians did rather successfully, nor in developing a revivalist right wing Hinduttva philosophy, conservative and fundamentalist to the core. It is the ancient Indian culture, dynamic in form and openness in outlook that provided a distinctive personality,[4] though irreducible

---

2 Sen, Amartya: *The Argumentative Indian: Writings on Indian Culture, History and Identity*, London 2005.

3 http://www.hindu.com/lr/2008/03/02/stories/2008030250010100.htm [11/06/2012]. The above observations depict Indians as actors, as it were, of a cosmic play with multiple roles that they voluntarily or involuntarily choose themselves with or without compulsion. An individual has different roles to play in a family – mother, father, brother, sister, in-laws, and a host of intricate designations with certain conventionally defined duties, though not everybody is bound by such obligations. Similar roles exist outside the domestic circles in different cultural settings.

4 Radhakrishnan, S.: *Indian Philosophy* (two volumes), London 1927.

perhaps to any stereotyped category. In one of his pieces of inspired writing, Frederick Max Müller appealed to the Western students of his time to turn to India, especially her 'ancient heritage', in the following words:

> "Whatever sphere of the human mind you may select for your special study, whether it be language, or religion, or mythology, or philosophy, whether it be laws or customs, primitive art or primitive science, everywhere, you have to go to India, whether you like it or not, because some of the most valuable and most instructive materials in the history of man are treasured up in India, and in India only".[5]

What India needs is not to reject her pre-modern tradition(s), but to refine and revitalize it in the context of modern civilizations and contemporary problems. I wish to suggest that it is this living cultural tradition(s) of ancient origin, reformed and reinforced in the modern context and contemporary challenges by such thinkers as Ramakrishna, Vivekananda, Tagore, Aurobindo, Gandhi and many others, that should form the main basis of India's intellectual engagement with the West or other cultures on issues like humanism. But this does not mean that the impact of modernism in India or the indigenous, ancient secular traditions, as manifested in the *Lokayata* system of thought[6] should be ignored. It is the synthesis of the two broad traditions that gives a more complete picture of India. In fact, M.N. Roy, who favored a radical humanism in more recent times, similar in spirit to the Western humanism (see below), thought that a critical and rational study of ancient Indian philosophical systems might do what the rediscovery of ancient Greek thought did for Europe during the Renaissance.

Cultural diversity has been an important feature of India, which is different from multiethnic structure of the United States of America where all the different groups are forced to show uniformity in language and customs. Modern India's cultural diversity involves not only peoples from different ethnic background and different faiths and creeds, but also of different linguistic backgrounds. Scholars are divided on the question whether there ever has been any unity. Actually unity as a nation or state has been a recent phenomenon; cultural unity varied in intensity from time to time. Those who claim India's cultural unity amidst differences explain it generally in terms of cultural factors like religion, social lineages and customs and festivals, including pilgrimage.[7]

5 Müller, F. Max: *India: What Can It Teach Us?*, New Delhi 1991, p. 11 (Originally published in 1883, Cambridge).

6 Chattopadhyaya, D.P.: *Lokayata: A Study in Ancient Indian Materialism*, Delhi 1959.

7 For further details, see Mookerji, Radhakumud: *The Fundamental Unity of India*, London 1914.

## 2.2 Facets of Indian Humanism

Any discussion of Indian cultural tradition here revolves around the central issues of humanism – the points shared by other cultures of the West and the East.[8] The first, and foremost, point of shared features involves the basic question: what has been the status of Man in India? Even if ancient Indian tradition is not particularly anthropocentric like its Western counterpart, did it show enough sensitivity to human existence, importance of Man in the creation, his aspirations and concerns? Did it evolve methods to address the problems of freedom from suffering? Apart from the metaphysical questions like 'who am I', did it also pay attention to ethical issues like what constitutes a good life? The answer is a positive one.

A second point of shared features relates to the question of 'reason', which too has been very well developed in India, as exemplified by such schools of philosophy as, Mimamsa, Nyaya, Vaiseshika, as well as the Jain and the Buddhist philosophies. However, in order to acquire higher forms of knowledge, emphasis has been placed to transcend the rational faculty. Indian culture has a unique capability to go beyond the dichotomies, contradictions and polarities. Rather than viewing the world in terms of religious-secular or material-spiritual polar opposites, a trend appearing since colonial times, traditional Indian way of thinking has highlighted the continuum of the life process, the continuum within a very wide range of human existence.

Traditional Western humanism emerged as one of the forms of creative resistance to the injustices and excesses meted at the hands of organized forms of religion, state machinery, and so on. It also changed its form during different periods of history – the Renaissance, the Age of Reason, the Age of Enlightenment, and today there are different variants. But all of them, whether secular/atheistic or theistic in orientation, converge on a common emphasis on the elevation of human dignity, human rights, and focus on Man's creative role in shaping his future. This last emphasis is best represented by what has been described, as 'Creative Humanism' expounded by Henri Bergson (France), and is also reflected in major Indian intellectual traditions. Notable Indian humanists grouped under this form of humanism are M.N. Roy and N.K. Devaraja.[9]

More or less all the major philosophical schools of India are in agreement with this idea of Man's 'creative' potentials. The ancient Indian education system emphasized that individuals should be encouraged to develop their thoughts independently. The modern education system has done just the opposite – in the

8 For excellent accounts of concepts relating to Indian humanism in an intercultural perspective, see Mukerjee, Radhakamal: *The Way of Humanism*, Bombay 1968; Radhakrishnan, S./Raju, P.T.: *The Concept of Man: A Study in Comparative Philosophy*, New Delhi 1995.

9 See Jatava, D.R.: *Social and Humanist Thinkers (Indian and Western)*, Jaipur 1998, chapter 4.

name of education, it has conditioned and restricted the growth of mankind to suit the interests of the dominant ideologies or power structures.[10] We shall come back to this while discussing the humanistic ideas of Vivekananda.

Humanism as a process or movement essentially relates to 'freedom' from all such unfavorable forces that cause suffering to mankind.

According to the Upanishads, perfection is one of the key characteristics of the *Brahman* or the Ultimate Reality, which is also the source of all creations including the mankind. The humans being a product of the Brahman also aspire to reach that state of perfection through complete growth, i.e. an all-round growth at material, mental/intellectual and spiritual levels, which is consistent with ideals or objectives of human life (*Purusharthas*) described in ancient law books (*Smrtis*) and the Epic and Puranic literature.[11] Any imbalance in the proportion of the three core dimensions might cause dwarfing of the individual, and hence of the human society. Growth also means growth of human capital or assets (beyond the culturally created financial one). While globalisation gives importance to financial capital alone, and recognizes human capital only in the context of the production process,[12] Indian systems of thought have reminded of other aspects of human capital – human potentials that have the power to liberate humans from suffering – e.g., knowledge, conscience (*Viveka*) and values like compassion and mutualism that lead to an all-round growth of the individuals and the society.

Indian humanism has been adequately described by various authorities, especially from the fields of philosophy, sociology, education, political sciences, but not history.[13] In the following pages Indian humanism and related concepts

10 Mayo, Peter: *Gramsci, Freire, and Adult Education. Possibilities for Transformative Action*, London 1999. Mayo places the mainstream educational systems squarely at the service of global capitalism. He asserts that schools and other educational programmes train a work force in performances that maintain and reproduce the current political order; they frame the dominant educational paradigms as subservient to the interests of those who control the planet's productive capacities.

11 The four *Purusharthas* or ideals of life are: 1. *Dharma* (righteousness, duty), 2. *Artha* (pursuit of material prosperity, as well as of meaning), 3. *Kama* (desire, generally interpreted in the sense of sexual pleasure), and 4. *Moksha* (liberation). See Basham, A.L.: *Wonder That Was India*, London 1954; Prabhu, P.H.: *Hindu Social Organization*, Bombay 1991 (First published in 1940).

12 Zula K./Chermack, T.J.: "Human Capital Planning: A Review of Literature and Implications for Human Resource Development", in: *Human Resource Development Review* 6.3 (2007): 245–262.

13 Bandiste, D.D.: *Humanist Thought in Contemporary India*, Delhi 1999; Crook, John H.: *World Crisis and Buddhist Humanism. End Games: Collapse or Renewal of Civilisation*, New Delhi 2009 (First Indian edition); Devaraja, N.K.: *Humanism in Indian Thought*, New Delhi1988; Jatava, D.R.: *The Dimensions of Humanism*, Agra 1970; Mohapatra, P.K. (Ed.): *Facets of Humanism*, New Delhi 1999; Mukerjee, Radhakamal: *The Way of Humanism: East and West*, Bombay 1968; Mukerji, D.P.: *Redefining Humanism: Selected Essays of D.P. Mukerji*, ed. by

will be discussed in two historical phases: a) the pre-modern and b) the colonial and post-colonial

### 2.2.1 The Pre-Modern India

Modern scholarship has divided the diverse philosophical traditions of India into two categories – the Orthodox and the Heterodox, depending upon whether or not they accept the authority of the Vedas – a group of texts composed over a long period between 2000 B.C. and 600 B.C.[14] The former includes the following philosophical schools: the Samkhya, the Yoga, the Nyaya, the Vaiseshika, the Mimamsa, and the Vedanta. The latter includes not only Buddhist and Jain philosophies but also the Lokayata system of thought that tried to substitute the spiritual basis of existence to the material basis and was accepted as a respectable system of thought.[15] Man, his growth, development and self-realisation constitute a perennial theme in all the philosophies belonging to the orthodox school as well as in Buddhism and Jainism.

Ashok Vohra elaborates the conception of Man in Indian tradition in contrast to the Biblical attitude where man has been condemned to be a sinner,[16] which was also perhaps a motivating factor behind the rise of humanism in modern Europe to recover faith in human dignity. In Indian tradition(s), men are reminded of their divine origin – *amrtasyaputrah*, i. e. children of the Immortal existence.[17]

A Vedic text, The *Aitareya Aranyaka* of the first millennium B.C., declares that man is the abode of Brahman (the Absolute): "*ayampuruso brahma-lokah*" (II.13). Lord Vishnu, an important (solar) deity of the Vedic period and an abstract principle, gained paramount importance in the later Brahmanical religious thought where he is described as having descended in ten incarnations from lower forms of life, fish, tortoise, boar, etc., through to the highest form of

---

Srobona Munshi, New Delhi 2009; Praharaj, D.M.: *Humanism in Contemporary Indian Perspective*, Meerut 1995; Saiyidain, K.G.: *The Humanist Tradition in Indian Educational Thought*, London 1966; Singh, Jaideep: *The Humanistic View of Man*, New Delhi 1979; Truong, Bhikkhu Duc: *Humanism in the Nikaya Literature*, Delhi 2005; Varma, V.P.: *Philosophical Humanism and Contemporary India*, Delhi 1979. See also Chattopadhyaya, U.: "Contemporary Challenges to Historical Studies: In Search of A 'Humanistic History'", in An Era of Global Crisis " in: *Taiwan Journal of East Asian Studies* 8.2 (2011): pp. 79–111.

14 Winternitz, Maurice: *History of Indian Literature*, trans. from German by Ketkar, S., vol. 1, Calcutta 1927.

15 Chattopadhyaya, D.P.: op. cit.; Chattopadhyaya, K.C.: "The Lokayata System of Thought in Ancient India", in: *Journal of the Ganganatha Jha Kendriya Sanskrit Vidyapeetha (Aditya Natha Jha Commemoration Volume)*, vol. XXXI (1–4), Allahabad 1975, pp. 137–155.

16 Vohra, Ashok: "Humanism in Indian thought", in: Mohapatra, P.K. (Ed.): *Facets of Humanism*, New Delhi 1999, p. 9.

17 Ibid.

Man.[18] In some of the versions, the historical Buddha (the enlightened Man) too has been included in the list of ten incarnations. This is a reflection of an evolutionary scheme of life recognized by the ancient Indians.[19] According to *Srimad Bhagavatam*, a text of the first millennium AD (XI.ix.28):

> "The Divine one having projected (evolved) with his own inherent power various forms such as trees, reptiles, birds, insects and fish was dissatisfied at heart with all these; [H] e projected the human form endowed with the capacity to realize *Brahman* (the universal Divine Self of all), and became extremely pleased".

India has had a rich narrative tradition and certain visions/ideas are expressed metaphorically through popular stories. Here the underlying message, not historical accuracy, which is important. The above narratives try to establish the following ideas: a) Evolution of life forms, b) Man as the highest form in this evolutionary process, and c) Man has a divine origin. They summarize Indian conception of Man and his place in the world. The impressions of such narratives have been so deep in the public perception that when Charles Darwin put forward his thesis of origins of species based on most scientific lines, it never came as a shock or surprise to the Indians.

In India there flourished a host of humanistic thinkers who held Man in a very high esteem. According to N.L. Gupta, Krishna DvaipayanaVyasa (or simply the Vyasa) who compiled the Great Epic *Mahabharata*, in all probability, during what Karl Jaspers defined as the Axial Age,[20] surpassed all other thinkers by proclaiming: "A man is the best of all creations, there is no object or idea better than man".[21] Gupta further says that "Vyasa stands as the fore-most thinker as far as the assessment of real worth of an individual and unity of mankind is concerned".[22]

But certainly this does not diminish the status of Mahavira and the Buddha, perhaps a near contemporary of Vyasa, as two of the foremost humanists of the world. The Buddha believed not in just generating thoughtful narratives like the Vyasa, but in transforming a theory or conviction of humanitarian concern into practice; he was like a self-less medical practitioner who could diagnose a disease and give an appropriate medicine for the well-being of mankind which it desperately needed. His prescriptions coming from deep inside of a compassionate heart had a deep and decisive impact on a large section of con-

18 Bhandarkar, R.G.: *Vaishnavism, Saivism and Minor Religious Systems*, Strasburg 1913.

19 Lord Rama and Lord Krishna, the respective heroes of the two epics, the *Ramayana* and the *Mahabharata*, too have been conceived as the incarnations of Lord Vishnu.

20 See Eisenstadt, S.N. (Ed.): *The Origins and Diversity of the Axial Age Civilizations*, New York 1986.

21 Gupta, N.L.: *Humanist Tradition of India*, New Delhi 1999, p. 2; *Mahabharata*, XII.288.20.

22 Ibid.

temporaneous and later societies from the powerful ruling and aristocratic classes and rich mercantile groups to the downtrodden. This in itself speaks volumes about his genuine humanitarian concerns.

*The Buddhist Philosophy*

There are two sides of Buddha's life – individual and social. In the Theravada Buddhism – an earlier form – Buddha is a man (an enlightened though) not God, a teacher and not a savior. The other side relates to his compassionate concerns with the sorrow of fellow men, eager to enter their lives, heal their troubles and spread his message for the good of the many: "*bahu-jana-hitaye*". The teachings of the Buddha have two complementary dimensions – the intellectual/philosophical and the moral/ethical. The main principle of Buddhist philosophy is the theory of causation or dependent origination. The Buddha recognized four noble truths: a) all existence is full of suffering, b) all suffering has a cause, c) suffering can be brought to an end, and d) there is a way to end the suffering.

It has also been recognized that our subjection to time, to *samsara* (the world), is due to *avidya* (unawareness) that leads to infatuation, depravity (*asava*). From *avidya* the mankind must rise to *vidya*, *bodhi*, enlightenment. The Buddha aims at a new form of existence that could be attained only through *jnana* or *bodhi*, i. e. absolute illumination. He declares: "I deem the highest goal of a man to be the stage in which there is neither old age nor fear, nor disease, nor birth, nor death, nor anxiety, and in which there is no continuous renewal of activity".[23] For him this realization is a growth from within. The Buddha raised his voice against the ignorance and superstition, the dread and the horror, that accompanied popular religions. Theistic views tend to generate dogmatism and intolerance. While most modernist traditions have tried to control and conquer the world through science and technology, time could never be controlled and it continues to remain a vital source of suffering. It is here that the Buddha has his own solution: "Our aim is to conquer time, overcome *samsara*, and the way to it is the moral path which results in illumination".[24] Radhakrishnan further notes:

> "While the *Karma* relates to the world of objects, of existence in time, nirvana assumes the freedom of the subject, of inwardness. We can stand out of our existential limits. We experience the nothingness, the void of the world to get beyond it. [...] The enlightened is free, having broken all bonds. [...] *The Buddha when he attained nirvana is far from being dissolved into non-being. It is not he that becomes extinct but the passions and desires*".[25]

---

23 *Buddhacarita* of Asvaghosa, XI.59, quoted by Radhakrishnana, S.: "Forword", in: *2500 Years of Buddhism*, ed. by P.V. Bapat, New Delhi 1956, p. ix.

24 Radhakrishnana, S.: Ibid., p. x.

25 Ibid., p. xi, emphasis added.

The result of such a state of existence reached by the Buddha is that "whatever he desires, that thought will he think, whatever thought he does not desire, that thought will he not think".[26]

Man is subject to old age, sickness and death, but ironically, out of ignorance and pride, he condemns the aged, sick and dead. Buddha taught that if we learn what pain is, we become the brothers of all who suffer. This is the highpoint of a compassionate humanism, as to be found in Buddhism.

Buddhism was also an attempt towards social reform against an existing order based on caste system and Vedic ritualism involving animal sacrifice. The Buddha was in favour of an egalitarian society and thus advised not to accumulate wealth. Being a humanist of the highest order, he was never harsh on any section of the society and thus commanded tremendous respect from all walks of life, including the rich corporate/mercantile groups that felt obliged to share their wealth for humanitarian causes. Buddhism had an international appeal as foreign Kings like Menander (Indo Greek) or Kanishka (Kushan) and other such rulers felt at home with Buddhism as their adopted religion. If Buddhism spread across a large part of the world, it was in recognition of its relevance to the contemporaneous societies; it did not have to move with the help of sword.

### *The Brahmanical Traditions*

The concept of Man in Indian (Brahmanical) tradition has been described in two ways (1) on the basis of *koshas* or sheaths, and (2) on the basis of *sariras* or bodies, as shown in the following chart:

| SCHEME 1 (5 *koshas* or Sheaths from outermost to innermost) | SCHEME 2 (3 Bodies) |
|---|---|
| *Annamaya* (equivalent to the physical body) | *Sthula* (the gross or physical body) |
| *Pranamaya* (the biospherical sheath) | *Sukshma* (the subtle body) |
| *Manomaya* (the psychical sheath) | |
| *Vijnanamaya* (the noospherical sheath) | |
| *Anandamaya* (the core; literally the "blissful") | *Karana* (It is immortal, eternal, unchanging, spiritual, conscious and blissful and the same as the *Atman*) |

Accordingly, the basic constitution of man has an enormous range – from the physical through to the all-powerful Atman, which is the same as the Brahman or the Absolute Reality. Life is an evolutionary process and the purpose of life is to

26 *Anguttara Nikaya* IV.35; *Majjhima Nikaya* XX.

move from the outermost sheath of the physical body (=*Sthulasarira*) to the core, the *Anandamaya* core. Since Man is ultimately linked with the Atman, there exists a divine element in him. Sankara, the great philosopher of the Advaitic School of Vedanta (788 – 820 A.D.), mentions in *Vivekacudamani* (121, 126):

> "There is some entity, eternal by nature, the basis of the experience of egoism, the witness of the three states (of waking, dream and sleep) and distinct from the five sheaths, who knows everything that happens in the waking, dream and sleep states, who is aware of the presence or absence of the mind and its functions; and who is the basis of the notion of egoism".

This is the Atman, the true self of man, which is also the self of the universe, i. e., Brahman or *Purusa* (literally Man). The Brahman has been described as the Omnipotent, Omniscient and Omnipresent and also as *Sat-chit-ananda* (Pure Existence, Intelligence and Bliss). I shall come back to this while discussing the philosophy of Vivekananda.

While Buddhism underwent a decline in India since early Medieval times, the Medieval period was marked by the rise of Bhakti tradition and Sufism after the advent of Islam.

### 2.2.2 The Colonial Period: Modernization of India and Modern Indian Humanism

With the advent of the colonial powers in India, one observes a process of transformation. While the new Western form of education changed the minds and attitudes of many young students, yet others became confused and questioned the virtues of Indian tradition, as certain weaknesses at social and religious levels were exposed. The nineteenth century was the Age of Awakening and marked the beginning of new reforms in an age of modernism. Raja Ram Mohan Roy of Bengal, a key figure of this period, fought against such social evils as the *Sati Pratha* (immolation of widows) and formed the Brahmo Samaj (= society) – a powerful socio-religious movement that maintained a distinctive identity from Hinduism and incorporated the best from the ancient Indian tradition and Christianity.[27] Certainly, such efforts by Roy and later social reformers like Ishvarchandra Vidyasagar (a Hindu), who fought for the remarriage of widows,[28] re-established the lost dignity of women in Bengal. Other key persons of the Brahmo Samaj tradition were Devendra Nath Tagore (father of Rabindra Nath Tagore) and Kesab Chandra Sen. One of the great contributions of the Brahmo Samaj was the education of women at par with men.

27 Joshi,V.C. (Ed.): *Rammohan and the Process of Modernization in India*, Delhi 1975.
28 Sen, Ashok: *Elusive Milestones of Ishwarchandra Vidyasagar*, Calcutta 1977.

Another reform movement during the Age of Awakening has been the Arya Samaj ("Noble Society"), founded by Dayananda in 1875. He emphasized the ideals of *Brahmacharya* (chastity) and *Sanyasa* (renunciation). A believer of the authority of the Vedas, Dayananda was instrumental in the revival of an ancient tradition with many social reforms.[29]

I shall discuss below the views of some of the greatest humanist thinkers of the 19th and early 20th centuries who not only clarified the 'misunderstandings' of Western colonial scholars about India, but also informed the fellow Indians their strength and dignity. Their works could be regarded both as reforms as well as guiding principles for political movements to secure "freedom" from the most mighty colonial power that had a deep and decisive impact on a large number of colonized nations of the world. But as we shall see, the philosophies of many such figures as Ramakrishna, his disciple Vivekananda, Aurobindo, and Tagore had a universal dimension.

*Ramakrishna*

Ramakrishna 'Paramahamsa' (1836–1886), the great mystic saint, occupies, according to V.S. Narvane "the same decisive position in the evolution of Indian thought that Socrates did in the development of Greek consciousness".[30] Both of them dawned at a time when their respective societies were witnessing an age of crisis.

Ramakrishna, whose real name was Gadadhar Chattopadhyaya, was born at Kamarpukur, a small village in the Hooghly district of Bengal, in a family of priests. During his childhood, he was prone to mystic visions. He possessed an unusually powerful sense of beauty and delighted in painting clay images. Ecstasy was the main feature of his childhood days that accompanied his mystic vision. Although he had no schooling, his intellectual equipment was remarkable.

That was the time when Indian society was fragmented into different cults and religions. He saw unity in all religions and himself practiced all the major forms of religion – Islam, Christianity as well as different sects within Hinduism. He believed that all religions ultimately teach one and the same truth. He possessed a store of very powerful similes and metaphors. He said, just as one and the same substance, water for example, is called by different names by different peoples (water, or aqua, or eau), so is one and the same Eternal Reasonable Bliss recognized as Allah by some, God by others, Brahman by still others. He declared (in his mother tongue, Bangla): "*Jatomatatatopatha*", i.e. as many views so many paths – all leading to the same Truth. According to him people who insist that

29 See Jordens, J.T.F.: *Dayananda Saraswati*, Delhi 1978.
30 Narvane, V.S.: *Modern Indian Thought*, Bomaby/New York 1964, p. 59.

only their religion is true, are like the blind men arguing about the appearance of the elephant, as in the well-known parable:

> "Four blind men went to know an elephant. One touched a leg of the elephant and said: 'The elephant is like a pillar'. The second touched the trunk and said: 'The elephant is like a club'. The third touched the belly and said: 'The elephant is like a jar'. The fourth touched the ears and said: 'The elephant is like a big winnowing-basket'".[31]

Pointing out that sectarian strife between different religions was meaningless and harmful, he stressed that God has an infinity of aspects. God is multiform – "He is formless and with form, and many are His forms which no one knows".[32] Being 'formless', He is indivisible existence-intelligence-bliss absolute (the *Sat-chit-ananda*).

Although Ramakrishna has been described as a follower of the Vedanta philosophy, his Vedanta was distinctly different from the previous forms advocated by such philosophers as Samkara ($8^{th}/9^{th}$ century). Ramakrishna could not accept the Advaitic thesis that the visible world and individual souls (viewed as independent entities with regard to the human body) are a set of merely illusory, phenomenal changes. Ramakrishna recognized the reality of the material world (the relative world), regarding it as a manifestation of Brahman (the Absolute). He believed that Brahman is only perceived in a super-conscious state called *samadhi*, when the flow of thought stops and absolute silence reigns in the soul. He said, "He who has realised Brahman, becomes silent".

An interesting point that emerges from his life and philosophy[33] is that knowledge cannot be fixed in space and time. The same truth expressed in ancient scriptures, such as the Vedas, Upanishads, Bhagavadgita and Puranas, can be rediscovered by any body – intellectual or otherwise – at any moment of time so long as one develops a zeal to understand and proper insights through meditation and several other methods. However, a proper study of the scripture is an added benefit, as it happened with Vivekananda, the disciple of Ramakrishna (see below). This fact counters the revivalist approach of the extreme right wing Hinduttva that helped its followers to develop more dogmatism and less insights on the essence of life and philosophy.

The humanistic angle of Ramakrishna's practical philosophy is clear from the fact that he placed his teachings at the service of man. He called on his disciples to serve man, seeing God in him. Each individual soul is immortal and potentially divine. This message was further elaborated by (Swami) Vivekananda.

31 *Memoirs of Ramakrishna*, Calcutta 1957, pp. 23–24.

32 Ibid., p. 25.

33 For an authentic account of the life and philosophy of Ramakrishna, see Rolland, Romain: The *Life of Ramakrishna*, Calcutta 1979. For preaching and parables of Ramakrishna, see Sen, Amiya P.: *His Words*, New Delhi 2010.

*Vivekananda*

Vivekananda (1863 – 1902), whose real name was Narendra Nath Dutta, was born in an educated family of Calcutta and was a brilliant student with a skeptical mind. When the English education began to germinate doubts in his mind about the Indian tradition, he met several Indian thinkers to know whether God at all exists as the tradition claimed. Dissatisfied by their answers and arguments he went to see Ramakrishna who not only convinced him about the existence of God but also changed the course of his life. He was destined to serve the suffering mankind.

Vivekananda reiterated with firm conviction in the First Parliament of Religions in Chicago (1893) what he imbibed from his Master – an enlightened vision which was also an embodiment of ancient philosophical traditions. He clarified many misunderstandings prevalent in the West about Hinduism, but what is so special about him is that he envisioned a radically different understanding of religion. He said that he is an atheist who believes and worships millions of gods but does not believe in himself. Self-belief is important for all individuals as that alone will release them from states of weakness. He declared: "Strength is felicity, weakness death". Being *Amrtasyaputrah* (children of the Immortal), an individual is endowed with all the latent talents that need to be made patent, first through self-belief and then through knowledge (*jnana*) and practice (detached *Karma*). He clearly said that calling a man 'sinner' is a permanent libel on humanity. He said that the powerful word that sprang from the Upanishads like a bomb and blasted like a bombshell was "fearlessness". It was possible for him to realize this also because he practised various forms of meditation to understand a much wider (in fact infinite) dimension of human existence. Work with devotion was very important for him and he said if means were noble, the end would take care of itself. Here one sees the impact of *Bhagavad Gita* where the Lord Krishna emphasized on *Nishkama Karma* (Work without the expectation of results). His active life devoted in the service of fellow human beings, including the poor and the downtrodden, was accomplished within fifteen years (1986 – 2001). Since he accomplished so much on a noble, humanitarian cause in such a short span of time, he was a gainer in the temporal capital. This revolutionary form of religion can hardly be said to go against humanism; on the contrary it complements it in a positive way.

Like his great teacher, Vivekananda realized that all individual souls are potentially divine and hence possess infinite potential to grow. This led to a radically different understanding of education. He defined education as the manifestation of knowledge already in man. He suggested that the role of a teacher or parents is not much greater than a gardener who only creates an incubatory environment for the seedlings and plants. He cannot pull the plant to grow; the capacity to grow is already there. Such dedicated gardeners have often shown more wisdom than a large section of human teachers (including religious teachers) who in the name of education change the direction of a child's natural growth, making him/her perpetually dependent so that it cannot develop self-belief properly. What a child could have grown into a huge Banyan tree, is often converted into bonsai that, though looks tamed and beautiful, does not have any intimidating effect on the authorities. Earlier teachers like the Buddha and Sankara too have emphasized that a student has to develop faculties so that s/he can get over a mediated and dependent kind of survival. Achievement of bliss through growth for Vivekananda is our birth right. If an individual grows, the society grows. So the humanism envisaged by Vivekananda prescribes a total growth for mankind, both men and women; all such actions and thoughts that impede growth are the sources of inhumanity that needs to be checked and discouraged.

It is interesting to note that the famous Indologist F. Max Müller, who did not have an opportunity to visit India, decided to meet Vivekananda in the West to learn about Ramakrishna directly from latter's pupil and a living representative of Indian wisdom.

*Aurobindo*

Aurobindo Ghosh (1872 – 1950), also known as Sri Aurobindo or simply Aurobindo, was a scholar (educated in India and Cambridge, U.K.) as well as a poet, evolutionary philosopher and a Yogi. He had a brief but intense career in politics in the freedom movement. He masterminded a powerful political movement soon after the partition of Bengal (1905) by the British rulers, but he underwent tremendous self-transformation during his period of imprisonment. He involved himself in the practice of a new spiritual path known as the Integral Yoga. The purpose behind this approach was to further the evolution of life by establishing spiritual consciousness (Supermind) that would lead to an eternal, divine life free from the fears of death.

The central point of Aurobindo's philosophical journey is "evolution" that he describes in his magnum opus, *The Life Divine.* Humanity represents a stage of development of mind in complex material forms of life. Evolution is an ongoing process and does not stop with the establishment of reason and intellect. Beyond mind exist higher levels of supra-mental consciousness. These higher levels of consciousness must emerge universally through the stages of evolution. Once they emerge, the earth will witness the appearance of a new species that will once again united in consciousness with *Sat-chit-ananda.* What happens at this stage can be summarized in his own words:

> "A dominant principle of harmony would impose itself on the life of the Ignorance; the discord, the blind seeking, the clash of struggle, the abnormal vicissitudes of ex-

> aggeration and depression and unsteady balance of the unseeing forces at work in their mixture and conflict, would feel the influence and yield place to a more orderly pace and harmonic steps of the development of being, a more revealing arrangement of progressing life and consciousness, a better life-order. A freer play of intuition and sympathy and understanding would enter into human life, a clearer sense of the truth of self and things and a more enlightened dealing with the opportunities and difficulties of existence".[34]

For Aurobindo, the spiritual goal of salvation is not confined to specific individuals or groups; the spirit of salvation should be open for anybody and everybody. In this sense, he seems to have accepted the general Vedantic ideal of *Lokakalyana* (Well-being of all). Herein one finds universalism in his spiritualistic framework.

It may be asked why Aurobindo's ideas, essentially spiritual in nature, should be regarded as a form of humanism. It may be said that his conception of religion and spirituality is not far from human considerations; it is certainly not anti-human. His specific view about life and living derived from a philosophical standpoint can be taken as having a deep human significance.

*Rabindranath Tagore*

Tagore (1861 – 1941), a poet, artist and philosopher of the Brahmo Samaj tradition, drew his inspiration more from nature and the Medieval Saints of India, such as Dadu and Kabir, than ancient religio-philosophical scriptures. The theme of humanism occupies a predominant place in his writings. In *The Religion of Man* he moves away from the traditional notion of religion.[35] For him religion should not be either ritualistic or confined to institutions like temples or churches. The realization of the divine within man is the most significant aspect of his religion. His views about God and religion are grounded in the humanistic persuasion. True religion, according to him, aims at unity of mankind and realization of divinity within.

Describing Tagore's thoughts under aesthetic humanism, V.S. Narvane cites Tagore's statement that God and man find themselves in tune with each other because they are both artists.[36] While the aim of man is to be united with God, it is God, the artist who finds the final fulfillment in mankind. The primary aim for Tagore is to view God as a dynamic immanent force in man, the aim of which should be to realize and thereby to attain enlightenment. His sense of God is not transcendent but very much living within human affairs. The 'sacred' element that is so prominent in theology is absent in Tagore's thought.

---

34 Aurobindo, Sri: *The Life Divine*, Pondicherry 1977, p. 969.

35 Tagore, Rabindranath: *The Religion of Man*, London 1931.

36 Narvane, V.S.: op. cit., chapter 5, pp. 111 – 167.

*M.K. Gandhi*

Mohandas Karamchand Gandhi (1869 – 1948) has been acclaimed as a theist as he imbibed Vaishnavism (a religious sect within Hinduism, centering on Vishnu as the Supreme deity) from family and was a devotee of Lord Rama. But he also appreciated the teachings of Vedanta. Although a spiritualist, he is also considered as a rational humanist for his untiring efforts at human upliftment with an appeal to reason. Gandhi's concept of 'Sarvodaya' which aims at the upliftment of all puts maximum emphasis on man.

Gandhi's aim has been to see man as a disciplined human being causing no harm to another being. The basic concept of *Ahimsa* (non-violence) on the moral plane provides rationalistic basis for the moral conduct of man. According to him there is no need for leaving this world and practicing any higher form of *yoga* for personal salvation. For him the practice of higher human value of causing no deliberate harm to others is important. This noble sense purifies a person and acts as a booster for the realization of God (i. e. feeling oneness with all). *Ahimsa* is not only a means employed for the freedom movement, it is an end in itself as a moral principle to be adopted for a better living.

Gandhi's attempts at removing discrimination amongst the colored peoples of South Africa and abolishing untouchability back home are some of the few remarkable items expressive of his humanistic temper. The five principles he supported as values of life are: truthfulness, celibacy, non-violence, non-stealing and non-hoarding. The absence of any one of these will cause human suffering and misery. His commitment to the eradication of misery of mankind is reflected in his statement that he does not want to be liberated so long all others are not liberated. He wants to take birth again to fight to alleviate human suffering. For Gandhi, *satyagraha* (an insistence on truth that leads to self-purification) is mandatory. It is the truth-force or love-force which is highly significant and can bring about major changes in human life. Gandhi's genius lay in his power to reconcile between spiritual humanism and rational humanism.

### 2.2.3 The Post-Independence Scenario

Under this section, we would study the contributions of M.N. Roy and the Dalit Movements with particular reference to the contributions of B.R. Ambedkar.

*M.N. Roy's Radical Humanism*

Manavendra Nath Roy (1887 – 1954) is one of the most prominent figures who fought all his life to champion the cause of humanism. He formulated his materialistic approach in 22 theses where he attempted to restore the $19^{th}$ century Radicalism and its humanist essence, and hence called his philosophy Radical

Humanism.[37] Roy's approach integrates the scientific attitude and the democratic spirit – democracy is not merely a process, it is a system of values. For the Radical Humanist, the quest for freedom and search for truth constitute the basic urge of human progress. The quest for freedom is the continuation (on a higher level) of intelligence and emotion, as well as of the biological struggle for existence.

The method and program of a social revolution must therefore be based on a reassertion of the basic principles of social progress. Hence, the program of the humanist revolution will be based on the principles of freedom, reason and social harmony. In this way, Radicalism gives to freedom a moral-intellectual as well as social content; and it also offers a comprehensive theory of social progress in which both the dialectics of economic determinism and dynamics of ideas find their due recognition; and it deduces from the same a method and program of social revolution in our time. Radical Humanism provides an approach to the reconstruction of the world as a commonwealth and fraternity of free men, by the collective endeavor of spiritually emancipated moral men.

Roy was not only a declared anti-traditionalist but also openly a rationalist who sought to transcend his own culture. Giving up one's own tradition and developing a rationale towards humanism uncolored by regional or cultural identities, however, placed him in a conflicting world of tension. Ashis Nandy has a point when he ventures to guess that Roy was unwittingly hinting at the "affirmation of traditions and cultural continuities in the face of the homogeneity that the modern world imposes in the name of universalism".[38] An important point about Roy is that he accepted, according to Nandy, "the limitations of the conventional concept of rationality and tried to be true to the full meaning of his own faith – that human reason and morality expressed the harmony of the cosmos".[39]

While Roy opposed the glorification of India's so-called spiritual heritage, he favoured a rational and critical study of ancient Indian philosophy. He thought it might do for India what the rediscovery of ancient Greek thought did for Europe during the Renaissance.

In 1948, he launched the Radical Humanist Movement, a nonpartisan political movement, to make India what he considered a true democracy. He was a founding Vice-President of the International Humanist and Ethical Union (IHEU); the Radical Humanist Movement was one of the original IHEU member organizations. The IHEU has in his honor created the M.N. Roy Human De-

37 Roy, M.N.: *Reason, Romanticism and Revolution*, Calcutta 1955.

38 Nandy, Ashish: *Traditions, Tyranny, and Utopias: Essays in the Politics of Awareness*, New Delhi 1992, p. 95.

39 Ibid., p.126. See Roy, M.N., op.cit., p. 301.

velopment Campus in Mumbai (Bombay).[40] Roy's humanist movement had an influence on a number of later humanists, including V.M. Tarkunde.[41]

*The Dalit Movement and Ambedkar*

A different kind of humanism developed during the post-independence era that did not bother so much about high philosophy; it demanded social justice and legitimate rights of the weaker and neglected sections of the society who were victims of the caste system of the Brahmanical order from very early times. The Dalit (literally downtrodden) movement has had a very long history, but the credit goes to the British rulers who brought a sense of liberty for the marginalized communities. One of the key figures of this movement was Jyotiba Phule who belonged to Mali (a low caste) community of Maharashtra. Pune's Chitpawan Brahmins would not allow any Dalit and backward to join schools. Phule realized that unless the community gets educated, they would not be able to emancipate themselves. So he started a massive work of education by starting various schools in and around Pune. Phule exposed the Brahamnical literature, wrote plays about the exploitation of the farmers and appreciated Christian missionaries for their noble work in school education.

B.R. Ambedkar (1891 – 1956), the major force behind the subsequent Dalit movement, took inspiration from Phule and emphasized the importance of education. But for him education must be rational and reasonable. Throughout his early life he suffered from the prejudices of the higher castes. He was an iconoclast and questioned the very essence of the Hindu Shastras (scriptures). In his letters to Gandhi he says that we should amend the Shastras because they talk of the caste system. Gandhi said that if we challenge the Shastras, the very foundation of Hinduism, then we have no business in calling ourselves Hindu. In fact, this led to a schism between Ambedkar and Gandhi. Ambedkar responded clearly that he was born as a Hindu but would not die as a Hindu.

*Ambedkar was one of the tallest intellectuals of the country.* He was an erudite person of extraordinary caliber and made a major contribution in the drafting of India's Constitution, which highlighted justice, liberty, equality, and fraternity. Secularism constitutes another highlight of modern Indian Constitution.[42]

40 See Nath, Ramendra: *M.N. Roy's New Humanism and Materialism*, Patna 2001.

41 For his life and works, see Rane, M.A. (Ed.): *V.M. Tarkunde 90: A Restless Crusader for Human Freedoms*, Mumbai 2000.

42 See Kashyap, Subhash C.: *Our Constitution: An Introduction to India's Constitution and Constitutional Law*, New Delhi 1994.

## 3. Conclusions

We have discussed the salient features of humanitarian attitudes in three different periods of Indian history – the pre-colonial, the colonial, and the post-independence. If we compare the Indian scenario with Western humanism, certain broad similarities as well as clear differences are apparent. For example, in India although humanitarian concerns have been expressed from time to time in the long period of history, it never manifested in the form of humanism as a movement until recently. We had a glimpse on the philosophical conception of man during the pre-modern period, as well as his aspirations (growth and freedom) and goal of life (liberation). Modernism, introduced during the colonial period, only intensified the overall humanistic thinking of pre-modern times, resulting in drives towards social reforms. The major thinkers and reformers of this period expressed their faith in the creative potential of humans and the dominant Upanishadic/Vedantic view, reiterated with force and conviction by Vivekananda, that man has an enormous potential and an infinite power to grow. This could be described under "creative humanism". This was also the stand taken by a modern Indian philosopher, N.K. Devaraja.[43] However, humanism based on materialistic philosophy (Lokayat, for example) co-existed with above lines of thinking during the ancient period of history.

Humanism as a revolutionary movement materialized with M.N. Roy in post-independence India, although he worked hard to this end from an earlier time. His Radical humanism was in the spirit of Western humanism, but he also questioned the limits of the Western concept of rationality. According to him human reason and morality were reflections of the 'cosmic harmony'. This can be taken to mean that human reason has a far wider range, than assumed, and is part and parcel of a greater cosmic intelligence system. In fact, reason is a function of the concentration of mind, and its range can enlarge in a situation of curiosity, crisis and challenge to understand what lies beyond the immediate sense perception. This distinguishes the levels of rationality of a truth seeking scientist or philosopher, on the one hand, and ordinary human beings, on the other. Unless one has the real desire to know the apparently unknown, a common man can misuse this natural gift (reason) only to reject what he does not like.

While modernism and conventional humanism of past generations considered 'reason' as the most precious gift to mankind that developed to its maximum capacity in the West, Indian intellectuals of all the three periods too highlighted its importance. Advanced Logic constitutes the basis of at least three major philosophical systems, the *Mimamsa*, the *Nyaya* and the *Vaiseshika*, that developed much before the Christian era and continuously refined and sharp-

43 Devaraja, N.K.: *Humanism in Indian Thought*, New Delhi 1988.

ened by commentators in the subsequent periods of history.[44] However, ancient Indian philosophers also pointed out the limits of reason and inform that to know higher realities, one requires other faculties that grow in course of deep meditation. The above study also shows that reason has to be considered in its dynamic/open form and linked with the power of imagination and willingness to understand, rather than for rejecting ideas that lay beyond the limits of reason.

So it is necessary to complement the faculty of reason with other faculties, including imagination, concentration of mind, and compassion, as well as a new positive attitude in order to meet the expectations of true understanding. Another human faculty highlighted in Indian forms of humanism is *Viveka* or conscience that needs to be incorporated in future education system to promote New Humanism.

Certainly, the reasoning power based on inductive and deductive forms of logic differs from individual to individual, as well as from culture to culture. But that should not serve as a limiting factor in New Humanism as it has a new responsibility, like the Buddha, in uplifting the individuals (and their cultures) who have been left behind in the race for progress. But the most important concept that cross-cuts cultural boundaries is the power of concentration – a real gift to mankind, as highlighted by Vivekananda. Once this faculty is developed, there is a hope for every individual, every culture to excel. It can come from detached action as prescribed in the *Bhagavad Gita* and from Yogic meditation.

Unity in difference is an important theme of New Humanism. Of course there is an underlying unity in mankind, but the beauty also lies in the diversity and difference, which has to be understood and appreciated before coming to the shared features. Here it may be suggested that like all organisms in the creation, all cultures have a unique role to play. The 'difference' is beautiful and cultural differences give unique identities to these cultures that could be used for mutual benefit. This part is *crucial to the question of New Humanism* and this will equip us in a better way to appreciate the fundamental unity of mankind.

44 Hiriyanna, M.: *Outlines of Indian Philosophy*, Delhi 1994, chapters X and XII.

Jörn Rüsen

# Classical Humanism – a Historical Survey

Why? Who? Where am I? For happiness.
A human being. On earth.

G.E. Lessing[1]

## 1. What is "Classical Humanism"?

Nowhere does there exist a culture in which some idea of what it means to be human does not play an important part in the way human beings make sense of and regulate their everyday lives. 'Humanity' is a concept that (among others) has come to designate one of the manifestations of such an idea. Humanism, in turn, gives a specific meaning to this with regard to the way individuals as well as social life is made meaningful. These terms are anything but clear. They rather cover a broad spectrum of meanings that the manner in which human beings live their lives has assumed for the practical purpose of providing some cultural orientation.[2]

This spectrum is demarcated by its two extremes: On one side *humanity* comprises the notion of everything men have in common as members of the species if *homo sapiens*. This common ground is less concerned with the natural equipment of the genre than with the cultural features humans share in terms of their various lifestyles. What is implied by this is that human beings invariably evolve meaningful operations for ordering their lives. 'Humanity' in a general sense defines the essence of being human as culturally determined. On the other hand this definition is confined to a specific form of this culturally defined essence, which in its turn concerns some central element of its array of norms. The term 'humanity' thereby acquires a decidedly normative connotation besides its empirical one. It grounds human existence in a few fundamentals, i. e. with reference to its specific relation with nature and the cosmos, which regu-

1 Lessing, Gotthold Ephraim: "Die Religion", in: *Werke*, vol. 1: *Gedichte, Fabeln, Lustspiele*, Darmstadt 1996, p. 171.

2 Cf. e. g. Giustiniani, Vito R.: "Homo, Humanus, and the Message of 'Humanism'", in: *Journal of the History of Ideas* 46.2 (1985): p. 167 – 195.

lates the way humans are dealing with each other. The cultural nature of being human in its most extreme form amounts to the constant choice of human action and suffering between inhumanity and humanity.

The most pronounced form of this interpretation of humanity is called 'humanism'. It is my concern in the following to make this specific variety visible and understandable in the context of its historical background. In doing so I am merging human beings with a more specific one, i. e., that of humanism as it has manifested itself in Western culture.

I regard the 'classical humanism' of the late 18th and 19th centuries as the most central manifestation of this. We are dealing here with a universal tendency that appeared in all of Europe, which however took on a different form in its various regional contexts. Tzvetan Todorov has expounded the French variety of this in a most impressive way.[3] I am therefore focusing on the German one, which inseparably connected with the names of Herder and Humboldt.[4]

In looking back from today's perspective this latter type of humanism can be understood as a constellation of intellectual tropes and a 'logic' of argumentation, that comprises and interconnects the most diverse aspects of cultural orientation.

The intellectual precondition for this constellation is formed by the anthropology of early modern history. Here, for the first time, the interpretation of man and the world is no longer grounded in a non-human authority of meaning-making (God or Nature) but is referring only to mankind itself as the ultimate goal. This has been aptly expressed by Kant in his famous formula whereby the three fundamental questions of philosophy, which also form the general guideline for the cultural orientation of human beings, – what can I know?, what must I do?, What can I hope? – converge into the one question: what is man?[5]

3 Todorov, Tzvetan: *Imperfect garden. The legacy of humanism*, Princeton 2002.

4 This historically specific definition of the term 'humanism', is not the dominant one in the international literature on the subject. In this context the term is meant in the sense of a philosophical dorm of discourse that is typical of early modern humanism, i. e. the way in which in those days the '*humanistas*' (people educated in classical antiquity) cultivated the '*humaniora*' (the intellectual disciplines in which the classical antiquity was researched and debated) in term of their critical distance from the discursive logic of scholasticism and its ties with ecclesiastical dogmatism. From this a more general intellectual attitude towards life can be distilled. An exemplar of this is Edward Said's definition of humanism as the liberal, open-minded and critical attitude of the humanities ("as open to all classes and backgrounds, and as a process of unending discourse, discovery, self-criticism, and liberation", *Humanism and Democratic Criticism*, New York 2004, p. 28 f.). In this definition humanism loses its historical specifity and becomes the stylized formula of intellectual liberalism – beyond all its concrete manifestations that are due to particular historical circumstances.

5 Kant, Immanuel: *Kritik der reinen Vernunft* 1781, 2nd ed. 1787, A 805, (*Werke* in 10 vols, ed. Wilhelm Weischedel, vol. 4, Darmstadt 1968, p. 677; Kant: *Logik* A. 26, (*Werke* in 10 vols, ed. Wilhelm Weischedel, vol. 5, Darmstadt 1968, p. 448).

This recourse to mankind itself as the sole source for the cultural definition of what it is to be human only becomes humanist in the truest sense if and when human beings are accorded specific value as a kind of anthropological principle, and if thereby being human acquires the status of an absolute norm when it comes to regulating any human practice.

Humanism in its modern form infuses the empirical dimension of human experience with a normative element. Immanuel Kant has formulated this in its most definite form:

> "...Man regarded as a person, i. e. a subject with a moral and practical reason, is exalted beyond anything, because in that capacity (*homo noumenon*) he is not just to be valued for achieving other people's or his own ends, but as an end in itself, i. e. he is possessed of a dignity (an absolute inner worth) whereby he deserves to be respected by all other rational beings, thus can measure up to all others of this kind and be on an equal footing with them."[6]

In classical humanism 'mankind' is held to be the ultimate criterion of any operation of creating meaning and as such is conceived of as applying universally both in an empirical sense (encompassing all of humanity existing in space and time) as well as in a normative one (ascribing to every subject the dignity of being its own end).

This criterion of meaning is also brought into play as the fundamental *criterion of legitimating* political rule. In humanism understood as a political variety the legal foundation of the state are formed by human and civil rights. This universalism is at the same time a universal *historicism*; as a principle man and world are interpreted and understood in historical terms.

For each human being and for the particular manner in which it conceives its life this kind of humanism takes on a specific form: that of *individuality.*

The universal as well as individualized quality of being human is only conceptualized as an anthropological potential; its realization is conditional upon being implemented via an individual process that at the same time has a social dimension. This process can be categorized under the heading of '*education*' (German '*Bildung*').

All these features are the essentials that characterize modern humanism as an intellectual construct. But this is more than just a mere idea. It has already become institutionalized in the life form of bourgeois civil society. The conviction that every religious belief in its various historical manifestations and its divergence from other beliefs can be integrated into a secular social order obliging all religious to coexist peacefully, ('*tolerance*') is an indispensable aspect of this form of life.

6 Kant: *Metaphysik der Sitten* A 93, (*Werke* in 10 vols, ed. Wilhelm Weischedel, vol. 7, Darmstadt 1968, p. 569).

The humanities are conceived by humanism as an organized system of interpretations that can lay claim to a degree of universal validity. Human and civil rights, as enshrined in modern constitutions, can be regarded as the most powerful institution of modern humanism, not least of all because of the claim to this universal validity.

In the following I am proposing to interpret this concept of humanism in a historical perspective, i. e. I would like to position it within the temporal scheme in which the current process of globalization has to be assessed.

## 2. Anthropological Premises

Any concept of what it means to be human[7] is determined by the fundamental difference existing between human and non-human creatures. In most of human life-forms the non-human qualities are distributed among two dimensions: the natural and the divine. Man is located somewhere in between – his place is where the two dimensions (natural, divine and human) are hierarchically ordered: the highest value is attributed to the divine world, the lowest to nature, and man who occupies the middle ground, is marked by the 'intermediate' quality of being capable of distinguishing between good evil, of even being compelled to do so. The quality of differentiate between good and evil – something that is unique to him – plus the resulting necessity of having to make practical choices under the term of his divine as well as natural attributes. The moral rules determining human behavior are defined by a clear-out distinction between good and evil. The ability to make such a distinction presupposed a certain idea of what it means to be human: human beings are defined as persons, they are individuals possessed of certain physical and psychological consistency, and as such they are responsible for their actions, at least as far as the sphere of their everyday lives is concerned. This responsibility endows every human being (to use the current diction) with the quality of dignity, which in turn demands that it should meet with respect and recognition in social contexts. The notion of human dignity is also connected with another human faculty that constitutes an anthropological universal, i. e. of changing one's own perspective of cognition and interpretation

7 For the following cf.: Antweiler, Christoph: *Was ist den Menschen gemeinsam? Über Kultur und Kulturen*, Darmstadt, 2nd ed. 2009; Antweiler, Christoph: *Mensch und Weltkultur. Für einen realistischen Kosmopolitismus im Zeitalter der Globalisierung* (= Der Mensch im Netz der Kulturen – Humanismus in der Epoche der Globalisierung, vol. 10) Bielefeld 2011. (English translation: *Inclusive Humanism. Anthropological Basics for a Realistic Cosmopolitanism*, Göttingen 2012).

by adopting that of another person. The dignity of man is anthropologically rooted in his discretion between good and evil plus the capacity for empathy.[8]

As regards its social dimension human life is anthropologically determined by a system of binary distinctions.[9] I am schematically listing them as follows:

- The distinction between up and down in social hierarchies
- The distinction between power and the lack of power
- The distinction between central and marginal places of cultural relevance
- The distinction between master and slave defining social inequality
- The distinction between man and woman that makes gender into a fundamental social category
- The distinction between old and young that goes beyond the merely biological difference, thereby defining social status and generating educational processes
- The distinction between having to die and the ability to kill
- The distinction between friend and foe that, in conjunction with the above-mentioned, regulates the use of power and force in social life, both in terms of its internal and external relations
- The distinction between interior and exterior, i. e. between a group of people with a sense of belonging together and with whom one forms a community – that means a collective identity with strong emotional and cognitive ties – on the one hand and those people whom one regards and treats and treats as the 'others' or 'strangers' on the other.

The last-mentioned distinction plays an important part in the historical development of mankind because it concerns a profound layer of human subjectivity and the formation of identity taking place at that level, which is of primary relevance for the idea of humanism. The relationship between one's social self and the otherness of the other is determined by an elementary as well as universal logic of differentiation: it is the logic of ethnocentric discrimination and, at the same time, of hospitality towards strangers. The cultural effort required in order to develop the sentiment of hospitality in the face of the quasi-natural aversion to what is different or strange, forcefully demonstrates the strength of the ethnocentrism that is at work in determining of cultural identity. In ethnocentrism the image of one's self is drawn exclusively in the shape and colour of positive values, which enable human beings to develop a sense of social cohesion as well as an affirmative attitude both to themselves and all the others belonging

8 This corresponds to certain norms of moral behavior whose status is equally universal: fairness in competition and a cooperative organization of labor.

9 The following reflections take up ideas propounded by Reinhart Kosellek: Koselleck, Reinhart: "Historik und Hermeneutik", in: Koselleck, Reinhart: *Zeitschichten. Studien zur Historik*, Frankfurt/Main 2000, p. 97 – 118.

to the same life form – something which is of vital importance. The otherness or alterity of those existing outside of this life form is, by the same logic, defined in terms of the lack, or at least the reduction of all those positive values in the alien life form. The most striking example of such a discriminatory mind-set is the distinction between civilisation and barbarity.[10]

## 3. Historical Change

It would be tempting to set these anthropological universals as the essential features of all life forms over against historical change. Such a facile opposition would prevent any deeper understanding of the changeability of human culture; which does not run counter to the anthropological universals but takes place inside these. They even permit us to determine the directedness of those changes in human life forms that usually foes by the name of 'history'. History is much more than arbitrary or accidental change. In terms of its quality as a process of development it is structured. This process derives its force from the continual attempts on the part of humans to achieve an acceptable balance among the distinctions listed above – distinctions which are also oppositions, and as such they are constantly generating tensions. Human life is driven onwards by the permanent struggle to overcome the destructive forces, "the anti-social sociability" (Kant), inherent in any social organisation, which are caused by the tensions generated between the alternatives that have been mentioned. In all social conflicts and struggles the ideal of a life form acceptable to all acts as the fundamental driving force of human social behaviour.

Which evolutionary tendency can one assume to be the most likely outcome of such an internal dynamics, or as one can also formulate it, of the historicity of human life? The only possibility of finding an answer to this question that is logically convincing consists in matching up present experience and future expectations and then look backwards at the experience of the temporal change humans and their world have undergone and then to explore the conditions of possibility for realizing the future as desired.[11] Two essential aspects of historical thinking have to be borne in mind.

When one proceeds in this manner: firstly the global dimension of human

10 The logic of ethnocentrism is dealt with more extensively in: Rüsen, Jörn: "How to Overcome Ethnocentrism: Approaches to a Culture of Recognition by History in the 21st Century", in: *Taiwan Journal of East Asian Studies* 1.1 (June 2004): 59 – 74; and in: *History and Theory* 43 (2004), Theme Issue "Historians and Ethics": 118 – 129.

11 The logic underlying historical thinking briefly outlined here is that of a reconstruction with a future orientation. It is an alternative to the long time prevailing but no longer plausible logic of a teleology that is grounded in same origin.

interaction, which these days makes the abstract collective concept of 'mankind' appears as a empirical fact, and secondly the requirement of establishing a viable coexistence between diverse traditions and ideas of being human. In accordance with this one can expect the future historical development to comprise essential processes of universalization, just as much as a tendency of emphasizing the difference as well as the interconnectedness between one's own self and he others.

Three essential stages in human development or cultural evolution can be differentiated:

1) Archaic forms of life where most, if not all, qualities of being human are based on kinship relations to the extent that all others with whom one is not connected by blood-ties are not regarded as human.
2) Life forms of a higher social complexity, in which the ethnic borders of being human are inevitably transgressed (as was the case in large empires). It is possible – as also happens here – to designate the step towards this type of universality by the term "axial time" ("Achsenzeit"), following suggestions made by Jaspers, Eisenstadt and other.[12] The universalizing tendencies resulting from axial times have manifested themselves in diverse cultures and independently of one another, quite literally 'side by side'.
3) The human life form within the system of "multiple modernities"[13], where the mental forms of cultural difference that have evolved are, or better: have to be, reconciled with the new form of an integrating universalism.

## 4. Archaic Societies

In archaic societies only members of the own community qualifies as human beings. All other people living outside their own sphere of life are not regarded as human; these are seen to be lacking in the essential features that define their own humanity.[14] This is made evident by the simple fact that a lot of the names that people living in such conditions give themselves testify to such a particularity:

12 Jaspers, Karl: *Vom Ursprung und Ziel der Geschichte*, Munich 1963 (first Zürich 1949); Eisenstadt, Shmuel N. (Ed.): *Kulturen der Achsenzeit. Ihre Ursprünge und ihre Vielfalt*, vol. I, II, III, Frankfurt/Main 1987, 1987, 1992; Arnason, Johann P./Eisenstadt, S.N./Wittrock, Björn (Eds.): *Axial Civilisations and World History*, Leiden 2005.

13 Eisenstadt, S.N.: "Multiple Modernities", in: *Daedalus* 129.1 (Winter 2000): 1 – 30; ibid.: *Die großen Revolutionen und die Kulturen der Moderne*, Wiesbaden 2006.

14 In order to designate this exclusive as well as particular universality of being human in archaic societies Klaus Müller has coined the fitting term "absoluteness of one's own world". (Müller, Klaus E. (Ed.): *Menschenbilder früher Gesellschaften. Ethnologische Studien zum Verhältnis von Mensch und Natur*, Frankfurt/Main 1983, p. 15).

one calls oneself 'man'. Names like 'Bantu', 'Khoikhoi', 'Apache' and numerous others have this meaning.

The cultural rules of these life forms are based on the one fundamental imperative of maintaining the tradition and perpetuating it under all circumstances in order to inculcate it in the minds and hearts of the people. Social relations are dominated by the principle of mutuality. There is a double standard: on the one hand the principles of how one treats one's own people prescribing mutuality, on the other hand the exploitation and subjection of the others, the strangers. Nothing proves this more strikingly than the fact cannibalism is a wide-spread strategy of forcibly acquiring the vital and mental power of the others.

## 5. Cultural Change in Axial Times

Following Karl Jaspers, the term 'axial time' designates a marked change of human life forms. It coincides with the emergence of the so-called 'high cultures'. As opposed to Jaspers I am not using this concept in the sense of a rigid chronological ascription of a turn-around that is valid across all cultures, but in due consideration of cultural differences (especially with regards to chronology) rather in the sense of an evolutionary boost of culture. Such boosts have not taken place across different cultures all at the same time, but their effect of causing a restructuring of the cultural organization of human life has been similar (in the sense of comparable) throughout. 'Axial time' is a time when a new understanding of man and his world emerges and manages to prevail (with long-term consequences as in the form of so-called 'world cultures' or 'civilisation').[15]

Three fundamental areas in which this manifests itself can be categorized: the (human) 'self', the (extra-human) 'world' and the (supra-human) 'God' (or The Divine). In consideration of this dual transcendency mankind became historically constituted as a non-natural, cultural category.

The new understanding of the 'human-ness' of humans evolved on the basis of the categories is brought about by a "transcendental breakthrough" (Eisenstadt) which causes profound changes in the fundamental categories that make up the human world and the conception humanity has of itself. This change mainly consists in the divine world acquiring a new (i. e. a "transcendental") quality removed from the reality of the world in which human beings are acting out their

15 Cf.: Eisenstadt, Shmuel N.: "Die Achsenzeit in der Weltgeschichte", in: ibid.: *Theorie und Moderne. Soziologische Essays*, Wiesbaden 2006, pp. 253 – 275, and in: Joas, Hans/Wiegandt, Klaus (Eds.): *Die kulturellen Werte Europas*, 4th ed., Frankfurt/Main 2006, pp. 40 – 68.

lives. To be more precise in philosophical terms one should actually say "transcendant" instead of "transcendental". The Divine assumes a form of existence that sets it apart from that of everyday life which thereby becomes utterly mundane. Those areas that in an archaic form of life were still closely interrelated now become separate units, and it is through their new character as a kind of intermediate, so to speak.

The new quality of being human can be defined as a heightened sense of subjectivity. This means that the added value of the beyond implicit in the idea of transcendence is now thought to inhere in mankind itself, thus marking out being human as a subjectivity whose meaning is derived solely from itself. In this sense the Jewish prophecy can be regarded as a paradigmatic example of how the world is located on one and the individual on the other side, separate from each other and related in an entirely new fashion. The human self is now thought to be contained within the 'heart' of each person. It thereby establishes a personal, even individual relationship vis-à-vis the divine world.[16] In a reversed perspective (in which the human appears in the light of the divine) man can then – as is the case in Judaism and Christianity – be defined as having been created in God's image.

Confucianism conceptualized this new subjectivity as 'ren', which in English is mostly translated as 'benevolence'. In German the term 'Menschlichkeit' seems to be an equivalent.[17] Ethical principles of universal validity, which can be summarized under the concept of Chinese humanism,[18] because integrated into the traditional world order and its ritual practices. This type of humanism caused the way the world was ordered to become more aligned with rational arguments than ever before.[19]

From now on the ethnic limits of being human were capable of being transgressed in the direction of new universality of mankind. The transcendental status of the source of all divine meaning leads to a new concept of mankind. This does not imply that the old ethnic limits had disappeared altogether (if that

16 The vocation of Jesaia is an impressive example of this: Jes. 6, 1 – 13.

17 See Chen, Yunquzan: "The Spirit of Renwen ('Humanism') in the Traditional Culture of China", in: Rüsen, Jörn/Laass, Henner (Eds.): *Humanism in Intercultural Perspective. Experiences and Expectations*, Bielefeld 2009, p. 56. Chen speaks from "the idea of regarding the people as the center, paying attention to their dignity and value…" (p. 49). See also Mittag, Achim: "Reconsidering *Ren* as a Basic Concept of Chinese Humanism", in: Meinert, Carmen (Ed.): *Traces of Humanism in China – Tradition and Modernity*, Bielefeld 2010, pp. 49 – 62.

18 Cf. numerous references in Chan, Wing-Tsit (Ed.): *A Source Book in Chinese Philosophy*, Princeton 1963, pp. 3 – 48; Meinert, Carmen (Ed.): *Traces of Humanism in China – Tradition and Modernity*, Bielefeld 2010.

19 Cf. Roetz, Heiner: *Die chinesische Ethik der Achsenzeit. Eine Rekonstruktion unter dem Aspekt des Durchbruchs zu postkonventionellem Denken*, Frankfurt/Main; ibid.: *Confucian ethics of the axial age*, Albany 1993.

is possible at all) but that they were accorded a new status with the area of collective identity. The others now also became human. This universalizing process finds its expression in the all-encompassing dimension of the divine world (Brahma, Jahve, Allah, God etc.). Independent of all social, political or gendered delimitations the individual gained an immediate access to, or an immediate encounter with, this universal and extra-mundane deity. This is neatly expressed in the words of Paulus: "Here is neither Jew nor Greek, neither bond nor free, there is neither male nor female: for ye are all one on Christ Jesus."[20] This universality of mankind extended to any single human being and could be claimed by it. It thereby became possible to (which is explicit in Judaism and Islam) that killing one single human being amounted to killing all of mankind.[21]

The power of ethnocentrism in the sense of its old and narrow ethnic definition of being human had been broken; this, however, did not cause it to disappear altogether but it reappeared in a new guise on the level of a generalized concept of humanity: Cultural identity that derived from this universality was able to lay claim to essentializing privilege of representing a 'civilized' concept of mankind, whereas the otherness of the others was conceived in terms of an only reduced form of humanity, i. e. a deficiency of 'true humanity'. And since the others follow the same logic in formulating their self-image, a "clash of civilizations" is the bitter consequence of competing ideas of humanity.

## 6. Steps towards Modernity

The new concept of man evolved during axial time has laid the foundation for the emergence of two new factors that have proved to be decisive for the latest epoch in the development of humanity: scientific rationality and the secular (i. e. not defined and legitimated in religious terms) ordering social life. The natural sciences and later also the humanities and social sciences were instrumental in demystifying the natural as well as the human world. This applied in an equal measure to the fundamental rules of social life and the concomitant rise of democracy as the organizing principle rule. This new culture of a secular civil society and in the concept of humanity it is based on finds its adequate expression in Kant's formulation that every human being is an end in itself and never only a means for the ends of other people, because of which it is endowed with an inalienable dignity. This dignity became institutionalized in the human

20 Letter to the Galatians 3, 28 (Authorized King James Version).
21 Thus in the Koran 5, 32 with reference to a Jewish saying.

and civil rights that formed the basis on which the political constitution of the newly formed modern societies was grounded.

It was in this secularized civil society that modern humanism emerged as the foundation of all cultural orientation. In its specific manifestation (briefly summarized above) it is the outcome of a long-term development in the history of Western civilization during the modern epoch. In the following paragraphs I wish to delineate this development in the form of a complex typology of various main trends in history.[22]

## 7. The Humanization of Mankind in Modern European History

The dawning of the Modern Age was marked by the appearance of various new tracts in philosophy and theology concerning 'mankind as such', its dignity, its risks as well as its potential. Giovanni Pico della Mirandola's *Oratio de hominis dignitate* (*Treatise on the Dignity of Man*) of 1486/87 became famous in this context.[23] In the early 17th century the term "anthropology" was also created. The Modern Age, however, is additionally marked by the concept of humanity becoming a matter of much controversy, which resulted in the various reflections upon its nature becoming more and more plural and divergent. In the 17th century the discipline of theology, which initially held the monopoly on defining what man is like, was superseded by philosophy , with which in turn the anthropological discourse of jurisprudence, medicine and the new sciences were competing. But the level of theoretical reflection aside, it was also in the field of cultural practice itself that changes in the concept of man occurred: in the religious, political and social areas of activity; since the 17th century in literature and the visual arts, which had become increasingly autonomous; finally in technology, which, based on scientific insights, became more and more dominant in everyday life and which gave rise to the human type of *homo faber*, of man thinking only in terms of what is technically feasible. In addition the concept of mankind was greatly influenced by the changes in people's material lives that were due to the advances in technology and later in industrial production, i. e. the successful fight against hunger, illness, infant mortality etc. as well as the growth in population resulting from this plus its consequences of migration and the colonial expansion of Europe.

The modern understanding of mankind rests on endowing the traditional

22 This description is based on the relevant remarks in the Enzyklopädie der Neuzeit: Rüsen, Jörn/Jordan, Stefan: "Mensch, Menschheit", in: Jaeger, Friedrich (Ed.): *Enzyklopädie der Neuzeit*, vol. 8: *Manufaktur-Naturgeschichte*, Stuttgart 2008, pp. 327 – 340.

23 Pico della Mirandola, Giovanni: *Oratio de hominis dignitate. Rede über die Würde des Menschen*, Latin-German, ed. and transl. by Gert von der Gönna, Stuttgart 1997.

grounding of humanity some transcendental authority with a new human quality, i.e. to transfer the spiritual quality implicit in this authority to the idea of man himself.[24] This process is of a universal historical relevance which can only be compared to the revolutionary changes in the concept of mankind during axial times: One could define this modern process as the *humanization of mankind*, however, without at the same time assuming that this – in the sense of moral progress – amount to the disappearance of inhumanity. 'Humanization' rather refers to a change in the understanding mankind has of itself, which process can be concretized and differentiated as: 1) secularization, 2) universalization, 3) naturalization, 4) idealization, 5) historicization, 6) individualization.

### a) Secularization

In the Modern Age the autonomy of a mankind acting as its own authority conflicted with the religious precepts of cultural orientation. The traditional Christian doctrine of salvation and its religious interpretation of the world was incapable of keeping pace with the ever increasing stock of knowledge provided by the sciences and the humanities. In the 17th century the traditional interpretation of the world became differentiated into various areas of knowledge in which empirical explanations without any reference to a transcendental authority became increasingly relevant for humanity's perception of itself. The most striking example of this is the Copernican turn in the sciences, which can be regarded as a philosophical-scientific revolution directed against the ancient geocentric world picture of what was 'natural' as sanctioned by the Christian Church.

The return back to classical antiquity was of decisive importance for this process of secularization. Ever since the Renaissance and the humanist movements associated with this it has played a vital role in forming the intellectual self-concept of the educated classes all over Europe.[25]

Without completely falling into oblivion as a source of meaning, the Christian religion, however, list its interpretative authority with regard to providing some orientation in the here and now. Morally and intellectually discredited through various religiously motivated civil wars, the Christian churches in the 17th century were submitted to a critique of religion, as a consequence of which the

24 Van Dülmen, Richard (Ed.): *Entdeckung des Ich. Die Geschichte der Individualisierung vom Mittelalter bis zur Gegenwart*, Cologne 2001.

25 Cf. Cancik, Hubert: "Die Rezeption der Antike – Kleine Geschichte des europäischen Humanismus", in: Rüsen, Jörn/Laass, Henner (Eds.): *Interkultureller Humanismus. Menschlichkeit in der Vielfalt der Kulturen*, Schwalbach/Taunus 2009, pp. 24–52.

subjectivity of Modern Man that had previously been grounded in the Christian religion was now solely defined in secular terms. Religious truth claims that had found their expression in various denominations ('positive' articulations of faith) were replaced with a universally human morality whose bases was formed by the law of reason (e.g. in G.E. Lessing's philosophical drama "Nathan der Weise" of 1779 with its "Parable of the ring").

With this morality secular cultural orientation of human life came into existence that derived its authority from civil society. In this context religious faith was conceived as a merely private matter because of the fundamental rule of tolerance. Due to the influence of the Enlightenment a secular understanding of man as a being that can freely dispose of his world in accordance with the precepts of reason became the very cultural foundation of modern civil society.

### b) Universalization

With the increased knowledge supplied by human and natural sciences the idea of the unity of the human race had to be reconsidered. In racial theory it was therefore possible to abandon the Unitarian concept altogether, e.g. in I. La-Peyrère, Voltaire, E. Long or Ch. Meiners.[26] In the end, however, the acknowledgement of the monogenetic unity of mankind prevailed against the idea of its polygeny.[27] This general frame of what humans have in common was the filled in with the ever increasing knowledge of the multiplicity of the cultural forms human life is capable of talking on. Especially travelogues played an important role in this process because with their description of the ways of human existence in areas of the world previously unknown of they manages to question the global claim to universality on the part of *homo europaeicus*. On the one hand the concept of humanity had to be adapted to the rapidly increasing knowledge the world that had been accumulated ever since the early Modern Age, on the other hand the newly gained knowledge had to be integrated into the task of drawing a generalizing picture of humanity that was up-to-date.

The interpretation of cultural difference continued to be governed by the typical assumption that all men were naturally endowed with the capacity to

26 La Peyrère, I.: *Prae-Adamitae*, 1655 (Reprint: Kessinger Publishing 2009); Voltaire: *Essai sur les moeurs et l'esprit des nations et sur les principaus faits de l'histoire depuis Charlemagne jusqu'a Louis XIII*, 1756 (repr.: Paris 1963, 2 vols.); Long, E.: *History of Jamaica*, 1774 (new print New York 2009); Meiners, Ch.: *Grundriß der Geschichte der Menschheit*, Lemgo 1785.

27 The anthropology of Johann Friedrich Blumenbach was typical of this as well as highly influential in discursive terms. (*De generis humani varietate nativa liber*, Göttingen 1775). On the cultural and historical context cf. Reill, Peter Hanns: *Vitalising nature in the Enlightenment*, Berkeley 2005.

freely as well as rationally choose their cultural identity. This assumption became part of political culture in the form of codified human rights that went back to a long-standing debate on natural rights. The history of this culture extends from the modern democratic constitutions, which were still confined to single nations, all the way to the "General Declaration of Human Rights" by the United Nations in 1948, which included all of mankind.

This amounted to a break-away from the ethnocentric asymmetry of the way in which cultural identity was constituted, and where inclusion or exclusion were charged with different positive or negative values. Even though the Western cultures claimed to process higher civilizatory standards than other cultures, the legitimization of exploitation and suppression that went along with this was clearly limited – at least on level of theological, philosophical, legal and moral reflection. In attributing also to the 'others' certain human qualities by including them in the human race, their barbaric treatment was (in the name of a higher civilization) laid open to critique in the light of minimal human standards and in the name of a higher kind of civilization, which in turn meant that it could be limited by legal means.

The political rule men over men thus became restricted in theoretical terms, and its legitimacy was premised upon the essential freedom of every individual subjected to such rule. This implied a fundamental claim to participation in political rule. The modern humanization of man had its political apogee, especially in Europe and the USA, in the evolution of constitutionally enshrined and sanctioned human and civil rights that is continuing until now.

Since human rights by definition were derived from and pertained to the entire human race, they could also be claimed for such individuals that, either on account of actual unfreedom (e.g. in the case of suppression) or the actual lack of some of the basic defining element of humanity (e.g. of reason in the case of small children or the mentally handicapped or of morality in the case of social deviants), did not come up to the standard definition of a free, reasonable and ethical human being. In the meantime the modern process of regulating political rule and social life by constitutional means that began in Western Europe and the USA has become globalized to some degree.

### c) Naturalization

Ever since the beginning of the Modern Age man discovered himself in terms of the sharp contrast and the dialectical mediation between his status as a natural and an intellectual creature all at the same time: On the one hand he thus became a thing, i.e. a corporeal object of rational analysis and, based on this, of technological domination and manipulation. On the other hand he became the very master of domination and manipulation. This distinction is due to the fact that man studying himself can never describe himself as such, but always in relational terms only: because of his natural qualities as an animal and because of his spiritual ones as a being related to God. Man thus was divided into an object of scientific observation on the one and a spiritual being on the other hand.

René Descartes expressed this dichotomy in man's relationship to himself and the world in a highly momentous formula by differentiating between "res cognitas" - an exclusively intellectual substance or a non-corporeal spirit - and "res externa" - a mere piece of matter. As *res extensia* man was considered to be on an equal footing with the material objects of the world, especially the non-thinking ones, and thus could be made the object of scientific research.[28]

The scientific dimension the reflection upon mankind had acquired through this can be seen as a special aspect of the process of naturalization and rationalization. Science became spit up into a variety of specialized disciplines. Until the late 18th century this resulted in a relatively rigid distinction between a purely scientific observation of mankind (e.g. in biology and anatomy) and its interpretation in the humanities (especially in philosophy and theology). Towards the end of the 18th century both approaches were conjoined in the form of a comprehensive philosophy of life. The spirit that belonged exclusively to man was now conceived as a natural drive or force which transformed and completed itself in the guise of moulding the human world (e.g. in J.F. Blumenbach and J.G. Herder). Classical humanism, - e.g. as propounded by Herder or the two Humboldt brothers, but especially by Goethe - was the attempt to reconnect human culture, which had been created by the non-material spirit, with material nature, thereby imparting to the latter a 'humane' dimension that was replete with normative meaning.

Since the middle of the 19th century new areas of science came into existence at the interface between the natural and cultural concepts of humanity with new methodological approaches, especially of an analytical nature, such as ethnology, psychology, psychiatry and sociology. Due to the specific focus of these disciplines the understanding of human life forms was extended to become a more comprehensive, even if specialized and methodologically heterogeneous study of the human sciences that far exceeded the old humanities with their paradigm of textual interpretation.

28 Descartes, R.: *Meditationes de prima philosophia. Meditationen über die erste Philosophie.* (Latin/German, ed. v. Gerhart Schmidt), Stuttgart 1985.

### d) Idealization

Concomitant and in a complex interchange with the naturalizing view of humanity the historical tendency of idealization evolved in the course of which the concept of human nature assumed a distinctly spiritual character. In the process the religious tradition of man being made in God's image mutated to become a secular, worldly divinity of man; it was characterized by term such as 'spirituality', 'good sense' (as opposed to reason) and 'person'. As early as the 15th century neoplatonic thinkers like Nicolaus Cusanus and Marsilus Ficino saw the human being as an artist, an "alter deus", who is capable of issuing forth the divine in nature, and thereby also in human nature.

In the early 16th century artists like Leonardo da Vinci and Albrecht Dürer created their works in accordance with this. Man now was not only regarded as the reified object of analysis and rational explanation (and consequently as dominated by technology), but at same he figured as their subject in the role of "maître et possesseur de la nature" (Descartes).[29] Even the human being reified as a vivisected corpse and as a source of scientific insight became an object of aesthetic fascination, especially the act of vivisection itself, e.g. in Rembrandt's "The anatonmy of Dr. Tulp" (1632). Leonardo, who himself conducted the vivisection of corpses, represented the human figure as a spiritual object of the highest order. The most comprehensive explanation and explication of this spiritualization of man as a natural being was supplied by German idealism.

The most important historical precondition for this anthropological concept of a moral personality was the idea of man being made in the image of God plus the religious practice – above all in Protestantism – of a direct as well as personal relationship with God. "Standing before God" now became part of humanity's concept of itself. Thus e.g. Dürer gave Christ-like traits to his self-portrait of 1500. This interiorization of the relationship with God on the part of the individual subject led to an idea of human subjectivity which is marked by the freedom of conscience and self-responsible action. Man now becomes aware of his ability to sink to the status of an animal or ascend to God-like spheres by means of his very actions. The cultural autonomy of mankind resulting from this act of religious emancipation with regard to determining itself and its world was succinctly expressed by G. Pico della Mirandola (1486), when, on the occasion of his creation of the world, he has God saying to humanity: "The limited nature of the others is circumscribed by the laws that I passed. Unfettered by any con-

29 Descartes, René: *Discours de la méthode*, 1637 VI, S. 2 (*Discours de la Méthode*, 6e partie. Paris 1966, p. 168; German translation: *Abhandlung über die Methode*, transl. Arthur Buchenau, Leipzig 1919, p. 51).

straints you shall determine your own nature according to your own will, whose power I have lent you".[30]

This concept of the spiritual nature of man also manifested itself in the systematic foundation of human self-interpretation. This is made evident by the hermeneutical turn of the humanities in the late 18th and early 19th century. They took up impulses from the philosophy of life and rationally evolved it into a specific method for investigating the human world in the variety of its historical manifestations.[31] Human cultures thus because the object of comprehensive research that was theoretically grounded in a "method of systematic understanding" (J.G. Droysen)[32] and the self-understanding of mankind was inextricably tied up with the ability to perceive and recognize cultural diversity both in terms human culture was produced because of the "educational drive" (Blumenbach)[33] of all natural beings – although far beyond the limits of nature. For Herder, who designated man as the first "emancipated being of creation",[34] human cultural achievement became measurable by the standard of how it realized the potential of being in short its "humanity". On the basis of this humanist conception of man being an end in himself the humanities were evolved at the end of the 18th century with a twofold approach that was anthropological and historical at the same time.

The aesthetization of the human perception of the self and the world forms a separate process in this development. In the medium of art the natural and spiritual qualities of human existence become reconciled and this humanist synthesis of nature and the human world is harmonized in such a way that it can be brought in line with the autonomous self-definition of mankind.

### e) Historicity

The temporization of the concept of mankind is specific to the Modern Age. Its nature was now conceived as the result of an evolutionary process, and consequently its culture became amendable to being interpreted in temporal terms: the exemplary mode of historical meaning-making that had found its traditional expression in the understanding of history as *magistra vitae* was replaced with a

30 See footnote 23.

31 Reill, Peter H.: *The German Enlightenment and the Rise of Historicism*, Berkeley 1975; Reill, Peter H.: *Vitalizing Nature in the Enlightenment*, Berkeley 2005.

32 Droysen, Johann Gustav: *Historik. Historisch-kritische Ausgabe*, ed. Peter Leyh, vol. 1, Stuttgart-Bad Cannstatt 1977, p. 22 and others.

33 Blumenbach, Johann Friedrich: *Über den Bildungstrieb*. 2. ed., Göttingen 1791.

34 Herder, Johann Gottfried: *Ideen zur Philosophie der Geschichte der Menschheit* (*Werke*, ed. Wolfgang Pross, vol. III/1), Munich 2002, p. 135.

genetic mode that emphasized the open future caused by the changes historical conditions underwent and that made progress into the essential aspect of historical evolution. This revolution in the concepts of mankind and its relationship with nature occurred during the "saddle time" around 1750 – 1850 and led to the idea of human nature's immutability being abandoned. Instead each person along with its own specific historical interest is understood to be the intellectual product of itself or of other peoples in other cultures and times.

This historicity appeared in different contexts. In connection with a theory of civil society, the Scottish Enlightenment of the late 18th century (e. g. D. Hume, A. Smith, A. Ferguson, J. Millar) transformed the foundation and legitimization of particular forms of life provided by natural law into a genuinely historical one. Within the framework of "theoretical history" the social nature of man was seen as being completely determined by historical. Man as an *animal sociale* goes through several stages of a universalizing historical evolution that finally culminates in the life form of modern civil society.[35]

As a consequence of the ever increasing knowledge about the multifariousness of human forms of life the idea of a generalizing and a temporal law applying to the way all humans regulate their lives came to be dispersed. Instead the concept of "humanity" as a fundamental category of defining human nature acquired a temporal dimension. To theorize about this condition initially became the task of the philosophy of history in the (early) Enlightenment). It provided the inherent temporality of human life forms with a general sense of direction. Being human was thereby dilated into the qualitative difference between past and future. The intellectual processing of past experience was considered to be the principle that enabled man to exceed this closed "experiential space" and transform it into an open "horizon of expectation" where he – due to his capacity for self-determination – was capable of opening up and realizing new human potentialities both in thinking as well as in acting.[36]

The movement of historism in the humanities of the 19th century was instrumental in making the historicity of mankind into the strategic basis of historical research. This strategy was guided by the insight that history amounted to the "*gnoti se auton*" ("understand yourself") of humanity (J.G. Droysen).[37] While initially referring to mankind in its entirety the focus of interest became increasingly narrowed down so as to eventually extend only to

35 Ferguson, Adam: *Versuch über die Geschichte der bürgerlichen Gesellschaft*, Frankfurt/Main 1986; Millar, John: *Vom Ursprung des Unterschieds in den Rangordnungen und Ständen der Gesellschaft*, Frankfurt/Main 1985.

36 Koselleck, Reinhart: "'Erfahrungsraum' und 'Erwartungshorizont' – zwei historische Kategorien", in: ibid., *Vergangene Zukunft. Zur Semantik geschichtlicher Zeiten*, Frankfurt/Main 1979, pp. 349 – 375.

37 Droysen: *Historik* (footnote 32), p. 41.

the European and national sphere. The potential ethnocentrism implicit in this was relativized, if not suspended, by the hermeneutical principle that each epoch was in itself valuable in terms of giving insights into the cultural nature of mankind, and also that any interpretation of past human life forms had to be systematically aware of their own cultural perception of themselves. Accordingly, the unity of mankind was held to manifest itself in the variety of its cultures.[38] Ranke expressed this idea as follows: "The principle of having the diversity of nations and individuals contributing to the idea of mankind as a whole is an absolute progress."[39]

### f) Individualization

As early as in the late Middle Ages a religiously motivated process of individualization set in whereby the uniqueness of each individual (before God and all other humans) became perceptible. The Reformation, the reform of Catholicism and the emergence of mystical forms of religiousness in all denominations all the way to Pietism or religious Enlightenment furthered this process that was to have far-reaching consequences for cultural practices. The individuality thus formed became absorbed, sometimes without problems, sometimes amidst a lot of struggle, by the concept of individual autonomy.

In the 17th and 18th centuries this gave rise to new ideas about the way man and mankind were related to each other. On the one hand this relationship was interpreted as a biological-anthropological one by recognizing each individual as part of the same human species. In the basis of this it was then possible in theoretical terms, to deduce the social cohesion of mankind from a fictitious social contract concluded by autonomous individuals for the sake of securing their common survival. This idea – first developed in an exemplary fashion by Thomas Hobbes in his "Leviathan" (1651) – found its classical expression in John Locke's "Two Treatises on Government" (1690) and above all in Jean-Jacques Rousseau's "Du contrat social" (1762). In this context the individual was perceived in the role of a patriarch, but what was decisive was his personal will to sociability as the very foundation of human society.[40]

This concept of human individuality was derived from the idea that, through the input of labour, was capable of acquiring the ownership of nature. The concept of humanity dominating the post-corporate life form of bourgeois so-

38 Jaeger, Friedrich, Rüsen, Jörn: *Geschichte des Historismus. Eine Einführung*, Munich 1992.
39 Ranke, Leopold von: *Über die Epochen der neueren Geschichte*, ed. Th. Schieder and H. Berding (*Aus Werk und Nachlaß*, vol. 2), Munich 1971, p. 80.
40 Van Dülmen, Richard: *Die Entdeckung des Individuums 1500–1800*, Frankfurt/Main 1997.

ciety had its basis in man's *equality* with all other men and the *freedom* to accumulate *property.* As the owner of property he associated himself with other property owners to form bourgeois society. By becoming part of this he was granted the status of a citizen who enjoyed the protection of his human rights as guaranteed by the constitution and who, together with all other citizens, was the very foundation of statehood and political rule.[41]

Parallel to this social individualism of bourgeois society there appeared theories concerning the existence of a spiritual link among human beings, e. g. in G.W. Leibniz' idea of a pre-established harmony, in G.F. Fichte's derivation of individual from absolute self-awareness and other representative of German Idealism, or in J.G. Herder's and W. von Humboldt's notion of the communality of all humans via their individual participation in certain transcendental ideas.[42] The experience of profound religious belief was the expression of man's personal relationship with God in the sense that his individualism as a human being was guaranteed by an authority beyond the here and now. The culturally determined nature of humanity – defined in terms of reason and freedom – now manifested itself in an unlimited plenitude both in space and time, as e. g. in the universal histories of the German Enlightenment historians A.L. Schlözer, J.Ch. Gatterer[43] or in J.G. Herder's philosophy of history.[44] The spiritual desire for creating culture ascribed to mankind in its entirety became noticeable in the multiplicity of life forms, and at the same time it became a precept for every human to individually regulate and give shape to his life. The specific achievement of such an individualization of mankind was termed "general education" ("*Bildung*"), and it became the guiding concept of human socialization as well as individualization informing educational programs and artistic practices. In Germany e. g. this was implemented through the reform of the education and university-systems at the end of the $19^{th}$ century, which was mainly influenced by Wilhelm von Humboldt and Friedrich Schleiermacher, or it manifested itself in the literary genre of the "*Bildungsroman*" that found its exemplary expression in

41 Macpherson, C.B.: *Die politische Theorie des Besitzindividualismus. Von Hobbes bis Locke*, Frankfurt/Main 1973.

42 Leibniz, G.W.: *Monadologie* (French/German, transl. by Heinrich Köhler), Frankfurt/Main 1996; Fichte, J.G.: *Die Bestimmung des Menschen*, 5th ed., Hamburg 1979; Fichte, J.G.: *Die Anweisung zum seligen Leben, oder auch die Religionslehre*, 4th ed., Hamburg 1994; Herder J.G.: *Auch eine Philosophie der Geschichte zur Bildung der Menschheit*, Frankfurt/Main 1967; Humboldt, Wilhelm von: "Über die Aufgabe des Geschichtsschreibers", in: *Werke*, ed. Andreas Flitner and Klaus Giel, vol. 1: *Schriften zur Anthropologie und Geschichte*, Darmstadt 1960, pp. 585 – 606 (*Gesammelte Schriften* [Akademie-Ausgabe] IV, pp. 35 – 56).

43 Schlözer, August Ludwig: *Vorstellung seiner Universalhistorie*, Göttingen/Gotha 1772. Newprint Hagen 1990; Gatterer, J.Ch.: *Abriß der Universalhistorie in ihrem ganzen Umfange. Bey dieser zwoten Ausgabe völlig umgearbeitet und bis auf unsere Zeiten fortgesetzt*, Göttingen 1773.

44 Cf. footnote 43.

Goethe's "Wilhelm Meister's Apprenticeship" ("*Wilhelm Meisters Lehrjahre*") (1795/96). This educational concept, which is still valid today, can be regarded, both structurally and genetically as the projection of the category of historicism onto that of individualization.

## 8. Steps towards the Future

The historicity plus the plurality of the idea of mankind – and especially the latter has given rise to the category of individuality – have had considerable repercussions for the use of this idea in the process of shaping personal identity.

First and foremost the power of individualization has increased enormously due to the process of globalization caused by world economy and the advance of technology. The Western notion of humanity was spread throughout the world due to colonization and imperialism, thus threatening the validity of other concepts of what is constitutive of mankind and other interpretations of the world connected with these. There were two ways of countering this threat by treating it as a challenge. One could adopt the Western way of thinking along with its conviction of man being able to dominate the world. The 4$^{th}$ of May Movement in China and the ideas propounded by Hu Shi may serve as an example of this.[45] Alternatively one could radically reject Western culture in the way Ghandi with his notion of Hindu Swaraj did.[46] The currently most wide-spread and influential intellectual trends in Subaltern Studies and Post-colonialism belong in this second alternative. In the same way as critique of Western intellectual dominance thus formulated may be understandable, the direct opposition to it is not very convincing because it is the exact counterpart to the Western ethnocentrism it is opposed to.

Postmodern cultural realism and relativism is another attempts to avoid the trap of ethnocentrism. It has certainly sharpened our view of the multi-fariousness of culture in human life while at the same time obfuscating the sway universalism holds in intercultural communication. Ethnocentrism becomes an unavoidable element in the shaping of cultural identity as along as human beings – as individuals as well as social formations ("communities") – conceive of themselves as different from others and treat others according this self-per-

45 Hu Shi: *Autobiographie mit Vierzig* (transl. from Chinese by Marianne Liebermann and Alfred Hoffmann), Dortmund 1998. See also Grieder, Jerome B.: *Hu Shih and the Chinese Renaissance*, Cambridge, Mass., 1999; Eglauer, Martina: *Wissenschaft als Chance. Das Wissenschaftsverständnis des chinesischen Philosophen Hu Shi (1891–1962) unter dem Einfluß von John Deweys (1859–1952) Pragmatismus*, Stuttgart 2001.

46 Gandhi, Mahatma: "Hindu Swaraj", in: Mukherjee, Rudrangshu (Ed.): *The Penguin Gandhi Reader*, New York 1993, pp. 3–66.

ception. In the process positive values are solely ascribed to the concept of the self while the otherness of the others is determined as a negative aberration from this norm.

But this does not mean that the manner in which universalizing definitions of humanity are employed in the process of identity formation is caught up in this binary logic. On the contrary, this logic is flexible, it is 'open'. It even offers the opportunity to humanize, if not to overcome, the "clash of civilizations". This chance rests upon altering the universalizing concept of what man is or should be from an exclusive into an inclusive one.

Through inclusion the otherness of the other is shifted from the sphere of everything that is outside the self into the area of our common humanity, of a diverse 'humanity' (in a synthesis of empirical and normative elements). Through this shift, this fundamental change in perspective, otherness becomes the specific manifestation of the human qualities of man that transcend all differences. Thereby it acquires a uniqueness that it has in common with the uniqueness of the self, and all this within a conceptual framework in which cultural difference as a determinant of one's own identity does not disappear but still plays an important role. In this sense the difference to the other becomes a way of becoming oneself through being reflected by the other, and the others pose to the self the challenge of being recognized.[47] An inclusive understanding of mankind is thus capable of mitigating the bitterness of ethnocentrism by turning it into an opportunity of humanizing both sides.[48]

This fundamental change is more than a theoretical postulate far removed from reality. There are some historical achievements in which this is already foreshadowed: Firstly of all in the enrichment of the idea of mankind through the aesthetic dimension. Within this sphere – but only here – the harshness of political and social differentiation is toned down by means of its imaginary resolution. Schiller's "Briefe über die ästhetische Erziehung des Menschen" amount to a classical formulation of this humanization of man through the influence of art.[49] Another manifestation of inclusive universalism is formed by the humanities and their hermeneutical method where a rich arsenal of understanding otherness and difference has been evolved. The principles of reconciling universalization and individualization applied there amount to a real-

47 Emmanuel Levinas has radicalized this argument in the sense of conceiving the self in terms of the other. (Levinas, Emmanuel: *Humanismus des anderen Menschen*, Hamburg 1989).

48 Cf. Rüsen, Jörn: "How to Overcome Ethnocentrism: Approaches to a Culture of Recognition by History in the 21st Century", in: *Taiwan Journal of East Asian Studies* 1.1 (June 2004): 59–74; also in: *History and Theory* 43 (2004) Theme Issue "Historians and Ethics": 118–129.

49 Schiller, Friedrich: "Über die ästhetische Erziehung des Menschen in einer Reihe von Briefen (1795)", in: *Sämtliche Werke in 5 Bänden*, ed. Peter-André Alt, Albert Meier and Wolfgang Riedel, vol. 5, Munich 2004, pp. 570–669.

istic chance of recognizing cultural difference. A very good example of this is Shmuel Eisenstadt's concept of "multiple modernities".[50] Meanwhile the humanities have also managed to point out hidden elements of otherness in one's own self.[51] Insights like these may tend to alternate the constraints that cause the self to project all those elements that are considered to be irreconcilable with the formation of its own subjectivity into those traits that constitute the otherness of the other. We have come to realize that traits are nothing but the exterritorialized shadow of ourselves. Finally, the secular life form of civil society has to be mentioned. In cultural terms based on the idea of human dignity it opens the opportunity of living with difference. The principle of tolerance was a first step in this direction. Over and above this the important step from tolerance to recognition is attempted in numerous contexts.[52]

Nevertheless, the idea of mankind founded on the principle of human dignity is under threat. Considering the overwhelming strength of market economy and the instrumental logic of technology the notion of the moral autonomy and self-determination of mankind seems to be but an illusion. Powerful political movements like Fascism or Communism were inspired by the idea of overcoming the given status of man in favour of a "new man" or "super-man" who were thought capable of leaving all the imperfections of human life as it existed in its present form behind in exchange for a brave new world.[53] The attractiveness of this idea was enhanced by the enormous opportunities that existed of manipulating not only human culture but also – due to the advances made in biology, artificial intelligence and brain research – even human nature itself. So far all these attempts have ended catastrophically. The same should apply to the current intellectual movements of transhumanism, which takes up all the dreams of happiness and salvation by promising to realize them via a change in the biological equipment of man and by enhancing his intellectual capacity by means of the artificial intelligence of computers hooked up with him.

What is man? This question has not lost anything of its tropicality, openness and the controversial attempts at answering it. If one sees the latest intellectual endeavours at providing an answer to the challenge issued by globalization to a sustainable cultural orientation in the light of the developmental boost concomitant with the universal theory of axial times, there are a lot of indications that Modern Humanism is a symptom of ourselves being right in the middle of a

50 Eisenstadt, Shmuel N.: "Multiple Modernities", in: *Daedalus* 129.1 (Winter 2000): pp. 1 – 30.

51 Waldenfels, Bernhard: *Vielstimmigkeit der Rede. Studien zur Phänomenologie des Fremden* 4, Frankfurt/Main 1999.

52 It, however, the life forms of secular civil society is pluralistically understood to be just one among others, the chance of making otherness livable is missed. Civil society is a meta-order that enables the pluralism of cultural orientation in the first place.

53 Cf. Küenzlen, Gottfried: *Der neue Mensch*, Frankfurt/Main 1997.

second axial time. What is at stake here is a revision (in the sense of a qualitative improvement) of all the achievements of the universalist concepts of humanity evolved in the first axial time. Such a revision requires a "Renaissance", a productive reception and further development of the concept of mankind that in modern humanism and to this day determines a variety of cultural traditions that in a decidedly intercultural communication are still vying with each other for an understanding so as not to be subsumed under the unitary culture of modernity.[54]

In whatever way the idea of humanity may be further developed there is one elementary as well as universal factor of human life that has brought into play anew since it so far had been totally underexposed in human thinking, if not even disregarded: human suffering. In view of numerous crimes against humanity, which, as ever, are depressing experience of our times and which the human and social sciences are still grapping with in order to understand, human suffering has to be focussed much more predominantly in terms of the question of where the opportunities but also the limits of our humanization are to be seen. Without systematically taking into account the universal as well as fundamental anthropological properties of man, his basic and inescapable fragility, fallibility and vulnerability any realistic reflection upon humanity is impossible.

54 Cf. Rüsen, Jörn/Laass, Henner (Eds.): *Humanism in Intercultural Perspektive. Experiences and Expectations*, Bielefeld 2009; Rüsen, Jörn/Laass, Henner (Eds.): *Interkultureller Humanismus. Menschlichkeit in der Vielfalt der Kulturen*, Schwalbach/Taunus 2009.

Oliver Kozlarek

# Man and World in Latin American Humanism

The so-called discovery of the New World quite literally opened up a *new* world to the Europeans. Whereas previously some idea, composed of empirical knowledge as well as fantasy, had been formed over the centuries concerning other civilizations in Africa or Asia, America offered the surprise of something absolutely new and unexpected. Such an encounter poses a tremendous challenge to any culture. Michel de Montaigne was so enthusiastic about the news reaching him from the other side of the Atlantic that he wanted to try out all the items of food and spices brought over by travelers and decorated his castle with Indian weapons and accessories.[1] Even though he never set foot on the new continent he must have been an ardent reader of travel writings and realized "that whatever knowledge we can gain from experiencing these peoples surpasses not only all the imagery with which the art of poetry has adorned the Golden Age, besides all the other inventions aimed at invoking a blissful state of mankind by poetic means, but also the speculative concepts of philosophy, and even its desire".[2]

Montaigne was not the only one to let himself be inspired by the discovery of the New World. It should rather become clear that the discovery of America must have had a tremendous influence on European culture, and that our understanding of present-day Europe cannot be separated from the new course it had been set on by the repercussions of this event. A lot of the ideas that nowadays are ascribed to the advent of modernity have originated from the transatlantic laboratory. This equally applies to modern humanism. Particularly the encounter with other human beings who were totally alien to the Europeans and with whom there existed no link in the previous knowledge of Europe revised a number of fundamental questions: Who and what are those people? Do they

1 Hamlin, William M.: *The Image of America in Montaigne, Spenser, and Shakespeare. Renaissance Ethnography and Literary Reflection*, New York 1995, p. 37.

2 Montaigne, Michel de: "Von den Menschenfressern", in: Montaigne, Michel de: *Essais* (ed. Ralph-Rainer Wuthenow), Frankfurt/Main 2001, p. 88.

qualify as human beings? How should we treat them? And finally, once again invoking the spirit of Montaigne: What can we learn from them?

The questions may have been prompted by a variety of motives: exoticism, the charm of what is novel and alien, but also the fear of what is strange. One thing, however, is certain: they rocked the foundations on which European culture in the 16th century rested, thus causing lively debates on either side of the Atlantic. Not only has humanism exerted some influence on these debates but consequently it was also put to a serious test itself and thus eventually acquired an altogether new complexion. In this process it has developed robust roots in Latin America and spawned a tradition of its own that has proved to be very much alive until today. In the following a few of the stages in the development of the specific brand of Latin American humanism will be introduced. In the following I will present a few stages of this Latin American humanism. I will particularly point to a certain the "world consciousness" that I believe to be relevant for us today.

## 1. Humanism and Politics

Montaigne as an adolescent had taken cognizance of the debate between Juan Ginés de Sepúlveda (1494–1573) and Bartolomé de las Casas (1484–1566) which took place in the Spanish city of Valladolid in 1550, creating quite a stir in Europe. The cause for this quarrel among scholars was Ginés de Sepúlveda's opinion that the Indios were barbarians and that thereby the Spanish rule over them was justified. Bartholomé de las Casas, who had for a long time lived in America as a priest and who a few years previously had written a famous indictment of the brutal and unjust conduct of the Spanish conquerors, was vehemently opposed to this.

This debate is a perfect example of how fundamental the discussions were that had been triggered by the discovery of these 'others'. What is at stake here is to ascertain the degree of humanity the Indios possess in comparison with the Europeans. While Ginés de Sepúlveda was prepared to regard the Indios as human beings of a lesser category, thus devaluing them vis-à-vis the Europeans, Bartholomé de las Casas insisted on the principle of *all* men being equal. Indios and Europeans should therefore be accorded the same rights. For this reason the philosopher Mauricio Beuchot regards Bartholomé de las Casas as an early defender of those human rights that were postulated only several centuries later.

Las Casas' thinking is derived from different sources. Nominalism and Thomism were of particular relevance for him, whereas humanism was less important. Beuchot thinks that Ginés de Sepúlveda was actually the real humanist. He bases this on the fact that Ginés de Sepúlveda had had a strictly humanistic education in Spain.[3] The debate of Valladolid therefore does not amount to a connection with or actualization of European humanism, but rather shows up its contradictions. Humanism offers no guarantee against injustice or contempt. It is on the contrary an invitation to discuss the question of what it means to be human again and again. Very often preconceived and limited views of mankind are responsible for abrogating from all those who do not correspond to such concepts their rights as a human being. The humanism of Sepúlveda is a good example of this. By contrast Las Casas could be viewed as the reformer of a European idea of mankind that had become too rigid and dogmatic. He saw the European humanism was no longer compatible with the new reality – which can be regarded as the very beginning of what nowadays is termed 'globalization' – and therefore had to be expanded. This makes Las Casas into a model for all future generations of humanists in Latin America. What they all have in common is that they draw on European humanism for their inspiration while at the same time seeing the need for its change.

Also the founder of the University of Mexico, the Augustinian Fray Alonso de la Veracuz (1507 – 1584) is a figure that stands out due to his humanism. Not only does he criticize the harsh rule of the Spaniards over the Indios, but he also declares it to be illegitimate. This is based on a theory of rule according to which all political power is vested in the people. Since the Indios have not ceded their political power to the Spanish King, he is not entitled to rule over them. The Mexican philosopher Ambrosio Velasco believes to have recognized in Fray Alonso de la Veracruz' thinking an amalgam of 'republicanism' and humanism. Although both schools of thought have their roots in Europe, Velasco emphasizes that from the Augustinian's ideas a new tradition of thinking originated that was to be characteristic of the philosophizing of the New World.[4]

For the drive for independence and the new Creole nationalism forming in Latin America, a recognition of the value and relevance of Indio culture gained in importance. The merging of political thought and humanism marked the course along which the new culture of the 17$^{th}$ century was to articulate itself. In 1609 Juan Zapata y Sandoval (1545 – 1630), who was also a member of the Augustinian order, published a book whose title has a surprisingly modern ring to it: *Sobre justicia distributiva* (On distributive justice). At the same time Zapata y Sandoval already formulates the desire for a separate nationhood that foreshadows that of the later Mexico. Also in the 17$^{th}$ century Latin American humanism finds an important expression in the poetry of Sor Juana Inés de la Cruz (1651 or

3 Cf. Beuchot, Mauricio: *Bartolomé de las Casas (1484 – 1566)*, Madrid 1995.

4 Cf. Velasco, Ambrosio (Ed.): *Significación política y cultural del humanismo iberoamericano en la época colonial*, Mexico 2008; idem: "Humanismo hispanoamericano", in: *Revista de Hispanismo Filosófico* 13 (2008): 13 – 30.

1648–1695). Octavio Paz regarded the poet as the "mother of a new culture" in which the search for the particular was matched by a striving for universality.

## 2. The Ambivalence of Enlightenment

The 18th century is generally considered to be the century that is marked by the Enlightenment. But it is also an age when European intellectuals, artists and scientists were proclaiming time and again the extent to which they were impressed by the influence and the consequences of the discovery of the New World. Jean-Jacques Rousseau and his concept of the 'noble savage' is only the most prominent example of how Europe began to view itself more critically in the mirror of these 'other' people and cultures. Such a positive assessment of non-European cultures is, however, contrasted by innumerable examples of how the New World and everything in it – people, animals, plant and inanimate objects – became devalued in comparison with the Old World, i. e. compared to what was familiar. The tenor of all these arguments is that in the New World everything is younger and therefore not yet fully developed. The most notorious examples of such anti-American exaggerations are the writings of the natural scientist George-Louis Leclerc de Buffon (1707–1788) and Corneille de Pauw (1739–1799).

All of these ideas are by no means incompatible with the rationalist claim of the Enlightenment. It is above all understood as the triumph of reason, and furthermore, if reason is conceived as a faculty that has to be developed in and by humans, then the anti-American exaggerations can also be seen as the attempt at explaining how the New World and its inhabitants cannot possibly participate in this triumph because they are still living in the state of "self-imposed tutelage" that Kant already mentioned in his famous essay "What is Enlightenment?" (1784). The anti-American arguments are, at least partially, the product of cultural arrogance, but they are equally part of a discursive strategy whose purpose it is to prove the allegedly 'natural' superiority of the Europeans by pseudo-scientific means.

Such notions can be countered again referring to Latin American humanism. The author of the *Historia Antigua de México* (The Ancient History of Mexico), the Jesuit Francisco Xavier Clavijero (1731–1787) wishes, and this is something he has in common with the European humanists of previous centuries, to revive the old traditions. However, the 'renaissance' he has in mind is not that of the ancient Greeks and Romans but that of the pre-Hispanic civilizations of America. At the same time Clavijeros history can be read as the exact counterpart of the anti-American exaggerations because it amply demonstrates that American people and nature are by no means of lesser value, but that primarily they are different. This is a first important step towards a differential logic that is no longer encoded in terms of categories like 'better' or 'worse'

## 3. The Long Road to Independence

The pride of the New World inspired by Clavijero's and others' writings led to a new nationalism which eventually was to culminate in liberation movements. Most of the states in Latin America known today gained their independence from their respective colonial powers at the beginning of the 19th century. Once formal independence had been achieved it was necessary to establish a new social order, a process which proved to be extremely lengthy and was to be interrupted by numerous setbacks. Still nowadays it is a matter of debate if Latin America has really succeeded in liberating itself from the yoke of colonialism. Neocolonial or, more recently, postcolonial theories still argue that the process of liberation, i. e. of 'decolonialization', has remained incomplete, in spite of all this formal independence.

Both in political and cultural terms the liberation movements drew their inspiration from liberalism. However, as the Mexican philosopher Leopoldo Zea maintains in an important book of his, liberalism became merged with positivism. Positivism eventually became the 'ideological instrument' of the new ruling classes, and by means of this ideology the newly formed societies of Latin America were to be set on course to the destination of 'order and progress'. Towards the end of the 19th century, according to Zea, positivism and the demand for order it stood for had gained the upper hand over liberalism. This tendency was reflected in the way the institutions of higher education were conceived. Thus Zea wrote: "The mission of liberalism had come to an end, and the rising generation in Mexico that had imbibed the ideology of positivism desired nothing more than order".[5] With this shift the idea of humanism was temporarily suspended, but not for long.

## 4. Humanism as a Critique of Positivism

Right in the early stages of the 20th century the world was thrown into a deep crisis. The most important events that in conventional historiography are constantly referred to in this context are the Russian October Revolution (1917) and the First World War (1914–1918). Even though these were events that affected the entire world, whether directly or indirectly, European historiography tended

5 Zea, Leopoldo: *El positivismo en México*, Mexico 1968, p. 179.

to overlook the fact that the ensuing crisis was not only a world-wide one, but also gave rise to different reactions in other parts of the world.

The Mexican revolution is a good example of this. It started in 1910 and ended about ten years later. Therefore the October Revolution was by no means the first revolution of the 20th century. Another prejudice on the part of conventional historiography has to be revised in this context: The Mexican revolution shows that not all revolutionary movements of the 20th century drew their inspiration from Marxism. On the contrary, the Mexican revolution was not based on any fundamental theory or ideology. As the historian Alan Knight has shown, it was mostly supported by 'simple people' and was not prepared by intellectuals who "wanted to prescribe a program or formulate a doctrine".[6] The revolution was not preceded by any kind of cultural programmatics. These were rather developed later during the course of the revolution. If, however, one wants to locate the coordinates by which this new cultural beginning was guided one can without any doubt identify an explicit humanism that was understood as a critique of positivism. This was most prominently formulated by a group of young intellectuals that became known by the name of *Ateneo de la juventud*. In the following I shall briefly introduce some of its members.

Antonio Caso (1883 – 1946) was a philosopher and at the same time one of the first sociologists in Mexico. He served twice (1920 and 1921 – 1923) as *rector* of the largest university in Mexico, the *Universidad Nacional de México* (today *Universidad Nacional Autónoma de México*), and the edition of his collected works runs to a proud 11 volumes. No matter if we regard Caso as a philosopher, sociologist or civil servant, in all the functions he served he proved himself above all to be a humanist. In some of his works there are explicit references to this effect, such as a programmatic text entitled *El nuevo humanismo* (The New Humanism).

In this new humanism Caso sees as the most important intellectual challenge to overcome the 'intellectualism' that in his opinion took its beginnings from Descartes' philosophy and proved to determine the entire "philosophical tradition of the Modern Age".[7] What Caso considered to be wrong with their tradition was its inability to understand man in his entirety. The separation of spirit and body or subject and object that is central to Descartes' thinking invariably leads to the idea of the separation of man and world. Caso, however, believed that man cannot be conceived of if divided from his world.

In addition to this, Caso charged the philosophers belonging to this tradition

6 Knight, Alan: "Intellectuals in the Mexican Revolution", in: Camp, Roderic A./Hale, Charles/Vázquez, Josefina Zoraida (Eds.): *Los intelectuales y el poder en México*, Mexico/Los Angeles 1991, p. 144.

7 Caso, Antonio: "El nuevo humanismo", in: idem: *Obras Completas* II, Mexico 1973, p. 66.

with searching for the truth without due consideration of man's role, of which positivism was an extreme example. Against this doctrine he maintains that the truth cannot be grasped at all without taking man into account. It is only accessible by and for mankind. In this sense "the most fundamental truth of all philosophy is an anthropological truth", he wrote.[8] This amounts to the claim that "every philosophical system in the strict sense should be a humanism".[9] Caso thereby advocates a philosophy where man quite definitely should be the focus of attention.

What determined Caso to pursue this course was his belief in the indissoluble link between man and world, i. e. the insight that man is always acting within his world. To view man and world as divided from each other appeared in the light of an action-centered anthropology, which was derived from the philosophy of North American pragmatism, as utterly devoid of sense. Caso considered the end of his humanism to be a dual one: a "discovery of man and the world".[10]

In another article entitled *Nuestra missión humana* (Our human mission) there are two complementary sentences that not only explicate the connection between man and world but also draw some moral consequences from this insight. The first sentence runs as follows: "The world is not yet complete".[11] In the second sentence it says: "Man is not yet complete".[12] Since world and man are still incomplete they are also headed towards perfection. Morality sees to it that mankind should remain on this course. In a perfect world with equally perfect people morality would be superfluous, but since we humans exist within a continuous process of perfecting both men and world, we require morality to keep us on course.

Like Caso the writer and essayist Alfonso Reyes (1889 – 1959) can be counted among the reformers of Mexican culture whose anti-positivism takes the form of a specific kind of humanism. Reyes as well sees the necessity of connecting humanism with the insight into the human need for agency. He thus emphasizes that these days the word 'humanism' no longer needs to be specified as to its content: "It is to be understood more in the sense of an orientation rather than in terms of a specific content. This orientation consists in putting all our knowledge and our actions to the service of everything that is good for mankind".[13] Humanism is not so much a theoretical or intellectual mindset as it is agency, i. e. a certain kind of interaction between men and the world.

Quite logically the insight into the practical dimension of humanism has to be

8 Caso: "El nuevo humanismo", p. 66.
9 Ibid.
10 Ibid, p. 68.
11 Caso, Antonio: "Nuestra misión humana", in: idem: *Obras Completas* IX, Mexico 1976, p. 55.
12 Ibid, p. 60.
13 Reyes, Alfonso: *Obras Completos de Alfonso Reyes* XX, Mexico 2000, p. 403.

complemented with the idea that man cannot be conceived of separate from the world. "Man is not isolated, freely floating in nothingness, but he forms part of the world".[14] Reyes does not pass over the ambiguity of the term 'world'. This is, however, one of its merits because in all the numerous worlds it is capable of referring to the innumerable facets of our humanity are manifesting themselves. Our definition of mankind is thus dependent upon the different concepts of the world referred to. If there were only one single definition of the world our freedom to define ourselves as humans would be greatly curtailed. "The world", writes Reyes, is for mankind "a second person".[15] World and man stand in a dialectical relationship and thereby determine each other.

Besides this existential and ontological notion of the world there is also the planetary world-concept that plays an important role in Reyes' humanism. Like so many other Latin American intellectuals Reyes was a cosmopolitan. Travels to, and the study of, other cultures for him were a matter of course. The awareness of the necessity to know the world is closely related with the cultural self-understanding of Latin America. This is distinguished by the idea of being a kind of melting-pot of two cultures: as a rule the respective 'autochthonous' pre-Hispanic culture on the one hand, and the European one on the other. In those countries where the pre-Hispanic cultures did not play an important part this role is filled by cultures which were brought to the New World (African slaves for instance) and which mingled with that of Europe. (This applies e.g. to Brazil and Cuba.) When, therefore, in the New World the cultures of Europe and America or Africa became blended, then such a blend (*mestizaje*) already results in a new transatlantic culture that straddles two continents. The theme of *mestizaje* – or hybridization, as it is called in more recent terminology – always occupied a place in most Latin American intellectuals' awareness, just like the intuition that this was undermining the barriers erected by ethnocentrism and nationalism. Seen from such a perspective the world already appears in an entirely different light. It is no longer the space where each ethnicity is confined to its own territory, its country or its culture. It is rather turned into a rich source of ideas and cultural diversity that potentially all people can draw on. For a lot of Latin American intellectuals the appropriation of elements from 'alien' cultures is a virtue that even nationalism proved to be unable to weaken.

Alfonso Reyes is distinguished by his expertise in the culture of ancient Greece. Admittedly it could be argued that this interest was not so much due to an interest in 'alien' cultures as to the fact that European culture was considered to be the hegemonial culture in Latin America and that Heleno-centrism was nothing but an aspect of the reproduction of Eurocentrism in Latin America.

---

14 Ibid., p. 406.
15 Ibid., p. 414.

However, the manner in which Reyes dealt with the legacy of ancient culture disproved this suspicion. Not only did he strive to reverently adopt the originals, but he rather used them as a mirror in which to reflect his own Mexican reality.

An example of this creative adaption is his play *Ifigenia cruel* (Cruel Iphigenia). In it Reyes does not only draw on the Greek matter but on Goethe's version of it, which the German poet already believed was something "devilishly humane". By analogy with Goethe Reyes uses the ancient model in order to reflect upon his own cultural experience. As the Romance philologist Ottmar Ette has already stated[16], the result is a cultural creation that consciously invokes universal themes and expands these by revitalizing them with the injection of topical themes. Ette writes: "If Mexican history also became part of the general historical process, an ongoing development which according to Alfonso Reyes had already begun with the humanization of mankind in the Eastern Mediterranean".[17] Reyes and other Latin American humanists regarded such a continuation of *world culture* as their mission.

Just like the humanists of the European Renaissance the Latin American humanists considered the study of ancient cultures as indispensable. The essayist and literary critic Pedro Henríquez Ureña, who is from the Dominican Republic, has mentioned several reasons for this. First and foremost studying the classics is a counterweight to the positivism already mentioned. But in a talk entitled *La cultura de las humanidades* (The culture of the humanities) Henríquez Ureña additionally emphasizes that the lesson Classical Antiquity teaches consists in being on the guard against the 'narrow' confines of one's own thinking.[18] For the Latin American present at the beginning of the 20th century, however, this also means that the study of the ancient Greeks and Romans has to be supplemented with the study of "Spanish, French, Italian, English and German literatures" as well as with "Arian, Semitic, Indian and Chinese" wisdom.[19] The task would be "to constantly judge, compare, search and experiment"[20] in order thereby to come closer to "the perfection of man". This "perfection" for Henríquez Ureña resides in the unity of mankind, and this could only be achieved in a veritable world culture which does not suspend all particularities and differences, but which succeeds in perceiving the universality lying behind these.

The philosopher Samuel Ramos (1987 – 1959) wrote in 1940: "In no epoch other that our own is it more appropriate to emphasize the unity of mankind

16 Cf. Ette, Ottmar: *Literatur in Bewegung*, Weilerswist 2001, p. 317 ff.

17 Ibid., p. 342.

18 Ureña, Pedro Henríquez: "La cultura de las humanidades", in: Ureña, Pedro Henríquez: *Obra Crítica*, Mexico 2001, p. 598.

19 Ibid., pp. 598 – 599.

20 Ibid., p. 599.

because today it seems to be absent more than ever before".[21] This sentence is from a book entitled *Hacia un nuevo humanismo* (Towards a New Humanism), in which Ramos wants to convince his readers that the increasing fragmentation of mankind can only be countered with a "New Humanism" in which the "central position of man" can be reconquered.[22] In his opinion we live in a fraudulent civilization that pretends to be good for humans, but which has long been "transformed into a monster that has shaken off its chains and now poses a threat to its master and creator". He concludes his critique by stating that "mankind is in a paradoxical situation since it has to defend itself against its own civilization".[23]

This brief summary of his work already shows that Ramos was strongly influenced by European cultural critique. Nietzsche, but above all Simmel are among the sources cited. What is remarkable is that Ramos does not fall into the trap of nihilism or normative skepticism. The reason for this lies in his firm trust in mankind, his humanism, which many of his European colleagues tended to forego rather carelessly.[24] In order to be able to understand this difference it is necessary to once more take the historical and geographical background into consideration: When in 1940 Ramos published his manifesto for a *New Humanism*, at a time when in Europe a new World War was raging, he was writing in Mexico, a country that at the time conceived of itself as a safe heaven, but also the laboratory for a world culture whose beginnings lay in Europe.

## 5. Humanism after the Second World War

After two world wars and the systematic annihilation of six million Jews and millions of other people it is difficult to believe that humanism, which was also invoked by the cultures participating in mass-murder, should be of any value at all. Those who – for different reasons – had always been opposed to it were only too willing to give the moribund humanism the coup-de-grace. An important critique was submitted by the German philosopher Martin Heidegger towards the end of the 1940s in his *Brief über den Humanismus* (*Letter on Humanism*), which by many was understood to be an abrogation of humanism.

A short while later a book appeared in Mexico that can also be read as an

21 Ramos, Samuel: "Hacia un nuevo humanismo", in: idem: *Obras Completas* II, Mexico 1990, p. 73.

22 Ibid., p. 72.

23 Ibid., p. 69.

24 This view is shared by Helmut Plessner, according to whom it was above all the Germans who broke away from European humanism. Cf. Plessner, Helmuth: *Die verspätete Nation*, Frankfurt/Main 1974.

eminent document of Latin American humanism after 1945. It is *The Labyrinth of Solitude* by the Mexican writer and intellectual Octavio Paz. The book is a collection of essays in which Paz (1914 – 1998), who in 1990 was awarded the Nobel Prize for literature, only at first sight treats of various aspects of Mexican culture. The purpose of the author, however, goes far beyond the claim of only writing a book about Mexico.

One must not overlook the fact that it was treating a topic that in those years was controversially discussed in European philosophy: i. e. the topic of desolation, or as Paz puts it: "solitude". This is for Paz the central experience of human existence, and therefore it is the fundamental condition of all humanity. He writes: "All men *feel* lonely from time to time; all humans sometimes *are* lonely. Living means to distance ourselves from what we used to be and to change into what in an unknown future we shall be, and therefore solitude is the very foundation of the *conditio humana*".[25]

This is where Paz differs from Heidegger: Heidegger believes that the feeling of desolation is due to the fact "that man continually contemplates and evolves only his being (*das Seiende*)".[26] That precisely is the main thrust of his critique, which is based on the conviction that the being (*Das Seiende*) obscures the view of what is relevant, i. e. 'Being' (*das Sein*). Paz, by contrast, believes that our sense of desolation can only be alleviated when lonely human beings become united with others. According to Paz the feeling of loneliness makes this insight obvious, because however much men may be tormented by a basic feeling of loneliness, it is also true that it is this very feeling itself that induces them to seek the 'communion' with other humans.

This humanism is the focal point where the diversity of themes the author touches upon in his work from 1950 becomes interconnected. All the different stories narrated there resemble a *labyrinth*. This metaphor is indicative of the method behind Paz' humanism: "Not only have we been dispelled from the center of the universe, but we are also condemned to find our way back to it as through a labyrinth of jungles and deserts, on steep paths and in dark passages".[27] Humanism thus confronts man with the constant task of searching for, and becoming united with, other human beings. One could also say: Paz' main objective was the way man can relates to the world – primarily with regard to the social world, but ultimately all other modes of the world. For Paz it was man's responsibility in the Modern Age to relocate himself vis-á-vis in the world and find his place in it.

---

25 Paz, Octavio: *Das Labyrinth der Einsamkeit*, Frankfurt/Main 1998, p. 189.

26 Heidegger, Martin: "Brief über den 'Humanismus'", in: Heidegger, Martin: *Gesamtausgabe. I. Abteilung: Veröffentlichte Schriften 1914 – 1970*, vol. 9, Frankfurt/Main 1976, p. 339.

27 Paz: *Das Labyrinth der Einsamkeit*, p. 202.

## 6. Perspectives: What We Can Learn from Latin American Humanism

After this cursory overview of humanism in Latin America the question of how relevant it is for the present age poses itself. What can its relevance be for the current problems that far exceed the spatial limits of Latin America? In my opinion this resides in the "world-consciousness" that forms an essential part of the Latin American variety of humanism. "World-consciousness" is a term coined by Alexander von Humboldt. According to Ottmar Ette[28] it could become the guiding concept of our current modernity. I tend to share this opinion.[29] In doing so I am not only thinking of the evident relevance of the term for the process of globalization that is going on presently. It is not only necessary to become conscious of the planetary dimension of the world, but what is also required is more "world-awareness" in its ontological and existential meaning, as e.g. with regard to the destruction of our environment that has gone completely out of control. All the mechanisms to halt this process are presumably doomed to failure unless we rediscover deep inside our civilization the cultural foundations for regulating man's relationship with the world.

This insight had been recently followed up by the US-American anthropologist Marshall Sahlins.[30] He comes to the conclusion that 'Western' thinking is plagued with a twofold illusion: Firstly, the assumption that man stands outside the world, and, secondly, that the world is essentially hostile towards him. From this arises the ambition to dominate or subjugate the world, a tendency Sahlins has observed especially in his own society, the United States. Whether Sahlins is correct in his assessment of 'Western' civilization in general this is not the place to expand on. However, I do see the necessity of revising our attitude towards the world – in its human, social as well as, 'natural' dimensions.

The Latin American brand of humanism has not only arrived at the conclusion that a humanism without world-consciousness is too abstract, but it is also an attempt to redefine the cultural terms on which man and world interact. The sources it draws on for inspiration are quite heterogeneous: While Luis Villoro refers to the world-view of the Aztecs according to whom the world is not a changeable object that is subject to man's will,[31] Antonio Caso's thinking is more along the lines of a form of existence that would realize the Christian

28 Cf. Ette, Ottmar: *Weltbewusstsein. Alexander von Humboldt und das unvollendete Projekt einer anderen Moderne*, Weilerswist 2002.

29 Cf. Kozlarek, Oliver: *Moderne als Weltbewusstsein. Ideen für eine humanistische Sozialtheorie in der globalen Moderne*, Bielefeld 2011.

30 Sahlins, Marshall: *The Western Illusion of Human Nature*, Chicago 2008.

31 Villoro, Luis: "Multiculturalismo y derecho", in: idem: *Los retos de la sociedad por venir*, Mexico: 2007, pp. 152–171, p. 171.

injunction of love for the world, and Octavio Paz insists that it is only the "poetic experience" that can sharpen our sense of being an integral part of the world.

What, more generally, all the different authors are mainly concerned with is to establish a more harmonious relationship with the world. This is done in a discursive mode that is surprisingly modern, which also makes it relevant for our current problems. The result is an alternative "project of modernity" that has gone more or less unnoticed until today.[32]

32 Cf. On this Miller, Nicola: *Reinventing Modernity in Latin America. Intellectuals Imagine the Future: 1900–1930*, New York 2008.

# III. Current Issues

Günter Dux

# Humanism and Its Interpretation in Secular Modernity – The Responsibility of Politics for Enabling a Humane Form of Life

## 1. Humanism as a Postulate of Political Ethics

The concept of humanism has a direct bearing on human forms of life. The person who invokes humanism is at the same time placing others under the obligation of realizing a humane form of life. The reason for this recursive as well as normative understanding of humanism is to be sought in the nature of a humane life form itself: It is capable of failing to be achieved. Its purpose can be missed in the way individuals conduct themselves, and also in the way social policies are shaped. It is therefore essential that the very meaning of humaneness should be reflected upon because it is currently under threat. A particular threat is posed by the way the market economy has evolved in the present age. This threat renders it necessary to make sure of what humanism really involves. Its true meaning can only be arrived at by clarifying the recursive-normative structure of the concept, i. e. its immediate referral to a humane form of life. It is therefore required to reach an understanding of what a humane form of life is all about. That is going to be my concern.

The explosive nature of the cognitive attempt at a recursive definition of humanism derives from the fact that, since the advent of the modern age and especially of Modernity, human life forms have come to be understood differently from what their conception used to be in the past. In our present modern times our idea of what constitutes a human life form is founded upon a world view that has become thoroughly secularized. What secularized world means can be stated precisely: whatever is found or occurs in the world has to be explained in terms of the mundane context of which it forms a part. This equally applies to humanity's form of life. It, too, is embedded in inner-worldly relations and has to be defined with reference to these relations. The secularized world of modernity has led to retrace ourselves on our own steps. This on the one hand applies to the evolutionary understanding of the biological nature of our form of life, but it also applies to the historical understanding of its cognitive dimension. The cognitive life form becomes evident in the way it has developed in connection with both the biological evolution as well with the historical process it underwent.[1] In a world defined in secular terms there is nothing that is not amenable to understanding.

The epistemological attempt to locate the cognitive life form in all its variety within a secularized world in such a way that it can be elucidated out of its innerworldly relationship stands in direct opposition to the prevailing epistemology, that is, a transcendental epistemology. Due to it there always remains a quantum that resists explanation. The modern epistemological claim is also opposed by an historical understanding that is informed by the concept of a counter-enlightenment which remains trapped within the epistemological constraints of pre-modern times. Given the epistemological premises of the modern age and also given the on-going progress of mankind's cognitive forms of life, their historical development also becomes comprehensible. It then becomes evident that their evolution follows a universal sequential order. That the human life form understood in modern secular terms is one that is amenable to cognitive understanding is the one insight that I am attempting to convey, the other being that along with this a concept of humaneness as a normative value can be arrived at in a rationally convincing manner.

## 2. The Historical Turning Point

*The Secularized Universe*

At all times human beings have considered their particular organizational form of life as one of the multifarious forms of life in the midst of nature. At all times they have sought to understand the ways in which they are related to nature. At all times they have known how to tell stories about how they came into the world and how their life form was located in the midst of nature. Myths and epics are the form these stories adopted in the dawn of history.

In all the past the place mankind occupied in nature was not a problem, at least not a structural one. The categories by means of which humans try to get a hold on nature have at all times been developed in the early stages of the ontogenesis of the members of the species. In this phase the social others represent the absolutely dominant "objects", the interaction with whom leads to the formation of those categories. The categorical forms, such as they were evolved in the early ontogenesis of the members of the species, therefore also bear the stigma of their social origin. Natural objects and natural events therefore have taken on the same structure as human actions and interactions. The objects and

1 Dux, Günter: *Historisch-genetische Theorie der Kultur. Zur prozessualen Logik im kulturellen Wandel*, Weilerswist [3]2007.

events in nature are thereby seen as being motivated by meaningful and intentional processes. This is exactly the way objects and events in nature were also regarded in the early stages of human history. In analogy with the actions, interactions and communication of humans the natural processes were also seen to be grounded in intentional and meaningful processes. The intentional and meaningful structure of human action however, is one that is determined by thought and language. It is precisely this structure that determines the structure of cognition in terms of which men lead their lives. Due to the assumed identity of the social and natural strata, the processes occurring in nature were also thought to be determined by their inherent meaningful and intentional structure. Throughout history the world in its totality was understood to be an intentional and meaningful cosmos regulated by an inherent mindfulness.

The comprehension of a natural world conceptualized in intentional and meaningful terms found its expression in the world view of the past. The notion that the world was regulated by subject-like agencies was thematized in religion. When in the course of history theological and philosophical thinking was trying to grasp the world in its totality it proceeded in the same way as one always does when seeking an explanation for a meaningful intentional process: One attempts to get hold of the subjectivity thought to be the source of the meaningful intention responsible for organizing it in order to understand the significance of what is expressed through the world. This source, however, is assumed to be exactly identical with the one underlying all action in pre-modern processes of the world: mind. "The mind takes precedence over everything", it says in the Shatapatha-Brahmana. In Christian theology this place is occupied by the mind of God. In philosophy the thinking founded upon an absolute mind has been expressed in Plato's doctrine of ideas in its most profound way. Plato locates all being in the idea of goodness.[2] This concept of the world and mankind as being grounded in an absolute mind extends, as is commonly accepted, all the way to Hegel and beyond.

In the modern age occurred a change in the understanding of the world and humanity that amounts to a real turning point in history. It manifested itself first in the understanding of nature which gained currency in the course of the scientific revolution of the 16$^{th}$ and 17$^{th}$ centuries. In its wake the intentional-meaningful paradigm that had thitherto dominated the natural processes was eliminated from the concept of nature. But not quite, though, because Newton still adheres to the notion of God as the great creator and preserver in his *Principia Mathematica* of 1687. However, in the subsequent scientific revolution this idea was dispensed. Just the same happened with the model of the machine,

2 Discussed in: Dux, Günter: *Von allem Anfang an: Macht nicht Gerechtigkeit. Studien zur Genese und historischen Entwicklung des Postulats der Gerechtigkeit*, Weilerswist 2009.

which at the beginning of the modern age served as the interpretive template of the universe. Much though a comprehensive model of natural processes on a micro-level may be currently under debate in theoretical physics, a restoration of the pre-modern intentional-meaningful paradigm has not materialized and is not even in sight. Nowadays we therefore have to put up with a physical universe that is conceived as a system whose processes are determined by its immanent laws. This is exactly what amounts to our secularized understanding of the universe. What a secularized world means can, therefore, be exactly defined in the light of the preceding insights: *A secularized world is one in which everything that exists and happens in the universe is the result of the interplay of its immanent processes and therefore can be explained in those terms.*

## 3. The Secular Understanding of Human Life Forms as Spiritual Forms of Life

How then, and that is the big question, can a universe from which any sense of mind has been eliminated accommodate the mind of man? Because the human form of life as one determined by thinking and language is by definition a life form determined by mind. A resolution of the aporetic understanding of the human life forms as they are determined by mind only becomes possible with the beginning of modernity. Darwin's theory of the evolution of the species is the basis for this. The relevance of Darwin's theory is insufficiently appreciated by thinking that human life forms are capable of being located within the biological stratum of man's anthropological equipment. The stratum of biological properties just forms the precondition for evolving human forms of life. Departing from this insight, the Darwinian theory of evolution offers a surprisingly simple way out of the aporia of connecting epistemology, nature and mind. We must assume that the biological equipment of man forms the constructive precondition for the human life forms determined by mind and created by mankind itself.

Human life forms are forms of organization constructed through the medium of thought and language. As such they are cognitive forms of life. Their base is a natural one, but they themselves are not part of nature. No such potential exists in nature any longer. They are the result of a cultural construct. Their formation of its categories occurs in each ontogenesis on the basis of a cultural degree zero of every subsequent member of the species. They have been further developed in the course of history.

The concept of cognitive life forms as forms of life that have been constructed by man himself proved to be revolutionary as regards his understanding of himself. It disperses all the essentializing definitions that were ascribed to him in the by now bygone understanding of humanism. Man is what he makes of himself by constructing his life form. The notion of life forms resulting from this is radical in nature. It is the manifestation of what we initially stated to be the consequence of a secular understanding of the world and mankind. Given the epistemological preconditions of modernity all the cognitive forms through which human beings give structure to their lives can be questioned as to the secular origins of their genesis and they can also be explained in these terms. Such a statement would be highly detrimental to the self-understanding of mankind and its life forms if it did not include an understanding of the historical development of the life forms and the world thus constructed. However, of primary importance for such a history is the fundamental insight: Through understanding human life forms as constructs we have retraced our own steps.[3]

## 4. The Part of History in the Historical-Genetic Understanding of Modernity

### 1. Historical Sequence of Developmental Stages

History, as understood in the historical-genetic terms of modernity, is equated with the unfolding of the organizational competence regarding the way humans live their lives, which is the result of the constructive capacity of mankind. This happens in an historical sequence of developmental stages that can also be reconstructed. It has evolved in this way because the organizational competence which was set in motion by the ontogenesis of the members of the human race was capable of being enhanced. In the same measure as the formation of life forms determined by mind on the part of every member of the species can be explained in terms of the conditions that caused it to come into existence and to follow an evident sequential order, history and its sequence of epochs equally proceeds along the lines of an evident processual logic of development. The stringency of this sequential development needs some explaining, because it was the stringency of this development that caused the secular world to emerge, and along with this process also the meaning of humanness as defined by secular modernity.

3 Dux: *Historisch-genetische Theorie der Kultur. Zur prozessualen Logik im kulturellen Wandel.*

## 2. The Logic of the Developmental Stages

The key to understanding the processual logic of human life forms and their history is provided by the condition under which the construction of cognitive sociocultural life forms was able to manifest itself in the early ontogenesis of the members of the species, that is in the interaction between the subject and the social as well as natural environment. Because the organizational forms of human life, the practical as well as the cognitive ones, are formed in the early ontogenesis through interacting with their environment, i.e. through experiencing it, does it become understandable why we humans are able to interact with our environment and live in a world that is our own construct.[4] A "constructivist realism" is the stuff from which our world is made. In exactly the same manner the unfolding and widening of our competence to interact with and organize our environment occurs, which in its turn finds it expression in the developmental sequence of the various forms of sociocultural organization. Ever since the virtual transition from natural history to history proper, i.e. the history of the cognitive sociocultural life forms, every form of social organization has created a new situation for interacting with the environment and constructing a more highly developed form of life. Every development of new structures of social organization has also formed the precondition for advancing the cognitive development of mankind. The developmental sequence can be traced along two different lines: the sequence of structural organization of society and the sequence of cognitive forms of mind. I have outlined elsewhere in a historical-genetic theory of culture the development from the early social organizations of hunters and gatherers via the archaic societies controlled by power and states and the societies of classical antiquity right up to the market-dominated societies of the modern age. However, what needs to be examined more closely is the sequence of cognitive development.

## 3. The Intrinsic Logic of the Development of Cognition

It is evident that at all times the basic kinds of knowledge have been formed during the early ontogenetic stages of the members of the human species. The relevance of this insight manifests itself when one determines the initial cognitive life forms in history. There, too, the forms of cognitive organization must have evolved from the early ontogenesis of the members of the species. There, too, the evolutionary process was predetermined by the early developmental

4 Dux: *Historisch-genetische Theorie der Kultur. Zur prozessualen Logik im kulturellen Wandel*, pp. 208–216.

logic that we have come to know in our own society. The universality of the early ontogenetic development of cognitive faculties counts as one of the most definite results of research in comparative culture.[5] Though in early societies the evolutionary process of cognition was set in motion by the ontogenesis of the members of the species in the same way as in later societies, this does not mean could evolve in the same measure. The evolutionary process is always conditioned by its natural and social environment. Until the beginning of the Modern Age it only extends as far as the environment demands the development of man's cognitive capacity. If the development of cognitive competence is measured by the operational yardstick of algebraic logic, the early organizational level of hunting and gathering only required the development of a cognitive competence that in later societies corresponded to that of a six-year old. Yet, the process takes more time. Then, however, the development is halted.

The finding that the process of development evolved thus far and not further has met with embittered resistance on the part of not few representatives of the disciplines of ethnology and anthropology. It is, however, incontrovertible for a way of thinking that is based on the assumption that human life forms are created or constructed by man himself. The cognitive of human life forms could not possibly have been fully evolved at the beginning of history. In that case it would have to be regarded as genetically predetermined. But nature does not know of cognition in the sense it develops by man. Especially the operative forms of logic are not inherent in it. The fact that the operational processes of cognition are the result of a cultural construct is not only confirmed by all theoretical explanations, but today we have unequivocal empirical proof of an only gradual evolution of operational competence in early societies pertaining to the development of causality or time as well as numerical thinking. Our own research into the development of how time and causality have become relevant categories does not permit any doubt of this.[6]

I have set out the development of the gradual enhancement of operative cognition in some detail because this has far-reaching consequences for the subsequent development. Assuming that the cognitive development takes as its point of departure the early ontogenesis of the members of the species, we must also premise that the ensuing development follows exactly the same lines as the ones come across in later societies, including our own. This development occurs with a certain stringency in that it implies a developmental logic. In other words,

5 For a discussion Dux: *Historisch-genetische Theorie der Kultur. Zur prozessualen Logik im kulturellen Wandel*, pp. 271 seq., 350 seq.

6 For a documentation of our empirical research Mensing, Joachim: "Die Zeit am Rio Uneiuxi (Amazonas)", in: Günter Dux, *Die Zeit in der Geschichte*, Frankfurt/ Main [2]1998, pp. 73–406; Dux, Günter/Puspha Kumari, V.: "Studien zur vorindustriellen Kausalität", in: Dux, Günter/ Wenzel, Ulrich (Ed.), *Der Prozess der Geistesgeschichte*, Frankfurt/Main 1994, pp. 436–471.

the logic of development is caused by the development of logic. The latter becomes indispensable for enhancing the knowledge of the world. Any development of thought processes originating from the ontogenesis of the members of the species can only be seen as arising from this development beyond its incipient stages. This is exactly what happened in history. This does not go to say that the developmental stages, such as we can now observe them in the ontogenetic development of today, correspond with any of the historical epochs. It required thousands of years until, with the cognitive level achieved in classical antiquity, a formal or operational competence of thinking had been achieved which, in the ontogenesis of our own culture, is normally that of an eleven-year old. There can be no doubt, however, that the achievement of formal and operational competence, such as it had been formed in antiquity and the Modern Age, is nothing but the continuation of the development of operational competence that is incipient in every ontogenesis.

If one follows the development of cognitive competence via a route starting with the early ontogenesis of the members of the species, this evolution can be traced, ever since the beginning of the era of agricultural production, along three distinct lines:

1) Along the line of algebraic competence, i.e. the competence of logically relating distinct entities.
2) Along the line of a material knowledge of the world that in the historical process becomes increasingly interrelated.
3) Along the line of reflexivity concerning human self-understanding, from which an enhanced agency and operational competence arise.

## 5. The Transparency of History

*Arriving in Modernity*

In a historical-genetic reconstruction of history, such as it has been expounded above, the course of history becomes evident in the succession of constructs that have been evolved ever since the beginnings of human history. Since man was capable of constructing its own practical lifestyles through the medium of thought and language under specific developmental conditions we are today able to retrace its own steps in the very process of historical development. This insight is indispensible for understanding ourselves in terms of the epistemological conditions of a world that has become secularized. A first powerful impetus for advancing the process of cognitive development was provided by the transition from the societies of hunter- gatherers to an agricultural mode of production and the organizational form of archaic societies determined by domination and state. The fact that the latter had to rely on extending the organizational competence both with regard to nature and social life triggered a first sustainable development of the cognitive domain. The invention of writing was a milestone in this development.[7] It did not just manage to improve the efficiency of organization, i. e. the logistics of rulership, but it was also a milestone because it was the act of fixing ideas in writing that enabled the development of human thought to become an intentional social process. Classical Antiquity occupies a key position in this process because here, too, the nature of rule as something socially constructed provided a major impetus for cognitive development.[8] How so?

The conflicts and the constitutional strife attendant upon the development of the polis in Athens from the 7th century B.C. onwards give rise to the awareness of living in a world whose social order was one that had been created by men themselves. Those belonging to the polis are conscious of the social order being at their disposal.[9] The consciousness thus gained of the world being a construct with regard to the social order finds its more comprehensive equivalent in the initial awareness of the constructedness of mind and cognition. From now on it becomes possible to shift the epistemological focus towards the medial organization of the mind and cognition without questioning its ontological status. It is this awareness that is fundamental to the rise of philosophy of classical antiquity.[10] This sets in train a critique of cognition that was resumed in the Middle Ages under the conditions of a different social structure. The progress of cognition in the Middle Ages is difficult to assess because in the Middle Ages human thought continues to be constrained by metaphysics as regards its concept of the natural as well as the social world.[11] What undergoes a dramatic change, though, is man's status in the world. This change manifests itself all of a sudden on the eve of the Modern Age with Montaigne.[12] It is the precondition for the complete turn-around in the world-view of early modernity that we talked about initially. This finally gains its full force with the discovery of the theory of evolution in modernity, as we have seen, because ever since it has been possible to explain the

7 Nissen, Hans-Jürgen/Damerow, Peter/Englund, Robert K.: *Informationverarbeitung vor 5000 Jahren. Frühe Schrift und Techniken der Wirtschaftsverwaltung im alten Vorderen Orient*, Berlin ³2004.

8 Dux,: *Historisch-genetische Theorie der Kultur. Zur prozessualen Logik im kulturellen Wandel*, pp. 400 seq.

9 Very clear Bleicken, Jochen: *Die athenische Demokratie*, Paderborn ⁴1995.

10 Dux, Günter: "Die Genese der Philosophie in der Geistesgeschichte der Menschheit", in: *Dialektik, Zeitschrift für Kulturphilosophie* (2003), pp. 125 – 155.

11 Maier, Anneliese: *Zwischen Philosophie und Mechanik. Studien zur Naturphilosophie der Spätscholastik*, Rom 1958; in regard to the social world Grabmann, Martin: "Das Naturrecht der Scholastik von Gratian bis Thomas von Aquin", in: *Archiv für Rechts und Wirtschaftsphilosophie* (1922), pp. 12 – 53.

12 Montaigne, Michel de: *Essais*, II, 12, Paris 1843, p. 284: "Nous ne sommes ny au dessus,ny au desous du reste".

logic inherent in cognitive development from the very beginning of history right up to the Modern Age. From now on one can no longer philosophize about the history of the human mind and cognition without reconstructing the actual process itself. In the secularized modern world there does not only exist the truth concerning the knowledge of the natural universe that has become the province of the natural sciences, but in addition to this there is the truth about the conclusiveness in the development of the human mind and cognition that the human and social sciences lay claim to. How this development went on from epoch to epoch may be a controversial issue, something that happens in all intellectual endeavor. Naturally, I do not claim to be immune against criticism for what I have said and how I have said it in the preceding argument. However, that there does exist a stringent logic in the way the social and intellectual development progressed cannot be doubted by an understanding of history that proceeds historically-genetically.

This insight meets with an objection one encounters again and again, i. e. that of ethnocentrism. A historical-genetic reconstruction of history that ends up in modernity is a reconstruction of history that terminates in the West. All the same, it is decidedly not ethnocentric because the sequential logic by which the constructive competence unfolded through the interaction between subject and environment was also set in motion in other cultures.[13] However, in them it occurred under circumstances and correspondingly took on a historical course that did not go beyond the organizational forms of early societies until they came under the influence of the different achievements of the West, however problematic these may be. How does all of this affect our understanding of humanness?

## 6. Humanness as a Problem in a Secularized World

### 1. The Historicity of Life Forms as Part of *conditio humana*

The lengthy though sketchy reconstruction of the historical development of human life forms has made one thing clear: When attempting to determine his anthropological make-up man is referred to the particular historical manifestations of his life forms. His existence is not ontologically determined by some kind of immutable essence, but he is always only what he has ultimately made himself into. This historical insight leads to the consequence that is fundamental for understanding humanness as a normative postulate: In order to do justice to

13 Courbage, Youssef/Todd, Emmanuel: *Die unaufhaltsame Revolution. Wie die Werte der Moderne die islamische Welt verändern*, Munich 2008.

his anthropological properties, man has to live up to the expectations of the life forms he has currently attained. He has to work his way up to the level of his day and age in order to fulfill the promise held out by his life form. This was no problem in the agrarian societies of the past. It is, however, a problem in the market-driven societies of our present age.

### 1.1. Self-Determination

In the modern age man, cognizant of the constructedness of human life forms, especially of their social organization, also has itself to take responsibility for this life form. This concept of its own self has manifested itself in the postulate of self-determination at the beginning of the modern age.[14]

Self-determination is a highly complex term; it is composed of three dimensions:

- Firstly it is the manifestation of an anthropological concept according to which human life forms have been created by man himself.
- In the postulate of self-determination the will of the subject to take an active part in shaping the social life forms of his time finds its expression. Self-determination forms the very basis of any kind of democracy.
- Finally the postulate of self-determination expresses the desire on the part of the subject to determine on its own how to live its live.

In each of these dimensions is manifested the modern consciousness of living in a universe that has no other constraints than those inherent in the human life form itself. This insight forms the very foundation of democracy. This insight, however, also is the basis for each subject's desire to lead a life whose meaning is determined by the developmental level of society and its specific operation of endowing life with meaning.[15] This very form of a self-determined life in a market-driven society is inhibited by its being dominated by economic system.

> We must face up to the fact that in modernity we have got entangled in a conflict arising from the human self-awareness generated by the history of the species being confronted with the real quality of life in a capitalist market economy.

This is the very problem of self-determination in our times; it is at the same time a problem of our humanity.

14 Gerhardt, Volker: *Selbstbestimmung. Das Prinzip der Individualität*, Ditzingen 1999; Krähnke, Uwe: *Selbstbestimmung, Zur gesellschaftlichen Konstruktion einer normativen Leitidee*, Weilerswist 2007.

15 Dux, Günter: "Wie der Sinn in die Welt kam und was aus ihm wurde", in: Müller, Klaus E./ Rüsen, Jörn (Ed.), *Historische Sinnbildung*, Reinbek 1997, pp. 195–217.

## 7. Humanism as a Problem in a Market-driven Society

A market-society is a systematically differentiated society. The system that society is founded upon is the economic one. This statement has historical implications. With market-production a process of forming society was initiated in which everybody is related with everybody through the intermediary of the market. The market-driven society has therefore created a society such as it never existed before. Rule in agrarian societies was organized in such a way that people were contained in small communities within the ambit of a rulership solely motivated by self-interest. Within the embracing society people were not at all connected in their daily practices of life. It is not until the advent of market-society that everybody is linked to everybody. This is primarily regulated by the market, and additionally by the other two major systems, the political and the cultural one. In a market-society people have to be integrated in each of the systems. Other than through being integrated into the total system of society subjects would find access to the economic system of subsistence, but also not gain access to the cultural system, especially to education. Both forms of integration, the inclusion via the system of labor and through culture, the market society is incapable to guarantee, at least not for everyone. The reason for this is obvious.

The formation of the economic system as the system forming the very basis of society is determined by the interest of those who are organizing the business enterprises within it. They are mainly profit-oriented, i. e. they are solely interested in the accumulation of capital. It is an exclusively individualistic interest whose declared purpose it is not to provide subjects with material goods and thereby to unite them in a society. The fact that subjects are provided for by the economic system and are included in a society is nothing but a side-effect of the economic system. This goes as far as it goes, but it does not extend sufficiently far to include everybody. Throughout the history of the market-society the economic system, dominated as it is by the logic of accumulating capital, has integrated the people only to the extent that their integration was compatible with capitalist interest and on the conditions taking into account capitalist interests. At no times everybody has been included, and in the past a lot of those who had been included were accorded this privilege only on condition of being insufficiently provided for. This is hardly surprising, given an understanding of the genesis of the system at large and of the logic of an economic system based on the accumulation of capital. It is simply the expression of the logic by which the economic system is formed. This insights seems to enforce a conclusion that in my view is incontrovertible: market-society has a basic fault in construction: Every one of its members has to be included in the economic system in order to survive, the economic system, however, is incapable of including everybody, and particularly not in a sufficient way.

The economic system of a market economy has its correlation in the political one, which is also – because of its inherent quality – its counterpart, because the political system, by its very nature, is designed to incorporate everybody into society. Especially in its democratic variety it is determined by the purpose to create the conditions suitable for everybody being capable of leading self-determined lives. The transformation of the absolutist into the modern state was already determined by the intrinsic logic of having everybody participate in the political organization of society and thereby creating living conditions enabling everybody to lead their lives under humane conditions. This claim already ran afoul of the bourgeois interest in an unfettered development of the economic logic of a market-society which had just been formed in France as early as the French revolution. The representatives of the bourgeoisie in the national assembly had already fully internalized the intrinsic logic of the market-society. Although the third estate claimed to speak for everybody they eventually left out the people.[16] Their resistance against the bourgeoisie and against a market-oriented policy was doomed to failure. It led to the reign of terror and ended in the dictatorship of Napoleon Bonaparte.

The demand on the part of the people to have their share in shaping the politics of society cannot be rejected. It is the expression, as we have seen, of the self-understanding of the modern subject leading its life under self-created organizational conditions. The realization of this, however, was blocked for as long as a century by bourgeois liberalism. In Germany liberalism knew how to come to terms with monarchical structures in those countries, which after the Vienna Congress and the Karlsbad resolutions, successfully resisted any process of democratization. It was not until the proletariat managed to organize itself in the form of workerite parties and trade unions that the idea of democracy asserted itself throughout Europe, in its wake bringing the recognition of universal and equal suffrage as well as the emergence of parliamentary democracy.[17] The proletariat had hoped to gain the majority in the political system within a democratic constitution of society, thereby being enabled to shape social relations in its own favor.[18] This expectation proved to be a failure. Even at the

16 Sieyés, Emmanuel: "Was ist der dritte Stand?", in: *Politische Schriften*, Darmstadt/Neuwied 1998.

17 Rueschemeyer, Dietrich/Stephens, Evelyne Huber/Stephens, John D.: *Capitalist Development and Democracy*, Chicago 1992; Eley, Geoff: *Forging Democracy. The History of the Left in Europe, 1850–2000*, Oxford 2002.

18 Lassalle, Ferdinand:"Offenes Antwortschreiben an das Zentralkommitee zur Berufung eines allgemeinen deutschen Arbeiterkongresses zu Leipzig, 1963", in: Dowe, Dieter/Klotzenbach,

general election of January 1919 during the Weimar Republic, the Social Democrats only managed to win 37.9 percent of the vote, while they never got beyond the 30 percent mark in subsequent years. Even if in post-war Europe a 'social democratization' of politics was observable, this was only due to the public consciousness still closely under the influence of a mode and form of production such as it had come into existence during the industrial revolution. The obvious deficits of this were to be mitigated by the welfare state. The welfare state, however, was, by the time it was properly implemented, i. e. during the two decades after World War II, a welfare state in withdrawal. In the present, the market-society has undergone a development in consequence of which both social formations, the proletariat and bourgeoisie as they had emerged in history, have become dissolved. The way the economic system has since evolved has led to the distribution of profit between labor and capital being newly determined in the market, and along with the ensuing redistribution of wealth the seat of power in the political system has been shifted. Under the terms of the neoliberal creed the aims of politics have been redefined quite dramatically. Today it is the task of politics to support the capitalist structure of a market society in such a manner that the constitution of the state is grounded in the principles laid down by the former. As an outcome of this development the original purpose of democracy, i. e. creating the conditions enabling people to lead self-determined lives, has been simply eliminated. What has been put in its place is a political program which overburdens the subject with the task of taking sole responsibility for its life, which, however, it is not able to take on because the rules of the game are determined by the forces of the market.

## Conclusion

*The Demands of Humanism*

1. Humanism, as we have stated, takes a humane form of life as the very basis of its organization. There is no other standard in a secularized world. What was initiated in classical antiquity has now become the normative foundation of society: Man is the measure of all things. Man, that is the individualized subject, seen however only in conjunction with all other humans. According to the standard evolved in modernity his way of life is determined by the demands exacted by a self-responsible life-style. In a secularized world there is just no authority capable of enjoining upon the subject any rules that are not proceeding from his own self-determination.

Kurt (Ed.), *Programmatische Dokumente der Deutschen Sozialdemokratie*, Bonn [4]2004, pp. 102–132.

In the modern age humanism as a normative postulate therefore amounts to the demand of creating social conditions that enable everybody to lead a self-determined life.

2. Self-determination as a postulate and maxim of a certain way of life is unthinkable without the category of meaning. For a life form capable of constructing its own organizational structures the category of meaning becomes of primary importance. Exactly because the constructedness of human life forms manifested itself at the beginning of the modern age, the category of meaning entered the political arena. But meaning requires an organization of life that is in tune with its historical development. Meaning as a relevant category of human life therefore amounts to the demand to be integrated into society in such a way as to enable every individual to satisfy the precepts of meaning inherent in its society. This is why justice has to be understood as a normative postulate.

A self-determined form of life for all can only be realized under the condition of a just society. Humanness is tantamount to social justice.

3. The definition of humanism by the standards of justice can be made more concrete. On the one hand there is the demand of ensuring by political means the participation in the economic resources, which would enable everybody to make full use of the opportunities in life opened up by modernity. According to this postulate it is not sufficient to just secure the most elementary form of subsistence.

Humanity requires a social state guaranteeing everyone's participation in the culture of modernity. The state has to take over the obligation of guaranteeing a humane form of life.

4. After all the effort expended on making it clear that a humane form of life demands from everybody that they work their way up to the level of the society they have been born into, it then becomes equally clear that this requirement in the modern age can only be achieved by investing substantially in education.

Humanism demands access to education, and notably an immeasurably more comprehensive form of education than the one provided by the elementary form of scholastic education of the past.

Ilse Lenz

# Differences of Humanity from the Perspective of Gender Research

The humanity of human beings is a fundamental issue of modernity which has to be reconciled with the profound diversity of human subjectivities, interests and desires.[1] In modernity the mainstream concept of humanity was grounded in the idea of a homogenous equality. The 'general' term for human beings was 'man', which however basically referred to the European male citizen or the 'male-man'. This male-dominant concept at first sight seems to be gender-neutral. But the "rights of man" were not automatically valid for women or colonial subjects, rather they were established as the standard by which these groups were defined as 'Others'.

When Olympe de Gouges published her "Declaration of the rights of women and female citizens" and thus proclaimed a notion of citizenship including women, this was perceived as a threat. "The (male white) citizens of the new nations stood for the common ground and for what was universal, whereas the 'women', the other half of humanity, were defined as the 'other' and as what was particular."

In modernity, equality became a recognized universal value. But mankind was analyzed and categorized in terms of anthropological differences which were used to legitimate inequality. In the $18^{th}$ and $19^{th}$ centuries gender differentiation was raised to the level of a fundamental anthropological difference.[2] From ethnological research we know that non-European societies interpreted the border separating the genders in a much more flexible way and acknowledged a plurality of gender-roles while they mostly recognized a basic difference between women and men. The phenomenon of "third" or "fourth" genders in some societies – such as the "Female husbands" in West Africa or the "Sworn virgins"

1 For discussions and new ideas I would like to thank Reinhart Kössler, Hinrich Rosenbrock, Jörn Rüsen, Claudia Ulbrich and Charlotte Ullrich. Any errors are of course my own responsibility.

2 Honegger, Claudia: *Die Ordnung der Geschlechter. Die Wissenschaften vom Menschen und das Weib 1750–1850*, Frankfurt/Main 1991; Frevert, Ute: *"Mann und Weib und Weib und Mann". Geschlechterdifferenzen in der Moderne*, Munich 1995.

in the Balkans, who bear a male name, wear trousers, smoke and drink – shows that diverse gender variations existed historically in several parts of the world.[3]

In European modernity, however, gender became established as a self-evidently dualistic category by which human beings were either classified as men or women without permitting interspaces and variations. On the basis of this gender-dualism new hierarchies and inequalities between persons were established, both on the micro- as well as the macro-level. With reference to the different nature of woman and man new social hierarchies and a polar division of labor became instituted in bourgeois society: women were "by nature" destined for the role of house-wife and mother within the domestic sphere of the family, while men had to compete in the economy and politics. In everyday life, women were close to men – in the family and the job, and yet on the basis of the "natural" gender-differences they were regarded and treated as different and thus non-equal subjects.

At the same time there emerged both in Europe and the USA influential schools of thought claiming an anthropological difference between groups of people according to their "race". From this they derived a fundamental difference between the "white" and the "other races". This racist ideology was used to legitimatize hierarchies and inequalities on the macro-level under the general heading of European colonialism and imperialism. Leading cultural anthropologists actually did turn against racism fairly early on by maintaining that all races were equal. Especially after the crimes committed by the Nazis, racism – both as a scientific approach and as an ideology – was largely discredited, although it still continues to be effective.

The categorization as "others" that were anthropologically distinct from the modern (man-male) subject had been contested from the very beginning. Time and again emancipatory social movements like the feminist movement and the Civil Rights Movements in the USA protested against these hierarchies based on difference. From the 1960s onwards this critique was rekindled by new social movements, with the Black liberation movement in the USA and anti-colonial thinkers like Frantz Fanon setting an example in this respect. The feminist movement was strongly influenced by the Civil Rights and Black Power movements in the USA, and both were emphasizing the social discrimination of the excluded groups of women and Blacks.

Their discourses of equality were tinged with communalist semantics. The own group was understood as a "we-group", as a community of one's own[4]

3 Schröter, Susanne: *FeMale. Über Grenzverläufe zwischen den Geschlechtern*, Frankfurt/Main 2002.

4 Elwert, Georg (1989): "Nationalismus, Ethnizität und Nativismus – über Wir-Gruppen-prozesse", in: Waldmann, Peter/Elwert, Georg Hg.: *Ethnizität im Wandel*, Saarbrücken; Fort Lauderdale, p. 21–60.

which was internally homogenized as well as dualistically set off against those outside it. The battle-cry of "we women", which was directed against gender-discrimination and oppression, equally gave rise to the tendency of constructing "women" as a homogeneous group that was demarcated from "men". Thereby the feminist movement remained within the binary confines of modern European thought that assumed the existence of two biologically distinct genders. Since the 1970s the critique of inequalities and differences has been strongly linked to communalist semantics, whereby different groups were dualistically opposed and related to each other: women vs. men, Blacks vs. Whites etc.

These discourses aimed at a fundamental critique of all kinds of domination. Their heritage, however, has proved to be problematic in view of individual differences as well as the cross- and "trans"-movements that are typical of the current trend of reflective modernization.[5] Thus women have diversified their individual life plans and biographies; they have attained professional and skilled jobs as well as positions of power. Many migrant women presently live in a transnational social space which is developing between their place of origin and their present location and are developing transnational and flexible identities. Homogenizing and dualistic understandings of gender or culture are not adequate for understanding present social changes, if they ever were.

In the following, a connected interconnected dual perspective will be adopted: Firstly, I will consider the possible contribution of gender research to the analysis of differences and inequalities in modernity. Secondly, gender research itself will be questioned in terms of its own dualisms and communalist concepts such as "gender", "race" or "culture" that, like other critiques of domination, it had adopted since the 1970s. The aim is to come to a more diverse, but still universal understanding of humanism – or in other words, a self-reflective humanism.

## Equality and Difference in International Gender Regimes and in Transnational Feminist Networks

How far have universal gender norms prevailed globally? Are cultural differences still central and main leading norms? In modernity, the international community has become agreed upon the fundamental equality of all human beings as well as upon the rights of women and human rights. These principles are enshrined in the General Declaration of Human Rights on the UN and its

5 Lenz, Ilse: "Geschlecht, Klasse, Migration und soziale Ungleichheit", in: Lutz, Helma (Ed.): *Gender Mobil? Vervielfältigung und Enträumlichung von Lebensformen – Transnationale Räume, Migration und Geschlecht*, Münster 2009, pp. 25–68.

amendment from 1948, the results of the UN Human Rights Conference from 1993 and the UN-Decade of Women after 1975.[6]

The UN-Decade of Women was initiated by the First UN World Conference of Women in Mexico in 1975, in which activists from the "North", the "South" and the "East" were engaged in lively debates concerning political and emancipatory strategies. The Fourth UN World Conference in Beijing 1995 agreed on the World Action Platform, which can be considered an international charter of women- and human rights endorsed by governments and feminist movements of most countries. The implementation of its principles was carried out and monitored after 1995 at a number of other conferences taking place at the UN head-quarters at five-year intervals. Thus the entire process of UN based institutional and international mobilization extended all the way from the 1970s to the new millennium. In its course a unified and international gender-regime[7] became established under the auspices of the UN.[8]

The main goals of the UN-Decade of Women were "equality, development and peace", thus providing a wide framework for discussing differences and convergences. At the Beijing conference of 1995 the empowerment of women, i. e. the formation of power and autonomous participation as well as Gender Mainstreaming were defined as further aims. Gender Mainstreaming is understood as the aim of achieving gender equality in all organizations and institutions, a process in which both men and women are actively engaged, and with both genders equally participating in making decisions. Currently this is largely being replaced by diversity-concepts according to which women, migrants and elderly people should be participants on an equal basis. After the initial focus on gender differences other differences resulting for example from culture, race or sexual orientation[9] have become recognized and are now being integrated into present equality concepts.

The UN decade and its conferences on gender brought three outstanding results which are still vital and effective. The first result was the creation of a

6 Lenz, Ilse: "Globalization, varieties of gender regimes, and regulations for gender equality at work", in: Gottfried, Heidi et al. (Eds.): *Gendering the Knowledge Economy: Comparative Perspectives*, London 2007, pp. 110–140; Zwingel, Susanne: *How do international women's rights norms become effective in domestic contexts? An analysis of the Convention on the Elimination of all Forms of Discrimination against Women (CEDAW)*, PhD Ruhr-University Bochum 2005 www-brs.ub.ruhr-uni-bochum.de/netahtml/HSS/Diss/ZwingelSusanne/diss.pdf.

7 The concept of an international regime refers to norms and regulations commonly agreed upon. But the implementation of the international gender regime is still lagging behind.

8 Lenz: "Globalization, varieties of gender regimes, and regulations for gender equality at work"; Pietilä, Hilkka: *The Unfinished Story of Women and the United Nations. United Nations. Non-Governmental Liaison Service* (UN-NGLS), Geneva 2007. http://www.un-ngls.org/pdf/UnfinishedStory.pdf (14.7.2012).

9 Class is integrated in the intersectional perspective but less frequently implemented in equality policies.

common language and semantics for gender equality. This enabled global feminist movements to negotiate and process international differences and power relations and to develop shared aims and demands. Especially the international women networks were successful in recognizing difference while at the same time defining equality in new ways. The women's and human rights' approach[10] enabled the articulation of different experiences within their specific socio-cultural contexts, and then to "translate" these for other groups, making their meaning accessible to others in the process. Women's action committees for instance were reporting on violence against women – a problem of global dimension but which takes on a different form of cultural articulation in different cultures. By working on these problems in a comparative perspective, it was possible to formulate common positions and demands in spite of and beyond differences.

The second result consists of the international agreements and norms on gender equality. Mainly the UN worked out and concluded a number of international conventions which were ratified by a large majority of the member states. These conventions established global equality norms while also respecting cultural differences. The most important of these are the Convention for the Eliminating all Forms of Discrimination Against Women (CEDAW) of 1979 and the World Action Platform of the Fourth UN World Conference in Beijing of 1995. CEDAW was formulated in the course of long negotiations, with the lines of conflict running between and inside the capitalist and socialist countries as well as between and inside Christian and Islamic or secular positions.[11] It was essential in establishing gender equality as a norm in the areas of political participation, of education, of work and the family. It also affirmed the social relevance of motherhood and the joint responsibility of both parents so that the care for children has to be shared between men and women both in society and in the family.[12]

The World Action Platform was decided on at the last great UN world women's conference in 1995, and it can be regarded as the international charter

10 Peters, Julie/Wolper, Andrea (Eds.): *Women's rights, human rights. International feminist perspectives*, New York 1995; Merry, Sally Engle: *Human Rights and Gender Violence. Translating international law into local justice*, Chicago 2006.

11 Zwingel: *How do international women's rights norms become effective in domestic contexts?*; Schöpp-Schilling, Hanna Beate/Flinterman, Cees: *The Circle of Empowerment. Twenty-Five Years of the UN Committee on the Elimination of All Forms of Discrimination against Women*, New York 2007.

12 Convention on the Elimination of All Forms of Discrimination against Women (CEDAW) (1979) http://www.un.org/womenwatch/daw/cedaw/text/econvention.htm; Zwingel: *How do international women's rights norms become effective in domestic contexts?*

of women's and human rights.[13] It defined targets and detailed steps to be taken in twelve essential fields, among others concerning equality in education, the economy, paid and unpaid work as well as politics. Violence against women was thematized in its various forms such as rape, sexual violence in war and armed conflict, and the trade in women and human beings in general. In addition, the women's and human right to peace and non-violence was recognized, across all cultures, both with regard to the private sphere of the family as well as society at large. The globalized feminist networks both in the North and the South with their commitment against violence had made a major contribution to this.

The third important result is the establishment of women's departments (now gender departments) in political, social and economic organizations. At the First World Women's Conference of 1975 and in CEDAW all ratifying governments committed themselves to establishing departments for equal opportunities or women's desks. Consequently in political, social or economic organizations, equal opportunities sections were formed that often cooperated with civic society as well as the women's movement. The norms of gender equality and gender justice have become globally established and recognized by now. They have been implemented in national policies in many parts of the world, and women's organizations as well as civil society actors are working towards realizing gender equality and justice at the local level.

## Equality and Difference in the Perspective of Gender Research

Gender research developed alongside this international social process. It evolved potential contributions to the core issue of this article, i.e. in which way difference, inequality or equality are relevant for humanism because these concerns have been at the center of its international development after 1970. New gender research has emerged in a continual exchange with diverse cultural and social approaches, and thus has been able to build bridges between the North, South and East. It received international impulses and absorbed them within the context of national and local gender studies according to the respective societal needs. Thus it created what I call "blended compositions": This term means processes in which global impulses are appropriated and blended with national/local knowledge in order to arrive at culturally contextualized concepts. One classical example is the research on female sexuality and the body. It was initially encouraged by international research pioneers, but then local discourses and

13 UN: *Report on the Fourth World Conference on Women (Beijing, 4–15 September 1995)*. A/CONF.177/20.

terminologies were developed by action research and model projects close to the NGOs active in the field.

Gender research aimed at the improvement of knowledge for analyzing gender relations and enhancing reforms and equality in the national and local context. Various transnational feminist networks and research organizations have participated in this exchange of knowledge and joint activities arising from it.[14]

In its critique of gender inequality, new women's studies turned against homogenizing approaches that regarded the adaption of women to male norms as the precondition for equality.[15] Women refused to conform to the model of the "male-man" or the one-dimensional *homo economicus*. They were critical of the ideal of the "working monad",[16] who is exclusively oriented towards the requirements of the labor market and its demands of individual flexibility while neglecting love and eros.

According to the modern gender division of labor, women were assigned unpaid care work for family members such as children, husbands and elder relatives. Due to this gender division of labor, they embodied difference and an ethics of care and human relationaliy. Both norms are highly relevant for humanism, because children, the weak and the elderly need care and human attention that are practiced and lived in everyday relations and that cannot be adequately provided by the market economy.[17] Women's studies analyzed the social construction of gender and gender difference while acknowledging care work and the relationality going along with it as one central issue of modern society. Therefore it was critical of modern homogeneous concepts of mankind and demanded the recognition of equality and difference in the conceptualization and valuation of human beings.[18]

But it also concerned itself with the international and intercultural differences of gender relationships. Towards the end of the 1970s it abandoned the idea of a world-wide patriarchy. It developed highly differentiated research of gender relations in various cultures, such as in China, Japan, Korea or Germany.[19] This

14 Lenz, Ilse: *Die Neue Frauenbewegung in Deutschland. Abschied vom kleinen Unterschied. Eine Quellensammlung*, Wiesbaden 2008, pp. 917–997; Moghadam, Valentine: *Globalizing Women. Transnational Feminist Networks*, Baltimore 2005.

15 Gerhard, Ute (Ed.): *Differenz und Gleichheit. Menschenrechte haben (k)ein Geschlecht*, Frankfurt/Main 1990.

16 Eckart, Christel: "Verschlingt die Arbeit die Emanzipation? Von der Polarisierung der Geschlechtscharaktere zur Entwicklung der Arbeitsmonade", in: *Widersprüche* 23 (1987): 7–18. http://www.widersprueche-zeitschrift.de/article365.html.

17 Folbre, Nancy: *The Invisible Heart. Economics and Family Values*, New York 2001.

18 Gerhard (Ed.): *Differenz und Gleichheit. Menschenrechte haben (k)ein Geschlecht.*

19 Chang, Pil-Hwa/Kim, Eun-Shil (Eds.): *Women's Studies in Asia Series. Women's Experiences and Feminist Practices in South Korea*, Seoul 2005; Du, Fangquing/Zheng, Xinrong (Eds.):

awareness of historical and cultural differences was subsequently further differentiated by postcolonial criticism and the intersectionality approach.

## Postcolonial Feminist Critique

Postcolonial feminist critics like Chandra Talpade Mohanty[20] blamed "Western feminists" for propagating a Eurocentric universalism and measuring the situation of women in the Third World by European standards instead of seeing it within its own socio-cultural context. The critique of such a Eurocentric universalism was definitely justified. But some authors also implied that equality and non-violence are less important or relevant for women in non-European cultures.[21]

Some of the postcolonial researchers had a tendency to interpret the critique of the oppression of women in non-European societies as an attack on and debasement of their culture. Along with their rejection of Eurocentric universalism they upheld nationalist or communalist positions in which the recognition of cultural groups in the final resort took precedence over gender issues. Sometimes this was linked with a certain cultural relativism: Thus the critique of the genital mutilation of girls in some African cultures was countered by the argument that in the "West" numerous women decide to have breast implants for the very same reason – i. e. in order to conform with some socially imposed and idealizing image of the body.[22] Thus, the dilemma of gender and interculturalism had been negotiated by turning gender into an element of communal "culture". The price to pay for this de-differentiation was a high one:

Firstly, the analytic distinction between gender relations in certain sociocultural contexts and the recognition of cultures was suspended or relativized.

---

*Women's Studies in China. Mapping the Social, Economic and Policy Changes in Chinese Women's Lives*, Seoul 2005.

20 Mohanty, Chandra Talpade: "Under Western Eyes Revisited: Feminist Solidarity through Anti-capitalist Struggles", in: *Signs* 28.2 (2003): 499 – 537.

21 For new feminist postcolonial approaches cf. i.a. Reuter, Julia/Villa, Paula (Eds.): *Postkoloniale Soziologie*, Bielefeld 2010; Kerner, Ina: *Postkoloniale Theorien zur Einführung*, Hamburg 2010; Spivak, Gayatri: *A Critique of Postcolonial Reason. Toward a History of the Vanishing Present*, Cambridge/London 1999; Steyerl, Hito/Gutiérrez, Rodriguez Encarnación: *Spricht die Subalterne Deutsch? Migration und postkoloniale Kritik*, Wien 2003. Since an adequate appraisal of this rich and innovative research is not possible in this context, I am confining myself to some of its critiques of universalism.

22 Cf. Saharso, Sawitri: "Gibt es einen multikulturellen Feminimus? Ansätze zwischen Universalismus und Anti-Essentialismus", in: Sauer/Strasser: *Zwangsfreiheiten. Multikulturalität und Feminismus*, pp. 11 – 28, here 21 – 22. The comparison neglects that the genital mutilation of the clitoris removes the very centre of female sexual sensitivity and is mostly experienced as highly traumatic.

However, it is possible and meaningful to differentiate between gender relations in certain socio-cultural contexts on the one hand and the recognition of cultures with their incompatible and diverse values and symbolic systems on the other. I would like to illustrate this by drawing on the example of Christianity: Jesus Christ advocated the equality of man and women in family and religion. In spite of this women were excluded from becoming priests in the Catholic Church because they were the embodiment of "hereditary sin". The position of women in Christian societies was, however, historically differentiated and it depended i.a. on various institutional factors, such as their position in the state, the family or the economy. Christian Church Fathers laid the groundwork of European culture with their patriarchal pronouncements. Still in the twentieth century the European Community has recognized gender equality to the status of one of its fundamental values. In other words: Equating "gender" with "culture" tends to disregard the innovative force and changeability of cultures, which on account of their internal contradictions are also capable of bringing about changes towards the equality of genders.

Secondly, the human rights of individuals – and especially of minorities – often tend to be neglected in nationalist or communalist discourses, but they are the very touch-stone of power relations among the genders. It is one of the indicators of the degree of the humaneness of a society whether women are traded or forced into marriage, whether homosexuals are persecuted or prostitutes excluded. Such violations of human/women's rights are often legitimated by referring to communal culture. Gradually a transcultural understanding of complex inequalities according to gender, culture/ethnicity and class is emerging. Here, gender research can learn from humanism, in which the individual and its dignity occupy center stage. Neither an isolated individual nor communal norms can claim absolute priority. On the contrary, it is important to strike a balance between the autonomy and dignity of the individual and a human community that is based on liberty, equality and diversity.

Therefore, I am pleading for re-establishing the analytical distinction between gender relations and the recognition of cultures and societies. This distinction permits to examine gendered inequalities and power relations, especially violence against women, in a comparative perspective without resorting to a pose of cultural superiority or gestures of self-assertion.

## The Perspective of Intersectionality

While postcolonial critique was mainly focused on international inequality, the intersectionality approaches are mainly concerned with examining the constellation and interdependency of inequalities due to class, gender, culture/

ethnicity or desire in local or national contexts. This approach was initiated by the Afro-American lawyer Kimberlé Crenshaw. In coining the term of intersectionality she referred to different types of social discrimination that, like the flow of traffic at an intersection, impinge on an individual: "If a Black woman is harmed because she is in the intersection, her injury could result from sex discrimination or race discrimination".[23] This approach was soon taken up and elaborated upon[24] because it emphasized the contextuality and the variability of inequality: Gender does not work everywhere in the same way, but is interrelated with other categories of inequality: A female manager may have more power than a worker at a production line or a migrant gardener, but in spite of this she is bound to experience sexual stereotyping, sometimes even discrimination, when it comes to her being promoted etc. As is evident in this example, the approach is also suitable for showing up the tension between different categories of discrimination such as gender, class, desire and ethnicity. Thus, the perspective on inequality is becoming dynamized as well as contextualized. Furthermore, the approach of intersectionality has enlarged our vision of the factors capable of generating inequality: Besides the classical trinity of class, genders and ethnicity/migration other factors such as homosexual or gay desire, disability or age have come into focus. Several theoretical approaches aim at explaining the interaction between class, "race" and gender. Cornelia Klinger and Gudrun Axeli Knapp differentiate between three structures of inequality in modernity along the lines of class, gender and ethnicity. Based on this they delineate in general terms how these differentiations are related to the underlying structures of capitalism, the patriarchy and nationalism.[25]

## Inequality and Gender Conflicts

So far the *structures* of gender difference and inequality have been outlined and some essential approaches in gender studies have been presented in view of their possible contributions to humanism. However, the processual perspective is

23 Crenshaw, Kimberlé: "Demarginalizing the Intersection of Race and Sex. A Black Feminist Critique of Antidiscrimination Doctrine, Feminist Theory and Antiracist Politics", in: *University of Chicago Legal Forum* (1989), pp. 138–167.

24 Cf. Lenz, Ilse: "Intersektionalität: Zum Wechselverhältnis von Geschlecht und sozialer Ungleichheit", in: Becker, Ruth/Kortendiek, Beate (Eds.): *Handbuch Frauen- und Geschlechterforschung. Theorie, Methoden, Empirie*, 3. ed., Wiesbaden 2010, pp. 158–165; Lutz, Helma et al. (Eds.): *Fokus Intersektionalität. Bewegungen und Verortungen eines vielschichtigen Konzeptes*, Wiesbaden 2010; Winker, Gabriele/Degele, Nina: *Intersektionalität. Zur Analyse sozialer Ungleichheiten*, Bielefeld 2009.

25 Klinger, Cornelia/Knapp, Gudrun-Axeli (Eds.): *Über-Kreuzungen. Fremdheit, Ungleichheit, Differenz*, Münster 2008.

relevant as well: One core processual issue is formed by the conflicts arising from inequality, as well as their compromises and resolutions. By this I mean the discursive and practical controversies concerning the forms, legitimization and limits of social inequality. Depending on the focus of their discourses and activities, they can be categorized as class, culture, ethnic and gender conflicts. However, even class and ethnic conflicts are interwoven with gender semantics. Thus the citizens or later on the workers are represented as men and fighters. In contrast to this women often symbolically represent ethnic groups as mothers of the nation, and their beauty and purity is made to stand for its honor. But gender conflicts are equally permeated by ethnic or class semantics, as is evidenced by the difference between middle class or working class women's movements. In the following I would like to sketch a preliminary and concise concept for understanding gender conflicts and subsequently relate it to humanism.

Gender conflicts are defined as the contentions which are enacted both in discourses and practices concerning what is "just" with regard to gender. The term does not refer to structures like e.g. the modern gender division of labor, but rather to the thinking and actions of actors who, within the framework of these structures, articulate and act out conflicts: Is it just that mothers are maintained by their husbands so that they can concentrate on their household or children, or that the state supports single mothers, or finally that married mothers should hold down their own job? These notions of justice represent different ideas concerning a relationship between gender and society considered as just or good – or in other words norms of gender justice. They arise from different intellectual and cultural sources and are undergoing considerable changes as a result of modernization. The breadwinner/housewife pattern that has just been mentioned as a first model was favored by various conservative movements both in Christianity and Islam, but it also influenced parts of the workers movement that demanded a living wage for the father so that "his wife" did not have to work. Currently the third model of mothers being entitled to independent gainful employment has prevailed worldwide in numerous regions and has become part of women's and human rights demands.[26] But it is strongly contested.

This approach of gender conflicts draws the notion of what is just from the meaning of the relevant actors: What do *they* consider to be just? Which meanings and aims do they relate to these ideas? If scientists impose their external value judgments, they may fall into the trap of normative (and not analytical) conclusions and also miss the actors' motives, interpretations and norms. A relevant framework for interpreting their meaning of justice are the

26 Cf. CEDAW 1979 UN: *Report on the Fourth World Conference on Women (Beijing, 4–15 September 1995).*

global gender norms of women's and human rights agreed upon by the UN and the international community.

In this article, I focus on current gender conflicts because we are dealing with the challenge issued to humanism by inequality and difference. The meanings and aims of different actors in gender conflicts can be classified into three main currents, which again embrace a broad range of diverse tendencies:

1. The first current is committed to *opening* the gender conflict in the sense of autonomy and equality for all people, aiming at symmetrical gender relations. It comprises the liberal, value-conservative and emancipatory religious currents of Modernity. Gianna Pomata has elaborated on their historical location within humanism.[27] In this sense, women and men in various societies have become involved in social movements extending from the women's anticolonial, humanitarian, anarchistic, socialist and liberal movements.[28] They aim for individual autonomy and equality of all human beings, while at the same time horizontal differentiations in terms of desire or culture are recognized. They recognize diverse varieties of gender and sexuality such as homosexuality, queer and heterosexuality which are seen as being equally legitimate and forming the basis of individual autonomy. In their view, gender thus should lose its influence as a structural category of inequality and become an individual matter. Liberal currents emphasize individual freedom, whereas transformative currents demand the dismantling of structural inequality.[29] Care feminists are thinking about societal models where the care of children and the elderly is perceived as a social, network and familial concern, emphasizing the importance of the civil society as an agent besides the state and the market economy.[30]
2. A second broad and diverse current aims at bringing the gender conflict to a *standstill*, i.a. by propagating that the ideal of equal and individual opportunities has become realized in global capitalism. These currents are in favor of a new gender contract in the spirit of neo-liberalism.[31] They argue that

27 Pomata, Gianna: "Feminism as Integral to the History of Humanism", in: Rüsen/Laass: *Humanism in Intercultural Perspective. Experiences and Expectations*, pp. 167–177.

28 Cf. Lenz, Ilse/Szypulski, Anja/Molsich, Beate: *Frauenbewegungen international. Eine Arbeitsbibliographie*, Opladen 1996.

29 Cf. Lenz: "Geschlecht, Klasse, Migration und soziale Ungleichheit", pp. 29–38.

30 Osawa, Mari: "The Livelihood Security System and Social Exclusion: The Male Breadwinner Model revisited", in: Lenz/Ullrich/Fersch: *Gender Orders Unbound. Globalisation, Restructuring, Reciprocity*, pp. 277–302; Pascall, Gillian/Lewis, Jane: "Emerging Gender Regimes and Policies for Gender Equality in a Wider Europe", in: *Journal of Social Policy* 33 (2004): 373–394.

31 These various branches differ, among other criteria, as regards their idea of the family. The liberal variety of neo-liberalism sees it as an alliance of fundamentally equal individuals who are capable of negotiating their relationship on the micro-level; as a result they largely ignore the relevance of unpaid care or even consider it as a liability (Cf. inter al McRobbie, Angela:

present institutions such as the family and the labor-market offer equal opportunities for all individuals, even though in gender specific ways. Within the family women and men should individually and privately determine the modes of gender divisions of labor and relationship they prefer. The inequalities arising from this are seen as the result of personal and free choices made on the micro-level. At the same time all individuals have equal access to the labor-market due to improved educational opportunities. This model of the neoliberal gender contract tends to obfuscate the structure of power relations and depreciates feminism as a collectivist and obsolete way of thinking.[32]

3. A third broad current aims to end the gender conflict by means of a rigid hierarchical reorganization. It is comprised of a heterogeneous spectrum of fundamentalist currencies of religious, nationalist and masculinist trends, such as right-wing Christian sects in the USA, Islamist networks or right-wing nationalists in Europe, the US, Japan and Korea. They aim at revoking modernity's pledge of individual freedom and equality for women and also for ethnic minorities. They are ultimately in agreement in calling for the re-establishing of neo-patriarchal gender hierarchy: Men should exercise their "natural authority" in politics and the economy as well as in the family and women should revert to their "natural role" as housewives and mothers. They are also upholding communalist norms, such as the honor of the nation or other groups. Often this honor is embodied by women so that it has to be defended by controlling the female body. Individualism is seen as decadent or it is attacked because of its "Western" affiliations, and homosexuality it tabooed and persecuted. The neo-patriarchal concept of authority is grounded in re-establishing a clearly demarcated gender dualism in which men are dominant, women have to be protected in their role of mothers, and homosexual desire is repressed.

Humanism has been historically aligned with the first current, i. e. the advocacy of equality, even though it has only recently tended to problematize the relationship between equality and difference. However, it seems to face problems in defining its position vis-à-vis the neo-liberal claim of the individual equality of opportunities, according to which structural inequality is diffused into results of individual choice, which may sometimes turn out to be unfortunate. It has even

*The aftermath of feminism. Gender, culture and social change*, London, Thousand Oaks 2009. Conservative neoliberal tendencies aim at re-establishing the neo-patriarchal family, assigning it the mission to compensate the risks of the market economy (cf. George, Susan: *Hijacking America. How the Religious and Secular Right Changed what Americans Think*, Cambridge 2008).

32 McRobbie: *The aftermath of feminism. Gender, culture and social change.*

more problems with the third position, i. e. that of neo-patriarchal self-assertion. It sometimes tends to support its claims for the equality of cultural recognition while it ignores its subordination of the rights of women to equality and non-violence.

The interlinking of ethnic and gender conflicts may generate fundamental and violent struggles for recognition. Such fights for recognition are typical of conflicts arising from inequality. They can be particularly violent when they involve the body, sexuality or sexual violence. The honor of the own group is then equated with the concept of female purity and its protection as symbolizing this honor, which can lead to "murders of honor". It may also motivate sexual violence against women from an opposing group in order to humiliate them and their men, as happened in the Yugoslavian war in the 1990s. Humanism is faced with the challenge of conflicting demands for recognition plus the respective logic informing these: the individual right to autonomy and equality versus communalist cultural assertion. It has not always taken the side of individual women, young people or dissidents who – like the conscientious objectors in the Yugoslavian war – refused to become complicit with violence.

## Reflective Universalism

Thus, humanism is confronted with a value conflict between universal human and women's rights and the rights of particular groups. I want to argue that reflective universalism could show a way beyond this dilemma. Enlightenment universalism proved to be Eurocentric because it was founded upon specific European values and it measured other cultures by this standard. Thus, it contributed to legitimating colonialism, imperialism and racism in dealing with non-European cultures. Due to this colonial complicity of Eurocentric universalism, poststructuralists and postcolonial critics tend to distance themselves and give precedence to the particular, the little narrations of the life world in contrast to the grand narrative and modernity's promise of freedom and equality. But the particular, the small world of the household, of village life or ethnic patronage are not free from domination, personal subjection and violence, as gender research has proved.

At the same time universalism does not forfeit its claim to global justice because of its Eurocentrism. Its legitimacy was disputed due to its narrow interest bound affiliation to European domination, or in other words because its range of application was restricted to privileging white men and women. But universalism is contradictory: While it proved exclusive and sometimes repressive in its historical narration and application, its basic ideas and promises of liberty, equality and solidarity are deeply inclusive and are now recognized as global needs and aspirations. Universalism has to be combined with critical and reflective global reflection. When universalism will acknowledge horizontal differences and criticize all kind of domination, it can overcome its historical and Eurocentric limitations.

A potential elective affinity between reflective universalism, humanism and feminism is indicated in diagram 1.

Diagram 1: Concepts of equality and hierarchy in the conflict between ethnicity and gender

| | | Gender concepts | |
|---|---|---|---|
| | | Universal gender equality | Gender hierarchy |
| Concepts of culture | Universal equality of cultures | - reflective universalism<br>- Global universalism<br>- humanism | - neo-patriarchalism based on cultural difference |
| | Communalism and ethnocentrism | - ethnocentric or racist gender policy<br>- ethnocentrism or racist feminism | - neo-patriarchal, ethnocentric or racist social organization |

Diagram 1: Concepts of equality and hierarchy in the conflict between ethnicity and gender

The diagram shows up the possible combinations between egalitarian and hierarchical concepts in the conflict between ethnicity and gender equality resulting in a range of constellations. When universal gender equality is combined with ethnocentrism or communalism one can speak of an ethnocentric feminism that asserts its own progressiveness by setting itself off against the "oppressed women in the other culture". It can be used in order to legitimize an ethnocentric or racist gender policy. These tendencies are currently emerging in liberal-conservative gender policies throughout Europe. If one argues in favor of all cultures being equal – irrespective of whether they are based on gender inequality and violence – neo-patriarchal gender relations can be reestablished. Relevant examples are the considerations to apply the sharia as municipal law in Canada or court sentences in France and Germany where in cases of marital violence or divorce husbands could plead for extenuating circumstances by referring to their "different culture".

When a hierarchical ordering of genders and cultures/ethnicities is advocated, this can result in an explosive mix of ethnocentrism and sexism, in which women's and human rights become restricted. The fundamentalist states of the Middle East like Saudi Arabia or Iran are examples of a neo-patriarchal order. Positions like these propose the maintenance or hierarchical reorganization of neo-patriarchal gender relations. The three currents outlined here may suggest that the question of a reflective universalism does not just constitute an academic problem; it could rather become highly relevant for the resolution of future conflicts arising from ethnic/gender inequalities. Finally, the diagram illustrates the elective affinity (*Wahlverwandtschaft*) between reflective universalism, humanism and feminism: accordingly reflective universalism is only viable if the equality of genders and cultures including their horizontal differences are recognized. Global feminism has aimed to work out the tensions and chances of relating and bridging these kinds of equalities. In this sense reflective universalism and global feminism may offer important contributions for the further differentiation and enrichment of humanism.

Jürgen Straub

# Personal Identity: A Concept in Humanist Tradition?

## Humanism and the Question of Psychological Identity

'The' humanism as such does not exist, not even if one limits one's focus to the territory and history of Europe while not considering those other regions where humanism in one of its numerous guises has long taken root and acquired a new form.[1] What we are, in fact, dealing with is a disparate and multifaceted, even *self-contradictory* tradition. Cancik lists a number of typical and often irreconcilable currents: the Western, atheist, Christian, dialectical, ethical, evolutionary, existentialist, Hebrew, classical, critical, socialist and secular brands of humanism.[2] Humanism is obviously highly heterogeneous and is capable of continually generating new variants.

In the 20th century, a "humanist psychology" emerged.[3] From the 1960s onwards it became most influential in forming the discourse and practice of an even if not totally new but decidedly altered concept of man. The human subject that began to *practice* and *interiorize* a *specifically psychological view* of itself and others is a creation of modern psychology. Humanist psychology made an im-

1 Cf. e.g. the contributions in Rüsen, Jörn/Laass, Henner (Eds.): *Interkultureller Humanismus*, Schwalbach/Ts. 2009, and also in the present volume.

2 As well as some others: cf. Cancik, Hubert: "Humanismus", in: Cancik, Hubert/Gladigow, Burkhard/Kohl, Karl-Heinz (Eds.): *Handbuch religionswissenschaftlicher Grundbegriffe*, vol. III: *Gesetz - Kult*, Stuttgart 1993; Cancik, Hubert: "Entrohung und Barmherzigkeit, Herrschaft und Würde. Antike Grundlagen von Humanismus", in: Faber, Richard (Ed.): *Streit um den Humanismus*, Würzburg 2003; Cancik, Hubert: "Die Rezeption der Antike - Kleine Geschichte des europäischen Humanismus", in: Rüsen/Laass: *Interkultureller Humanismus.*

3 For a survey cf. Schneider, Kirk J./Bugental, James F./Pierson, J. Fraser (Eds.): *The Handbook of Humanistic Psychology. Leading Edges in Theory, Research, and Practice*, Thousand Oaks/London/New Delhi 2001; on its rather idiosyncratic 'humanist' program cf. Straub, Jürgen: "Wissenschaftliche Psychologie als Humanismus? Rekonstruktion eines hybriden Programms zur Errettung der modernen Seele", in: idem (Ed.): *Der sich selbst verwirklichende Mensch. Über den Humanismus der Humanistischen Psychologie*, Bielefeld 2012, pp. 15-68.

portant contribution to this – long before and alongside psychoanalysis as founded by Sigmund Freud and some other of its branches.[4]

This equally applied to the program of a continuous practice of *self-thematization* and *self-alteration* for the purpose of maximizing personal happiness and achieving certain social aims, all of which has manifested itself in various psychotherapies and practices of "psychoboom". As a rule, such processes have been, and will be, accompanied and even furthered by "facilators" with a supporting or manipulating role (consultants, therapists, pedagogues, trainers, coaches, group-dynamic instructors, psychoanalysts etc.). Quite frequently, the measures taken are given a technological interpretation. In such a case they are (over-) simply accepted as scientifically proven forms of optimizing by instrumental means experience and behavior of 'souls' that are seen to be in need of improving or correcting, and sometimes are also greatly suffering.

These technological approaches to human beings, these instructions and interventions also mostly lay the emphasis of the 'work' on the emotions of their addressees (for quite some time people have actually been talking about "emotional work" or "the work of grieving"). As a principle, they do not shy away from interfering with all kinds of psychological structures or functions (perceptions, thinking, desire, wishes, demands – almost anything can be turned into an object of self-thematization and self-optimizing). The aims pursued by the relevant interventions and instructions – especially in humanist psychology and the concomitant world view – go under the resounding names of such promises as: health happiness, self-experience and self-realization, emancipation and responsibility, independence and autonomy, freedom and justice, interpersonal relationship and the ability to love as well as a host of other accomplishments and "competences" are prominent examples of an ever widening range of offers. Basically everything revolves around a question that seems quite innocuous – the so-called question of identity. In its temporalized form it sounds as follows: "Who am I, how did I become who I am, who do I want to be or shall I be?"

The modeling of modern man along the lines of psychology, psychoanalysis, psychotherapy or psychotechnology is anything but a harmless enterprise that is something universally acceptable and pleasant to all people concerned. This

4 For us contemporaries, the psychological view is something highly familiar and literally inscribed into our body. It constantly structures our perception, thinking, feeling and acting. This at least applies to all those belonging to the so-called Western world. In spite of all the problems that arise when it comes to defining a generally accepted concept of "Modernity", one can state with certainty: even in the *modern* societies of the Orient, Western psychology, psychoanalysis and psychotherapy have so far scarcely taken root. This is another aspect that the numerous studies devoted to multiple modernities should take into account more than they have done until now.

sometimes brutal but mostly subtle *making* and *modifying* of human beings in the name of – as they claim – a continually *self-optimizing process of optimization* is foreshadowing the *individualized individuals* of late- or post-modernist societies.[5] The psychologised, psychoanalyzed and psychotherapized subject is not, as we know, necessarily happier than the person that has been spared such (self-) therapy. Moreover, sometimes he or she may not even end up being more competent (in whatever respect). Even this type of subject, or especially this one, will be unable to find its way out of its notorious sense of unease with and in an inhospitable Modernity and frequently just waits for the fulfillment of great promises.[6]

In the end, the individual that has been psychologized, psychoanalyzed and psychotherapized remains dependent on those institutions and persons who hold out the promise of self-realization, freedom and autonomy and their subsequent consummation. The psychological perspective on oneself and others can also be regarded as a controlling and disciplinary dispositive.[7] It has acquired the status of a disposition that is deeply embedded in the inner lives of late- and post-modern human beings. It has been *interiorized* and *practiced* by millions and millions of people (and is barely felt to be something particular, strange, peculiar or even alienating). It is perceived as a matter of course and something that has been *gradually* 'acquired', painfully 'striven for' and dearly 'bought' in a process of social normalization that is the result of relations of power and domination.

The *imperative of the psychological view* that has been internalized as a disposition and been integrated into the habitus of countless groups is without doubt an appropriate aspect of the reflective lifestyle on the part of late- or post-modernist subjects; it may often turn out to be useful, sometimes even unavoidable, mostly helpful for living one's life, and occasionally indispensable for survival. The relevant, even necessary critique of this imperative, and especially of its subtle and "subcutaneous" effects, does not alter this in the least. Therefore there are well-founded and justifiable ways of not exclusively interpreting the 'subjection' of modern subject by the meandering imperative of psychology, psychoanalysis and psychotherapy as the result of *pure* domination and mere repression (as Foucault does with regard to psychoanalysis at the end of the first volume of his work *Sexuality and Truth*, thereby pouring out the baby with the

5 Beck, Ulrich/Beck-Gernsheim, Elisabeth: *Riskante Freiheiten. Individualisierung in modernen Gesellschaften*, Frankfurt/Main 1994.

6 The analyses by Illouz, Eva: *Saving the Modern Soul: Therapy, Emotions, and the Culture of Self-Help*, Berkeley 2008, for several years have been very pertinent to this complex of issues.

7 As elaborated by Michel Foucault; cf. e. g. Foucault, Michel: *Dits et Écrits*, 4 vols., Frankfurt/Main 2001–2005; Kammler, Clemens/Parr, Rolf/Schneider, Ulrich Johannes (Eds.): *Foucault Handbuch. Leben – Werk – Wirkung*, Stuttgart/Weimar 2008.

bathwater[8]). Instead of such a pathetic and pseudo-radical critique of the progressive intentions and emancipatory aims of modern psychology, psychoanalysis and psychotherapy, a more balanced and sober strategy seems appropriate whereby the appraisal and assessment of this whole field could be more differentiated. Psychological, psychoanalytical and psychotherapeutic theories and practices are *by all means capable* of enriching human lives. Not least of all they *may* assist individuals to free themselves from obscure constraints, thus making them into more liberated, self-confident and autonomous persons. They may also help people order the life they share with others according to the principles of reciprocity, equality and justice. Psychologically grounded and supported processes of self-experience, self-reflection and self-formation undoubtedly *also* serve the purpose of practicing empathy and the ability to adopt another person's view. This may not completely ensure compassion and solidarity. It is, however, the absolute precondition for the practical application of such humanist values. In conclusion one can say that modern psychology (including psychoanalysis and psychotherapy) is in many respects interwoven with the most relevant concerns of humanist tradition, even in those cases where it does not expressly designates itself as "humanist". This becomes evident by the point to be elaborated on in the following: the psychological view of oneself and others assists in the formation of a subject that is characterized by a *specifically structured understanding of itself and the world.* The name for such a communicatively acquired understanding of the self and the world, which in psychology (and some of its neighboring disciplines) has been elevated to the status of a theoretical concept, is *identity.* Therefore there are good reasons for asking oneself if the complex theoretical construct of *personal identity* belongs within a pragma-semantic field in which the traces of the humanist tradition – at least of certain types of humanism – cannot be overlooked.

Since more than a hundred years, modern psychology, psychoanalysis and psychotherapy have been busy crafting – regardless of their differences concerning certain details – a 'neo-humanist' image of man (and have been involved in its practical acceptance in all kinds of social sub-systems as well as in the life world). This ever more detailed image refuses to conform to the naïve illusion and idealizing heroism of man "as such", as it is still to be met with in superannuated anthropologies. It is opposed to all formerly glorified ideas of a strong subject (be it the subject of consciousness, reason or desire). This concept of mankind that is closely allied with notions of identity tends to replace and dismantle such ideas in the process of an irreversible deconstruction and decentring of the *supposed* 'subject of previous centuries'. This idea of an ever more distinct view of a *soggetto debole* that is more self-effacing and reticent and that

8 Foucault, Michel: *The History of Sexuality*, vol. 1: *An Introduction*, New York 1978.

is no longer relying on its will and agency is about to gain a new 'strength' and 'autonomy' just by realizing its weakness and limitations, its neediness, emotionality and inescapable dependency.[9]

The following thoughts on the concept of identity are going to present an interpretation of the theoretical notion of personal identity which in the exuberance of postmodern excitement and in the often too enthusiastic adulation of fragmentariness has become side-lined by the social and cultural sciences and their propagation in the mass-media. The postmodern pathos has become somewhat diminished by now, and the aesthetic, ethical or political celebration of fragmentariness has lost a great deal of its splendor. This particularly applies to the relish or celebratory spirit with which the fragmented (dissociated, multiple, polyphrenic, rhizomatic etc.) personality and its 'existence' that was broken into thousands of disconnected pieces had been praised (something that one should at most call a kind of 'subsistence' in the turbo-capitalist fight for survival). Nonetheless the postmodern penchant for what is fragmentary is not completely over yet. Insofar as this liking completely ignores the actual suffering of really fragmented (dissociated, multiple, polyphrenic) people, it forms part of a cold cynicism that has lost its connection with reality. Whoever commingles and confuses the fascinating beauty of the fragment and fragmentariness in art (in the fine arts as much as in literature and music) with the painful suffering of people who are headed for a breakdown or who are hopelessly divided, is fostering an inhumane indifference which is forsaking all the achievements of the humanist tradition that are still worth preserving. The concept of personal identity advanced in the following is firmly embedded within this tradition and can only be understood in its terms. At this juncture one nevertheless has to pose the question which tradition or which kind of humanism is being referred to.

If one adheres to the historical development of the concept the line extends all the way from Roman *humanitas*, i. e. humanness or humanity, and via later variations of the same to the term *humanism*, which was first introduced by Friedrich Niethammer (1766 – 1848) as late as the 19th century. With Niethammer the concept referred to a reforming pedagogy that aimed at "the general and non-vocational preparation for university studies, the care 'for the humanity of the pupil'".[10] Only many decades after the original proclamation of this educational program of reform the term gained currency as the designation of an historical epoch – i. e. the Italian renaissance (as propounded by George Voigt and Jacob Burkhardt). Finally it came to refer to *all kinds of* intellectual currents of some practical relevance (see above) that were based on certain *anthro-*

9 Not least of all upon the recognition of others; cf. Todorov, Tzvetan: *Abenteuer des Zusammenlebens. Versuch einer allgemeinen Anthropologie*, Berlin 1996.
10 Cancik: "Humanismus", p. 174.

*pologies* and *concepts of mankind* while propagating a corresponding world view and political or pedagogical aims. In the process, the reference to Greco-Roman antiquity which was central for classical humanism tended to recede into the background or vanished altogether.

The inherent *double* meaning of humanity (*humanitas*), which also left its imprint on numerous projects and movements (and still continues to do so), gives a first helpful indication, even though it still may be somewhat general and abstract, of what one might these days understand by humanism – especially with regard to a *psychological* neo-humanism that counts "personal identity" among its key concepts. Humanity, as Cancik[11] points out, has always denoted "education" (*erudition, litterae, scientia*) and also "mildness of manners" (*mansetudo, comitas, benignitas* as well as intellectual erudition' (*eruditio*) and '(active) mercifulness' (*philanthropia*) all in one. This concept, along with the various philosophical-humanist programs derived from it, comprises, roughly speaking,

- the attempt at a *universal (anthropological) definition* of mankind as a species,
- *ethical and moral reflections* that in Modernity are concerned with the universal dignity of mankind and general human rights, around questions of equality and justices,
- the pedagogically and politically motivated appeal to subjecting mankind, and each individual, to a *process of formation as well as education*, thereby working upon the continuous and never ending perfection of human beings as integrated wholes,
- the injunction to always orientate human life and its practices by *human principles*, i. e. devoting special care and support to those who are in need of help.

Of course, the concept of "personal identity" appears in none of the humanisms that had emerged until the early 20th century. It is the product of a more recent late modernist or postmodernist age in which the theoretical reflection upon *differences* and *tensions within the subject itself*, such as they are experiences in everyday life, has acquired an intensity hitherto unknown as well as a depth that had been previously unexplored. European psychoanalysis and American pragmatism (also rooted in Europe) were decisive in paving its way and shaping its profile. Alongside with these more profound insights into the contingent and complex as well as the dynamic and fragile structure of the late and postmodern

11 Cancik: "Die Rezeption der Antike – Kleine Geschichte des europäischen Humanismus", p. 32.

subjects' communicative relation to the self and the world, the theory of personal identity appears on the scene.

It is tantamount to the endeavor, so far unfinished, to conceive of the unity of the individual person, an entity that cannot be reified, can never be attained and that defies stabilization as the (also temporalized) synthesis of something highly heterogeneous. It is the attempt to theoretically conceptualize a subject that in a splintering and continually changing world remains at least somehow capable of judgment, orientation and action. All of this is not a matter of course. The theory of personal identity is attempting to supply an answer to the question of what the desirable options are in the face of such a predicament. Its response unmistakably takes up the demands and norms of the multifaceted humanist tradition by transporting, specifying and renewing it.

The multiplicity of humanist world views and their respective ideas of humanity render it somewhat difficult to link up the concept of *personal identity* with any one particular tradition or to conceive of it as a humanist project on a determinate sense. How could one, given present conditions, arrive at a meaningful neo-humanist definition of "personal identity"? The ensuing argument may be read as supplying an answer to this very question. It attempts to outline the contours of a psychological humanism in the age of post- and late modernity. For good reason, such a neo-humanism, which is aware of its antecedents, is focusing its interest on the concept of *personal identity.* It is evident that such an idea of humanity that is decidedly inspired by a psychological (as well as historical and culture-specific) anthropology can contribute to correcting some *supposedly* universalizing assumptions about mankind 'as such'. This precautionary measure is a protection against (time-specific) eurocentric humanism which is not qualified to speak on behalf of all mankind. The psychology of personal identity also wishes to make a contribution to the globalized intercultural dialogue upon what constitutes our common humanity. This also raises the question if certain aspects of the psychology of personal identity – whether based upon empirical, ethical, moral or political considerations – might not be amenable to being universalized in the era of globalization. It is thereby also an invitation to all those interested in this problem to reflect upon the question whether the concept of personal identity might not be a particularly adequate and attractive way of indicating the modalities of an up-to-date human self-understanding. These are attractive and convincing at once because they may point out a viable path towards the aim of a more self-critical and modest perfection of mankind. Should it turn out to be successful, this hesitant, but by no means procrastinative perfection of humans would be closely connected with education and formation of individuals capable of openly interacting with one another in a world that is growing ever more complex.

The theory of personal identity is unique in embracing more than any other the idea of *openness*, which is very demanding in psychological terms. As we shall demonstrate, the "self-identical" person does not shut her- or himself off neither from the external other and stranger nor from what is other and strange within the self. It rather displays an unbiased and open-minded attitude towards, and interest in, whatever is new. This is not an easy thing to achieve. On the contrary, such openness is the result of a life-long process of learning. New experiences, in whatever content and shape, are by their nature unforeseeable and are therefore something of an imposition which can go beyond the bound of what a person may be capable of tolerating, thereby overtaxing it. "Identity" in this context designates that kind of communicative behavior in persons confronted with such a situation that enables them to encounter whatever is novel without *too much fear* and – when it turns out to be disturbing or upsetting – to cope with the situation by drawing on the creative resources available to oneself.

## Identity: Heterogeneous Meanings, First Determinations[12]

As early as the 1970s, the concept of identity became increasingly diffused with regard to its cultural pragmatics and semantics, which was due to its omnipresence. Its various functions became dissociated. Ever since critics have objected to the descriptive, analytical and explanatory potential of the term having become exhausted. One thing is undeniable: a proliferating polyvalence and an untameable polyfunctionality are its hallmark.[13]

The "identity of a person" refers to subjects that are capable of *distancing* themselves from, and *situating* themselves vis-à-vis, their own selves. The idea of identity is based on the elementary insight that every feeling and every thought of an individual *being identical with oneself* – i. e. of *being like oneself* in a non-trivial and more than tautological sense – inevitably presupposes change in the perspective on (a life's) history and an intrinsically multifaceted self in the present, therefore entailing an inherently *differential, transitory* and *heterogeneous* structure of the subject (see below). The physical manifestation, the practical articulation and symbolic reflection of this *complex structure* (in temporal, social, cultural and factual terms) is the most basic logical implication of any sophisticated (modern) identity. An identity defined as the *unity of differences* is not a quality in the sense of an 'external' feature that can be ascribed to human beings in the same way as to objects. The question of identity is premised on a subject capable of speaking and acting.

12 Some of the following passages are largely identical with their previous publication in *Handbuch für Kulturphilosophie*, Stuttgart 2012.
13 Straub, Jürgen: *Theorien der Identität*, Hamburg 2013.

However, this does not imply that identity is a kind of private matter that is independent from what others have to say and that can do without their recognition. There can be no identity without the experience and expectations *shared* by others. Accordingly, the identity of a person has to be distinguished from her or his *individuality*, uniqueness and distinctiveness (and to a certain degree her or his ineffability: *individuum ineffabile est*). This also does not mean that the subject has an immediate and unlimited access to its own identity or is conscious of it. In this regard, too, there is the possibility of self-delusion or of superior insight on the part of others. In spite of all this one thing is certain: in the most fundamental sense, identity is a personal matter. Accordingly, Ricœur[14] speaks of *ipse*-identity (ipse; selfhood; ipséité, *Selbstheit*) and distinguishes it from *idem*-identity (idem; sameness; mêmeté; *Selbigkeit*). The question of identity from the perspective of *ipse*-identity is the *who*-question motivated by the practical self-concern of human being: "who am I (or have I become) and who do I (actually, now and in the future) wish to be?", which means that this is not an impersonal *what*-question that can only be posed from the perspective of any outside observer whose concern is the *idem*-identity: "what is something (at certain points in time $t_1$, $t_2$, … $t_n$)?"

Such a concept of selfhood presupposes no constancy of 'something', but it inquires after the identity of a person or a group under the *paradoxical* and at the same time *constitutive* premise that everything in this person's life is basically capable of changing, that a lot actually has changed and that quite a few things will change (in a contingent, often unforeseeable way). Additionally, in each life there are quite a few synchronical elements that do not quite cohere and that give rise to latent 'inner' tensions and sometimes even manifest themselves as conflicts (e.g. conflicting orientations and inclinations, wishes and desires, irreconcilable convictions, conflicting interests etc.). Within this language game, identity and difference are *by no means logically* disjunctive categories or mutually exclusive concepts. Rather, they presuppose each other and cannot exist separately. One can even say that the identity of a person can only be defined as the dynamic as well as fragile *unity of its* (*diachronical and synchronical*) differences. Such a definition does not require any essentialist and substantialist assumptions about a constant core of a person's selfhood (*simper idem*).

14 Ricœur, Paul: *Das Selbst als ein Anderer*, Munich 1996, p. 141 ff., 173 ff.

## The Historical, Cultural and Social Context

The question of identity arises only when considerable *and continuous differentiations of the self in a dynamically changing world* prompt it with great urgency. It only becomes virulent in a context where the answer is no longer obvious or even pre-given, but, rather, is to be supplied by the subjects themselves and is therefore intricate, remaining, moreover, provisional. The question of identity is an *indicator of a problem.* It points to the incertitude and uncertainties that have been empirically diagnosed in many regards, to the need for orientation and to the crisis of meaning which in the 20th century became notoriously typical of a rapidly growing number of people.[15]

It is well known that the conditions under which the question of identity flourishes (and becomes functional) has at least in some respects become "globalized" or "glocalized", particularly over the last few decades. This has led to the range of problems where the concept of identity can be 'legitimately' applied having become considerably extended. And yet its *specific* pragma-semantics, i.e. its socio-cultural *relativity* has to be taken into consideration. Even today, a fairly small proportion of mankind is suffering from problems of identity or is going through a crisis of identity. The practical concern of the majority of people is of a different order. This does, by the by, pertain to an indeterminate part of the members of modern societies. Among them there are persons whose self is by no means structured along the lines of the concept of identity that has been developed in our context.[16]

The idea of identity originated in the Western world of industrialized societies in the 19th century, deriving its specific meaning within that very context. For

15 Berger, Peter L./Berger, Brigitte/Kellner, Hansfried: *The Homeless Mind. Modernization and Consciousness*, New York 1973; Eagleton, Terry: *The Meaning of Life*, Oxford 2007; Giddens, Anthony: *Modernity and Self-Identity. Self and Society in the Late Modern Age*, Cambridge 1991; Taylor, Charles: *Sources of the Self: The making of the modern identity*, Cambridge 1989; idem: *The Ethics of Authenticity*, Cambridge, MA, 1991; Willems, Herbert/Hahn, Alois (Eds.): *Identität und Moderne*, Frankfurt/Main 1999.

16 For reasons of space, a comparison with theories of the self from other cultures, whereby our theories of identity could be confronted with alternatives, must be passed over. The differentiation between (primarily 'Western') *independent* and a (primarily 'Non-Western', 'Eastern') *interdependent* self is one of the most popular ones. This pair of opposites (amounting to a crude contrast between both sides that also homogenizes either) is part and parcel of an equally simple differentiation between individualistic cultures (corresponding on the personal level with an individuocentric/ideocentric orientation) and collectivist cultures (with a sociocentric/allocentric orientation). The as yet most influential theory of cultural self-concepts is the one propounded by Markus, Hazel/Kitayama, Shinobu: "Culture and the self: Implications for cognition, emotion, and motivation", in: *Psychological Review* 98 (1991): 224–253; cf. Straub, Jürgen/Chakkarath, Pradeep: "Identität und andere Formen des kulturellen Selbst", in: *Familiendynamik* 36 (2010): 110–119.

that reason, it is simply wrong to use this term as a universal anthropological category by applying it to all kinds of people in the past and present. Whoever speaks of identity in the sense developed in our context, is referring to late or postmodernist societies, which in the social and cultural sciences are characterized by certain diagnostic terms that have by now acquired the status of catchwords: temporalization, dynamics, acceleration, division of labor as part of a process of industrialization based on science and technology, (functional) differentiation, mobility, flexibility, (social and cultural) plurality, deontologization, de-traditionalization and individualization.[17] Not least, it is the awareness of an increasing sense of contingency.

## Theory of Identity: Basic Differences

Since so far there has never been evolved a sufficiently elaborated concept of identity in any of the theoretical traditions, one has to keep on looking for a concept that is acceptable in practical and, not least of all, normative-political terms. There are some trendsetting starting points, especially in the tradition of American pragmatism (e.g. William James, George H. Mead) and symbolic interactionism (e.g. Anselm Straus), in psychoanalysis (e.g. Heinz Lichtenstein), in phenomenology and hermeneutics (e.g. Paul Ricœur), but also in analytical philosophy (e.g. Michael Quante), or in integrating approaches (e.g. Jürgen Habermas).[18] In what follows we shall recall the relevant meaning that the concept of identity has acquired within this interdisciplinary field.

When we speak of personal identity, we refer to a unity that has been constructed in practical and symbolic terms and comprises diachronical as well as synchronical differences, which is why in view of further possible differentiations of the self it is inevitably of a transitory nature.[19] Theories of identity relate to this unity on the way of a *form* and *structure* that can be precisely delineated. From this the *qualitative* identity, as regards the *content* of a subject's personality, has to be distinguished (e.g. characteristic features, values, orientations, interests). Whoever is not concerned with such content matters and

17 Cf. Beck/Beck-Gernsheim: *Riskante Freiheiten. Individualisierung in modernen Gesellschaften*; Beck, Ulrich/Giddens, Anthony/Lash, Scott: *Reflexive Modernisierung. Eine Kontroverse*, Frankfurt/Main 1996; Giddens, Anthony: *The Consequences of Modernity*, Stanford, Cal., 1990.

18 For a survey and the relevant literature cf. Straub, Jürgen: "Identität", in: Jaeger, Friedrich/Liebsch, Burkhard (Eds.): *Handbuch der Kulturwissenschaften. Grundlagen und Schlüsselbegriffe*, Stuttgart 2004, pp. 277–303, Straub: *Theorien der Identität.*

19 Straub, Jürgen/Renn, Joachim (Eds.): *Transitorische Identität. Der Prozesscharakter des modernen Selbst*, Frankfurt/Main, New York 2002.

fundamentally regards identity as the problem of shaping and maintaining a unified form or structure, is taking a decidedly *theoretical* stance vis-à-vis the problem of identity. Some of the constituent elements of such a complex theoretical construct will be considered in the next paragraph.

## Identity and Autonomy

In *pragma-semantic* terms, the concept of personal identity is closely linked with the notion of a person's potential for *experience* and *action.*[20] This potential for action is rooted in so-called *experiences of self-determination.* It ultimately refers – in the later stages of ontogenesis from adolescence onwards – to the kind of autonomy that includes a certain, although never complete *independence* of the individual from those material, social and cultural conditioning factors that it was exposed to while growing up or has to live with the present. Autonomy is always conditional and limited, and in concrete cases it is a personal matter where inter- and intra-individual comparisons provide a standard for assessing the quality and the degree of *partial* independence that has been achieved.

However, the realization of such a project of successively attaining partial autonomy is *only possible* if and as long as a person succeeds in evolving a psychological structure that has been shaped by a process of *self-transformation*, and further if it is successful in *differentiating* this structure into numerous transitional stages, thereby *keeping it stable.* Hence this dynamic structure that we have designated as *identity* is *open* for new experiences and consequently for the various modalities of creative *self-transcendence.*[21] A person having an *open psychological* structure (especially in social terms), the cultural and historical relevance of which can hardly be overestimated, is an integral part of the modern concept of identity. Open-mindedness requires being receptive to what is other and strange. It also calls for the willingness to change oneself as well as for a certain amount of that kind of courage (premised upon some degree of self-assurance), which enables people to admit to others that they are vulnerable.

A theoretically complex and sophisticated concept of identity incorporates the idea of *decentered autonomy* and *subjectivity*, which is still relevant in a *normative*, but not least of all in a *political* sense. Upon closer inspection such an idea proves to be, with regard to *the theory of the subject*, the *analogon* and

20 Cf. Straub, Jürgen/Zielke, Barbara: "Autonomie, narrative Identität und die postmoderne Kritik des sozialen Konstruktivismus: 'Relationales' und 'dialogisches' Selbst als zeitgemäße Alternativen?", in: Jaeger, Friedrich/Straub, Jürgen (Eds.): *Was ist der Mensch, was Geschichte? Perspektiven einer kulturwissenschaftlichen Anthropologie. Jörn Rüsen zum 65. Geburtstag*, Bielefeld 2005, pp. 165 – 210.

21 Joas, Hans: *Die Entstehung der Werte*, Frankfurt/Main 1997.

*complement* to the political concept of an *open society* (not only *in the sense of* Popper but also and even more so in the sense of Cornelius Castoriadis or Ernesto Laclau, whose political philosophy and sociology draws its inspiration from psychoanalysis). This was by the way already known to the psychoanalytic ego-psychologist Erikson, to whom we owe the popularization of the lexeme "identity". It was he who established his influential pragma-semantics by integrating it in a *triadic* conceptual scheme within which the metaphor of openness occupies a key position. This conceptual definition can already be found in other, older writings, notably the American pragmatists.

## The Triadic Pragma-semantics of Identity, Totality, Multiplicity (Diffusion, Dissociation, Fragmentation)

The pragmatics and semantics of our concept does *expressly not* work out in the tension between the *duality of identity and non-identity.* Over many decades, this just as common as it is misguided *binary encoding and dualistic construction* has resulted in the entire debate being led into a dead end. This was based on the assumption that the person in question could be determined through contrasting it with its exact opposite, and nothing else. "Identity" was thereby solely conceived as the counterpart of the non-identical (or difference). This binary logic, however, is insufficient. Difference has to be become part of a *triadic* system if the meaning of personal identity is to be adequately defined. This tri-partite structure takes the form of a *continuum* whose extremes are demarcated by *totality* on the one hand and *multiplicity* (*diffusion, dissociation, fragmentation*) on the other. In a topological perspective, the concept of identity is located right *in the middle* between these extremes.

Only by taking into consideration both ends of the continuum does one understand what lies in the middle, where it had already been placed by Erikson.[22] In his definition he was always referring to *both contrastive horizons of comparison,* i.e. the opposite horizons of totality and multiplicity (diffusion, dissociation, fragmentation) in order to clarify the concept of identity. He was consequently envisaging a triad of sociocultural and psycho-social options of structuring a person's communicative relationship with the self and the world when he spoke of identity. On the one hand, he distinguished identity from non-identity in the form of multiplicity (diffusion, dissociation, fragmentation), which was undermining (subverting, destroying) a person's ability to act and orientate her- or himself. As an analyst experienced in dealing with the suffering

22 Erikson, Erik H.: *Identity and the Life Cycle. Selected Papers,* New York 1959.

of the patients, he recognized there an *excess* of so-called *dystonic* forces at work that were threatening the psychosomatic integrity of a person and could result in a ruptured self. However, the borderline separating identity and multiplicity is a fluid one. *No* (modern) identity is ever entirely free from dystonic forces. The non-identical is not just the counterpart, but also – in a paradoxical fashion – an integral part of personal identity. As the integrative unity of its differences, the latter is a dynamic and open-ended synthesis of the heterogeneous, which is constantly threatened by tensions, conflicts and crises that now and then also "colonize" it.[23] On the other hand, Erikson distinguished his concept of identity from a totality symbolizing that violent confinement which is capable of generating violence both 'internally' and 'externally' and which has been grotesquely misunderstood by some critics of modern theories of identity as generally amounting to "identity".[24] Totality is a *closed* structure that is rigidly intent on its own reproduction, its possibly *inflexible solidification* and *unyielding affirmation:* nothing from outside, at least nothing that is other or strange, is allowed inside, and nothing from inside is allowed out – at the very least it should neither get into contact nor enter into a *co-modificatory exchange* with the other and the strange. If possible, totality confines any exchange to the auto-reproductive 'invocation' of an identificatory self and of what is familiar. It prohibits, avoids and blocks off communication as such. Totality stands for the resistance to change, the repulse and exclusion of whatever is new or strange.[25]

Identity by contrast functions as a mode of practical self-realization whereby what strangeness is, at least in principle, acknowledged as a welcome challenge to selfhood. An identity orientated towards "the subjective realization of communality"[26] does not close itself off from what is other of strange, but is in need of these – especially because they are capable of taking the self beyond the limits of its subjectivity, thereby enriching the horizon, the orientation and the experiential or active potential of a person. This is often concomitant with trouble, fear and anxiety, and will probably be a constant source of worries. And yet it is not simply blocked off psychologically and avoided physically.

23 Ricœur, Paul: *Das Selbst als ein Anderer*, Munich 1996; Straub: *Theorien der Identität.*

24 Of course, a person *can* experience ascription of identity (whether imposed by itself or from the outside) as an *unreasonable demand*, from which it *suffers*. Equally, however, people can be damaged both physically and psychologically by having their identity diffused or taken away, even in the day and age of "flexible human beings" who are characterized by *non-committal commitments.* Marcia, James E./Waterman, Alan S./Matteson, David R./Archer, Sally/Orlofsky, Jacob L.: *Ego Identity. A Handbook for Psychosocial Research*, New York 1993; Sennett, Richard: *The Corrosion of Character: The Personal Consequences of Work in the New Capitalism*, New York/London 1998.

25 Erikson: *Identity and the Life Cycle*; Straub *Theorien der Identität.*

26 Theunissen, Michael: *Selbstverwirklichung und Allgemeinheit. Zur Kritik des gegenwärtigen Bewusstseins*, Berlin/New York 1981, p. 6.

To all appearances, the terms "identity" and "totality" are ideal types. Unfortunately, this is not the case with "multiplicity" (diffusion, dissociation, fragmentation), which *in effect* can lead to the *complete* disintegration of personality structures and the total destruction of the potential for experiencing and acting. Identity is located in the middle of this continuum. This theoretical topology unequivocally determines the pragma-semantics of the term in question within a scientific context. Depending on the spirit of the age and *the real empirical living conditions*, the debates on the theory of identity sometimes center around the risks involved in an approach to the extreme pole of totality, and at other times around the dangers of an unconditional surrender to the extreme 'option' of multiplicity and fragmentation. From a psychological perspective, both possibilities have their (at times) quite attractive aspects since they offer short-term (pseudo-) solutions to rather urgent problems – however high the price may be that a totalitarian structuration of the self just as its diffusion, dissociation, fragmentation or multiplication will exact sooner or later. Identity is an aspiration, a kind of longing that is capable of imparting form and direction to a person's self-formation. Human beings that are located within the framework provided by the *normative* semantics of the open and mobile self usually aim to exert some influence on this contingent process of self-formation. In doing so they inevitably encounter the limits of their capacity: self-withdrawal is a part of that self that the theories of transitory identity have been trying to come to terms with for more than a century.

## Continuity, Consistency, Coherence

For an answer to the question of how identity as selfhood, as the dynamic and fragile unity of person can be defined more precisely three concepts (whose use is by no means standardized) are decisive. They all possess a 'contra-intuitive' meaning. They emphasize anew that identity is specified as the *integrative structure of difference* or as the *synthesis of the heterogeneous.* All the basic terms of the theory of identity do not designate *states* but *processes* that represent the essentially temporary and unstable result of the practical, symbolic or mental actions of a subject (among which can also be counted the 'perception' and 'processing' of contingencies, both of these being the result of an interpretive effort). The person concerned about her or his identity has to ensure the continuity, consistency and coherence of her or his life. For this purpose it can draw on an unlimited host of conscious or unconscious behavioral strategies.

Some of them are striving for relating, integrating and synthesizing whatever is discontinuous in a temporal dimension, in other words for *continuity.* This term that is very important for the theory of identity therefore by no means implies that a human being remains the same throughout its life (*semper idem*) because nothing has changed in its life, nor is likely to change today or tomorrow. Rather, continuity can only exist under the theoretical and empirical precondition of *change* throughout the cycle of a life. This term designates a specific way of integrating temporal *differences*. Continuity thus amounts to constant *acts of self-continuation* in a life that is inescapably structured in a temporal dimension. This activity alone is capable of creating a connection or relationship that is not given *per se* and that would come about without the interference of a subject. It is the person her- or himself that perceives and experiences her- or himself as a *changing subject* and then *relates* such differences with one another along the time axis – doing so always from the perspective of a changing present (i. e. as something that is forever new). The person *creates* that connection which in the theory of identity is designated as continuity. It thereby integrates memories from its life, present experiences and impressions as well as expectations of an imagined future, whether it may be hoped for or fraught with anxiety. Of course, certain permanent 'elements of life' can be relevant for this purpose (such as one's mother tongue or repetitive actions in the form of habits, routines or rituals). Apart from the fact that a lot of things change and therefore have to be processed in the way mentioned, even what remains permanent has to be *actively preserved* and integrated into a time context that is emotionally experienced, cognitively represented and/or symbolically articulated.

A particularly relevant, albeit not the only form of active self-continuation is the narrating of stories (of the self). Narratives thematize change, they describe and explain them *uno actu* in their *own proper fashion*. Self-narrations are also capable of rendering change plausible without eliminating contingency, and they make it understandable why a subject, in spite of all the changes it underwent in its life, has managed to remain the same person that is still (or has remained) self-identical. Under special consideration of narratives' capacity to conceptualize and organize temporal dimension, for some time now one speaks of *narrative* identity. Meanwhile, the narrative dimension of temporally complex identities is the best researched aspect in a number of different disciplines.[27]

*Consistency* refers to the logical 'coherence' of enunciations, that is, to the non-contradictoriness in the linguistic self-thematization of a subject in particular. Even though this aspect may not be irrelevant for personal identity (for its articulation, its communication, and its recognition by others etc.), human beings are not 'logical automates' and therefore are not always concerned with

27 Brockmeier, Jens/Carbaugh, Donald (Eds.): *Narrative and Identity: Studies in Autobiography, Self and Culture*, Amsterdam 2001; Bruner, Jerome S.: *Acts of Meaning*, Cambridge, MA/London 1990; Ricœur: *Das Selbst als ein Anderer.*

consistency, nor strongly dependent on it in respect of their awareness or consciousness of themselves. This does not mean that blatant contradictions are irrelevant and are of no consequence for the individuals and their social environment. And yet the observance of the requirement of logical consistency is incapable of resolving the practical conflicts and the psychological tensions that are *constitutive* of a personality.

What is much more important for the theory of personal identity is the notion of *coherence*. This designates a meaningful context for, or, else, the compatibility of, social roles and positions that a person currently occupies in various areas of life and fields of activity (both professional and private), e. g. as a single father, a general in the army, a homosexual after a late coming out, president of the local chapter of the Rotary Club, a professional high sea sailor, techno fan, etc. Such diverse roles are linked with action- and life-orientations that harmonize with each in varying degrees. At the most profound level, it is all about the reconcilability of such orientations.[28] Obviously, this criterium cannot be reduced to the purely logical compatibility of linguistic utterances. It is rather dependent upon socio-cultural, institutional and informal ideas of what in a life can be made to cohere and fit together (i. e. which orientations or maxims can be coherently integrated into a system and which cannot). A devout Catholic or priest could not at any time get away with the coming out of the general without getting into problems of coherence and thereby identity (quite apart from the veritable difficulties with his church). These days, in many countries a homosexual orientation of a general, a secretary of state or a CEO of Deutsche Bank is no longer, at least in principle, a problem that would confront the individual concerned with cultural and social demands for coherence. (Quite apart from this, the continuing discrimination and stigmatization, to which homosexuals are still exposed, might present a problem.)

What becomes evident is that the criteria by which we measure coherence are socio-culturally variable and subject to considerable changes; additionally, they are open to the creative input of innovative individuals who are joining together 'things' that others had so far considered to be irreconcilable (e. g. the descriptive feature of 'female gender' with the institutional role reserved for Catholic priests).

Identity is directly dependent on continuity and coherence, and these are intimately connected with the idea of personal autonomy. Without identity, the capacity for judgment, autonomy and experience is unthinkable. Identity and

28 That can be reconstructed as maxims in the sense of Immanuel Kant – see Straub: *Theorien der Identität.*

autonomy are mutually interdependent. This connection is an important aspect of the *political* semantics of "personal identity".[29]

## Final Remarks

Does there exist a viable (neo-) humanism in the present and for the future of an ever more closely related humanity? In case it does and should exist, one should try and find out if the concept of *personal identity* might not be one of the indispensable theoretical and basic concepts of such a complex world view. One thing seems undeniable: a renewed humanism will not – and not only in the regions of the Western world – be able to do without an up-to-date and psychologically defined concept of humanity. Perhaps it would be wise of today's humanists to examine what modern psychology has to offer, assessing its merits in the context of an intercultural dialogue, in which Western psychology is merely one indigenous psychology among others, and revising it if necessary. One is certainly not advocating a Eurocentric arrogance by surmising that the concept of personal identity belongs to the most sophisticated and interesting ideas at the disposal of humans who want to understand themselves and others. The concepts dealt with here are not universal, and do not form part of a universal anthropology. It is, however, a proposal for conceptualizing man within the context of an intercultural dialogue that has only become possible fairly recently.

29 Cf. Straub, Jürgen: "Personale Identität als Politikum. Notizen zur theoretischen und politischen Bedeutung eines psychologischen Grundbegriffs", in: Henry, Barbara/Pirni, Alberto (Eds.): *Der asymmetrische Westen. Zur Pragmatik der Koexistenz pluralistischer Gesellschaften*, Bielefeld 2012, where theories of personal identity are considered as the subjective analogon of theories of democracy.

Helwig Schmidt-Glintzer

# Chances for a Global Humanism in the Conflict of Cultures

## Preliminary Remarks

That man is wolf to man has long been a commonplace. The justification for this view was not so much supplied by man's biological constitution and genetic disposition. It was rather European civilization, which had proved to be decisive of mankind's fate over the last few centuries that provided the basis for the success of this assessment of man. While Immanuel Kant had still linked the concept of enlightened autonomy with an awareness of communal life,[1] Thomas Hobbes (1588 – 1679) had already resolved goodness "into the process of self-preservation and self-enhancement on the part of the individual's social behaviour".[2] Alois Haas has summed this up as follows:

> "For Hobbes the social impetus which causes human beings to form communities is not provided by any form of legalized rules of peaceful interaction that would indicate a natural human inclination for sociability, but "man does not by nature seek [...] any company for the sake of company, but only in order to gain honour and advantage."[3] Furthermore the state of socialization among men has to be regarded as *bellum omnium contra omnes* – everybody seeks their own advantage and uses all others as a means to that end.[4] It is obvious that such an individualistic anthropology – everybody has 'a right to everything'[5] – as the realization of *homo homini lupus*[6] at the very

1 Cf. Theunissen, Michael: *Selbstverwirklichung und Allgemeinheit. Zur Kritik des gegenwärtigen Bewußtseins*, Berlin 1982, p. 7; cf. also. Haas, Alois M.: "Selbstverwirklichung", in: *Georges Bloch Annual* 13/14 (2006/2007): 545 – 565, p. 549.

2 Theunissen: ibid.

3 Hobbes, Thomas: *Vom Menschen, Vom Bürger*, Hamburg 1994, p. 77.

4 Ibid., p. 83.

5 Ibid., p. 82.

6 Ibid., p.59. – Haas draws particular attention to Jüngel, Eberhard: "Zum Wesen des Friedens. Frieden als Kategorie theologischer Anthropologie", in: Jüngel, Eberhard: *Ganz werden*, Tübingen 2003, pp. 1 – 39, especially 3. *Homo homini lupus*, pp. 18 – 22.

beginning of modernity could not possibly encourage a positive theory of self-realization.[7]"

It was hard to counter such a general tendency, particularly because the conditions resulting from a people being constrained as though in a cage – all those who would go against this would thereby put themselves outside the mainstream. The problem of how one could get out of this deadlock will be resumed towards the end of this article.

In general the rise of Europe and the ensuing 'Europeanization' of the world went along with a dehumanization of the racial or cultural other, and in spite of this it did not clash with the love of nature, of animals or with romantic love, all of which experienced – in a kind of compensatory move – a new heyday. Enemy-concepts went hand in hand with European expansion, and the demonization of the opponent is still not unknown in Europe as late as the beginning of the 21st century, and all this in spite of a long-lived Enlightenment discourse. And yet, and this is another aspect of European Enlightenment, fairly early on the European policy of violence and conquest also came under severe criticism.[8]

## Man at the Centre

The idea of a new humanism is based on merely an extended knowledge of mankind and its history, and it focuses its attention on man as a member of the entire human race. This inclusive trope is very ancient and finds its most pronounced expression in the Chinese tradition where it historically manifests itself in the genre of biography.[9] But it is also to be found in the Stoa and the discourse of natural rights in the early Modern Age. Such a new humanism is dominated by the principle of viewing all humans as part of the same species, and it considers all the variations of the attempts that have been made to exclude people from human society, because such acts of exclusion are obviously as unavoidable as they are on occasion for reflecting upon the possibility of inclusion or, where this proves to be impossible, of reconciling 'humanity' with a certain guarded distance.

The humanism referred to in this context is grounded in the basic human capacity for empathy, to destroy which has been attempted time and again and at

7 Haas, Alois M.: op.cit., p. 549.

8 Cf. Pierre Kodjio Nenguié: "Rasse, Alterität und Humanität: Anmerkungen über die Afrikapolitik der Goethezeit. Zu Karl von Eckartshausens *Isogin und Celia, eine Geschichte von einem unserer schwarzen Brüder aus Afrika, von einem Mohren* (1786)", in: *Das achtzehnte Jahrhundert* 33.1 (2009): pp. 26–41.

9 Mann, Susan: "Scene-Setting: Writing Biography in Chinese History", in: *The American Historical Review* 114.3 (June 2009): 631–639.

all levels. Especially for the process of drilling soldiers, some kind of kind of negative conditioning has become the standard procedure, but it also figures in the rhetoric justifying torture as the ultimate means for state agencies to obtain information.[10] The discourse of criminal psychology in the $18^{th}$ century, the link between Enlightenment discourse and the formation of man belong in this context,[11] as much as the utter willingness to fight and kill on the part of the German officer corps with its 'humanist' education.[12]

The new humanism, however, is guided by the principle of including all humans without exception while at the same time being conscious of this claim being constantly under threat. It lives by its hope of the civilizing effect of democracy. Because in the same measure that other features of modernity will eventually prevail and prove their worth throughout the world, the hope becomes justified of attaining a world culture founded on the peaceful negotiation of conflicts. The need for difference in the search for identity and for self-assertion, even at the price of denigrating the Other or entire groups of people, are accepted as part of reality. This acceptance is accompanied by the absolute resolve always to set off against it the capacity for empathy. This means that in education also it will be important to instil a 'culture of empathy'. At the same time this process will require institutions and, more generally, supra-individual agencies in order to be able to minimize evil.[13]

Another dimension to be considered in this context is the way we treat our dead, because "without a culture of burial and remembrance there can be no humaneness".[14] This comes under the category of care in general, but then in a more special sense it means the care we take of the dead as well as of children since both birth and death are an integral part of human existence. "This is why our custom of paying tribute to the dead also amounts to providing for the future."[15] Robert Harrison's observation that man only became human after having been driven out of paradise is highly pertinent. It is important to foster

10 Cf. on the debate of torture Stallknecht, Michael: "Sie oder wir", in: *Süddeutsche Zeitung* 147 (30. June 2009): 12.

11 Cf. Schott, Heinz: "'Born Criminals', 'Degenerates' and 'Psychopaths'. On the History of Criminal Psychology in Germany" in: *Transactions in Medicine & Heteronomous Modernization*, Tokyo 2009, pp. 33–47.

12 Cf. also the scrupulous reflection by Himmler, Katrin: *Die Brüder Himmler: eine deutsche Familiengeschichte*, Frankfurt/Main 2005.

13 Cf. Thomä, Dieter: "Gespiegelte Perspektiven", in: *Frankfurter Allgemeine Zeitung* 147 (29. June 2009): 6 as a review of Breithaupt, Fritz: *Kulturen der Empathie*, Frankfurt/Main 2009. – Rizzolatti, Giacomo/Sinigaglia, Corrado: *Empathie und Spiegelneurone. Die biologische Basis des Mitgefühls*, Frankfurt/Main 2008.

14 Robert Harrison in interview with Köhler, Andrea, in: *Neue Zürcher Zeitung* 146 (27./28. June 2009): 31.

15 Ibid.

this conviction, as well as the insight that man is man and not God.[16] In this regard there is wide agreement between Christian and Chinese religiousness, because after all the awareness of a lost Golden Age formed the basis of the Confucian world view. It is therefore not surprising that the Neoconfucians should have attempted to ascribe to the Confucian tradition "a strained relationship with the world".[17] Thus it is not our concern to regain paradise. On the contrary, it is life in the here and now that gets affirmed. At the same time it has to be acknowledged that there are asymmetrical processes of change that move at different rates of speed, which results in there being winners and losers of modernization. Thus the temporal dimension has always to be taken into account.

I am therefore proposing the following thesis: it is only by acknowledging the "clash of civilizations", to use Samuel Huntington's formula, that there is a chance of realizing a global humanism. This means that we also have to know how to deal with inequality, with guilt and fate, with responsibility and to whom it is to be attributed, but in an equal measure with forms of compensation, of forgetting, of forgiveness, of expiation and of pardon.[18] This will also be a matter of opening up possible choices of action with practical consequences. Such a comprehensive approach will enable us to conceive of the conflict of interests and the potential of the sciences in terms of a unified knowledge that is modelled on the ancient concept of *humanitas*, and thereby make our principles of action subservient to the requirement of a 'humane' life of the entire world community.

## Humanism: More than a Period-term

In our understanding humanism is strongly determined by its origin as a term designating an epoch, and in connection with this the transition from the Middle Ages to the Modern Age and right up to the present – i. e. our twentieth century that witnessed a relapse into barbarity in the middle of Europe. This implies that in spite of all its new interpretations humanism still remains a period-term.

This has caused whatever is designated as humanism to acquire what Karl

16 Cf. Jüngel, Eberhard: "'Wir sollen Menschen und nicht Gott sein. Das ist die summa'. Zum Wesen des Christentums", in: *Weltreligionen. Verstehen, Verständigung, Verantwortung*, ed. by Karl Kardinal Lehmann, Frankfurt/Main 2009, pp. 113 – 134.

17 Cf. Metzger, Thomas A. : *Escape from Predicament. Neo-Confucianism and Chinas Evolving Political Culture*, New York 1977.

18 Cf. Kodalle, Klaus-Michael: *Annäherungen an eine Theorie des Verzeihens*, Stuttgart 2006.

Jaspers has called "a very wide meaning", and therefore we speak in this context, following other authors, of a 'new' humanism.[19]

It should be agreed that – ever since each point of the globe can be reached within a few hours and since the early-warning interval of intercontinental missiles and intelligent high-precision weapons has dwindled to a very short time – it is now a matter of urgent necessity to reconstitute the older idea of *one* humanity on a global scale. One should therefore take into consideration whether the concept of humanism might not form a bridge between earlier discourses on humanity on the one hand and new ideas for the future under novel conditions on the other. This attempt might be aided by the fact that not only in the European tradition, but also in the cultures of East Asia that were influenced by Chinese thought, specific concepts of humanity and humanism have been evolved that could be joined together to form a new idea of humanism in an intercultural perspective. In Chinese culture the tradition of preserving human memory and personal history that is evidenced by the genre of biography might form a point of departure for such an enterprise as well as the customary role of the scholar, who with the sounds of the Zither emulates the harmony of the spheres, and who with brush, ink and paper inscribes himself in the intellectual tradition, and through doing both strives to perfect the formation of his personality. These activities, one could argue, come perhaps closest to realizing something one could designate as humanism. However, since it is a fact that the discourse of humanity, the concept of world literature, of world peace or even of "eternal peace"[20] was initially a result of the European Enlightenment, which brought in its wake an unprecedented domination of the world,[21] we have to start with Europe. This is not to deny that in the history of mankind there have been similar processes of globalization, understood as the "intensification and acceleration of cross-border transactions accompanied by their extension in space" (Ulrich Menzel).[22] To name but one example: The rationalization period during the epoch of separate states that resulted in the foundation of the unitary Chinese empire in 221 B.C. was notable for a similar dynamic and ever since the 6$^{th}$ pre-Christian century generated similar concepts of humanity and universality.

19 Jaspers, Karl: *Über Bedingungen und Möglichkeiten eines neuen Humanismus. Drei Vorträge*, Stuttgart 1962, p. 21.

20 Cf. Kant's essay of 1795 "Zum ewigen Frieden. Ein philosophischer Entwurf".

21 It is no surprise that the idea of universality should originate in that part of the world from which the dynamics of change proceeded.

22 Menzel, Ulrich: "Tausend Jahre Globalisierung im Rückblick aus der aktuellen Globalisierungsdebatte", in: Schmidt-Glintzer, Helwig (Ed.): *Neue Blicke auf alte Karten und die Dynamik der europäischen Kulturgeschichte*, Wiesbaden 2007, p. 137–209, hier p. 139. – "intensification" means "that such cross-border activities are developing more rapidly than those that remain within national boundaries." (Ulrich Menzel).

## Doubt and the Disappointment of War

It only makes sense to talk of global humanism if at the same time the existence of conflicts is acknowledged. Another aspect that is novel in the 20th and 21st centuries compared with all other previous processes of globalization resides in the fact that the globality we have now attained is irreversible, at least as far as we can imagine. It is true that processes of globalization have always alternated with critical counter-movements – something which can also be expected for the present or the near future and which has often been due to the circumstance that as a rule there are always winners and losers in the process of globalization. However, there are some signs that for the benefit of most people – if not for the survival of the species – it is necessary and sensible to do everything we can in order to avoid relapsing into a period of time before our present technological achievements, while at the same time reaffirming and guaranteeing the value system of universal human rights.

One obstacle to this is due to the concept of humanism itself, because from early on it had been systematically confined to European culture and was thereby withheld from mankind in its entirety as well as certain individuals, even though some thinkers like Kant, Herder and Humboldt emphatically sought to encompass all of the human race.[23] The failure of this project led to a disappointed humanism.[24] Thus Sigmund Freud in 1915 was justified to speak of the "disappointment of war".[25] The concept also came under criticism from another perspective. In the lecture notes from a propaedeutic seminar on Schiller's *Letters on the Aesthetic Education of Man*, dated 4 November 1936, the following statement can be found:

"What does humanism want? The spiritual perfection of man?" For this one

23 The confinement to national culture can also be found in Hans Georg Gadamer's on "The meanıng ot the humanist tradition". Cf. Gadamer, Hans-Georg: *Wahrheit und Methode*, Tübingen ²1965, pp. 1–39, esp. p. 6 below and p. 7 above. – I do not wish to gloss over counter-positions such as that of Giambattista Vico (1669–1744). Cf. Vico Giambattista: *Die neue Wissenschaft über die gemeinschaftliche Natur der Völker*. Edition from 1744 translated and introduced by E. Auerbach with an epilogue by W. Schmidt-Biggemann, Berlin/New York ²2000.

24 Accordingly to this an understanding of what is alien is not impossibly although seldom achieved. Cf. on this Osterhammel, Jürgen: *Die Entzauberung Asiens*, Munich 1998, pp. 24–25.

25 Cf. Freud, Sigmund: "Zeitgemäßes über Krieg und Tod (1915)", in: Sigmund Freud, *Studienausgabe*, vol. IX, Frankfurt/Main 1974, pp. 33 ff. – It is recommended to everybody to study the period around 1914 when the century that has not yet ended actually begins. Just read Thomas Mann's "Gedanken im Krieg" or simply consult the second volume of the journal "Neue Rundschau" from that first year of war.

would have to know first what man is and what his perfection or imperfection consists in.[26]

This was said at a time when men who had had the benefit of a 'humanist' education were planning the Shoa, so that Albert Camus was right in remarking that "today's executioners are, as everyone knows, humanists. Therefore one cannot … be sufficiently distrustful of the humanitarian ideology."[27]

In spite of the prevailing tendency in the 20th century to discredit the concept of humanism, certain thinkers have tried to reconceptualise humanism. This was done in the face of the Moscow trials or the Shoa, and Maurice Merleau-Ponty remarked that "the realization of humanity utterly depends on the successful creation of meaning initiated by humans in and through history", even though this does not guarantee any progress towards more humanity.[28] Theologians like Eberhard Jüngel have countered this kind of despondency by referring to the coming of God's kingdom as a realistic utopia. Maintaining the four relations of man with God, his social and natural environment as well as with himself not only plays an important role in Christian theological discourse,[29] but also has a determining influence on the religiosity of other cultures such as in China. And the very recognition of other beings in their otherness emanating from the insight that in all its relations the human subject, especially with regard to its connection to God, must never aspire to be *like God*, is a central of all religions throughout history.

## The New Humanism in Posttraditional Societies

A new humanism will not be able to confine itself to only recognizing certain abstract norms of behaviour, but it must also acknowledge the concrete needs and requirements of posttraditional societies, which comprises their self-interpretation in the light of their own specific tradition. We also assume that "human community has really become established without being limited to a

26 Heidegger, Martin: *Übungen für Anfänger. Schillers Briefe über die ästhetische Erziehung des Menschen*, ed. by Ulrich von Bülow. (=Marbacher Bibliothek 8), Marbach am Neckar 2005, p. 10.

27 Camus, Albert: "Die Guillotine. Betrachtungen zur Todesstrafe", in: idem: *Fragen der Zeit*, Hamburg 1960, p. 177. See also Himmler: *Die Brüder Himmler. Eine deutsche Familiengeschichte.* – Sartre's debate of the concept of humanism is also important, beginning with his mockery in his novel *La Nauseé* from 1938 right up to his later statements. – cf. Wroblewsky, Vincent von: "Wie humanistisch ist Sartres Existentialismus?", in: Faber, Richard/Rudolph, Enno (Eds.), *Humanismus in Geschichte und Gegenwart*, Tübingen 2002, pp. 119–137.

28 Cf. *Historisches Wörterbuch der Philosophie*, vol. 3, column 1229–1230.

29 Jüngel, Eberhard: op.cit. (in: Karl Lehmann), p. 126.

specific nationality".[30] In this context the demand that "the self-realization required from us [...] today [...] [is made concrete] in the way we are concerned about hunger in the world or world-peace."[31] But this appeal is not sufficiently far-reaching. The concern for the whole is a necessary but not a sufficient reason. This is evident quite clearly in the Chinese example where currently the unity of the world is being proclaimed as the basis of all explanations of the world and the production of meaning, as in the concept of religion as defined by Zhuo Xinping.[32] This demands an insight into multifarious interests, the recognition of which can only be attained through participation; what is at stake here is not just the insight into this connection as such, but also a change of the cognitive process itself that has to be brought about. It must be accepted that we are incapable of putting ourselves in the shoes of every other because as human beings we are of limited capacity.

## The Individual and its World

I am referring at this juncture to the theory of *normative individualism* (Dietmar von der Pfordten) and confront it with the demands of human rights, both in a historically reconstructive as well as a synchronous perspective relevant to our own present. It would be worthwhile to empirically verify this theoretical construct in a comparative perspective from the 16th century onward, taking into account its various social, governmental and institutional specifities. In Von der Pfordten's view the 17th century from its very beginnings has been dominated by one "central idea" which has contributed to the "development of constitutional government, the rule of law as well as well as human rights", which is summed up in the idea of a *normatively legitimated individualism*, i. e. "the idea that the use of political power in the final resort can only be justified through its being legitimated by every individual involved."[33] After surveying some specific theories of how to justify political decision-making he develops his *Three-Zone Theory of Political Justice*.[34] After having examined a number of terms like law, freedom, human abilities, self-preservation, and preference, the concept of *interest* becomes of crucial relevance for him.[35] In his Three-Zone theory there are certain interests which only depend on individuals, then there are others which

30 Theunissen: op.cit., p. 45.
31 Ibid.
32 Cf. Schmidt-Glintzer, Helwig: *Wohlstand, Glück und langes Leben. Chinas Götter und die Ordnung im Reich der Mitte*, Frankfurt/Main 2009, p. 240.
33 Von der Pfordten, Dietmar: *Rechtsethik*, Munich 2001, p. 293.
34 Ibid., pp. 436 ff.
35 Ibid., p. 441.

are exclusively dependent on communities, whereas in a third zone there exist interests which are only partially dependent on communities.[36] In the Chinese context this discourse could be further pursued by reconstructing the reflections upon the relationship between the "common good" (*gong*) and personal or particular interest (*si*). With regard to Buddhism a similar tension would have to be negotiated between the monastic community, the individual monk and society at large.

In addition to negotiating between communal and individual interests the distinction between a state under the rule of law and a tyrannical regime is relevant, however in the sense of gradual differences between both,[37] and not in the shallow sense propagated these days by party politicians. When von der Pfordten defines a state under the rule of law in terms of "the observation of human rights, the principle of democracy, the principle of majority rule, legal protection and compensation in the case of disappropriation etc."[38], then all premodern states fall outside the category of rule of law. This also raises the question of which individual rights define the standard by which this can be judged. As John Rawls has argued, hierarchical and thereby illiberal societies can recognize liberal societies and vice versa. Nonetheless the hierarchical societies have to fulfil three minimal conditions:[39] "*firstly* they have to be peaceful and non-expansionist; *secondly* their legal system has to be guided by a notion of justice that is orientated towards safeguarding the common good, and which can plausibly and credibly demonstrate that this common good reflects the interests of all members of society. – The People's Republic of China is a prominent example of such a society."[40]

## Four Preconditions for Humanism as a Guiding Concept

The *first precondition* for a new humanism therefore consists in recognizing the networks created in the process of globalization as the elements enabling understanding and management, especially considering that they are forms of subjective affiliation. The League of Nations, the United Nations and the human rights debate, but also international networks, non-governmental organizations

36 Ibid., p. 452.

37 Ibid., p. 524.

38 Ibid., p. 524

39 Schubert, Gunter: "Zwischen Konfuzius und Kant. Ansätze zur Operationalisierung eines inter-kulturellen Menschenrechtsdialogs mit Ostasien", in: idem (Ed.): *Menschrechte in Ostasien. Zum Streit um die Universalität einer Idee II*, Tübingen 1999, p. 19–51, p.4 3.

40 Cf. Schubert: op.cit., p. 43.

and initiatives[41] as well as forms of transnational security alliances come under this category. The idea of humanity is indissolubly linked with the long-past experience of global wars such as the Thirty Years' War, the first real world war properly speaking, and most certainly with the so-called First World War in the 20th century, and it is reflected in the mention of the inalienability of human dignity in the constitution of the Federal Republic of Germany of 1949. However, humanism is also associated with numerous wars of liberation, including the liberation of Germany from its self-imposed Nazi-loyalty.

The *second precondition* is formed by recognizing the fact that in European Modernity the concept of humanity that was deemed to be universal has remained 'incomplete' because on the one hand even enlightened societies can be profoundly inhumane,[42] but above all because incompleteness is the constituent element of humanism in the first place. If, for instance, in an edition of the *American Historical Review* the reasons are listed for why the rate of murder and manslaughter in the USA is so much higher than in Europe,[43] then the topic of the vastly different conditions influencing humanism throughout the world is addressed, which is always associated with ideas of freedom.[44]

The *third precondition* consists in recognizing that not only humanism but any other kind of identity formation and sense-making is a referral to its own specific pre-history and thereby poses the question – and I am here expanding Merleau-Ponty's theory – whether there can be a human past which is capable of integrating its own past events in the manner of collective memories. This also applies to the past of 'victims' and 'winners'. At this point one also is compelled to ask to what extent collectives are capable of being held responsible, because they are much more susceptible to delusions than individuals and therefore, are

41 An example of this is the 'Clinton Global Initiative' founded in 2005 by the former President of the USA Bill Clinton. Cf. "Das bessere Gesicht Amerikas", in: *Der Spiegel* 14 (2006): 116–117.

42 The deficit associated with this also consists in the relevant debates only taking place within certain cultures. Cf. Höffe, Otfried: *Vernunft und Recht. Bausteine zu einem interkulturellen Rechtsdiskurs*, Frankfurt/Main 1996, p. 53.

43 The "Problem of American Homicide", in: *American Historical Review* 11.1 (February 2006): 75–114.

44 This historicity is of course, constitutive of all the cultures that one has to take into account when examining notions of humanism. It would therefore be relevant to connect the concept of humanism with the traumata of other cultures. In his book, *A Nation among Nations. America's place in World History.* Thomas Bender has argued against the concept of "American Exceptionalism" and emphasized: "If we can begin to think about American history as but one local instance of a general history, as one history among others, not only will historical knowledge be improved, but the cultural foundations of a much-needed cosmopolitanism will be enhanced. We do not want to reinforce a narrow and exclusive notion of citizenship, but encourage and sustain a cosmopolitan citizenry, at once proud nationals and humble citizens of the world", quoted after http://hnn.us/articles/23913.html [04/17/2006].

not completely accountable, in the sense of Friedrich Nietzsche's dictum: "Madness is quite rare with individuals, but in the case of groups, parties, peoples and eras it is the rule."[45] By inverting this argument, it is all about the question if collectives are not *per se* ambivalent, and are thus capable of being humane just as much as they are inhumane.

The *fourth precondition* is formed by a much-needed revision of the concept of religion or, respectively, by overcoming the peculiar distance between humanism and religion.[46] For a long time humanism was seen as a "turning away from the Beyond" and a "turning towards the here and now,"[47] and it is therefore no coincidence that the relationship between humanism and Christianity, but especially the "relation between humanism and the Reformation",[48] should have been variously debated and been the subject of a lot tension.[49] Over against Etienne Gilson, who designated the Renaissance as the "Middle Ages without God", Enno Rudolph insists on calling the Renaissance "God without the Middle Ages". The humanist ideal of education prevalent during that epoch – Rudolph estimates this to have covered the period from 1300 to 1600 – according to him was the "emancipation of the individual from the tutelage imposed from outside".[50]

These then are the *four preconditions*, and what is at stake here is the *condition humaine* within the ambit of a global concept of mankind that essentially lives by accepting the variety and the social conditioning as well as the individuality and uniqueness of men, including their historicity. Of these four preconditions I would like to make a few specific remarks on the last one.[51]

45 Nietzsche, Friedrich: "Jenseits von Gut und Böse", in: *Werke*, vol. 2, ed. von Karl Schlechta, Munich 1966, p. 637.

46 We should like to warn, however, against easy remedies, since difference is most clearly manifested between religions, which justifiably try to resist the process of levelling in a highly complex society. Very illustrative of this is the comment on the world-ethos project of Hans Küng by Klaus Berger: *Von der Schönheit der Ethik*, Frankfurt/Main 2006, pp. 24 f.

47 *Religion in Geschichte und Gegenwart*, 1st ed., "Humanismus", column 191, Tübingen 1912.

48 This is the introduction to Kampschulte, F. W.: *Die Universität Erfurt in ihrem Verhältnisse zu dem Humanismus und der Reformation. Erster Theil: Der Humanismus*, Trier 1858, p. VII.

49 That 'relations' of humanism and Christianity have always been 'conflictual' is an argument also propounded by Stegemann, Ekkhard W.: "Das unaufhebbar Befremdliche am Menschlichen. Einige Gedanken über Humanismus und Christentum", in: Faber, Richard/Rudolph, Enno (Eds.), *Humanismus in Geschichte und Gegenwart*, Tübingen 2002, pp. 167–186, here p. 167.

50 Rudolph here is referring to Blumenberg, Hans/Kristeller, P.O.: *Humanismus und Renaissance*, Munich 1973 and more others. Rudolph, Enno: "Der Renaissance-Humanismus als Epochenstifter", in: Faber/Rudolph: *Humanismus in Geschichte und Gegenwart*, pp. 3–15, esp. p. 3.

51 In this context I am expressly referring to Jörn Rüsen's contribution "Die Erziehung des Menschengeschlechts – ein Rückblick in die Zukunft der Vergangenheit", in: Schmidt-Glintzer, Helwig (Ed.): *Aufklärung im 21. Jahrhundert*, Wiesbaden 2004, pp. 67–92.

## Humanism in Functional Terms

In this sense a global new humanism cannot afford to be just a continuation of the European concept of humanism. Much though the idea of humanism may be linked with character formation and education as in the Latin term *studia humaniora* that has been in use in Germany since the 17th century, it nevertheless remains closely associated with "a spiritual attitude that is making it clear that it is modelling the striving of the Modern Age for humanity on the example of the ancient Greeks and Romans."[52] What can be meant by 'global humanism' considering the definitions given so far? It is certainly not what Julian Nida-Rümelin understands by a "renewed humanism" which merely consists of invoking other previous stages of humanism, such as the humanist movement of the late Middle Ages and the early Modern Age or the neo-humanism of the 19th century. Nida-Rümelin also thinks that a "new definition as regards its content" is required and is thus focussing on "the fundamental dimension of culture": social interaction, communication, self-determination, self-formation, aesthetic and musical education.[53] In addition to this he is concerned with rationality, liberty and responsibility[54] plus "humanistic revolutions" from Plato to the present. If we wanted to run the whole gamut of such ideas, and if we decided to take up Sartre's "Existentialism is a Humanism" ("*L'existentialisme est un humanisme*") as well as ring all the changes of the discourse on nihilism from Nietzsche to Gottfried Benn we would still remain within the confines of European thought.[55] If we really want to arrive at a concept of humanity that would be globally accepted, this would have to be based on notions of humaneness from diverse cultures.[56] Because too much self-centred confidence would be at best nothing but emotional enthusiasm, as Gotthold Ephraim Lessing remarks in his work "Die Erziehung des Menschengeschlechts" ("On Educating the Human Race") from

52 "Humanismus", in: *Historisches Wörterbuch der Philosophie*, vol 3, column 1217 – 1230, s.v. column 1217. – The recourse to Classical Antiquity led to new coinages like "neo-humanism" (F. Paulsen) and "third humanism" (L. Helbing), and, throughout the 19th and 20th centuries, to a variety of specializations such as "pragmatic, technical, national, modern, real, social, socialist, existentialist, personal, Christian humanism."

53 Nida-Rümelin, Julian: *Humanismus als Leitkultur. Ein Perspektivenwechsel*, ed. by Elif Özmen, Munich 2006, p. 26.

54 Ibid., p. 30.

55 In this context I do not wish to refer to the European rhetoric of superiority of the last two hundred years, and also do not wish to invoke the concepts of separatism or exclusionism of all other non-European cultures, but I do want to point out very briefly that even the concepts of 'European' or 'Asian' themselves are constructs representing a one-sided view of the world.

56 The opposite perspective to this would be to simply designate the Other as evil and attempt to eradicate it – something that has been reflected upon a lot but has been justifiably and above all plausibly rejected.

1780 (§§85 ff.). However, can it possibly be our purpose, and above all, is it realistic to expect that "men do what is good […] because it is good" (§85)? That matters would not be as easy as this Lessing was already cognizant of.

## The Obstinacy of Cultures

Of course, as has already been indicated, one does come across the spirit of self-critique besides that of arrogance in the writings about other peoples throughout the early Modern Age. This became more accentuated since the end of the 18th century. At the same a certain arrogance vis-à-vis the human race started to manifest itself. This induced Father Albert Maria Weiss to differentiate between humanity and humanism. According to him the "honourable term of humanity" should be accorded "exclusively to that endeavour which strives to attain the perfection of man", whereas humanism designates every aspect of human life and activity in all its dire reality.[57] As Father Weiss puts it very concisely: "Humanity is the healthy part of human nature, humanism its sick and fallen part."[58] It is remarkable how Weiss negatively contrasts the whole variety of cultures with the humanity of Christianity, and on those occasions when he cannot fail to notice signs of humanness he discounts them by saying: "Buddhism has also suspended human sacrifice. Does this really testify to religious perfection? God beware! Such a diluted religion, if it deserves that name at all, is only capable – apart from its general abhorrence of all bloodshed – of making sacrificial offerings of flowers, milk, tea, biscuits and butter."[59]

However, one cannot limit oneself to the inter-religious dialogue, because the respective traditions must become mutually negotiable, Chinese and Germans, Italians, French – to name but one example – will have to start entering into a debate on their particular and differing religious or cultural traditions as well as their socio-psychological contexts. One of the preconditions for this is to be open to what the other thinks about oneself. This is a mere starting point, and it is conditional upon ourselves enquiring after the tradition of the other.[60] In the process we will make the experience that Lessing has formulated in §38 of his

57 Weiß, Albert Maria: *Humanität und Humanismus. Grundzüge einer Kulturgeschichte erster Theil*, Freiburg i. Br. 1879 (= the same, *Apologie des Christenthums vom Standpunkte der Sittenlehre*, 2. vols., Freiburg i. Br. 1878 – 1884), p. 3.

58 Ibid., p. 5.

59 Ibid., p. 141.

60 If only we had got that far already so that we in Europe could talk about the Chinese literary tradition in the same way that Chinese Germanists and Romanists are capable of talking about German, Italian or French literature.

work “Die Erziehung des Menschengeschlechts” (1780)[61] according to which our limited focus will not just be returned back on our own tradition, but in addition it will be widened in such a way that we can better understand ourselves. Our concern is therefore with both our own tradition as well as with that of the other, and consequently with the contingency of our own position, and without acknowledging this any kind of trans-cultural humanism will not be viable.[62]

Whatever it is that still remains recognizable beyond all the differences is the continuity of what we will designate as *humanum*, i. e. the principle that human beings are generally capable of understanding, reciprocal recognition, love and empathy. In order to make possible the education of mankind in this spirit towards self-formation, mutual recognition, general accountability, and – to employ a modern concept – a global civil society, the process of globalization itself has to be critically reflected upon. This does not imply that we wish to deny those values we usually connect with the concept of humanism any degree of universality, but every culture has to come to the realization that it has to arrive at the idea of humanity and human rights from within its own context.[63]

However, we always have to reckon with institutions, self-perceptions, demands, and therefore the recourse to being human alone is no solution. This is no surprise, because human beings consist of more than just their basic equipment. Man is a cultural creature. This is exactly the context where it makes sense to conceive of humanism in the terms of one’s own tradition, but only to the extent that mankind still perceives itself as a unity, whereby the claim to universality is not just limited to its Enlightenment sense, and that its various traditions and their provenance are remembered and reflected upon.[64]

---

61 “The child that had been sent to foreign parts encountered other children who knew more, who lived more decently, and it was shamed into thinking: Why do I not know this, too? Why do I not live like this, too? Could they not have taught me this in my father’s house? Could they not have brought me up like this, too? Then it looked at its schoolbooks again, for which it had long ago developed an aversion, in order to put the blame on its school books. But behold! It recognized soon that the books are not to blame, that it only has got itself to blame for not knowing these things and not living this kind of life.”

62 In this work *Philosophischer Glaube* (Frankfurt/Main 1958, p. 80) Karl Jaspers has described this situation as follows: “The consequence of such a faulty perspective (the perspective of the historically formed unconditionality of one’s own belief in a universal truth for all) is the self-deception about what I really am and desire, is intolerance (not accepting anything except one’s own dogmatic view) and the inability to communicate (not listening what others have say, not being willing to have one’s own view questioned.” Cf. Wen-chao Li, *Die christliche China-Mission im 17. Jahrhundert*, Stuttgart 2000, p. 311.

63 This is also emphasized by Otfried Höffe, cf. Höffe, Otfried: *Vernunft und Recht. Bausteine zu einem interkulturellen Rechtsdiskurs*, Frankfurt/Main 1996, p. 83.

64 In this context I would like to propound four theses: *Firstly*, human beings have always accepted their kind, and the abhorrence of the Other is secondary phenomenon. – *Secondly*, reflecting upon the part is not unique to the European cultural tradition, but other cultures also have their history, their historiography, and their traditions of symbolic meaning. –

Reflection upon and remembrance of the past as well as reciprocal recognition and agreement upon common values are all faced with the undeniable problem that all humans come from cultural backgrounds that are highly different. These differences in their turn are the result of multiple and partially explicable causes and effects. Therefore a global realization of humanism can only be imagined as a process conducted on the spirit of mediation and justice.

In order to facilitate communication this requires the clarification of one's own humanistic tradition, concepts of humanity, as well as ideas of freedom, self-determination and necessity. This will only be successful and practicable if, besides diachronically studying the various traditions, we maintain a synchronous discourse. How could this function in practice? I shall give an example of this.

## The Clash of Cultures and the Demographic Factor

There have always been and always will be clashes of culture. But there are also lines of conflict within each culture. In this context the debate conducted in Europe comes to mind when period-terms became linguistic weapons. The debate on the Gothic period in Germany, which is reflected in titles like "Die Renaissance, das Verhängnis der deutschen Cultur" ("The Renaissance, the Doom of German Culture") by Richard Benz (Jena 1915) is a case in point by way of demonstrating how such concepts carried a normative charge in their function as linguistic weapons.[65] This equally applies to the concept of Baroque and numerous others, but also to such phenomena as iconoclastic movements, especially during the period of the *Kulturkampf* when Germany was riven by strife among the major religious denominations. There are numerous ways conflicts can be conceived and carried out, and all cultures have devoted some thought to this. Sigmund Freud concludes his text from 1915 about "The Disappointment of War" with this statement :

> "It will remain a mystery why national individuals should despise, hat, abhor one another, even in peace-time, and every nation the other. I cannot explain this. It seems as if in such a case all moral restraints on the part of the individuals become removed

*Thirdly*, there s no reasonable argument for justifying the precedence of one cultural tradition over another. – *Fourthly*, we assume – and I think justly – the universality of human rights as we know them: Of course it is totally unresolved by which means this utopia can be achieved.

65 On the "spirit of the Gothic period" cf. Claussen, Peter Cornelius/Mondini, Daniela (Eds.): "Wohin weht der "Geist der Gothik"? Über einen Stilbegriff der Deutschen Moderne", in: *Georges-Bloch-Jahrbuch des Kunsthistorischen Instituts der Universität Zürich* 9/10 (2002/03): 223–347.

> when they form part of a majority or even of millions of people, and only the most primitive, primal and crudest mental attitudes are left over. Such a sorry state of affairs will perhaps only be altered in the course of some later development. But a modicum of truthfulness and sincerity among men, and between the people and those who govern them might pave the way for such a change."[66]

In all these considerations one should be mindful of the fact that the idea of humaneness, the basic element of any concept of humanism, only seems to have become a necessity after its actual disappearance. But it has already been mentioned at the beginning that we live in a post-paradisiacal era.

66 Freud: op.cit., pp. 47–48.

## Notes on Contributors

Prof. Dr. phil., Dipl. geol. Christoph Antweiler

Director of the Institute for Oriental and Asian Studies (IOA) at the University of Bonn, Germany, cultural anthropologist and Prof. of Southeast Asian Studies, Board of Bonn Center for Asian Studies (BAZ); Board Member EUROSEAS (European Association of Southeast Asian Studies), Board Member for Germany; Member Academia Europea (London).

*Fields of Research:* Urbanity, decision-making, cognition, local Knowledge, societal evolution, human universals, applied anthropology; regional: Southeast Asia, especially Indonesia.

*Recent publications:* Handbook of Evolution. Vol. 1: The Evolution of Cultures and Societies (with F.M. Wuketits, eds.) 2004; Was ist den Menschen gemeinsam? Über Kultur und Kulturen $^{2}$2009; Inclusive Humanism. Anthropological Basics for a Realistic Cosmopolitanism 2012; Environmental Uncertainty and Local Knowledge. Southeast Asia as a Laboratory of Global Change (ed., with A.-K. Hornidge) 2012.

Prof. Dr. Dr. h.c. Hubert Cancik

Prof. emeritus for classics at the Eberhard-Karls-University Tübingen, Germany. Editor in chief and cooperator in different research and publication projects, as there are: "Religionsgeschichte Deutschlands"; "Handbuch religionswissenschaftlicher Grundbegriffe"; "Der Neue Pauly" (engl. ed.: Brill's New Pauly Encyclopedia); "Römische Reichs- und Provinzreligion"; "Religion in Geschichte und Gegenwart" (engl. ed.: Religion Past & Present); "Franz Overbeck. Werke und Nachlaß".

*Fields of research:* Greek and Roman cultures; history of ancient religions; history of the reception and scholarship of classical antiquity, humanism.

*Recent publications:* Römische Religion im Kontext. Gesammelte Aufsätze I, ed. Hildegard Cancik-Lindemaier 2008; Religionsgeschichten. Gesammelte Aufsätze II, ed. Hildegard Cancik-Lindemaier 2008; Europa – Antike – Humanismus. Humanistische Versuche und Vorarbeiten, ed. Hildegard Cancik-Lindemaier 2011.

Prof. Dr. Umesh Chattopadhyaya (Ph.D., Cantab.)

Professor in the Department of Ancient History, Culture and Archaeology, University of Allahabad, India.

*Fields of research:* His area of specialization is history and archaeology with a focused interest in New Humanism. With a background in Physics, his other areas of interest include Philosophy of Science. He has participated in various international conferences in Germany, U.K. and Egypt.

*Publications:* Chattopadhyaya has published widely in English and German and is currently in the process of publishing his Indian Humanism: A Source Book.

Prof. Dr. Günter Dux

Professor emeritus of sociology at the University of Freiburg, Germany. In 1995 Leibniz-professor at the University of Leipzig. In 1997/98 head of the research group on the theory of cultural and social change at the Center for Interdisciplinary Research (ZiF) at the University of Bielefeld.

*Fields of research:* sociology of epistemology; historico-genetical theory of culture and society; ontogenetical and historical development of cognition in preindustrial societies; sociology of normative structures: morality and justice; political sociology; sociology of religion.

*Recent publications:* Why Justice. The Logic of Capitalism 2009; Since the Very Beginning: Power and not Justice 2009; Democracy as Human Lifeform 2013.

Prof. Dr. rer. nat. Dr. med. habil. Gerald Hüther

Professor for Neurobiology at University of Göttingen, Germany.

*Fields of research:* His interests include the influence of early experiences on brain development and the effects of fear and stress and the meaning of emotional reactions.

*Publications:* He is the author of numerous scientific publications and popular books on scientific themes. For further informations: www.win-future.de, www.nelecom.de, www.sinn-stiftung.eu, www.forum-humanum.eu, www.gerald-huether.de

Prof. Dr. Oliver Kozlarek

Doktor der Philosophie (Free University Berlin, Germany) and Doctor en Humanidades (Universidad Autónoma Metropolitana, Mexico). Oliver Kozlarek teaches political and social philosophy as well as social theory at the Institute for Philosophical Research at Universidad Michoacana de San Nicolás de Hidalgo in Morelia, Mexico. He has been a visiting fellow at the Kulturwissenschaftliches Institut in Essen at the New School for Social Research and at Stanford University. He was Cantemir Senior Fellow with the Berendel Foundation.

*Fields of research:* theories of modernity and globalization, critical theory, globalization and humanism, Latin American political and social thought.

*Recently edited and authored books include:* De la Teoría Crítica a una crítica plural de la modernidad 2007; Entre Cosmopolitismo y "conciencia del mundo" 2007; Humanismo en la época de la globalización: Desafíos y horizontes 2009 (with Jörn Rüsen); Octavio Paz: Humanism and Critique 2009; Moderne als Weltbewusstsein. Ideen für eine humanistische Sozialtheorie in der globalen Moderne 2011; and Shaping a Humane World. Civilizations, Axial Times, Modernities, Humanisms 2012 (with Jörn Rüsen and Ernst Wolff).

Prof. Dr. Ilse Lenz

Professor for Sociology (social inequality/gender) at the Ruhr-University Bochum (Germany); coordinator of the Marie-Jahoda-Chair for International Gender Studies.

*Fields of research:* globalisation, gender and work, complex social inequalities (class, gender, migration, desire), women's and global justice movements in comparative perspective (Germany, Japan).

*Recent publications:* Gender Orders Unbound. Globalisation, Restructuring, Reciprocity Lenz, Ilse, (eds., with Charlotte Ullrich; Barbara Fersch) 2007; Die Neue Frauenbewegung in Deutschland. (The new women's movement in Germany) 2. ed. 2010; Anders und gleich in NRW – Gleichstellung und Akzeptanz sexueller und geschlechtlicher Vielfalt. (Different and equal in North-Rhine Westfalia – Equal Opportunity and acceptance of sexual and gender diversity (ed., with Katja Sabisch and Marcel Wrzesinski) 2012; Frauenbewegung in Japan. Gleichheit, Differenz, Partizipation (The women's movement in Japan. Equality, difference, participation) (with Michiko Mae), 2013 i.E;

PD Dr. Dr. Georg W. Oesterdiekhoff

Private lecturer at the Institute for Technology Karlsruhe, deputy chair for sociology at the universities of Aachen and Erlangen-Nürnberg,Germany; visiting professor at the Universidad Nacional de Colombia, Colombia. *Fields of research:* Theory programme "structure-genetic sociology" as general theory of humanities and social sciences and as general theory of the development of humankind, culture, and history. The theory programme consists of a link between developmental psychology and historical disciplines. Furthermore, sociology of religion, culture, knowledge, and economics.

*Recent publications:* Mental Growth of Humankind 2009; The Steps of Man Towards Civilization 2011; Was Pre-Modern Man a Child? 2012; Ontogeny and History 2012; Die geistige Entwicklung der Menschheit 2012; Die Entwicklung der Menschheit von der Kindheitsphase zur Erwachsenenreife 2013.

Prof. Dr. Heiner Roetz

Professor for Chinese History and Philosophy at Ruhr-University, Bochum, Germany.

*Fields of research:* Classical Chinese philosophy, Chinese ethics, human rights in China, intercultural philosophy.

*Recent publications:* Konfuzius 2006; (with Hubert Schleichert) Klassische chinesische Philosophie 2009; edited: (with Lena Henningsen) Menschenbilder in China 2009; (with Wolfgang Ommerborn and Gregor Paul); Das Buch Mengzi im Kontext der Menschenrechtsfrage 2011.

Prof. Dr. Dr. h.c. Jörn Rüsen

Senior Fellow at the Kulturwissenschaftliches Institut (Institute for Advanced Study in the Humanities) at Essen, Germany; Professor emeritus for General History and Historical Culture at the University of Witten/Herdecke, head of the research project (2006 – 2009) on "Humanism in the era of globalisation – an intercultural dialogue on culture, humanity, and values" at the Kulturwissenschaftliches Institut in Essen.

*Fields of research:* theory and methodology of history, history of historiography, strategies of intercultural comparison, intercultural communication in modern societies; humanism in a globalizing world.

*Recent publications:* History: Narration – Interpretation- Orientation 2005; edited: (with Henner Laass) Humanism in Intercultural Perspective 2009; (with Stefan Reichmuth and Aladdin Sarhan) Humanism and Muslim Culture 2012; (with Oliver Kozlarek and Ernst Wolff) Shaping a Humane World 2012; (with

Michai I.Spariosu) Exploring Humanity – Intercultural Perspectives on Humanism 2012.

Prof. Dr. Helwig Schmidt-Glintzer

Director of the Herzog August Bibliothek Wolfenbüttel, Germany (Research Library for Medieval and Early Modern Humanistic Studies) since 1993. 1981 through 1993 chair for East Asian Culture and Languages at the University of Munich. Thought at the Universities of Bonn, Hamburg, Munich, Göttingen and Hannover.

*Fields of research:* Chinese History and Culture; Ideology of the Chinese Literati; changes of value systems and spheres of knowledge.

*Recent publications:* China – Eine Herausforderung für den Westen. Plädoyer für differentielle kulturelle Kompetenz 2011.

Prof. Dr. phil. Jürgen Straub

Since 2011 he has been serving as Dean of the faculty for social science at the Ruhr University of Bochum (RUB, Germany), where he has also been a tenured professor with the chair in social theory and social psychology since the summer term of 2008. Presently, he is involved in the introduction and advancement of a cultural psychological emphasis in teaching and research. Prior to his tenure at the Ruhr University, he had been holding a chair in intercultural communication at the Technical University of Chemnitz (2002–2008) where he designed and mentored the masters study programme "Intercultural communication and competence".

*Fields of research:* intercultural communication and competence, social and cultural psychology, interdisciplinary social and cultural theory, comparative social research and analysis of culture, action theory, theory of identity, mnemonic and biographic theory, historical consciousness, violence in modern societies, psychosocial consequences of Shoah, psychology of religion, research in psychotherapy, history of psychology and psychologisation of the sociocultural sphere as well as theory, methodology and methodic analysis in qualitative and interpretative research.

*Recent publications:* Edited: Narration, Identity and Historical Consciousness: The Psychological Construction of Time and History 2005; Pursuit of Meaning: Theoretical and Methodological Advances in Cultural and Cross-Cultural Psychology (ed. with D. Weidemann, C. Kölbl and B. Zielke) 2006; Handbuch Interkulturelle Kommunikation und Kompetenz (ed. with A. Weidemann and D. Weidemann) 2007; Wie lehrt man interkulturelle Kompetenz? Theorien, Methoden und Praxis in der Hochschulausbildung. Ein Handbuch (ed. with A. Weidemann and S. Nothnagel) 2010; Dark Traces of the Past. Psychoanalysis and Historical Thinking (ed. with J. Rüsen) 2011; Der sich selbst verwirklichende Mensch. Über den Humanismus der Humanistischen Psychologie 2012; Menschen machen. Die hellen und dunklen Seiten humanwissenschaftlicher Optimierungsprogramme (ed. with A. Sieben and K. Sabisch-Fechtelpeter) 2012.

# Bibliography

Abalealard, Peter: *Gespräch eines Philosophen, eines Juden und eines Christen.* Latin-German edition: *Peter Abailard.* Ed. and transl. by Hans-Wolfgang Krautz, Darmstadt 1995.

Adamopoulos, J./Lonner, W.J.: "Absolutism, Relativism and Universalism in the Study of Human Behavior", in: Lonner, Walter J./Malpass, Roy S. (Eds.): *Psychology and Culture*, Boston etc. 1994, pp. 129 – 134.

Adams, William Yewdale: *The Philosophical Roots of Anthropology.* (= CSLI Publications: CSLI Lecture Notes, 86), Stanford, Cal. 1998.

Andreae, Bernard: *Odysseus. Archäologie des europäischen Menschenbildes*, Frankfurt/Main [2]1984.

Antweiler, Christoph: "Analogisierung als spezielle Form von Vergleich: eine nützliche Methode der interdisziplinären Evolutionsforschung", in: *Erwägen, Wissen, Ethik. Deliberation, Knowledge, Ethics* 16.3 (2005): 370 – 371.

Antweiler, Christoph: *Grundpositionen interkultureller Ethnologie.* (= Interkulturelle Bibliothek, 79), Nordhausen 2007.

Antweiler, Christoph: *Heimat Mensch. Was uns alle verbindet*, Hamburg 2009.

Antweiler, Christoph: *Mensch und Weltkultur. Für einen realistischen Kosmopolitismus im Zeitalter der Globalisierung* (Der Mensch im Netz der Kulturen – Humanismus in der Epoche der Globalisierung, vol. 10), Bielefeld 2011 (English translation: *Inclusive Humanism. Anthropological Basics for a Realistic Cosmopolitanism*, [= Reflections on (In)Humanity], Göttingen 2012.)

Antweiler, Christoph: *Was ist den Menschen gemeinsam? Über Kultur und Kulturen*, Darmstadt ([1]2007), [2]2009.

Arnason, Johann P./Eisenstadt, S.N./Wittrock, Björn (Eds.): *Axial Civilisations and World History*, Leiden 2005.

Aurobindo, Sri: *The Life Divine*, Pondicherry 1977.

Aust, Stefan and Gerhard Spörl: "Das bessere Gesicht Amerikas", in: *Der Spiegel* 14 (2006): 116 – 117.

Back, Jean/Bauret, Gabriel (Eds.): *The Family of Man. Témoignages et documents*, Luxemburg 1994.

Back, Jean/Schmidt-Linsenhoff, Victoria (Eds): *The Family of Man –2000. Humanism and Postmodernism. A Reappraisal of the Photo Exhibition by Edward Steichen*, Marburg 2004.

Baker, Nicholson: *Human smoke. The beginnings of World War II, the end of civilization*, New York 2008.

Bandiste, D.D.: *Humanist Thought in Contemporary India*, Delhi 1999.

Barthes, Roland: "Die große Familie des Menschen", in: idem: *Mythen des Alltags*, Frankfurt/Main 1974, pp. 16–19.

Basedow, Johann Bernhard: *Vorstellung an Menschenfreunde und vermögende Männer über Schule, Studien und ihren Einfluß in die öffentliche Wohlfahrt* (1768). (= Neudrucke pädagogischer Schriften 14), Leipzig 1893.

Basham, A.L.: *Wonder That Was India*, London 1954.

Beck, Ulrich/Beck-Gernsheim, Elisabeth: *Riskante Freiheiten. Individualisierung in modernen Gesellschaften*, Frankfurt/Main 1994.

Beck, Ulrich/Giddens, Anthony/Lash, Scott: *Reflexive Modernisierung. Eine Kontroverse*, Frankfurt/Main 1996.

Bender, Thomas: *A Nation among Nations. America's place in World History.* http://hnn.us/articles/23913.html [04/17/2006].

Berger, Klaus: *Von der Schönheit der Ethik*, Frankfurt/Main 2006.

Berger, Peter L./Berger, Brigitte/Kellner, Hansfried: *The Homeless Mind. Modernization and Consciousness*, New York 1973.

Bergsträsser, Gotthelf: *Hunain ibn Ishaq und seine Schule*, Leiden 1913.

Beuchot, Mauricio: *Bartolomé de las* Casas (1484–1566), Madrid 1995.

Bhandarkar, R.G.: *Vaishnavism, Saivism and Minor Religious Systems*, Straßburg 1913.

Bielefeldt, Heiner: "Menschenrechtliche Universalität und Entwicklungs-Zusammenarbeit", in: Habisch, André/Pöner, Ulrich (Eds.): *Signale der Solidarität. Wege christlicher Nord-Süd-Ethik*, Paderborn etc. 1994, pp. 31–47.

Bleicken, Jochen: *Die athenische Demokratie*, Paderborn [4]1995.

Blumenbach, Johann Friedrich: *Über den Bildungstrieb*. 2. ed., Göttingen 1791.

Blumenback, Johann Friedrich: *De generis humani varietate nativa liber*, Göttingen 1775.

Boehm, Christopher: "Ambivalence and Compromise in Human Nature", in: *American Anthropologist* 91 (1989): 921–939.

Böhme, Gernot: "Kant und die Family of Man. Wie begründet sich die Universalität der Menschenrechte?", in: *Lettre Internationale* 25 (1999): 23–26.

Boster, James Shilts/D'Andrade, Roy: "Natural and Human Sources of Cross-Cultural Agreement in Ornithological Classification", in: *American Anthropologist* 91 (1989): 132–142.

Boster, James Shilts: "Cultural Variation", in: Wilson, Robert Anton/Keil, Frank C. (Eds.): *The MIT Encyclopedia of the Cognitive Sciences*, London 1999.

Boster, James Shilts: "Human Cognition as a Product and Agent of Evolution", in: Ellen, Roy F./Fukui, Katsuyoshi (Eds.): *Redefining Nature. Ecology, Culture and Domestication.* (= Explorations in Anthropology), Oxford and Washington, D.C. 1996, pp. 268–289.

Bovet, Pierre: *Le sentiment religieux et la psychologie de l'enfant*, Neuchâtel/Paris 1951.

Brockmeier, Jens/Carbaugh, Donald (Eds.): *Narrative and Identity: Studies in Autobiography, Self and Culture*, Amsterdam 2001.

Brown, Donald Edward: "Human Universals, Human Nature/Human Culture", in: *Daedalus* (Fall 2004): 47–54.

Brown, Donald Edward: "Human Universals", in: Levinson, David/Ember, Melvin (Eds.): *Encyclopedia of Cultural Anthropology*, vol. 1, New York 1996, pp. 607 – 613.

Brown, Donald Edward: "Human Universals", in: Wilson, Robert Anton/Keil, Frank C. (Eds.): *The MIT Encyclopedia of the Cognitive Sciences*, London 1999, pp. 382 – 384.

Brown, Donald Edward: *Human Universals*, New York etc. 1991.

Bruner, Jerome S.: *Acts of Meaning*, Cambridge, MA, London 1990.

Burkhardt, Jacob: *Die Kultur der Renaissance in Italien* (1860), Frankfurt/Main 1989.

Byrne, Richard W.: "Social and Technical Forms of Primate Intelligence", in: de Waal, Frans B.M. (Ed.): *Tree of Origin. What Primate Behavior Can Tell Us about Human Social Evolution*, Cambridge, Mass./London 2001, pp. 145 – 172.

Campbell, Donald T.: "The Two Distinct Routes Beyond Kin Selection to Ultrasociality: Implications for the Humanities and Social Sciences", in: Bridgeman, Diane L. (Ed.): *The Nature of Prosocial Developoment. Interdisciplinary Theories and Strategies*, New York 1983, pp. 11 – 41.

Camus, Albert: "Die Guillotine. Betrachtungen zur Todesstrafe", in: idem: *Fragen der Zeit*, Hamburg 1960, p. 177.

Cancik, Hubert: "Die Rezeption der Antike – Kleine Geschichte des europäischen Humanismus", in: Rüsen, Jörn/Laass, Henner (Eds): *Interkultureller Humanismus. Menschlichkeit in der Vielfalt der Kulturen*, Schwalbach/Taunus 2009, pp. 24 – 52.

Cancik, Hubert: "Entrohung und Barmherzigkeit, Herrschaft und Würde. Antike Grundlagen von Humanismus", in: Faber, Richard (Ed.): *Streit um den Humanismus*, Würzburg 2003.

Cancik, Hubert: "Humanismus", in: Cancik, Hubert/Gladigow, Burkhard/Kohl, Karl-Heinz (Ed.): *Handbuch religionswissenschaftlicher Grundbegriffe*, vol. III: *Gesetz–Kult*, Stuttgart 1993.

Caso, Antonio: "El nuevo humanismo", in: idem: *Obras Completas* II, Mexico 1973, pp. 65 – 71.

Caso, Antonio: "La existencia como economía, como desinterés y como caridad", in: idem: *Obras Completas* III, Mexico 1972.

Caso, Antonio: "Nuestra misión humana", in: idem: *Obras Completas* IX, Mexico 1976, pp. 55 – 62.

Cassin, René: *La pensée et l'action*, [...], Boulogne-sur-Seine 1972.

Chan, Wing-Tsit (Ed.): *A Source Book in Chinese Philosophy*, Princeton 1963.

Chang, Pil-Hwa/Kim, Eun-Shil (Eds.): *Women's Studies in Asia Series. Women's Experiences and Feminist Practices in South Korea*, Seoul 2005.

Chattopadhyaya, D.P.: *Lokayata: A Study in Ancient Indian Materialism*, Delhi 1959.

Chattopadhyaya, K.C.: "The Lokayata System of Thought in Ancient India", in: *Journal of the Ganganatha Jha Kendriya Sanskrit Vidyapeetha (Aditya Natha Jha Commemoration Volume)* 31.1 – 4 (1975): 137 – 155.

Chattopadhyaya, U.: "Contemporary Challenges to Historical Studies: In Search of A 'Humanistic History' in An Era of Global Crisis" in: *Taiwan Journal of East Asian Studies* 8.2 (2011): 79 – 111.

Chen, Yunquzan: "The Spirit of Renwen ('Humanism') in the Traditional Culture of China", in: Rüsen, Jörn/Laass, Henner (Eds): *Humanism in Intercultural Perspective. Experiences and Expectations*, Bielefeld 2009.

Chomsky, Noam: *The New Military Humanism. Lessons from Kosovo*, London 1999.

Claussen, Peter Cornelius/Mondini, Daniela (Eds.): "Wohin weht der 'Geist der Gothik'?

Über einen Stilbegriff der Deutschen Moderne", in: *Georges-Bloch-Jahrbuch des Kunsthistorischen Instituts der Universität Zürich* 9/10 (2002/03): 223–347.

Cole, Michael/Scribner, Sylvia: *Culture and thought*, New York 1974.

*Convention on the Elimination of All Forms of Discrimination against Women* (CEDAW) (1979) http://www.un.org/womenwatch/daw/cedaw/text/econvention.htm.

Courbage, Youssef/Todd, Emmanuel: *Die unaufhaltsame Revolution. Wie die Werte der Moderne die islamische Welt verändern*, Munich 2008.

Crook, John H.: *World Crisis and Buddhist Humanism. End Games: Collapse or Renewal of Civilisation*, New Delhi 2009. (1st Indian edition).

D'Andrade, Roy: "Moral Models in Anthropology", in: *Current Anthropology* 36.3 (1995): 399–408.

Dasen, Pierre (Ed.): *Piagetian psychology. Cross-cultural contributions*, New York 1977.

Dasen, Pierre/Berry, John W. (Eds.): *Culture and cognition. Readings in cross-cultural psychology*, London 1974.

Dawkins, Richard: *Der Gotteswahn*, Berlin 2008.

Dawkins, Richard: *The god delusion*, London 2006.

De Waal, Frans B.M.: *Der Affe und der Sushimeister. Das kulturelle Leben der Tiere*. Munich 2005; orig. "The Ape and the Sushi Master. Cultural Reflections by a Primatologist", New York 2001; London 2001.

De Waal, Frans B.M.: *Der Affe in uns. Warum wir sind wie wir sind*, München 2006 (orig. *Our Inner Ape. A Leading Primatologist Explains Why We are Who We are*, New York 2006).

Descartes, René: *Discours de la méthode*, 1637 VI. (*Discours de la Méthode*, 6e partie, Paris 1966). German translation: *Abhandlung über die Methode*, transl. Arthur Buchenau, Leipzig 1919.

Descartes, René: *Meditationes de prima philosophia. Meditationen über die erste Philosophie*. Latin/German, ed. v. Gerhart Schmidt, Stuttgart 1985.

Devaraja, N.K.: *Humanism in Indian Thought*, New Delhi 1988.

Diderot, Denis/d'Alembert, Jean le Rond (Eds.): *Encyclopédie ou Dictionnaire raisonné des sciences, des arts et des métiers* (1751–1780), vol. 8, 1765.

Diels Hermann/Kranz, Walther (Eds.), *Die Fragmente der Vorsokratiker*, Berlin 1952/60)

Dissanayake, Ellen: *Homo Aestheticus. Where Art comes from and why?*, New York etc. 1992.

Droysen, Johann Gustav: *Historik. Historisch-kritische Ausgabe*, ed. Peter Leyh, vol. 1., Stuttgart-Bad Cannstatt 1977.

Du, Fangquing/Zheng, Xinrong (Eds.): *Women's Studies in China. Mapping the Social, Economic and Policy Changes in Chinese Women's Lives*, Seoul 2005.

Duerr, Hans-Peter: *Nacktheit und Scham*, Frankfurt/Main 1988.

Dunbar, Robin I.M.: "Coevolution of Neocortical Size, Group Size, and Language in Humans", in: *Behavioral and Brain Sciences* 16 (1993): 681–694.

Dunbar, Robin I.M.: *The Human Story. A New History of Mankind's Evolution*, London 2004.

Dutschke, Rudi: *Versuch, Lenin auf die Füße zu stellen*, Berlin 1974.

Dux, Günter: "Die Genese der Philosophie in der Geistesgeschichte der Menschheit", in: *Dialektik. Zeitschrift für Kulturphilosophie* (2003): 125–155.

Dux, Günter: "Die ontogenetische und historische Entwicklung des Geistes", in: Dux,

Günter/Wenzel, Ulrich (Eds.), *Der Prozess der Geistesgeschichte*, Frankfurt/Main 1994, pp. 175 – 224.

Dux, Günter: *Historisch-genetische Theorie der Kultur. Zur prozessualen Logik im kulturellen Wandel*, 3. ed., Weilerswist 2007.

Dux, Günter: *Von allem Anfang an: Macht nicht Gerechtigkeit. Studien zur Genese und historischen Entwicklung des Postulats der Gerechtigkeit*, Weilerswist 2009, pp. 124 – 144.

Dux, Günter: "Wie der Sinn in die Welt kam und was aus ihm wurde", in: Müller, Klaus E./ Rüsen, Jörn (Eds.), *Historische Sinnbildung*, Reinbek 1997, pp. 195 – 217.

Dux, Günter/Puspha Kumari, V. (1994): "Studien zur vorindustriellen Kausalität", in: Dux, Günter/Wenzel, Ulrich (Eds.), *Der Prozess der Geistesgeschichte*, Frankfurt/Main 1994, pp. 436 – 471.

Eagleton, Terry: *The Meaning of Life*, Oxford 2007.

Eckart, Christel: "Verschlingt die Arbeit die Emanzipation? Von der Polarisierung der Geschlechtscharaktere zur Entwicklung der Arbeitsmonade", in: *Widersprüche* 23 (1987): 7 – 18. (http://www.widersprueche-zeitschrift.de/article365.html). Shortend reprint in Lenz, Ilse (Ed.): *Die Neue Frauenbewegung in Deutschland. Abschied vom kleinen Unterschied. Eine Quellensammlung*, Wiesbaden 2008, pp. 391 – 398.

Eglauer, Martina: *Wissenschaft als Chance. Das Wissenschaftsverständnis des chinesischen Philosophen Hu Shi (1891 – 1962) unter dem Einfluß von John Deweys (1859 – 1952) Pragmatismus*, Stuttgart 2001.

Ehrlich, Paul R.: *Human Natures. Genes, Cultures, and the Human Prospect*, Harmondsworth 2002.

Eibl, Karl "Warum der Mensch etwas Besonderes ist. Einige evolutionsbiologische Aspekte", in: *Literaturkritik.de* 2 (2007) (www.literaturkritik.de/public/rezension, php; consulted 11.02.2013)

Eibl, Karl: *Animal Poeta. Bausteine der biologischen Kultur- und Literaturtheorie.* (= Poetogenesis. Studien und Texte zur empirischen Anthropologie der Literatur), Paderborn 2004.

Eisenberg, L.: "The social construction of the human brain", in: *Am. J. Psychiatry* 152 (1995): 1563 – 1575.

Eisenstadt, Shmuel N.: "Die Achsenzeit in der Weltgeschichte", in: ibid.: *Theorie und Moderne. Soziologische Essays*, Wiesbaden 2006, pp. 253 – 275, and in: Joas, Hans/ Wiegandt, Klaus (Eds.): *Die kulturellen Werte Europas*, 4th ed., Frankfurt/Main 2006, pp. 40 – 68.

Eisenstadt, Shmuel N.: *Die großen Revolutionen und die Kulturen der Moderne*, Wiesbaden 2006.

Eisenstadt, Shmuel N. (Ed.): *Kulturen der Achsenzeit. Ihre Ursprünge und ihre Vielfalt*, vol. I, II, III, Frankfurt/Main 1987, 1987, 1992.

Eisenstadt, Shmuel N.: "Multiple Modernities", in: *Daedalus* 129. 1 (Winter 2000): 1 – 30.

Eisenstadt, Shmuel N. (Ed.): *The Origins and Diversity of the Axial Age Civilizations*, New York 1986.

Elias, Norbert: *Power and civility*, New York 1982.

Elwert, Georg: "Nationalismus, Ethnizität und Nativismus – über Wir-Gruppenprozesse", in: Waldmann, Peter/Elwert, Georg (Eds.): *Ethnizität im Wandel*, Saarbrücken/Fort Lauderdale 1989, pp. 21 – 60.

Engels, Friedrich/Marx, Karl: "Die heilige Familie" (Paris, Brüssel 1884/1845), in: *Marx-Engels-Werke* (MEW) 2,7, Berlin 1959.

Erikson, Erik H.: *Identity and the Life Cycle. Selected Papers*, New York 1959.

Ette, Ottmar: *Literatur in Bewegung*, Weilerswist 2001.

Ette, Ottmar: *Weltbewusstsein. Alexander von Humboldt und das unvollendete Projekt einer anderen Moderne*, Weilerswist 2002.

Evans-Pritchard, Edward Evan: *Witchcraft, oracles, and magic among the Azande*, Oxford 1976.

Ferguson, Adam: *Versuch über die Geschichte der bürgerlichen Gesellschaft*, Frankfurt/Main 1986.

Feuerbach, Ludwig: *The essence of Christianity*, New York 1985.

Fichte, J.G.: *Die Anweisung zum seligen Leben, oder auch die Religionslehre*, 4th ed., Hamburg 1994.

Fichte, J.G.: *Die Bestimmung des Menschen*, 5th ed., Hamburg 1979.

Flynn, James: *What is intelligence?*, London 2007.

Folbre, Nancy: *The Invisible Heart. Economics and Family Values*, New York 2001.

Fortune, R.F.: *Sorcerers of Dobu*, London 1932.

Foucault, Michel: *Dits et Écrits*, 4 vols., Frankfurt/Main 2001 – 2005.

Foucault, Michel: *The History of Sexuality*, vol. 1: *An Introduction*, New York 1978.

Franz Rosenthal, *Das Fortleben der Antike im Islam*, Zürich/Stuttgart 1965. (English translation: *The classical heritage in Islam*. Transl. from German by Emile and Jenny Marmorstein, London 1992)

Freud, Sigismund Schlomo: *Vorlesungen zur Einführung in die Psychoanalyse*. (= Sigmund Freud, *Gesammelte Werke*, 11), Frankfurt/Main $^{5}$1969 (first 1917).

Freud, Sigmund: "Zeitgemäßes über Krieg und Tod (1915)", in: Sigmund Freud, *Studienausgabe*, vol. IX, Frankfurt/Main 1974, pp. 33 ff.

Frevert, Ute : *"Mann und Weib und Weib und Mann". Geschlechterdifferenzen in der Moderne*, Munich 1995.

Gadamer, Hans-Georg: *Wahrheit und Methode*, 2nd ed., Tübingen 1965

Gandhi, Mahatma: "Hindu Swaraj", in: Mukherjee, Rudrangshu (Ed.): *The Penguin Gandhi Reader*, New York 1993, pp. 3 – 66.

Gatterer, J.Ch.: *Abriß der Universalhistorie in ihrem ganzen Umfange. Bey dieser zwoten Ausgabe völlig umgearbeitet und bis auf unsere Zeiten fortgesetzt*, Göttingen 1773.

Geertz, Clifford James: *The Interpretation of Cultures*. New York 1972.

George, Susan: *Hijacking America. How the Religious and Secular Right Changed what Americans Think*, Cambridge 2008.

Gerhard, Ute (Ed.): *Differenz und Gleichheit. Menschenrechte haben (k)ein Geschlecht*, Frankfurt/Main 1990.

Gerhardt, Volker: *Selbstbestimmung. Das Prinzip der Individualität*, Ditzingen 1999.

Giddens, Anthony: *Modernity and Self-Identity. Self and Society in the Late Modern Age*, Cambridge 1991.

Giddens, Anthony: *The Consequences of Modernity*, Stanford, Cal., 1990.

Giedd, J.N./Blumenthal, J./Jeffries, N.O. et al.: "Brain development during childhood and adolescence: a longitudinal MRT study", in: *Nature Neuroscience* 2.10 (1999): 861 – 863.

Gieselmann, Martin/Seebold, Irmtraud: *Der Humanismus in der Epoche der Globalisierung. Ein interkultureller Dialog über Kultur, Menschheit und Werte. Arbeitspapier,*

Essen: Kulturwissenschaftliches Institut (KWI), unpubl. mscr., n.y. (ca. 2006), (http://humanismus@kwinrw.de/cms/index.php?t=126&sid=a622b977f26d7e992c78ffd0bf d7b648; consulted: 13.10.2011)

Giustiniani, Vito R.: "Homo, Humanus, and the Message of 'Humanism'", in: *Journal of the History of Ideas* 46.2 (1985): 167 - 195.

Goethe, Johann Wolfgang: "Italienische Reise. Italian Journey", 3rd Dec. 1786, in: Johann Wolfgang Goethe, *Sämtliche Werke*, Zürich 1977 (=1950), vol. II, p. 160; cf. p. 157; p. 179.

Grabmann, Martin: "Das Naturrecht der Scholastik von Gratian bis Thomas von Aquin", in: *Archiv für Rechts und Wirtschaftsphilosophie* (1922): 12 - 53.

Gregor, Thomas A./Tuzin, Donald F.: "Comparing Gender in Amazonia and Melanesia: A Theoretical Orientation", in: idem (Eds.): *Gender in Amazonia and Melanesia. An Exploration of Comparative Method*, Berkeley 2001, pp. 1 - 16.

Gregorovius, Ferdinand: *Geschichte der Stadt Rom im Mittelalter* (1859/1860), Darmstadt 1953/1957 (= Munich 1978.

Grieder, Jerome B.: *Hu Shih and the Chinese Renaissance*, Cambridge, Mass., 1999.

Grossmann, Klaus E./Grossmann, Karin: "Universale Bedingungen für die Entwicklung kultureller Vielfalt: Eine verhaltensbiologische Perspektive", in: Trommsdorff, Gisela/Kornath, Hans-Joachim (Eds.): *Theorien und Methoden der kulturvergleichenden Psychologie.* (= Enzyklopädie der Psychologie, Themenbereich C, Theorie und Forschung, Serie VII, Kulturvergleichende Psychologie, vol. 1), Göttingen etc. 2007, pp. 221 - 285.

Guo Qingfan, *Zhuangzi jishi, Zhuzi jicheng*, vol. 2, Beijing 1985, pp. 172 f.

Gupta, N.L.: *Humanist Tradition of India*, New Delhi 1999.

Haas, Alois M.: "Selbstverwirklichung", in: *Zürich Studies in the History of Art. Georges Bloch Annual* 13/14 (2006/2007): 545 - 565.

Habermas, Jürgen: "Philosophische Anthropologie. Ein Lexikonartikel", in: idem: *Kultur und Kritik. Verstreute Aufsätze*, Frankfurt/Main 1973, pp. 89 - 111.

Habermas, Jürgen: *Zur Rekonstruktion des Historischen Materialismus*, Frankfurt/Main 1976.

Hallpike, Christopher: *Foundations of primitive thought*, Oxford 1978.

Hallpike, Christopher: *The evolution of moral understanding*, London 2004.

Hamlin, William M.: *The Image of America in Montaigne, Spenser, and Shakespeare. Renaissance Ethnography and Literary Reflection*, New York 1995.

Hauck, Gerhard: *Kultur. Zur Karriere eines sozialwissenschaftlichen Begriffs.* (= Einstiege. Grundbegriffe der Sozialphilosophie und Gesellschaftstheorie, 16/17), Münster 2006).

Hauschild, Thomas: "Ethnologie als Kulturwissenschaft", in: Stierstorfer, Klaus/Volkmann, Laurenz (Eds.): *Kulturwissenschaft interdisziplinär.* (= Narr Studienbücher), Tübingen 2005, pp. 59 - 79.

Heidegger, Martin: "Brief über den 'Humanismus'", in: Heidegger, Martin: *Gesamtausgabe. I. Abteilung: Veröffentlichte Schriften 1914 - 1970*, vol. 9, Frankfurt/Main 1976, pp. 313 - 364.

Heidegger, Martin: *Übungen für Anfänger. Schillers Briefe über die ästhetische Erziehung des Menschen*, ed. by Ulrich von Bülow. (= Marbacher Bibliothek 8), Marbach am Neckar 2005.

Hejl, Peter M./Antweiler, Christoph: "Kooperation und Konkurrenz", in: Roth, Gerhard (coord.): *Antrag auf eine internationale Konferenz Transkulturelle Universalien am Hanse-Wissenschaftskolleg in Delmenhorst*, unpubl. ms. (Delmenhorst) 2004, pp. 11–13.

Hejl, Peter M.: *Introduction – Culture: Universals and Particulars.* Paper, Conference "Media and Universals 2005, Focus on Film and Print", SFB/FK 615 Medienumbrüche, Teilprojekt A 3: Soziale und Anthropologische Faktoren der Mediennutzung, Siegen: 3.2.–5.2.2005.

Hepp, Andreas: *Transkulturelle Kommunikation*, Konstanz 2006.

Herder Johann Gottfried: *Auch eine Philosophie der Geschichte zur Bildung der Menschheit*, Frankfurt/Main 1967.

Herder, Johann Gottfried: *Ideen zur Philosophie der Geschichte der Menschheit* (*Werke*, ed. Wolfgang Pross, vol. III/1), Munich 2002, p. 135.

Himmler, Katrin: *Die Brüder Himmler: eine deutsche Familiengeschichte*, Frankfurt/Main 2005.

Hiriyanna, M.: *Outlines of Indian Philosophy*, Delhi 1994.

Hobbes, Thomas: *Vom Menschen, Vom Bürger*, Hamburg 1994.

Hobbins, A.J. (ed.): *On the Edge of Greatness: The Diaries of John Humphrey, First Director of the United Nations Division of Human Rights*, Montreal 1995–2001

Höffe, Otfried: *Vernunft und Recht. Bausteine zu einem interkulturellen Rechtsdiskurs*, Frankfurt/Main 1996.

Holenstein, Elmar: "Interkulturelle Beziehungen – multikulturelle Verhältnisse. Im Ausgang von Japan-Berichten in der westdeutschen Presse", in idem: *Menschliches Selbstverständnis. Ichbewußtsein – Intersubjektive Verantwortung –_Interkulturelle Verständigung*, pp. 104–180.

Holenstein, Elmar: *Kulturphilosophische Perspektiven. Schulbeispiel Schweiz, Europäische Identität auf dem Prüfstand, Globale Verständigungsmöglichkeiten*, Frankfurt/Main 1998.

Holenstein, Elmar: *Menschliches Selbstverständnis. Ichbewußtsein – Intersubjektive Verantwortung – Interkulturelle Verständigung*, Frankfurt/Main 1985.

Holenstein, Elmar: "Sprache und Gehirn. Phänomenologische Perspektiven", in: Schnelle, Helmut (Ed.): *Sprache und Gehirn. Roman Jacobsen zu Ehren*, Frankfurt/Main 1981, pp. 197–216.

Holenstein, Elmar: *Zur Begrifflichkeit der Universalienforschung in Linguistik und Anthropologie.* (= Akup. Arbeiten des Kölner Universalien-Projekts, 35), Cologne 1979.

Honegger, Claudia: *Die Ordnung der Geschlechter. Die Wissenschaften vom Menschen und das Weib 1750–1850*, Frankfurt/Main 1991.

Hu Shi: *Autobiographie mit Vierzig* (transl. from Chinese by Marianne Liebermann and Alfred Hoffmann), Dortmund 1998.

Humboldt, Wilhelm von: "Über die Aufgabe des Geschichtsschreibers", in: *Werke*, ed. Andreas Flitner and Klaus Giel, vol. 1: *Schriften zur Anthropologie und Geschichte*, Darmstadt 1960, pp. 585–606 (*Gesammelte Schriften* [Akademie-Ausgabe] IV, pp. 35–56).

Humphrey, John P.: *Human Rights and the United Nations: A Great Adventure*, New York 1984.

Huntington, S.: *The Clash of Civilizations*, New York 1996.

Huntington, S.: *Who Are We?*, London 2004.

Hüther, G./Doering, S./Rüger, U./Rüther, E./Schüssler, G.: "The stress reaction process and the adaptive modification and reorganization of neuronal networks", in: *Psychiatry Research* (1999): 83 – 95.

Hüther, G.: "Stress and the adaptive self-organization of neuronal connectivity during early childhood", in: *Int. J. Devl. Neuroscience* 16 (1998): 297 – 306.

Hüther, G.: "The central adaptation syndrome", in: *Progress in Neurobiology* 48 (1996): 569 – 612.

Hüther, G.: *The compassionate brain*, Boston 2006.

Illouz, Eva: *Saving the Modern Soul: Therapy, Emotions, and the Culture of Self-Help*, Berkeley 2008.

Jacob, François: "Evolution and Tinkering", in: *Science* 196 (June 1977): 1161 – 1166.

Jacob, Margaret: *Scientific culture and the making of the industrial west*, Oxford 1997.

Jaeger, Friedrich/Rüsen, Jörn: *Geschichte des Historismus. Eine Einführung*, Munich 1992.

Jaeger, Werner: *Paideia. Die Formung des griechischen Menschen* (1933/34; 2nd edition 1936), vol. I, Berlin 4th ed. 1959.

Jaeger Werner (Ed.): *Das Problem des Klassischen und die Antike* (1933), Darmstadt 1951.

Jaspers, Karl: *Philosophischer Glaube*, Frankfurt/Main 1958.

Jaspers, Karl: *Über Bedingungen und Möglichkeiten eines neuen Humanismus. Drei Vorträge*, Stuttgart 1962.

Jaspers, Karl: *Vom Ursprung und Ziel der Geschichte*, Munich 1963 (first Zürich 1949)

Jatava, D.R.: *Social and Humanist Thinkers (Indian and Western)*, Jaipur 1998.

Jatava, D.R.: *The Dimensions of Humanism*, Agra 1970.

Joas, Hans: *Die Entstehung der Werte*, Frankfurt/Main 1997.

Jordens, J.T.F.: *Dayananda Saraswati*, Delhi 1978.

Joshi V.C. (Ed.): *Rammohan and the Process of Modernization in India*, Delhi 1975.

Jüngel, Eberhard: "'Wir sollen Menschen und nicht Gott sein. Das ist die summa'. Zum Wesen des Christentums", in: *Weltreligionen. Verstehen, Verständigung, Verantwortung*, ed. by Karl Kardinal Lehmann, Frankfurt/Main 2009, pp. 113 – 134.

Jüngel, Eberhard: "Zum Wesen des Friedens. Frieden als Kategorie theologischer Anthropologie", in: idem: *Ganz werden*, Tübingen 2003, pp. 1 – 39.

Kammler, Clemens/Parr, Rolf/Schneider, Ulrich Johannes (Eds.): *Foucault Handbuch. Leben - Werk - Wirkung*, Stuttgart/Weimar 2008.

Kampschulte, F.W.: *Die Universität Erfurt in ihrem Verhältnisse zu dem Humanismus und der Reformation. Erster Theil: Der Humanismus*, Trier 1858.

Kant, Immanuel: "Zum ewigen Frieden. Ein philosophischer Entwurf" (1795), ed. by Theodor Valentiner, Stuttgart 1963.

Kant, Immanuel: *Kritik der reinen Vernunft* (1781), 2nd ed. 1787, A 805, *Werke* in 10 vols, ed. Wilhelm Weischedel, vol. 4, Darmstadt 1968.

Kant, Immanuel: *Logik* A. 26, *Werke* in 10 vols, ed. Wilhelm Weischedel, vol. 5, Darmstadt 1968.

Kant, Immanuel: *Metaphysik der Sitten* A 93, *Werke* in 10 vols, ed. Wilhelm Weischedel, vol. 7, Darmstadt 1968.

Kashyap, Subhash C.: *Our Constitution: An Introduction to India's Constitution and Constitutional Law*, New Delhi 1994.

Kearney, Michael: "World View", in: Levinson, David/Ember, Melvin (Eds.): *Encyclopedia of Cultural Anthropology*, vol. 4., New York 1996, pp. 1380 – 1384.

Kearney, Michael: *World View.* (= Chandler & Sharp Publications in Anthropology and Related Fields), Novato, Cal. 1984.

Keesing, Roger M./Strathern, Andrew J.: *Cultural Anthropology. A Contemporary Perspective*, Fort Worth etc. [3]1998 ([1]1976, [2]1982).

Kelley, Lawrence: *War before civilization*, Oxford 1996.

Kennedy, John Stodart: *The New Anthropomorphism*, Cambridge 1992.

Kerner, Ina: *Postkoloniale Theorien zur Einführung*, Hamburg 2010.

Keupp, Heiner/Hohl, Joachim (Eds.): *Subjektdiskurse im gesellschaftlichen Wandel: Zur Theorie des Subjekts in der Spätmoderne*, Bielefeld 2006.

Klinger, Cornelia/Knapp, Gudrun-Axeli (Eds.): *Über-Kreuzungen. Fremdheit, Ungleichheit, Differenz*, Münster 2008.

Kluckhohn, Clyde Kay Maben/Murray, H.A.: *Personality in Nature, Society and Culture*, New York 1953.

Knight, Alan: "Intellectuals in the Mexican Revolution", in: Camp, Roderic A./Hale, Charles Vázquez/, Zoraida, Josefina Zoraida (Eds): *Los intelectuales y el poder en México*, Mexico/Los Angeles 1991, pp. 141 – 171.

Kodalle, Klaus-Michael: *Annäherungen an eine Theorie des Verzeihens*, Stuttgart 2006.

Koenersmann, Ralf: *Handbuch der Kulturphilosophie*, Stuttgart 2012.

Köhler, Andrea: "Im Garten des Menschlichen. Der amerikanische Literaturwissenschaftler Robert Harrison im Gespräch", in: *Neue Zürcher Zeitung* 146 (27./28. June 2009): 31.

Köpping, Klaus-Peter/Welker, Michael/Wiehl, Reiner (Eds.): *Die autonome Person. Eine europäische Erfindung?*, Munich 2002.

Koselleck, Reinhart: "'Erfahrungsraum' und 'Erwartungshorizont' – zwei historische Kategorien", in: ibid., *Vergangene Zukunft. Zur Semantik geschichtlicher Zeiten*, Frankfurt/Main 1979, pp. 349 – 375.

Koselleck, Reinhart: "Historik und Hermeneutik", in: Koselleck, Reinhart: *Zeitschichten. Studien zur Historik*, Frankfurt/Main 2000, p. 97 – 118.

Kozlarek, Oliver: "Towards a Humanist Turn", in: *The Unesco Courier* (October-December 2001): 18 – 20.

Kozlarek, Oliver: *Moderne als Weltbewusstsein. Ideen für eine humanistische Sozialtheorie in der globalen Moderne*, Bielefeld 2011.

Kraemer, Joel L.: *Humanism in the Renaissance of Islam*, Leiden 1986.

Krähnke, Uwe: *Selbstbestimmung. Zur gesellschaftlichen Konstruktion einer normativen Leitidee*, Weilerswist 2007.

Kristeller, P.O.: *Humanismus und Renaissance*, Munich 1973.

Kroeber, Alfred Louis: "Totem and Taboo in Retrospect", in: *American Journal of Sociology* 55 (1939): 446.

Küenzlen, Gottfried: *Der neue Mensch*, Frankfurt/Main 1997.

Kulturwissenschaftliches Institut Essen (KWI) 2005: "Graduiertenkolleg 'Der Humanismus in der Epoche der Globalisierung. Ein interkultureller Dialog über Kultur, Menschheit und Werte'", in: *Die Zeit* 52 (21.12.2005): 38.

La Peyrère, I.: *Prae-Adamitae*, 1655 (Neudruck: Kessinger Publishing 2009).

Lai Yanyuan, *Hanshi waizhuan jinzhu jinyi*, Taipei 1972.

Landshut, Siegfried (ed.): *Karl Marx – Die Frühschriften*, Stuttgart 1964.

Leach, Edmund Ronald: "Magical Hair", in: *Proceedings of the Royal Anthropological Institute of Great Britain and Ireland* 88.2 (1958): 147 - 164.

Leach, Edmund Ronald: *Social Anthropology.* (= Fontana Master Guides), London 1982 (also New York 1985).

Lechner, Frank J./Boli, John: *World Culture. Origins and Consequences*, Oxford etc. 2005.

Lee Ming-huei [Li Minghui]: "Rujia chuantong yu renquan" [Confucian tradition and human rights], in: *Yuandao* 7 (2002): 36 - 55.

Lee Shui-chuen: "A Confucian Assessment of 'Personhood'", in: Döring, Ole/Chen, Renbiao (Eds.), *Advances in Chinese Medical Ethics: Chinese and International Perspective*, Hamburg 2001.

Leibniz, G.W.: *Monadologie* (French/German, transl. by Heinrich Köhler), Frankfurt/Main 1996.

Lenz, Ilse: "Geschlecht, Klasse, Migration und soziale Ungleichheit", in: Lutz, Helma (Ed.): *Gender- Mobil? Vervielfältigung und Enträumlichung von Lebensformen - Transnationale Räume, Migration und Geschlecht*, Münster 2009, pp. 25 - 68.

Lenz, Ilse: "Globalization, varieties of gender regimes, and regulations for gender equality at work", in: Gottfried, Heidi et al. (Eds.): *Gendering the Knowledge Economy: Comparative Perspectives*, London 2007, pp. 110 - 140.

Lenz, Ilse: "Intersektionalität: Zum Wechselverhältnis von Geschlecht und sozialer Ungleichheit", in: Becker, Ruth/Kortendiek, Beate (Eds.): *Handbuch Frauen- und Geschlechterforschung. Theorie, Methoden, Empirie*, 3. ed., Wiesbaden 2010, pp. 158 - 165.

Lenz, Ilse: *Die Neue Frauenbewegung in Deutschland. Abschied vom kleinen Unterschied. Eine Quellensammlung*, Wiesbaden 2008.

Lenz, Ilse: "Transnational social movement networks and transnational public spaces: Glocalizing Gender Justice", in: Pries, Ludger (Ed.): *Rethinking Transnationalism. The Meso-link of Organisations*, London et al. 2008, pp. 104 - 126.

Lenz, Ilse/Szypulski, Anja/Molsich, Beate: *Frauenbewegungen international. Eine Arbeitsbibliographie*, Opladen 1996.

Lenz, Ilse/Ullrich, Charlotte/Fersch, Barbara (Eds.): *Gender Orders Unbound. Globalisation, Restructuring, Reciprocity*, Leverkusen 2007.

Lessing, Gotthold Ephraim: "Die Religion", in: *Werke*, vol. 1: *Gedichte, Fabeln, Lustspiele*, Darmstadt 1996.

Levinas, Emmanuel: *Humanismus des anderen Menschen*, Hamburg 1989.

Lévi-Strauss, Claude: *Das wilde Denken*, Frankfurt/Main 1968 (orig. *Le pensée sauvage*, Paris 1962).

Lévy-Bruhl, Lucien: *How natives think*, Princeton 1985.

Lévy-Bruhl, Lucien: *L'éxperience mystique et les symboles chez les primitives*, Paris 1938.

Lévy-Bruhl, Lucien: *Le surnaturel et la nature dans la mentalité primitive*, Paris 1931.

Lewontin, Richard Charles: *Menschen. Genetische, kulturelle und soziale Gemeinsamkeiten.* (= Spektrum-Bibliothek, 10), Heidelberg 1986 (orig. *Human Diversity.* [= Scientific American Books], New York 1982).

Li Ruiquan (Lee Shui-chuen): *Rujia shengming lunlixue* (Confucian Bioethics), Taipei 1999.

Li, Wen-chao: *Die christliche China-Mission im 17. Jahrhundert*, Stuttgart 2000.

Libera, Alain de: *Der Universalienstreit. Von Platon bis zum Ende des Mittelalters*, München 2005 (orig. *La querelle des universeaux*, Paris 1996).

Lichtenstein, Heinz: *The Dilemma of Human Identity*, New York 1977.

Liu, D./Diorio, J./Day, J.C./Francis, D.D./Meaney, M.J.: "Maternal care, hippocampal synaptogenesis and cognitive development in rats", in: *Nature Neurosci.* 3 (2000): 799–806.

Loizos, Peter/Heady, Patrick (Eds.): *Conceiving Persons. Ethnographies of Procreation, Fertility and Growth.* (= London School of Economics Monographs on Social Anthropology), London 1999.

Long, E.: *History of Jamaica*, 1774 (new print: New York 2009).

Lonner, Walter J.: "The Psychological Study of Culture: Issues and Questions of Enduring Importance", in: Friedlmeier, Wolfgang/Chakkarath, Pradeep/Schwarz, Beate (Eds.): *Culture and Human Development. The Importance of Cross-Cultural Research to the Social Sciences*, Hove and New York 2005, pp. 10–29.

Lonner, Walter J.: "The Search for Psychological Universals", in: Triandis, Harry Charalambos/Lambert, William Wilson (Eds.): *Handbook of Cross-Cultural Psychology*, vol. 1: *Perspectives*, Boston 1980, 143–204.

Lonner, Walter J: "Das Aufkommen und die fortdauernde Bedeutung der kulturvergleichenden Psychologie", in: Trommsdorff, Gisela/Kornath, Hans-Joachim (Eds.): *Theorien und Methoden der kulturvergleichenden Psychologie.* (= *Enzyklopädie der Psychologie, Themenbereich C, Theorie und Forschung*, Serie VII, vol. 1: *Kulturvergleichende Psychologie*), Göttingen etc.: 2007, pp. 97–117.

López, Austin A./Atran, Scott/Coley, J./Medin, Douglas/Smith, E.: "The Tree of Life. Universals in Folk-Biological Taxonomies and Inductions", in: *Cognitive Psychology* 32 (1997): 251–295.

*Lunyu*, in: *Harvard-Yenching Sinological Index Series, A Concordance to the Analects of Confucius*, reprint Taipei 1972.

Lurija, Alexander R.: *Cognitive development. Its cultural and social foundations*, Cambridge, Mass., 1982.

Lutz, Helma et al. (Eds.): *Fokus Intersektionalität. Bewegungen und Verortungen eines vielschichtigen Konzeptes*, Wiesbaden 2010.

Mach, Ernst: *Die Mechanik in ihrer Entwicklung*, Leipzig 1883.

Macpherson, C.B.: *Die politische Theorie des Besitzindividualismus. Von Hobbes bis Locke*, Frankfurt/Main 1973.

Mae, Michiko/Lenz, Ilse: *Die Frauenbewegung in Japan. Eros, Gleichheit, Differenz. Quellen und Analysen*, Wiesbaden 2010.

Maier, Anneliese: *Zwischen Philosophie und Mechanik. Studien zur Naturphilosophie der Spätscholastik*, Rom 1958.

Mann, Susan: "Scene-Setting: Writing Biography in Chinese History", in: *The American Historical Review* 114.3 (June 2009): 631–639.

Marcia, James E./Waterman, Alan S./Matteson, David R./Archer, Sally/Orlofsky, Jacob L.: *Ego Identity. A Handbook for Psychosocial Research*, New York 1993.

Markl, Hubert: *Evolution, Genetik und menschliches Verhalten. Zur Frage wissenschaftlicher Verantwortung.* (= Serie Piper 623), Munich and Zürich 1986.

Markus, Hazel/Kitayama, Shinobu: "Culture and the self: Implications for cognition, emotion, and motivation", in: *Psychological Review* 98 (1991): 224–253.

Marshall, Thomas H.: *Bürgerrechte und soziale Klassen. Zur Soziologie des Wohlfahrtsstaats*, Frankfurt am Main 1992.

Marx, Karl: "Ökonomisch-philosophische Manuskripte (1844)", in: *Marx Engels Werke*, Berlin 1964.

Marx, Karl: "Zur Kritik der Hegelschen Rechtsphilosophie", in: *Marx Engels Werke*, vol. I, Berlin 1976.

Marx, Karl/Engels, Friedrich: "Die großen Männer des Exils (Manchester 1852)", in: *Marx Engels Werke* 8, Berlin 1960, p. 279.

Mayo, Peter: *Gramsci, Freire, and Adult Education: Possibilities for Transformative Action*, London 1999.

McAdams, Dan P.: *The Stories We Live By: Personal Myths and the Making of the Self*, New York 1993.

McCrum, M./A.G. Woodhead: *Documents of the Principates of the Flavian Emperors* (A.D. 68–96), Cambridge 1966.

McGrew, William C.: "The Nature of Culture. Prospects and Pitfalls of Cultural Primatology", in: de Waal, Frans B.M. (Ed.): *Tree of Origin. What Primate Behavior Can Tell Us about Human Social Evolution*, Cambridge, Mass., and London 2001, pp. 229–254.

McRobbie, Angela: *Top Girls. Feminismus und der Aufstieg des neoliberalen Geschlechterregimes*, Wiesbaden 2010.

Medin, Douglas L./Ross, Norbert/Atran, Scott/Burnett, Russel C./Blok, Sergey V.: "Categorization and Reasoning in Relation to Culture and Expertise", in: *The Psychology of Learning and Motivation* 41 (2002): 1–41.

Meiners, Ch.: *Grundriß der Geschichte der Menschheit*, Lemgo 1785.

Meinert, Carmen (Ed.): *Traces of Humanism in China – Tradition and Modernity*, Bielefeld 2010.

*Mengzi*, in: *Harvard Yenching Institute Sinological Index Series, A Concordance to Meng Tzu*, Reprint Taipei 1973.

Mensing, Joachim (1998): "Die Zeit am Rio Uneiuxi (Amazonas)", in: Dux, Günter: *Die Zeit in der Geschichte*, 2. ed., Frankfurt/Main, pp. 373–406.

Menzel, Ulrich: "Tausend Jahre Globalisierung im Rückblick aus der aktuellen Globalisierungsdebatte", in: Schmidt-Glintzer, Helwig (Ed.): *Neue Blicke auf alte Karten und die Dynamik der europäischen Kulturgeschichte*, Wiesbaden 2007, pp. 137–209.

Merry, Sally Engle: *Human Rights and Gender Violence. Translating international law into local justice*, Chicago 2006.

Merton, R.K.: *Auf den Schultern von Riesen* (1965), Frankfurt/Main 1983.

Metzger, Thomas A.: *Escape from Predicament. Neo-Confucianism and Chinas Evolving Political Culture*, New York 1977.

Mez, Adam: *Renaissance des Islam*, Heidelberg 1922.

Michelet, Jules: *Histoire de France*, vol. 7, Paris 1855.

Millar, John: *Vom Ursprung des Unterschieds in den Rangordnungen und Ständen der Gesellschaft*, Frankfurt/Main 1985.

Miller, Nicola: *Reinventing Modernity in Latin America. Intellectuals Imagine the Future: 1900–1930*, New York 2008.

Mittag, Achim: "Reconsidering *Ren* as a Basic Concept of Chinese Humanism", in: Meinert, Carmen (Ed.): *Traces of Humanism in China – Tradition and Modernity*, Bielefeld 2010, pp. 49–62.

Moghadam, Valentine: *Globalizing Women. Transnational Feminist Networks*, Baltimore 2005.

Mohanty, Chandra Talpade: "Under Western Eyes Revisited: Feminist Solidarity through Anti-capitalist Struggles", in: *Signs* 28.2 (2003): 499–537.

Mohapatra, P.K. (Ed.): *Facets of Humanism*, New Delhi 1999.

Montaigne, Michel de: *Essais*, II, 12, Paris 1843.

Montaigne, Michel de: "Von den Menschenfressern", in: Michel de Montaigne, *Essais* (ed. Ralph-Rainer Wuthenow), Frankfurt/Main 2001.

Mookerji, Radhakumud: *The Fundamental Unity of India*, London 1914.

Mou Zongsan, *Zhengdao yu zhidao* [Politics und Government], Taipei 1961.

Mukerjee, Radhakamal: *The Way of Humanism, East and West*, Bombay 1968.

Mukerji, D.P.: *Redefining Humanism: Selected Essays of D.P. Mukerji*, ed. by Srobona Munshi, New Delhi 2009.

Müller, F. Max: *India: What Can It Teach Us?*, New Delhi 1991. (Originally published in 1883, Cambridge).

Müller, Klaus E. (Ed.): *Menschenbilder früher Gesellschaften. Ethnologische Studien zum Verhältnis von Mensch und Natur*, Frankfurt/Main 1983.

Müller, Klaus E.: "Das Unbehagen mit der Kultur", in: idem (Ed.): *Phänomen Kultur. Perspektiven und Aufgaben der Kulturwissenschaften.* (= Kultur und soziale Praxis), Bielefeld 2003: 13–47.

Murdock, George Peter: "The Common Denominator of Cultures", in: Ralph Linton (Ed.): *The Science of Man in the World Crisis*, New York 1945, pp. 123–140 (also in: George Peter Murdock (Ed.): *Culture and Society: Twenty-four Essays*, Pittsburgh 1964, pp. 88–110).

Nandy, Ashish: *Traditions, Tyranny, and Utopias: Essays in the Politics of Awareness*, New Delhi 1992.

Narvane, V.S.: *Modern Indian Thought*, Bomaby/New York 1964.

Nath, Ramendra: *M.N. Roy's New Humanism and Materialism*, Patna 2001.

Nenguié, Pierre Kodjio: "Rasse, Alterität und Humanität: Anmerkungen über die Afrikapolitik der Goethezeit. Zu Karl von Eckartshausens *Isogin und Celia, eine Geschichte von einem unserer schwarzen Brüder aus Afrika, von einem Mohren* (1786)", in: *Das achtzehnte Jahrhundert* 33.1 (2009): 26–41.

Nida-Rümelin, Julian: *Humanismus als Leitkultur. Ein Perspektivenwechsel*, ed. by Elif Özmen, Munich 2006.

Nie Jing-Bao: "The Plurality of Chinese and American Medical Moralities", in: *Kennedy Inst Ethics J* 10.3 (2000): 239–260.

Niethammer, Friedrich Immanuel: *Philanthropinismus, Humanismus: Texte zur Schulreform*, ed. by Werner Hillebrecht. (= Kleine pädagogische Texte 29), Weinheim 1968.

Nietzsche, Friedrich: "Der griechische Staat. Weihnachtgabe an Cosima Wagner, 1872", in: Colli, Giorgio/Montinari, Mazzino (Eds.), *Friedrich Nietzsche. Sämtliche Werke. Kritische Studienausgabe*, Munich 1980, vol. 1, pp. 764–777.

Nietzsche, Friedrich: "Jenseits von Gut und Böse", in: *Werke*, vol. 2, ed. von Karl Schlechta, Munich 1966, p. 637.

Nisbett, Richard E.: *The Geography of Thought. How Asians and Westerners Think Different … and Why*, New York etc. 2003; London 2003.

Oerter, Rolf: "Das Menschenbild im Kulturvergleich", in: idem. (Ed.): *Menschenbilder in der modernen Gesellschaft. Konzeptionen des Menschen in Wissenschaft, Bildung,*

*Kunst, Wirtschaft und Politik.* (= Der Mensch als soziales und personales Wesen, 15) Stuttgart 1999, pp. 185 - 198.

Oerter, Rolf: "Menschenbilder im Kulturvergleich", in: Trommsdorff, Gisela/Kornath, Hans-Joachim (Eds.): *Theorien und Methoden der kulturvergleichenden Psychologie.* (= *Enzyklopädie der Psychologie, Themenbereich C, Theorie und Forschung*, Serie VII, vol. 1: *Kulturvergleichende Psychologie*), Göttingen etc. 2007, pp. 487 - 530.

Oesterdiekhoff, Georg W.: "Das archaische Prozeß- und Beweisrecht und die immanente Gerechtigkeit", in: *Zeitschrift der Savigny-Stiftung für Rechtsgeschichte, Germanistische Abteilung* 119 (2002): 175 - 192.

Oesterdiekhoff, Georg W.: "The arena games in the Roman empire: a contribution to the explanation of the history of morals and humanity", in: *Narodna Umjetnost. Croatian Journal of Ethnology and Folklore Research* 46.1 (2009): 177 - 202.

Oesterdiekhoff, Georg W.: *Die Entwicklung der Menschheit von der Kindheitsphase zur Erwachsenenreife*, Wiesbaden 2013.

Oesterdiekhoff, Georg W.: *Die geistige Entwicklung der Menschheit*, Weilerswist 2012.

Oesterdiekhoff, Georg W.: *Entwicklung der Weltgesellschaft. Von der Steinzeit zur Moderne*, Hamburg/Münster 2005.

Oesterdiekhoff, Georg W.: *Kulturelle Bedingungen kognitiver Entwicklung. Der strukturgenetische Ansatz in der Soziologie*, Frankfurt/Main 1997.

Oesterdiekhoff, Georg W.: *Kulturelle Evolution des Geistes. Die historische Wechselwirkung von Psyche und Gesellschaft*, Hamburg/Münster 2006.

Oesterdiekhoff, Georg W.: *Mental growth of humankind in history*, Norderstedt 2009.

Oesterdiekhoff, Georg W.: *The steps of man towards civilization. The key to disclose the riddle of history*, Norderstedt 2011.

Oesterdiekhoff, Georg W.: *Traumzeit der Menschheit. Ursprung und Wesen der Religion*, (forthcoming).

Oesterdiekhoff, Georg W.: *Zivilisation und Strukturgenese. Norbert Elias und Jean Piaget im Vergleich*, Frankfurt/Main 2000.

Oesterdiekhoff, Georg W./Rindermann, Heiner: *Kultur und Kognition*, Hamburg/Münster 2008.

Ommer, Uwe: *1000 Families. Das Familienalbum des Planeten Erde. The Family Album of Planet Earth. L'album de famille de la planète Terre*, Cologne 2000.

Osawa, Mari: "The Livelihood Security System and Social Exclusion: The Male Breadwinner Model revisited", in: Lenz/Ullrich/Fersch: *Gender Orders Unbound. Globalisation, Restructuring, Reciprocity*, pp. 277 - 302.

Osterhammel, Jürgen: *Die Entzauberung Asiens*, Munich 1998.

Parsons, Talcott: "Evolutionary Universals in Society", in: *American Sociological Review* 29 (1964): 339 - 357.

Pascall, Gillian/Lewis, Jane: "Emerging Gender Regimes and Policies for Gender Equality in a Wider Europe", in: *Journal of Social Policy* 33 (2004): 373 - 394.

Paulsen, Friedrich: *Geschichte des gelehrten Unterrichts auf den deutschen Schulen und Universitäten vom Ausgang des Mittelalters bis zur Gegenwart. Mit besonderer Rücksicht auf den klassischen Unterricht*, Berlin (1844; $^{2}$1895) 3rd enlarged edition, ed. by Rudolf Lehmann, Leipzig 1919 - 1921.

Payne, Harris/Gray, Susan: "Exploring Cultural Universals", in: *Journal of Geography* 96 (1997): 220 - 223.

Paz, Octavio: *Das Labyrinth der Einsamkeit*, Frankfurt/Main 1998.

Peacock, James Lowe: "Challenges Facing the Discipline", in: *Anthropology Newsletter* 35.9 (1995): 1 ff.

Peters, Julie/Wolper, Andrea (Eds.): *Women's rights, human rights. International feminist perspectives*, New York 1995.

Philipp, Claudia Gabriele: "Die Ausstellung 'The Family of Man' (1955). Fotographie als Weltsprache", in: *Fotogeschichte* 23 (1987): 45 – 61.

Piaget, Jean/Garcia, Rolando: *Psychogenesis and the history of sciences*, New York 1989.

Piaget, Jean/Inhelder, Bärbel: *The growth of logical thinking from childhood to adolescence*, New York 1958.

Piaget, Jean/Inhelder, Bärbel: *The psychology of the child*, New York 1969.

Piaget, Jean: *Introduction à l'épistémologie génétique*. Vol. 1: *La pensée mathematique*, vol. 2: *La pensée physique*, vol. 3: *La pensée sociologique*, Paris 1950.

Piaget, Jean: *Judgment and reasoning in the child*, New York 1959.

Piaget, Jean: *The child's conception of the world*, New York 1975.

Piaget, Jean: *The moral judgment of the child*, New York 1997.

Piaget, Jean: *The psychology of intelligence*, London 1950.

Pico della Mirandola, Giovanni: *Oratio de hominis dignitate. Rede über die Würde des Menschen*, Latin-German, ed. and transl. by Gert von der Gönna, Stuttgart 1997.

Pietilä, Hilkka: *The Unfinished Story of Women and the United Nations. United Nations. Non-Governmental Liaison Service* (UN-NGLS), Geneva 2007. http://www.un-ngls.org/pdf/UnfinishedStory.pdf.

Pinker, Steven: *Wörter und Regeln. Die Natur der Sprache*, Heidelberg/Berlin 2000 (orig. *Words and Rules*, New York 1999).

Platenkamp, Josephus D.M.: "Natur als Gegenbild der Gesellschaft. Einige Betrachtungen zu einer paradoxen Idee", in: Mohrmann, Ruth-Elisabeth (Ed.): *Argument Natur – Was ist natürlich?* (= Worte – Werke – Utopien. Thesen und Texte Münsterscher Gelehrter, 7), Münster 1999, pp. 5 – 16.

Plessner, Helmuth, *Die verspätete Nation*, Frankfurt/Main 1974.

Pomata, Gianna: "Feminism as Integral to the History of Humanism", in: Rüsen/Laass: *Humanism in Intercultural Perspective. Experiences and Expectations*, pp. 167 – 177.

Porter, Roy: *The creation of the modern world*, New York 2000.

Prabhu, P.H.: *Hindu Social Organization*, Bombay 1991. (First published in 1940).

Praharaj, D.M.: *Humanism in Contemporary Indian Perspective*, Meerut 1995.

Pries, Ludger *Die Transnationalisierung der sozialen Welt. Sozialräume jenseits von Nationalgesellschaften*, Frankfurt/Main 2008.

Qiu Renzong (Ed.): *Bioethics in Asia – a Quest for Moral Diversity*, Dordrecht 2006.

Radhakrishnana, S.: "Forword", in: *2500 Years of Buddhism*, P.V. Bapat (Ed.), New Delhi 1956.

Radhakrishnan, S.: *Indian Philosophy* (2 vols.), London 1927.

Radhakrishnan, S./Raju, P.T.: *The Concept of Man: A Study in Comparative Philosophy*, New Delhi 1995.

Ramakrishna: *Memoirs of Ramakrishna*, Calcutta 1957.

Ramos, Samuel: "Hacia un nuevo humanismo", in: Ramos, Samuel: *Obras Completas* II, Mexico 1990, pp. 4 – 75.

Rane, M.A. (Ed.), *V.M. Tarkunde, 90: A Restless Crusader for Human Freedoms*, Mumbai 2000.

Ranke, Leopold von: *Über die Epochen der neueren Geschichte*, ed. Th. Schieder and H. Berding (= *Aus Werk und Nachlaß*, vol. 2), Munich 1971.

Redfield, Robert: *The Primitive World and Its Transformations*, Ithaca, N.J., 1953.

Reill, Peter Hanns: *The German Enlightenment and the Rise of Historicism*, Berkeley 1975.

Reill, Peter Hanns: *Vitalising nature in the Enlightenment*, Berkeley 2005.

Rensch, Bernhard: *Das universale Weltbild. Evolution und Naturphilosophie*, Darmstadt [2]1991 (first: Frankfurt/Main [1]1977).

Reuter, Julia/Villa, Paula (Eds.): *Postkoloniale Soziologie*, Bielefeld 2010.

Reyes, Alfonso: *Obras Completos de Alfonso Reyes* XX, Mexico 2000.

Richerson, Peter J./Boyd, Robert: "Institutional Evolution in the Holocene: The Rise of Complex Societies", in: Runciman, Walter Garrison (Ed.): *The Origin of Human Social Institutions.* (= Proceedings of the British Academy, 110), Oxford etc. 2001, pp. 197–234.

Richerson, Peter J./Boyd, Robert: "Complex Societies: The Evolutionary Origins of a Crude Superorganism", in: *Human Nature* 10 (1999): 253–290.

Richerson, Peter J./Boyd, Robert: *Not by Genes Alone. How Human Culture Transformed Human Evolution*, Chicago/London 2005.

Ricœur, Paul: *Das Selbst als ein Anderer*, Munich 1996 (franz. 1990).

Ritter, Joachim (Ed.): *Historisches Wörterbuch der Philosophie*, Basel 1971 ff.

Rizzolatti, Giacomo/Sinigaglia, Corrado: *Empathie und Spiegelneurone. Die biologische Basis des Mitgefühls*, Frankfurt/Main 2008.

Robertson, Roland: *Globalization. Social Theory and Global Culture.* (= Theory, Culture & Society), London etc. 1992.

Roetz, Heiner: "Confucianism between Tradition and Modernity, Religion, and Secularization: Questions to Tu Weiming", in: *Dao* 7.4 (2008): 367–380.

Roetz, Heiner: *Die chinesische Ethik der Achsenzeit. Eine Rekonstruktion unter dem Aspekt des Durchbruchs zu postkonventionellem Denken*, Frankfurt/Main 1992.

Roetz, Heiner: *Confucian Ethics of the Axial Age*, Albany 1993.

Roetz, Heiner: *Konfuzius*, Munich 2006.

Roetz, Heiner: "On Nature and Culture in Zhou China", in: Dux, Günter/Vogel, Hans Ulrich (Eds.), *Concepts of Nature. A Chinese-European Cross-Cultural Perspective*, Leiden 2010, pp. 198–219.

Roetz, Heiner: "The end of ethical universalism? Bioethics in the age of globalization and the case of China", in: Sitter-Liver, Beat (Ed.): *Universality: From Theory to Practice, An intercultural and interdisciplinary debate about facts, possibilities, lies and myths*, Fribourg 2009, pp. 177–190.

Rolland, Romain: *The Life of Ramakrishna*, Calcutta 1979.

Rorty, Richard: *Contingency, Irony, and Solidarity*, Cambridge 1989.

Ross, Norbert: *Culture and Cognition Implications for Theory and Method*, Thousand Oaks etc. 2004.

Roy, M.N.: *Reason, Romanticism and Revolution*, Calcutta 1955.

Rudolph, Enno: "Der Renaissance-Humanismus als Epochenstifter", in: Faber, Richard/ Rudolph, Enno (Eds.), *Humanismus in Geschichte und Gegenwart*, Tübingen 2002, pp. 3–15.

Rüsen, Jörn: "Die Erziehung des Menschengeschlechts – ein Rückblick in die Zukunft der Vergangenheit", in: Schmidt-Glintzer, Helwig (Ed.): *Aufklärung im 21. Jahrhundert*, Wiesbaden 2004, pp. 67–92.

Rüsen, Jörn: "How to Overcome Ethnocentrism: Approaches to a Culture of Recognition by History in the 21st Century", in: *Taiwan Journal of East Asian Studies* 1.1 (June 2004): 59–74 and in: *History and Theory* 43 (2004), Theme Issue "Historians and Ethics": 118–129.

Rüsen, Jörn (Ed.): *Perspektiven der Humanität. Menschsein im Diskurs der Disziplinen*, Bielefeld 2010.

Rüsen, Jörn: "Traditionsprobleme eines zukunftsfähigen Humanismus", in: Martin Vöhler and Hubert Cancik (Ed.): *Humanismus und Antikerezeption im 18. Jahrhundert.* Vol. 1: *Genese und Profil des europäischen Humanismus*, Heidelberg 2009, pp. 201–216.

Rüsen, Jörn/Jordan, Stefan: "Mensch, Menschheit", in: Jaeger, Friedrich (Ed.): *Enzyklopädie der Neuzeit*, vol. 8: *Manufaktur-Naturgeschichte*, Stuttgart 2008, pp. 327–340.

Rüsen, Jörn/Laass, Henner (Eds): *Humanism in Intercultural Perspektive. Experiences and Expectations*, Bielefeld 2009.

Rüsen, Jörn/Laass, Henner (Eds.): *Interkultureller Humanismus*, Schwalbach/Ts. 2009.

Sachße, Christoph/Tennstedt, Florian: *Geschichte der Armenfürsorge in Deutschland*, Stuttgart/Berlin 1980.

Saharso, Sawitri: "Gibt es einen multikulturellen Feminimus? Ansätze zwischen Universalismus und Anti-Essentialismus", in: Sauer/Strasser: *Zwangsfreiheiten. Multikulturalität und Feminismus*, pp. 11–28.

Sahlins, Marshall: *The Western Illusion of Human Nature*, Chicago 2008.

Said, Edward: *Humanism and Democratic Criticism*, New York 2004.

Saiyidain, K.G.: *The Humanist Tradition in Indian Educational Thought*, London 1966.

Salisbury, John of: *Metalogicon*, ed. C.C.J. Webb, Oxford 1929.

Sanderson, Stephen King: *Evolutionism and Its Critics. Deconstructing and Reconstructing an Evolutionary Interpretation of Human Society*, Boulder, Col./London 2007.

Satre, Jean-Paul, *La Nauseé*, Paris 1938.

Sauer, Birgit/Strasser Sabine (Eds.): *Zwangsfreiheiten. Multikulturalität und Feminismus*, Wien 2008.

Schaeder, Hans-Heinrich: "Der Orient und das griechische Erbe (1928)", in: idem, *Der Mensch in Orient und Okzident. Grundzüge einer eurasiatischen Geschichte*, Munich 1960, pp. 107–160.

Schaeder, Hildegard: *Moskau, das Dritte Rom. Studien zur Geschichte der politischen Theorien in der slawischen Welt*, Darmstadt$^2$ 1957, (thesis Hamburg 1927; first printing Prague 1929).

Schiefenhövel, Wulf: "Kognitions- und Entscheidungsmuster in Melanesien", in: Schmidinger, Heinrich/Sedmak, Clemens (Eds.): *Der Mensch – ein "animal rationale"? Vernunft – Kognition – Intelligenz.* (= Topologien des Menschlichen, 1), Darmstadt 2004, pp. 275–292.

Schild, Wolfgang: *Alte Gerichtsbarkeit*, München 1980.

Schiller, Friedrich: "Über die ästhetische Erziehung des Menschen in einer Reihe von Briefen (1795)", in: *Sämtliche Werke in 5 Bänden*, ed. Peter-André Alt, Albert Meier and Wolfgang Riedel, vol. 5, Munich 2004, pp. 570–669.

Schlözer, August Ludwig: *Vorstellung seiner Universalhistorie*, Göttingen/Gotha 1772. Newprint Hagen 1990.

Schmidt, Julia: "Edward Steichens 'The Family of Man'", in: *Kunstchronik* 8 (1996): 365–370.

Schmidt-Glintzer, Helwig: *Wohlstand, Glück und langes Leben. Chinas Götter und die Ordnung im Reich der Mitte*, Frankfurt/Main 2009.

Schneider, Hermann: *Kultur und Denken der alten Ägypter*, Leipzig 1909.

Schneider, Kirk J./Bugental, James F./Pierson, J. Fraser (Eds.): *The Handbook of Humanistic Psychology. Leading Edges in Theory, Research, and Practice*, Thousand Oaks/London/New Delhi 2001.

Schöfthaler, Traugott: "Kultur in der Zwickmühle. Zur Aktualität des Streits zwischen kulturrelativistischer und universalistischer Sozialwissenschaft", in: *Das Argument* 139 (1983): 333–347.

Schöpp-Schilling, Hanna Beate/Flinterman, Cees: *The Circle of Empowerment. Twenty-Five Years of the UN Committee on the Elimination of All Forms of Discrimination against Women*, New York 2007.

Schott, Heinz: "'Born Criminals', 'Degenerates' and 'Psychopaths'. On the History of Criminal Psychology in Germany", in: *Transactions in Medicine & Heteronomous Modernization*, Tokyo 2009, pp. 33–47.

Schröder, Inge: *Wege zum Menschen. Theoretische Beiträge zur evolutionären Anthropologie*, Göttingen 2000.

Schröter, Susanne: *FeMale. Über Grenzverläufe zwischen den Geschlechtern*, Frankfurt/Main 2002.

Schubert, Gunter: "Zwischen Konfuzius und Kant. Ansätze zur Operationalisierung eines inter-kulturellen Menschenrechtsdialogs mit Ostasien", in: idem (Ed.), *Menschrechte in Ostasien. Zum Streit um die Universalität einer Idee II*, Tübingen 1999, pp. 19–51.

Sen, Amartya: *The Argumentative Indian: Writings on Indian Culture, History and Identity*, London 2005.

Sen, Amiya P.: *His Words*, New Delhi 2010.

Sen, Ashok: *Elusive Milestones of Ishwarchandra Vidyasagar*, Calcutta 1977.

Sennett, Richard: *The Corrosion of Character: The Personal Consequences of Work in the New Capitalism*, New York, London 1998.

Sherry, John F. Jr.: *Contemporary Marketing and Consumer Behavior. An Anthropological Sourcebook*, Thousand Oaks etc. 1995.

Sicks, Kai Marcel: *Bericht zur Konferenz 'Das Planetarische. Kultur – Technik – Medien im postglobalen Zeitalter' an der Universität zu Köln, 8.10.–10.10.2008*. H-Soz-u-Kult, http://hsozkult.geschichte.hu-berlin.de/tagungsberichte/id=2351< (consulted: 11.02.2013).

Sieyés, Emmanuel: "Was ist der dritte Stand?", in: idem, *Politische Schriften*, Darmstadt/Neuwied 1988.

Silverman, Sydel: *The Beast on the Desk. Conferencing with Anthropologists*, Walnut Creek, Cal., etc. 2002.

Singh, Jaideep: *The Humanistic View of Man*, New Delhi 1979.

Spivak, Gayatri: *A Critique of Postcolonial Reason. Toward a History of the Vanishing Present*, Cambridge/London 1999.

Spranger, Eduard: "Aufruf an die Philologie (1921)", in: idem, *Der gegenwärtige Stand der Geisteswissenschaften und die Schule*, Leipzig 1922, pp. 5 – 13.

Stallknecht, Michael: "Sie oder wir", in: *Süddeutsche Zeitung* 147 (30. June 2009): 12.

Stegemann, Ekkhard W.: "Das unaufhebbar Befremdliche am Menschlichen. Einige Gedanken über Humanismus und Christentum", in: Faber, Richard/Rudolph, Enno (Eds.), *Humanismus in Geschichte und Gegenwart*, Tübingen 2002, pp. 167 – 186.

Steichen, Edward: *The Family of Man. The Greatest Photographic Exhibition of All Time – 503 Pictures From 68 Countries*, New York 1955.

Stern, William: *Psychology of early childhood up to the sixth year of age*, New York 1924.

Steyerl, Hito/Gutiérrez, Rodriguez Encarnación: *Spricht die Subalterne Deutsch? Migration und postkoloniale Kritik*, Wien 2003.

Strathern, Andrew J./Stewart, Pamela J. (Eds.): *Identity Work. Constructing Pacific Lives.* (= Association of Social Anthropologists of Oceania Monograph), Pittsburg 2000.

Straub, Jürgen (Ed.): *Erzählung, Identität und historisches Bewußtsein. Zur psychologischen Konstruktion von Zeit und Geschichte*, Frankfurt/Main 1998.

Straub, Jürgen (Ed.): *Der Humanismus der Humanistischen Psychologie*, Bielefeld 2012.

Straub, Jürgen: "Identität", in: Jaeger, Friedrich/Liebsch, Burkhard (Eds.): *Handbuch der Kulturwissenschaften. Grundlagen und Schlüsselbegriffe*, Stuttgart 2004, pp. 277 – 303.

Straub, Jürgen: "Personale Identität als Politikum", in: Henry, Barbara/Pirni, Alberto (Eds.): *Der asymmetrische Westen. Zur Pragmatik der Koexistenz pluralistischer Gesellschaften*, Bielefeld 2012.

Straub, Jürgen: *Theorien der Identität*, Hamburg 2012.

Straub, Jürgen: "Wissenschaftliche Psychologie als Humanismus? Rekonstruktion eines hybriden Programms zur Errettung der modernen Seele", in: idem (Ed.): *Der sich selbst verwirklichende Mensch. Über den Humanismus der Humanistischen Psychologie*, Bielefeld 2012, pp. 15 – 68.

Straub, Jürgen/Chakkarath, Pradeep: "Identität und andere Formen des kulturellen Selbst", in: *Familiendynamik* 36 (2010): 110 – 119.

Straub, Jürgen/Renn, Joachim (Eds.): *Transitorische Identität. Der Prozesscharakter des modernen Selbst*, Frankfurt/Main, New York 2002.

Straub, Jürgen/Zielke, Barbara: "Autonomie, narrative Identität und die postmoderne Kritik des sozialen Konstruktivismus: 'Relationales' und 'dialogisches' Selbst als zeitgemäße Alternativen?", in: Jaeger, Friedrich/Straub, Jürgen (Eds.): *Was ist der Mensch, was Geschichte? Perspektiven einer kulturwissenschaftlichen Anthropologie. Jörn Rüsen zum 65. Geburtstag*, Bielefeld 2005, pp. 165 – 210.

Strier, Karen B.: "Beyond the Apes: Reasons to Consider the Entire Primate Order", in: de Waal, Frans B.M. (Ed.): *Tree of Origin. What Primate Behavior Can Tell Us about Human Social Evolution*, Cambridge, Mass., and London 2001, pp. 69 – 93.

T'ang Chun-I: *Essays on Chinese Philosophy and Culture*, Taipei 1988.

Tagore, Rabindranath: *The Religion of Man*, London 1931.

Tang Junyi, *Zhongguo renwen jingshen zhi fazhan* [The Development of the Chinese Humanist Spirit], Hongkong1958, partly translated in T'ang Chun-I, *Essays on Chinese Philosophy and Culture*, Taipei 1988, pp. 257 – 289.

Taylor, Charles: *Sources of the Self: The making of the modern identity*, Cambridge 1989.

Taylor, Charles: *The Ethics of Authenticity*, Cambridge, MA 1991 (first published as *The Malaise of Modernity*).

Theunissen, Michael: *Selbstverwirklichung und Allgemeinheit. Zur Kritik des gegenwärtigen Bewußtseins*, Berlin 1982.

Thomä, Dieter: "Gespiegelte Perspektiven", in: *Frankfurter Allgemeine Zeitung* 147 (29. June 2009): 6.

Todorov, Tzvetan: *Abenteuer des Zusammenlebens. Versuch einer allgemeinen Anthropologie*, Berlin 1996.

Todorov, Tzvetan: *Imperfect garden. The legacy of humanism*, Princeton 2002.

Tomasello, Michael: "The Human Adaptation for Culture", in: Wuketits, Franz M./Antweiler, Christoph (Eds.): *Handbook of Evolution*, vol. 1: *The Evolution of Human Societies and Cultures*, Weinheim 2004, pp. 1–23 (orig. in: *Annual Review of Anthropology* 28 [1999], pp. 509–529).

Treadgold, Warren T.: *The Nature of the 'Biblioteca' of Photius*, Dumbarton Oaks 1980.

Truong, Bhikkhu Duc: *Humanism in the Nikaya Literature*, Delhi 2005.

Tu Weiming: "A Confucian Perspective on the Core Values of Global Community", in: *The Review of Korean Studies* 2 (1999): 55–70.

Tu Weiming: "The Ecological Turn in New Confucian Humanism: Implications for China and the World", in: *Daedalus* 130.4 (2001): 243–264.

Uhl, Matthias/Kumar, Keval J.: *Indischer Film. Eine Einführung*, Bielefeld 2004.

UN: *Report on the Fourth World Conference on Women (Beijing, 4–15 September 1995)*. A/CONF.177/20.

Ureña, Pedro Henríquez: "La cultura de las humanidades", in: Ureña, Pedro Henríquez: *Obra Crítica*, Mexico 2001, pp. 595–603.

Van der Walt, Sibylle: "Die Last der Vergangenheit und die kulturrelativistische Kritik an den Menschenrechten. Ursprung und Folgen der westlichen Alteritätsobsession", in: *Saeculum* 57.2 (2006): 231–253.

Van Dülmen, Richard: *Die Entdeckung des Individuums 1500–1800*, Frankfurt/Main 1997.

Van Dülmen, Richard (Ed.): *Entdeckung des Ich. Die Geschichte der Individualisierung vom Mittelalter bis zur Gegenwart*, Cologne 2001.

Varma, V.P.: *Philosophical Humanism and Contemporary India*, Delhi 1979.

Velasco, Ambrosio: "Humanismo hispanoamericano", in: *Revista de Hispanismo Filosófico* 13 (2008): 13–30.

Velasco, Ambrosio (Ed.): *Significación política y cultural del humanismo iberoamericano en la época colonial*, Mexico 2008.

Vico, Giambattista: *Die neue Wissenschaft über die gemeinschaftliche Natur der Völker*. Edition from 1744 translated and introduced by E. Auerbach with an epilogue by W. Schmidt-Biggemann, Berlin/New York [2]2000.

Villoro, Luis: "Multiculturalismo y derecho", in: idem: *Los retos de la sociedad por venir*, Mexico 2007, pp. 152–171.

Villoro, Luis: *Los retos de la sociedad por venir*, Mexico 2007.

Villoro, Luis: "Una vía negativa hacia la justicia", in: idem: *Los retos de la sociedad por venir*, pp. 15–41.

Vohra, Ashok: "Humanism in Indian Thought", in: Mohapatra, P.K. (Ed.): *Facets of Humanism*, New Delhi 1999, pp. 3–12.

Voltaire: *Essai sur les moeurs et l'esprit des nations et sur les principaus faits de l'histoire depuis Charlemagne jusqu'a Louis XIII*, 1756 (repr.: Paris 1963, 2 vols.).

Von der Pfordten, Dietmar: *Rechtsethik*, Munich 2001.

Waldenfels, Bernhard: *Vielstimmigkeit der Rede. Studien zur Phänomenologie des Fremden* 4, Frankfurt/Main 1999.

Weiß, Albert Maria: *Humanität und Humanismus. Grundzüge einer Kulturgeschichte erster Theil*, Freiburg i. Br 1879 (= the same, *Apologie des Christenthums vom Standpunkte der Sittenlehre*, 2. vols., Freiburg i. Br. 1878 – 1884.

Welsch, Wolfgang: "Transkulturalität. Lebensformen nach der Auflösung der Kulturen", in: Luger, Kurt/Renger, R. (Eds.): *Dialog der Kulturen. Die multikulturelle Gesellschaft und die Medien*, Wien 1994, pp. 147 – 169.

Welsch, Wolfgang: "Über den Besitz und Erwerb von Gemeinsamkeiten", in: Brinkmann, Claudia/Scheidgen, Hermann Josef/Voßhenrich, Tobias/Wirtz, Markus (Eds.): *Tradition und Traditionsbruch zwischen Skepsis und Dogmatik. Interkulturelle philosophische Perspektiven.* (= Studien zur Interkulturellen Philosophie, 16), Amsterdam/New York 2006, pp. 113 – 145.

Welsch, Wolfgang: "Wandlungen im humanen Selbstverständnis", in: Schmidinger, Heinrich/Sedmak, Clemens (Eds.): *Der Mensch – ein 'animal rationale'? Vernunft – Kognition – Intelligenz.* (= Topologien des Menschlichen, 1), Darmstadt 2004, pp. 48 – 70.

Werner, Heinz: *Comparative psychology of mental development*, New York 1948.

Willems, Herbert/Hahn, Alois (Eds.): *Identität und Moderne*, Frankfurt/Main 1999.

Wilson, Edward Osborne: *Die Einheit des Wissens*, Berlin 1998 (orig. *Consilience. The Unity of Knowledge*, New York 1998).

Winker, Gabriele/Degele, Nina: *Intersektionalität. Zur Analyse sozialer Ungleichheiten*, Bielefeld 2009.

Winternitz, Maurice: *History of Indian Literature*, trans. from German by S. Ketkar, vol. 1, Calcutta 1927.

Wiredu, Kwasi: "Gibt es kulturelle Universalien?", in: Hejl, Peter M. (Ed.): *Universalien und Konstruktivismus*, Frankfurt/Main 2001, pp. 76 – 94 (= Delfin 2000); orig. in: *The Monist* 78.1 [1995]).

Wiredu, Kwasi: *Cultural Universals and Particulars. An African Perspective.* (= African Systems of Thought), Bloomington/Indianapolis 1996.

Wrightsman, Lawrence S.: *Assumptions about Human Nature. A Social-Psychological Approach*, Monterrey, Cal., 1975.

Wroblewsky, Vincent von: "Wie humanistisch ist Sartres Existentialismus?", in: Faber, Richard/Rudolph, Enno (Eds.), *Humanismus in Geschichte und Gegenwart*, Tübingen 2002, pp. 119 – 137.

Wulf, Christoph: *Anthropologie. Geschichte, Kultur, Philosophie*, Cologne 2009 (earlier ed. Reinbek bei Hamburg = Rowohlts Enzyklopädie 2004).

Yang Xiangzhong: "An embryonic nation. Liberal views on human-embryo technology make China ideal to become a world leader in this field", in: *Nature* 428 (11. March 2004): 210 – 212.

Yearbook of the United Nations, *Special Edition – UN Fiftieth Anniversary*, 1945 – 1995

Zea, Leopoldo: *El positivismo en México*, Mexico 1968.

Zeininger, Wolfgang: *Magische Geisteshaltung im Kindesalter und ihre Bedeutung für die religiöse Entwicklung*, Leipzig 1929.

Zula, K./Chermack, T.J.: "Human Capital Planning: A Review of Literature and Implications for Human Resource Development", in: *Human Resource Development Review* 6.3 (2007): 245–262.

Zwingel, Susanne: *How do international women's rights norms become effective in domestic contexts? An analysis of the Convention on the Elimination of all Forms of Discrimination against Women (CEDAW)*, PhD Ruhr-University Bochum 2005 www.brs.ub.ruhr-uni-bochum.de/netahtml/HSS/Diss/ZwingelSusanne/diss.pdf.

# Index of Names